TEACHING
READING
AS
A
THINKING
PROCESS

HARPER & ROW, PUBLISHERS
New York, Evanston, and London

TEACHING
READING
AS
A
THINKING
PROCESS

RUSSELL G. STAUFFER

Director
The Reading Study Center
University of Delaware

Dedicated to Hilda Stauffer

Library of Congress Catalog Card Number: 69-10060

Illustration
Acknowledgments

All illustrations, with the exception of the one on page 36, are from the Winston Basic Readers by Russell G. Stauffer *et al.*, New York, Holt, Rinehart and Winston, by permission. The date of the individual publication is given in parentheses after each title.

PAGES

29, 79 124	*Away We Go* (1960), p. 101, 120, 121, 124.
31	*Skyways to Tomorrow* (1962), p. 45.
36	Adapted from C. K. Ogden and I. A. Richards, *The Meaning of Meaning,* New York, Harcourt, Brace & World (1946), p. 11.
65	*Teacher's Manual for Away We Go* (1960), p. 8.
72, 78 81, 82 84	Redrawn from *Away We Go* (1960), pp. 119, 120, 121, 122, 123, 124.
94-95	*Above the Clouds* (1962), pp. 42-45. Photos from John Deere.
125, 126 127	Studybook pp. 31, 79, 80 as they appear in *Teacher's Manual for Away We Go* (1960), pp. 25, 27, 29.
143	By the author from *Teacher's Manual for Above the Clouds* (1960).
216-217 220-221 224-225 232-233 236-237 240-241 246-247 250-251	Redrawn from *Teacher's Edition for Ready To Go* (1960).
226-227 229, 231 235, 244	*Teacher's Edition for Ready To Go* (1960).

Contents

Foreword

This book is intended for use as a textbook in courses on the foundations of reading instruction offered by colleges and universities. The detailed accounts of practices and procedures should make it especially practical for undergraduates. The carefully documented chapters provide the wherewithal for making the book useful as a text for a first course in the art of reading instruction. In addition, the book may serve as a manual of information for teachers in service.

The chief concern of the author was to acquaint pre-service and in-service teachers with a philosophy of reading instruction. Reading must be taught as a thinking process if sound reading-study skills are to be mastered. Reading instruction must be differentiated so that each child may attain his full potential. In addition, an attitude toward reading as a source of entertainment and knowledge must be fostered. Above all, the findings of research must be applied to the reading instruction of all children.

The book is divided into five parts. Part I's thesis is that the foundation of reading instruction is thinking. It provides the reader with a focus and declares essential perspectives. Part II describes how group instruction is to be accomplished and why. A group provides a medium for the meeting of minds and basic readers and the like can provide the materials. Part III gives detailed accounts of how reading instruction can be individualized and why. Individual differences in ability, in interests, in tastes, and in ambitions must be taken into account if self-reliant, resourceful, and self-activated students are to be prepared.

Part IV presents a discussion on beginning reading instruction. Here the value of reading as a facet of language, of child development as a matter of learning and maturity, of phonics as a skill collateral to comprehension, and of reading as a process of comprehension are described. Part V provides an exhaustive treatment of the need for skill attainment in word recognition, a discussion of concept development, and an evaluation of the role of testing and reporting.

A unique feature of this text is its coordination and synthesis with a second text, *Directing Reading Maturity as a Cognitive Process,* which was designed for use at the graduate level. Certain portions of the first volume also appear in the second, but the differences that exist are considerable. The amalgamation permits the alert undergraduate to turn to the second text and grasp basic concepts at greater depth and thoroughness than might be otherwise possible. The second volume deals exhaustively with concept attainment and the cognitive processes, as well as the role of the library in a comprehensive reading program. It also discusses speed reading and how to prepare versatile readers and keep them on the road to reading maturity.

Preface

The noblest freedom we can give our children is freedom from fear. The way to do this is to teach them to face fear boldly, to look at it, analyze it, and act on it. The noblest skill we can give a reader is the freedom to examine his own thinking, to raise his own questions, to seek answers diligently and boldly, to analyze and act. The only fear a scholar should have is the tyranny of his own decisions. He must be thorough and diligent in seeking the facts, judicious in weighing them, and fearful only that he must face the consequences of his own decisions.

Democracy and ignorance do not go together. A citizen must be able to read and to judge what he reads. He must read widely and frequently. He must judge the value of what he reads against his own experience and the statements of others. His mind rather than his memory must be trained, so that for him learning to read and to make educated decisions will be a continuing process.

Reading is a man's bulwark against loneliness—his window on life, his unending delight. Reading gives access to life's robe and miter. It provides a bishop's crook. It brings yesterday and tomorrow into now.

This book was written that every boy and girl might have a better chance to learn the freedoms of self, of a scholar, of a citizen, and of mankind. It reflects much careful thinking about reading and reading instruction and is based on many years of teaching, clinical experience, lecturing, consultations, and editorship. It advances certain convictions and does so in various contexts, even at the risk of being redundant.

First and foremost is the belief that the reading process is akin to the thinking process. Not only is this belief spelled out in all its facets, but also ways of teaching children to be thinking readers are numerously detailed. Children must learn to ask questions, to analyze questions others raise, to seek answers with judgment suspended until all the facts are in, to make wise decisions, and to act.

Second is the belief that group reading instruction is as essential as individualized reading instruction. It is in the dynamcs of a group situation that the thinking-reading skills can be honed and polished. Inquiring minds, focused on the same content, under the direction of a skilled teacher provide the wherewithal. In the foundation years of reading instruction, basic readers can supply the materials needed for Directed Reading-Thinking Activities. Basic readers can be most useful, if controls of vocabulary give way to control of concepts, if *memoriter* processes give way to cognitive processes, if so-called companion readers give way to the library, and if skill activities in boxes give way to functional reading-skill activities. Individualized reading instruction, with its focus on self-responsibility, self-knowledge, and sharing, requires at least equal instruction time with group instruction. Any basic-reader program represents but a poor abridgment of a library. No basic-reader system should at any time be thought of as *the* reading program.

Third is the belief that reading is one facet of language, and one means of communication. From the very beginning, reading instruction should be focused on the language-experience approach. Children can learn to read much as they learned to talk.

Fourth is the belief that a school library is more essential to sound reading instruction than any basic-reader series can ever be. It must have more than equal time and attention. Steps have been defined to show how this can be accomplished by word and deed as well as by thought.

Fifth, is the belief that word-attack skills can be taught in a functional way at a rate and depth not allowed by boxed-skill activities with forged contexts. Attention is focused on meaning clues or context clues because of the primacy of communication. Phonic clues or sound clues and structural clues or sight clues can be excellent auxiliary aids. The dictionary needs to be recognized and used as early in a reader's life as circumstances permit and require. This instruction can be initiated in first grade for many children.

Sixth is the belief that concept development and cognitive structures require early emphasis and soon take precedence over the mechanical aspects of word recognition. This is so because reading in all phases of the curriculum becomes a principal source of knowledge and cognitive structures. The semantic and syntactic aspects of the developmental process of learning-to-read are essentially one.

Seventh is the belief that the major purpose of most reading instruction is to improve comprehension. A problem solver seeking answers makes inferences, tests the inferences, and changes the inferences as he meets new contingencies. The reader's purpose for reading primarily determines how he will read, what he will read, and what he expects from what he reads, and his purpose is largely determined by his level of conceptual development and his cognitive functioning. The ideal is to obtain understanding with the greatest cognitive economy.

Eighth is the belief that the mature reader is a versatile reader. The mature reader knows how to adapt his rate of reading to the purposes for which he is reading and the nature (science, social science, fiction) and difficulty (readability) of the material. The mature reader does not read everything at the same rate; he is versatile and adapts.

Ninth is the belief that, as a person reads and comprehends, he acquires new concepts and learns to objectify reality. At the same time, he acquires an increasingly undistorted knowledge of *self*. This self-realization goes on throughout life. Egocentrism appears in various forms from childhood through adulthood. Clarity comes about only as one learns to see things from points of view other than one's own.

Tenth is the belief that the hard-to-measure outcomes of critical and creative reading must be measured and must replace tests that measure only superficial evidence of reading performance. The accuracy of the measuring rod pretty well determines what will be brought forth to be measured. Both formal (standardized tests) and informal tests must do more than focus on symptoms of reading difficulty. Reports to pupils should be the foundation for reports to parents.

This book is by no means perfect. It may at points appear oversimplified and too detailed, or too technical and sophisticated, or too redundant and evangelistic. These isolated liabilities, however, blend together into an organized and interrelated whole.

Without a doubt, the book reflects the thinking and writing of many people. This is why it is so abundantly documented. When quotations were used, care was taken not to violate the integrity of the original. Throughout, it should be apparent that ideas are built upon ideas.

The book was three years in the writing and many more years in the thinking. It required infinite pains and industrious drudgery. Hard work alone does not make this book a good book, but it is a common thread that is woven into the fabric of every sentence, every paragraph, every page, and every chapter.

Well, there you have it. And I must warn you, it may require some labor and thought on your part. This is clearly the *sine qua non* (the "without which not") of comprehension.

R. G. S.

PART I ❧ FOUNDATIONS OF READING INSTRUCTION

Chapter I
Reading: A Thinking Process

"I have found the answer to my question, and I can read the line that proves it," said a six-year-old first grader, rising to her feet. The warmth and eagerness with which she spoke reflected the passion of the scholar who has achieved.

This six-year-old girl was taking a major step toward achieving reading maturity. She was judging the relevance of a statement or sentence or thought to a purpose. She had wanted to know if Susan, the girl in the story, had found the penny she had lost or had found another penny. The sentence she read orally to prove her point was: "Susan found the penny." At once a boy in the group challenged her: "How do you know it was the penny Susan lost?" The girl replied: "It said 'the penny.' It didn't say 'a penny' or 'another penny.'"

This pointed incident occurring in a group-type Directed Reading-Thinking Activity illustrates many of the basic essentials of both intelligent reading and sound reading instruction. To be able to tell when the answer found fits the question asked is truly a major skill, one essential to reading for meaning. It is evident, too, from the girl's words "I have found the answer to *my* question," that she had been thinking prior to the reading.

There is almost unanimous agreement among reading specialists that *motivation, set,* or *purpose* influences productive reading. Apparently, this girl had declared earlier that she wanted to know whether the penny that was found was the penny that was lost. For the girl to have so clearly stated her purpose implies that she must already have known some of the story facts, that she must have reacted to these facts, that she must have associated the facts in the story with her knowledge and experiences, and that she must have made judgments about events that might reasonably follow. A skilled reader differs from others largely because of what he does in order to read (22). [Numbers in parentheses refer to the works cited at the end of the chapter.] As a result, how and what he reads are different from an unskilled performance. He examines all available clues, reflects about them in terms of his experience and knowledge, and then sets his purposes according to his informed judgments.

When this six-year-old stood at her desk in the presence of the other members of the group and the teacher, she was displaying the vigor and vitality and conviction of a person who has found the truth and is prompted to say so. To be sure, there was an emotional aspect to her response, but it was of the type that includes others in the group in an activity that to a large degree is purposive, conscious, or planned in character (4). It is during such a meeting of minds—which occurs when purposes are set, confirmed, or revised—that true individual differences can be observed and that each pupil can be directed to read more efficiently. This is also the time to study individual reading behavior, individual change, participation patterns, and group development. And it is the time too when a well-directed, Group-Type Reading-Thinking Activity can be seen to be consciously determined, deliberative, reality-bound, and goal-seeking.

The oral reading by the six-year-old of the line that proved her point was smooth and clear and done with an enthusiasm and spirit that would have roused a smile on the lips of any teacher who could have heard the performance. This young lady was out to prove her point and this was her preoccupation—not the pronouncing of words. She had a message to communicate to her audience, and she wanted to be sure they heard the words and were convinced. Could any teacher ask for more?

The give and take of a group situation provides an intellectual setting that can stimulate thinking and productive reading. When a boy challenged the girl and she met the challenge, the air was bristling with small but rapidly developing intellectual sabers. It is remarkable—and yet so true—that even six-year-olds, rather than argue pointlessly, can discusss a situation with astonishing objectivity. Children can think and read critically about matters related to their experiences. A six-year-old may not be motivated, or intellectually able, to comment on the validity of an historical doctrine, but she may, as this girl did, think critically about a lost penny and the language used to describe it.

Six-year-olds can think; they can size up a situation; they can put together the two and two of setting and plot and predict the outcome; they can evaluate findings in terms of their relevance to a set purpose; and they can integrate the knowledge gained with their prior knowledge. This single illustration supports the idea that reading is a phenomenon of mental activity akin to thinking. As such, it is an interplay of "response to outer, or realistic, and inner, or imaginative and artistic, forces which occurs in relation to the mental context, or personalizing factors" (28, p. 358). In other words, reading, like thinking, rests upon three principal aspects, "namely (1) *realistic thinking,* or reasoning, (2) *imaginative* thinking, and (3) *personalized* thinking" (29, p. 358). Also, like problem solving, purposeful reading has three phases: (1) confrontation by a problem, (2) reading to find a solution, and (3) finding the solution or failing to find it.

WHAT IS READING?

For some years I have asked the students in a graduate course on reading instruction for a written answer to the question, "What is reading?" Usually the class consists of teachers with from one to twenty-five years of teaching experience. Though their answers are quite varied, all seem to grasp the fundamental idea that to read is to comprehend what is read. Following are some representative definitions I have received.

Reading is complex process.
Reading means to get information from the printed page.
Reading is the ability to pronounce and comprehend the printed word.
Reading is interpreting signs, letters, or symbols by assigning meanings to them.
Reading is receiving ideas and impressions from an author via the printed word.

These definitions are probably typical of the way most classroom teachers define reading. If this is true, it is essential that teachers acquire a better understanding of the concept of *reading.* In 1936, William S. Gray said that a clear understanding of the nature of reading was fundamental to sound reading instruction. The development of programs that will serve adequately the needs of contemporary life "presupposes a clear understanding of the nature of reading and of the fundamental processes involved" (11, p. 23).

Early writers regarded reading as a synthesis of letters into a spoken word standing for an idea. The ABC method of which the Swiss educational reformer Johann Heinrich Pestalozzi wrote persisted for centuries. Though this method was vehemently denounced by Horace Mann as long ago as 1838, it continues to be used in some of our modern schools, with the result, according to Mann (19),

that more than eleven-twelfths of all the children in the reading classes in our schools do not understand the meaning of the words they read; that they do not master the sense of the reading lessons, and that the ideas and feelings intended by the author to be conveyed to, and excited in, the reader's mind, still rest in the author's intention, never having yet reached the place of their destination.

Even as late as 1955 one author, Rudolf Flesch, defined reading as "getting meaning from certain combinations of letters. Teach the child what each letter stands for and he can read" (8, p. 2).

In 1886, G. Stanley Hall, in his book on the psychology and pedagogy of reading, discussed the synthetic and the analytic methods of teaching reading (13, p. 3): "The synthetic [method] . . . proceeds from letters or sounds to words, sentences, etc.; and the analytic . . . begins with pictures, words or sentences and descends to visual or vocal elements. . . ." Even though Hall, like Mann, favored beginning with whole words, he pointed out that there were still many differences of opinion and practice respecting the most practical of these ways. Also, like Mann, Hall wrote about reading as thought-getting.

In 1913, Edmund B. Huey went a step further when he wrote, in his now classic *The Psychology and Pedagogy of Reading* (15, p. 350), "until the insidious thought of reading as word-pronouncing is well worked out of our heads, it is well to place the emphasis strongly where it really belongs, on reading as *thought-getting,* independently of expression." Then he went on to say (15, p. 359) that by silent-reading practice in getting meanings from the page "the rate of reading and thinking will grow with the pupil's growth and with his power to assimilate what is read."

Word and Phrase Method

The word-whole method and the phrase method of B. Erdmann and R. Dodge (7) and others including Charles H. Judd and Guy T. Buswell (17) led to defining reading as a process of recognizing printed words by units of recognition or by phrases. Although none of these authorities seemed to lose sight of the need to read for meaning, the attention they gave to other factors was diverting. Reading became a matter of span of recognition, fixation pause, duration of the fixation, fixations per line, regressive movements, and accurate return sweeps. Though studies of eye movements did throw additional light on the reading process, the teaching of reading was limited in objectives and was concerned primarily with the mechanics of reading. Reading, as a school subject, continued to be, as Edmund Huey put it, "an old curiosity shop of absurd practices" (15).

Starting in 1879 with Emile Javal (16), a French oculist, and continuing through the 1940s, extensive research was done concerning eye movements. The initial apparatus used to measure eye movements was a plaster of Paris cup molded to fit the cornea and having a round hole to permit reading, and an aluminum pointer tracing eye-movement records on the smoked-paper surface of a revolving drum cylinder. The first eye-movement camera using corneal reflection was invented by R. Dodge. The ophthalmograph, a small portable camera now available from the American Optical Company, has been used recently.

The eye-movement studies led to the development of the metronoscope, the tachistoscope, and reading films to improve the skill of poor readers. The metronoscope is essentially a triple-shutter tachistoscope that trains poor readers to read a line with only three pauses or three fixations. Reading films like the Harvard Films aimed to accomplish the same purpose by a motion-picture method. The tachistoscope is a short-exposure device whereby exposure time can be controlled. Words, phrases, or sentences may be used.

One of the most remarkable and enlightening findings of all the work on eye movements and the subsequent pacing training is Miles A. Tinker's report that *fixations* (not eye movements) take up about 90 percent of the total reading time in rapid reading and about 95 percent in slow reading (27). In other words, the rate at which the eyes move is of less importance to productive reading than the mental activity that occurs during the fixation pauses. Stated differently, it is the thinking that occurs during the pauses that dictates the length of the pauses and also the frequency of the pauses. Little wonder, then, as Irving H. Anderson and Walter I. Dearborn say, that "research has not conclusively demonstrated that any lasting benefit is derived from eye-movement training as such. The whole approach requires reexamination" (3, p. 131).

Equally as interesting is the fact that Miles A. Tinker, who has done extensive eye-movement research at the University of Minnesota, devotes only parts of two pages in his text *Teaching Elementary Reading* (26) to eye movements. The use of gadgets and techniques to train eye movements, he says, are symptoms of reading efficiency and not fundamental contributors to it. Another statement by Tinker presents the crux of the issue most succinctly (26, pp. 15–16):

Furthermore, rate of reading should vary according to the purpose of the reading and according to the difficulty and nature of the material. Some materials should be read rapidly, others slowly and even reread if the reading is to be efficient. The able reader is the versatile reader, the one who changes his pace to fit the requirements of the materials and the reading purpose. In fact, rapid reading has no practical significance in itself except that sometimes the task calls for expedition while at other times slow reading is in harmony with the requirements of the specific task. And the ability to vary speeds will be part of the repertory of the versatile reader. So the emphasis should be upon efficient rather than upon rapid reading per se. . . . This does not mean that there should be no training to improve rate of reading. Occasionally, pupils should be encouraged to work rapidly with the understanding that comprehension is not to be sacrificed.

Much of what has been said here regarding the value of eye-movement training and rapid-reading exercises could be said, too, about the widespread current practice of teaching readers so-called new words prior to their meeting them in a story context. The practice of writing new words on the chalkboard so as to "prepare" the reader for them is absurd and asinine. It has no practical significance. A similar comment could be made about teaching phonetic skills in isolation, and the comment is just as applicable if the skills are taught in isolation after the reading.

Another view of reading was expressed in the Twenty-fourth Yearbook. Part I, of the National Society for the Study of Education. William S. Gray says there that reading as formerly taught was determined largely by three aims: "to master the mechanics of reading, to develop habits of good oral reading, and to stimulate keen interest in, and appreciation of, good literature" (10, pp. 9–10). While this view may have been appropriate to the decades before 1920 when social organization was less complex and education was largely limited to the Three R's, it did not fit the changing times after World War I. According to the Yearbook Committee, the purpose of reading is "to extend the experiences of boys and girls, to stimulate their thinking powers, and to elevate their tastes," and the ultimate end of reading instruction is "to enable the reader to participate intelligently in the thought life of the world and appreciatively in its recreational activities" (10, p. 9). Of special interest here is the phrase "to stimulate their thinking powers." Through the ages, sound thinkers about reading have always recognized the need for reading for meaning, but it is significant that a publication that might materially influence practices has at last recognized the same need.

By 1936, the new Committee on Reading of the National Society for the Study of Education had taken an even broader view of the nature of reading. The new definition was spelled out by William S. Gray: "The reader not only recognizes the essential facts or ideas presented, but also reflects on their significance, evaluates them critically, discovers relationships between them, and clarifies his understanding of the ideas apprehended" (11, p. 26). Gray went on to say that:

The Yearbook Committee believes that any conception of reading that fails to include reflection, critical evaluation, and the clarification of meaning is inadequate. It recognizes that this very broad use of the term implies that reading includes much that psychologists and educators have commonly called thinking. The Committee . . . takes the position . . . that since efficient readers do think about what they read while they are reading it, the teacher should provide needed stimulus and guidance both in securing ideas from the page and in dealing reflectively with them. (11, p. 26.)

The implications of this definition are clear. Without a doubt, Gray's reference to what William H. Pyle[1] had said a few years before is aptly pointed: "It is not what is presented to the child that promotes growth but rather the reaction that he makes to what is presented" (11, p. 26). And it follows, too, that clear thinking and weighing of ideas during reading as well as after it are needed from the earliest grades. It is to be wished that at this point the Committee had also added the phrase, "as well as antecedent to it," for it is this aspect of the total reading act that is in much greater need of emphasis and clarification. Purposes for reading—the way in which they are determined and clarified and the way in which they dictate depth and rate of comprehension—contribute immeasurably to the total task involved in the art of reading.

By the time the Forty-eighth Yearbook, Part II, was published, so much additional research on reading had been accomplished that Arthur I. Gates gave a new account of the reading process.

---

[1] William H. Pyle, *The Psychology of the Common Branches* (Baltimore: Warwick and York, 1930).

Reading is not a simple mechanical skill; nor is it a narrow scholastic tool. Properly cultivated, it is essentially a thoughful process. However, to say that reading is a "thought-getting" process is to give it too restricted a description. It should be developed as a complex organization of patterns of higher mental processes. It can and should embrace all types of thinking, evaluating, judging, imagining, reasoning, and problem-solving. Indeed, it is believed that reading is one of the best media for cultivating many techniques of thinking and imagining. (9, p. 3.)

Gates goes on to say that the reader "does more than understand and contemplate; his emotions are stirred; his attitudes and purposes are modified; indeed, his innermost being is involved" (9, p. 4). This definition of the reading process is so compelling and persuasive that it makes a sharp contrast to the crude analogy of the mechanistic eye-movement era. Furthermore, it is sufficiently comprehensive to include situations in which reading is done for entertainment as well as for learning, thus allowing for some of the more subtle aspects of personal and social growth to which reading may contribute or in other words to what Dora V. Smith refers to as a neglected phase of current education (21, p. 205).

One of the best discussions on reading is Ernest Horn's book on methods of instruction in the social studies (14), Chapters III, IV, and V of which are at the top of my required reading list for graduate courses in reading. Reading, Horn says, "includes those processes that are involved in approaching, perfecting, and maintaining meaning through the use of the printed page" (14, p. 152). In discussing his definition, Horn recognizes the varieties and gradations of reading and of purposes for reading, methods for achieving understanding, and organizing knowledge in order to be functional. It is in his discussion of the symbolic character of language, however, that he goes beyond the definitions so far presented:

The author, moreover, does not really convey ideas to the reader; he merely stimulates him to construct them out of his own experience. If the concept is already in the reader's mind, the task is relatively easy, but if, as is usually the case in school, it is new to the reader, its construction more nearly approaches problem-solving than simple association. Moreover, any error, bias, or inadequacy in the author's statement is almost certain to be reflected in the ideas formed by the student. (14, p. 154.)

Once teachers grasp the significance of this statement, they will understand that they cannot make their students learn simply by assigning them a story or by requiring them to read on in the text to answer specific questions. The result of such assignments is usually a verbatim or slightly paraphrased report, because the pupil's attitude is mechanical rather than thoughtful, because it has been assumed that the author has ideas to convey through the straight and narrow sensory passageway afforded by the eye, and because it has been assumed that repetition can be equated with knowledge. An active search for meaning is best fostered in a situation in which the pupils are encouraged to act upon their own questions. The lively give and take of ideas, experiences, and knowledge in the prereading session produces questions that require of the reader an ordering and reordering, a testing and retesting, of his own ideas as he deals with the knowledge and experiences reported by the authors.

Another of the best discussions of reading appears in a book written by a man who received a doctorate in psychology from Columbia University, who was associate professor of law at the University of Chicago, and who is at present director of the Institute for Philosophical Research in San Francisco. Mortimer Adler's *How To Read a Book* should be required reading of all teachers from the preschool level to the postgraduate level. According to Adler,

> The art of reading . . . includes all the same skills that are involved in the art of discovery: keenness of observation, readily available memory, range of imagination, and, of course, a reason trained in analysis and reflection. . . . To whatever extent it is true that reading is learning, it is also true that reading is thinking. (1, p. 43.)

Earlier, Adler had distinguished between two types of reading and had indicated that the line of distinction between the two types frequently is hazy:

> The first sense is the one in which we speak of ourselves as reading newspapers, magazines, or anything else which, according to our skill and talents, is at once thoroughly intelligible to us. . . . The second sense is the one in which I would say a man has to read something that at first he does not completely understand. . . . The writer is communicating something which can increase the reader's understanding. (1, p. 31.)

He goes on to say:

> I am not pretending that the job is an easy one. I am only insisting that it is not an impossible one. If it were, no one could read a book to gain in understanding. The fact that a book can give you new insights or enlighten you indicates that it probably contains words you may not readily understand. If you could not come to understand these words by your own efforts, then the kind of reading we are talking about would be impossible. It would be impossible to pass from understanding less to understanding more by your own operations on a book. (1, pp. 202–203.)

It might be thought that Adler overestimates the value of getting the meaning of a word from other words and underestimates the value of experience, but in *What Man Has Made of Man* he says "What is crucially important . . . is the basic proposition: *All human knowledge arises from the operation of the sense, and most human knowledge goes beyond sense. i.e., has a reflective development.*" [Italics in original.] (2, p. 9.)

Reading to learn is a demanding task. It requires a command of thinking skills as well as reading skills. It also requires knowledge of grammar, syntax, and logic. This is especially so when the reader encounters something that at first he does not understand. And, as Ernest Horn has pointed out, this is usually the case in school (14, p. 154). Students need to be taught to read and with material that is intelligible to them. As Adler indicates, in general the ground plan for reading narrative material resembles that for reading scientific or expository works. Gradually, however, the reading program through the intermediate and secondary schools should give more and more training in reading the latter type of material. Reading matter designed to develop basic reading-thinking skills at the intermediate level and beyond should reflect this shift of emphasis.

THE PROCESS OF THINKING

What does it mean to consciously direct thinking? What happened, for example, in the following situation when the six-year-old reader finally located the line that seemed to support his point? In a group-type Directed Reading-Thinking Activity, a six-year-old boy exclaimed, "I was right. They are going to paint the house." The picture on the first page of the story showed two bears dressed like people, walking toward a house that was rather obviously in need of paint. This boy had examined certain facts at hand and had predicted that the bears would paint the house. When the teacher asked him to read the line that proved his point, he started to skim the page eagerly. He reached the bottom of the page, seemed considerably puzzled, and then started reading the page again—this time more slowly and carefully. At last he paused and looked up, saying: "It doesn't really say that they will paint the house, but this is where I got the idea." Then he read the line: "The bears will work on the house." What occurred when this young fellow realized that the answer he had predicted and found was not stated specifically but was only implied? What gave direction and organization to his reading-thinking process? How can an individual's reading-thinking process become increasingly deliberate and controlled?

In the 1910 edition of *How We Think*, John Dewey analyzed reflective experience and declared that thought may be directed by five steps:

(i) a felt difficulty; (ii) its location and definition; (iii) suggestion of possible solution; (iv) development by reasoning of the bearings of the suggestion; (v) further observation and experiment leading to its acceptance or rejection; that is, the conclusion of belief or disbelief. (5, p. 72.)

In the 1933 edition of the same work, Dewey listed the five phases of reflective thought as follows:

(1) Suggestions, in which the mind leaps forward to a possible solution; (2) an intellectualization of the difficulty or perplexity that has been felt (directly experienced) into a *problem* to be solved, a question for which the answer must be sought; (3) the use of one suggestion after another as a leading idea, or *hypothesis*, to initiate and guide observation and other operations in collection of factual material; (4) the mental elaboration of the idea or supposition as an idea or supposition (*reasoning*, in the sense in which reasoning is a part, not the whole, of

inference); and (5) testing the hypothesis by overt or imaginative action. (6, p. 107.)

Later Dewey adds that the five phases need not follow one another in a set order. Each step does something to perfect ideas that lead to new observations and data, and each helps the mind to judge more accurately the relevancy of the facts at hand. The way the five phases are managed depends upon the intellectual tact and sensitivity of the individual. Over and over, Dewey suggests that reflective thinking involves a look into the future, a forecast, an anticipation, a prediction, a prognosis, as well as the individual's knowledge and past experience.

David H. Russell lists six steps that may occur in the thinking process (20, pp. 15–16):

1. The *child's environment stimulates mental activity.* . . . Sense perceptions and memory are often the initial stage in thinking.
2. *The orientation or initial direction of the thinking is established.*
3. *The search for related materials takes place.*
4. *There is a patterning of various ideas into some hypothesis or tentative conclusion.*
5. *The deliberative, or critical, part of the thinking process is developed.*
6. *The concluding stage of the thinking process takes place when the hypothesis selected above is subjected to the test of use.*

According to Russell, these six steps parallel Dewey's analysis. He also points out that the degree of direction and the amount and type of organization influence the thinking process because of the nature of the stimulus patterns or problems encountered and because of the characteristics of the thinker himself.

STEPS IN THE READING-THINKING PROCESS

Certain steps akin to thinking and to reading can now be defined. The steps are essential to the reading-thinking process, especially when reading for information.

Declaring Purposes

Regulating reading by purposes—by questions to be answered—sets up a perplexity that demands a solution. This need to resolve a perplexity steadies and guides the reader-thinker and controls the rate and type of reading undertaken. In other words, the nature of the purposes to be achieved fixes the answers being sought and regulates the rate and scope of the reading-thinking process.

Self-declared purposes are a special significance. As directive influences and motivators, they are authoritative and trustworthy, especially to the degree that they are promoted by the facts at hand and the reader's motives, attitudes, and experiences. They avoid the pitfalls of assigned purposes and the artificiality of ready-made questions. They make the reader a student of what he is reading rather than a servant to recitation. They develop traits of open-mindedness, whole heartedness, and responsibility, of alertness, flexibility, and curiosity. Possession of the ability to declare purposes makes the difference between an able reader and an intellectual bungler.

Reasoning While Reading

As Edward L. Thorndike indicated some years ago, reading is reasoning. He pointed out that the word *reason* comes etymologically from the word *ratio,* meaning to balance. As the reader proceeds, he balances what he finds against his purposes, experiences, and knowledge. Thorndike concluded that:

Understanding a paragraph is like solving a problem in mathematics. It consists in selecting the right elements of the situation and putting them together in the right relations, and also with the right amount of weight or influence or force for each. The mind is assailed, as it were, by every word in the paragraph. It must select, repress, soften, emphasize, correlate, and organize, all under the influence of the right mental set or purpose or demand. (25, p. 329.)

This is to say that the reader manipulates the ideas to discover logical relations, or he rearranges logical patterns in such a way that a conclusion can be reached. To the degree that the reader has acquired certain standards or patterns, he can synthesize information and draw conclusions. Such reasoning will range from being simple and easy to accomplish to being complex and difficult to accomplish. Thus, the first grader who challenged the author's statement about a long parade of ducks by pointing out that three ducks in a line did not make a long parade was making a valid judgment. He was comparing the facts at hand against a standard obtained from examined experience.

As used in psychology today, the term *reasoning* usually refers to the solution of problems by logical operations. Reasoning is productive thinking and is to be contrasted with a mechanical response to previously learned stimuli or reproductive thinking.

Judging

Making judgments is a process with definite antecedents and consequences. As instanced above, the purposes to be achieved are the preparation for judgment, and they determine to a large degree what kind of judgments should be made. In this respect, the set for judgment is a productive task and alerts the reader to the kind of reading needed, so that a judgment can be made, helps the reader decide about materials to be read, and helps the reader decide the nature of the judgment to be made. The judgment might be a straightforward Yes or No, an estimate, or a decision that is specified only partially and involes evaluating alternative solutions.

Judgment is an evaluative process by which the reader draws conclusions.

The judgments made must be relevant to the purposes declared, and they must be correct. To judge, the reader must select and weigh the facts and make decisions that are pertinent and discriminate.

Not all reading requires complex judgments. In situations where there is not much doubt, the response is merely a perception or an act of recognition. Thus, when the reader judges a simple, clearly specific aspect of the total reading context—such as the size of a city, the amount of rainfall in a country, or a friend's telephone number—he does it quickly and on sight. But when there is something doubtful, when the different aspects or points at issue are not distinctive, when there is controversy consisting of alternate claims, when there is a question about how the claims are to be interpreted, estimated, appraised, and placed, the judgment is not at all simple, but complex. For example, a story about a lost dog without an identification collar and tag puzzled a group of first graders. Should the boys who found the dog try to locate the owner and, if so, how? Was the procedure described in the story one that could serve in future cases? Should other courses have been followed and, if so, why and how?

Declaring purposes, reasoning, and judging, the three aspects of the reading-thinking process, are fundamental to the reading-to-learn process, yet a fourth aspect, refining and extending ideas, is also necessary. Research on concept formation indicates that many people are reluctant to discriminate between the particular qualities of a concept or to sort and assimilate the qualities so that a standard of reference can be obtained. Yet it is precisely at this point that good teaching of reading becomes outstanding instruction and makes of the good reader a superior and mature reader. William S. Gray and Bernice Rogers say of the mature reader that he

> may be said to possess (1) . . . unique characteristics . . . that predispose him to reading; (2) a focus, or radix, of interest . . . which serves as an inner drive or motivating force; (3) awareness of himself as a responsible group member . . . ; (4) an ever expanding spiral of interest . . . ; (5) a high level of competence in reading, which enables him to proceed with reasonable ease and understanding in grasping and interpreting meanings, in reacting rationally to the ideas apprehended, and in applying his ideas with sound judgment and discrimination. (12, pp. 236–237.)

The authors go on to say that the foregoing statements do not explain how such maturity may be acquired. As they analyzed their cases, they discovered that, while home background was a contributing factor of large importance, the amount of schooling was more closely related to competence in reading. The crucial point along this route to maturity was the point at which reading ceased to be "a mere intellectual exercise of grasping and remembering meanings. . . . it is the point at which reading begins to bring about significant conversions, to make changes in one's core of values, to broaden interests, to open up new horizons, and to provide new and improved ways of thinking about things . . . . the process has become self-generating" (12, p. 237). To this they add that, while little can be done to change the reader's capacity to learn to read, much can be done to stimulate and direct reading activities so as to ensure maximum progress.

SUMMARY

A teacher's "point of view" regarding reading is extremely important. As L. Susan Stebbing says (23, p. 38), "The expression 'point of view' is metaphorical. . . . Mountains seen across the bay look very different from those same mountains as they are being climbed" or as they appear from an airplane.

Fortunately, the points of view of authorities concerning reading are pretty much in agreement. What is hoped is that the point of view about reading as a thinking process as developed in this chapter may be accepted and understood by all who read it. If you agree that muddled thinking ends in bungled doing and that to think clearly is useful for the sake of achieving even our most practical aims, if you agree that muddled reading ends in bungled verbalisms, if you agree that to read meaningfully is useful for achieving even our most practical day-to-day needs, then we agree that reading should be taught as a thinking process.

The roots of our beliefs and practices are deep in the traditions of the past. Even as teachers, we are not completely rational beings. That practices have lagged behind sound theory by as much as a generation or two is not too astonishing. We have after half a century come a long way toward breaking the lock step in classroom instruction. We have also come a long way toward breaking the round-the-robin comprehension alluded to by Horace Mann and so roundly denounced by present-day writers. A first step toward breaking the comprehension lock step is to believe that reading is a thinking process; a second step is to believe that people can be trained to read critically and reflectively.

REFERENCES

1. Adler, Mortimer J., *How To Read a Book*, New York, Simon & Schuster, 1940.
2. Adler, Mortimer J., *What Man Has Made of Man*, New York, Ungar, 1937.
3. Anderson, Irving H., and Walter F. Dearborn, *The Psychology of Teaching Reading*, New York, Ronald, 1952.
4. Bion, W. R., "Group Dynamics: A Re-View," *International Journal of Psychoanalysis, 33* (1952), 235–247.
5. Dewey, John, *How We Think*, Boston, Heath, 1910.
6. Dewey, John, *How We Think*, Boston, Heath, 1933.
7. Erdmann, B., and R. Dodge, *Psychologische Untersuchungen uber das Lesen, auf Experimenteller Grundlage*, Halle, 1898.
8. Flesch, Rudolf, *Why Johnny Can't Read and What You Can Do About It*, New York, Harper & Row, 1955.
9. Gates, Arthur I., "Character and Purposes of the Yearbook," *Reading in the Ele-*

mentary School, Forty-eighth Yearbook of the National Society for the Study of Education, Part II, Chicago, University of Chicago Press, 1949.

10. Gray, William S., "Essential Objectives of Instruction in Reading," *Report of the National Committee on Reading,* Twenty-fourth Yearbook of the National Society for the Study of Education, Part I, Bloomington, Ill., Public School Publishing Co., 1925.

11. Gray, William S., "The Nature and Types of Reading," *The Teaching of Reading: A Second Report,* Thirty-sixth Yearbook of the National Society for the Study of Education, Part I, Bloomington, Ill., Public School Publishing Co., 1937.

12. Gray, William S., and Bernice Rogers, *Maturity in Reading,* Chicago, University of Chicago Press, 1956.

13. Hall, G. Stanley, *How To Teach Reading, and What To Read in School,* Boston, Heath, 1886.

14. Horn, Ernest V., *Methods of Instruction in the Social Studies,* New York, Scribner's, 1937.

15. Huey, Edmund Burke, *The Psychology and Pedagogy of Reading,* New York, Macmillan, 1913.

16. Javal, Emile, as reported by Edmund Burke Huey in *The Psychology and Pedagogy of Reading,* New York, Macmillan, 1913.

17. Judd, Charles H., and Guy T. Buswell, *Silent Reading: A Study of the Various Types,* Supplementary Educational Monographs, No. 23, Chicago, University of Chicago Press, 1922.

18. McKee, Paul, *The Teaching of Reading in the Elementary School,* Boston, Houghton Mifflin, 1948.

19. Mann, Horace, "Second Annual Report of the Secretary of the Board of Education, 1838," in *Life and Works of Horace Mann,* vol. II, New York, Lothrop, Lee and Shepard, 1891.

20. Russell, David H., *Children's Thinking,* Boston, Ginn, 1956.

21. Smith, Dora V., "Literature and Personal Reading," *Reading in the Elementary School,* Forty-eighth Yearbook of the National Society for the Study of Education, Part II, Chicago, University of Chicago Press, 1949.

22. Stauffer, Russell G., "A Directed Reading-Thinking Plan," *Education, 79* (May, 1959), 527–532.

23. Stebbing, L. Susan, *Thinking To Some Purpose,* Hammondsworth, England, Penguin, 1939.

24. *The Teaching of Reading: A Second Report,* Thirty-sixth Yearbook of the National Society for the Study of Education, Part I, Chicago, University of Chicago Press, 1937.

25. Thorndike, Edward L., "Reading as Reasoning: A Study of Mistakes in Paragraph Reading," *Journal of Educational Psychology, 8* (June, 1917).

26. Tinker, Miles A., *Teaching Elementary Reading,* New York, Appleton-Century-Crofts, 1952.

27. Tinker, Miles A., "Time Taking for Eye-Movements in Reading," *Journal of Genetic Psychology, XLVIII* (June, 1936), 468–471.

28. Vinacke, W. Edgar, *The Psychology of Thinking,* New York, McGraw-Hill, 1952.

PART II ✦✦✦✦ GROUP INSTRUCTIONS AT VARIOUS LEVELS✦✦✦✦

Chapter 2 ❧❧ Group Directed Reading-Thinking Activities

A DIRECTED READING-THINKING ACTIVITY PLAN

Emmett A. Betts was quite right when he said that in general authors of basal readers were in agreement on the basic principles and assumptions regarding directed reading activities. He described the plan on which there was general agreement as follows:

> First, the group should be prepared, oriented, or made ready, for the reading of a story or selection. Second, the first reading should be *guided silent* reading. Third, word-recognition skills and comprehension should be developed during the silent reading. Fourth, the reading—silent or oral, depending upon the needs of the pupil—should be done for purposes different from those served by the first, or silent, reading. Fifth, the follow-up on the "reading lesson" should be differentiated in terms of pupil needs. (3, p. 492.)

The Directed Reading-Thinking Activity plan presented on pp. 20–21 contrasts sharply with the plan commonly endorsed and described above because of the following underlying assumptions.

1. Children can think. Within the limits of their experiences and language facility, they can size up a situation, conjecture about it, and they can reach conclusions.

2. Children can act purposefully. They can anticipate, plan, enjoy realization, and remember.

3. Children can examine. They can study a situation or a set of circumstances, note details, make associations, ask questions, modify their concepts, and form new concepts.

4. Children can use their experiences and knowledge. They are able to recall related experiences, remember ideas learned, and make meaningful associations and discriminations.

5. Children can weigh facts and make inferences. They can put together the two and two of a situation, sense subtleties, and be guided thereby.

6. Children can make judgments. They can decide between right and wrong, between fairness and unfairness, between yes and no, between success and failure.

7. Children can become emotionally involved. If they are active participants in a situation, they can become involved to the degree that enthusiasm is evident.

8. Children do have interests. Their likes and dislikes have been studied and catalogued many times. What is equally as important about their interests is that they are quick to recognize what they want and do not want, and that they are quite straightforward about saying so.

9. Children can learn. About the only difference in the learning of children and adults may be attributed to motivation and previous experience. The laws of learning do not distinguish between children and adults.

10. Children can make generalizations. Research has shown that, when children have mastered a principle on one kind of material, they can apply the principle to other kinds of materials.

11. Children can understand. As William A. Brownell and Verner M. Sims (4, pp. 38–40) point out, however, their understanding depends largely upon the degree to which they are motivated by a recognized need or purpose, to the background of relevant experience they possess, to the degree to which pupils direct or have their attention directed to the important aspects of a situation, to their stating what they have learned in their own words, to the degree to which they actively and aggressively approach learning, and to the degree to which the teacher involves them as active participants in setting purposes, in accomplishing the purposes, and in evaluating success or failure. These and kindred items make for wise and wholesome understandings essential to the directing of a reading-thinking process.

Certain basic steps underlie the effective development of a group Directed Reading-Thinking Activity (D-R-T-A), and these can be used whenever a group of children are dealing with the same material at the same time under teacher guidance. The plan is especially useful when basic readers are used as source material to develop skills essential to the reading-thinking process.

I. Identifying Purposes for Reading
  A. Examining clues available in the
    1. Title and subtitles
    2. Pictures, maps, graphs, and charts
    3. Material: adjusting to information as it is read, and to readability
  B. Declaring purposes in terms of the
    1. Reader's background of experience, intellect, language facility, interests, and needs
    2. Experience, abilities, interests, and needs of the group

      3. Content of the material: concepts of time, place, people, number, science, aesthetics, and humor

II. Guiding the Adjustment of Rate to Purposes and Material
    A. Skimming: to read swiftly and lightly
    B. Scanning: to read carefully from point to point
    C. Studying: to read and reread so as to pass judgment

III. Observing the Reading
    A. Noting abilities to adjust rate to purpose and material
    B. Recognizing comprehension needs and providing help by clarifying
        1. Purposes
        2. Concepts
        3. Need for rereading (silent or oral)
    C. Acknowledging requests for help with word-recognition needs by providing immediate help in the use of
        1. Context clues: meaning clues
        2. Phonetic clues: sound clues
        3. Structural clues: sight clues
        4. Glossary clues: meaning, sound, and sight clues

IV. Developing Comprehension
    A. Checking on individual and group purposes
    B. Staying with or redefining purposes
    C. Recognizing the need for other source material
    D. Developing concepts

V. Fundamental Skill-Training Activities: Discussion, Further Reading, Additional Study, Writing
    A. Increasing powers of observation (directed attention)
    B. Increasing powers of reflection by
        1. Abstraction: reorganizing old ideas, conceiving new ideas, distinguishing between ideas, generalizing about ideas, and making inductions and analyses
        2. Judgment: formulating propositions and asserting them
        3. Reasoning: inferring and demonstrating, and systematizing knowledge inductively
    C. Mastering the skills of word recognition: picture and language context analysis, phonetic and structural analysis, and dictionary usage
    D. Developing adeptness in the use of semantic analysis: levels of abstraction, shifts of meaning, referential and emotive language, definite and indefinite terms, and concept development

It should be evident at once that this D-R-T-A plan is not a process standing alone, to be used only in directing the reading of material in a basal reader. Its doctrines are fundamental to problem solving, abstracting and analyzing information, and propaganda analysis and similar frequently occurring activities in which reading serves as an aid in the lives of both children and adults in their search for truth and beauty. The attitude of straight thinking required to draw inferences, to evaluate relevancies, to grasp sequences, to draw tentative conclusions, to suspend judgment, to evaluate and make decisions of judgment can be taught and acquired through suitable classroom procedures in most curricular areas.

Everyone is agreed that in the process of becoming educated a student may not rely on the unsystematic, catch-as-catch-can sort of thinking of everyday living. The literate man differs from the illiterate man in what he does about learning (1). A student starts with a problem or purpose to be resolved or accomplished. Then he collects relevant facts, groups the facts, and uses the facts to predict, control, and determine a means to an end. Similarly, the skilled reader differs from the unskilled reader by what he does in order to read. The *purposes* he sets determine *how* and *what* he reads. The literate man and the skilled reader when reading for information perform like a researcher. They set up the equivalent of a null hypothesis and are as interested in evidence that disproves the hypothesis as they are in evidence that supports it.

To understand how this plan for directing a reading-thinking activity can be used effectively, particularly for group-type instruction using basic readers, it will be necessary to take a look at the "basic reader." This needs to be done in some detail, since basic readers provide the source material for reading instruction in well over 90 percent of the schools in the United States.

WHAT IS A BASIC READER?

A basic-reader series is a set of books and related materials planned and prepared to be used in a unique way for reading instruction at successive stages of reading development and consisting of a selected content of a specialized nature. An interesting discussion of *basic* and *basal* appears in the Sixtieth Yearbook of the National Society for the Study of Education (12, pp. 165–188). Even though *basal* is the term preferred there, both terms have been used interchangeably by reading experts through the years (11, p. 49).

A basic-reading series is supposed to provide materials and define methodology needed to develop fundamental habits, attitudes, and skills essential to reading. As Virgil E. Herrick indicates, such a sweeping and all-embracing definition rests on two assumptions, "first, that a set of essential or fundamental habits and skills is generally known; second, that these habits and skills are of such a nature that a series of books and materials specially prepared are essential to their development" (12, p. 167).

In 1950, in preplanning for the writing of a new series of basic readers, I made a thorough analysis of "skill programs" and professional writings currently available. The study indicated that comprehension skills to be taught numbered in the hundreds, as did word-attack skills.

Similar findings were obtained on the stages that schoolchildren typically go through in developing reading abilities. The most comprehensive single statement on this subject appeared in Chapters II and IV of the Thirty-sixth Yearbook of the National Society for the Study of Education, both of which were prepared by William S. Gray (9, 15). We concluded, with David Russell, that, while such descriptions appear valid, "at best, they are general descriptions giving rough approximations of a child's reading status" (17, p. 229).

The finding of our study that impressed us most was the lack of agreement on "systematic sequences" and on the *when* and *how* of teaching specific skills. As Russell (17) brings to light, there are many blocks, both of a general administrative nature and of a psychological nature, to accomplishing a developmental reading program. These same blocks, blocks to articulation, transition, and continuity, need to be dealt with by those who prepare a series of basic readers. It is this, we concluded, that results in the lack of agreement between the various series. It also means, however, that the words "systematic" and "sequential" should always appear within quotation marks because of the many meanings they have and the various procedures they imply.

Insofar as reading for meaning is concerned, the major difference between reading at the primary level and reading at the high-school level and beyond is the individual's reading maturity. That children can think and can think critically even at six years of age, the time when most begin formal reading instruction, is now widely accepted. This means that comprehension skills embracing the finding and using of facts, integrating facts, going beyond facts, generalizing, making judgments, discriminating, appreciating character feeling, clarifying and extending concepts, and drawing conclusions are all taught at all levels or stages of progress and vary only in degree and kind. Furthermore, a grasp of these skills can be accomplished only to a limited degree in any basic reading series. The limitations are those of the materials.

A basic-reader series at its very best could be representative of the source material of a library only on an extremely limited basis. In fact, even a superior series exaggerates to call itself an *abridged* library, for it does not compare as favorably as an abridged dictionary tends to compare with an unabridged dictionary. Contrast, if you wish, a dictionary like the *Winston Dictionary for Schools* with *Webster's New International Dictionary (Unabridged)* or with *The Oxford English Dictionary*. Then compare the content of a basic series of readers with the central library of a school, city, or university. The comparison points up sharply the severe limitations of a series of basic readers, and the importance of source material for reading instruction takes on the dimensions that it should.

In the area of word-attack skills and vocabulary building, there is closer, but not total, agreement among the various basic-reader series and phonetic programs concerning skills to be accomplished and systematic sequences. In general, what may be said about basic-reader programs is that "continuity is achieved best in terms of gradual change from easy to difficult materials" (17, p. 247). These changes reflect arbitrarily declared controls of word introduction, word repetition, words per sentence, words per page, word difficulty, and so on. Even so, this continuity in difficulty is not nearly so apparent at the intermediate-grade levels as it is at the primary levels. And continuity in content is not as apparent at either level as continuity in difficulty.

Content can be examined, though, in terms of interest areas, type (narrative or expository, fiction or fact) and structure (plot development or compendiousness). Interest areas range in kind and degree from the typical experiences of primary-level children (home, family, neighborhood, toys, animals, objects, vehicles, and the like) to the more varied, unusual, and numerous experiences of the upper-intermediate-level child (arts and crafts, astronomy and astronauts, history and geography, law and ethics, the sciences, and so on). Story types range from realistic and imaginary, fact and fantasy, mysteries and riddles, comedy and fable to biography and autobiography, essays and reviews, history and current events, natural and social sciences, and so on. Material structure varies from plots that are simple and straightforward in their relating of events to plots that involve flashbacks and subtleties and unique arrangements of details to editorials, essays, articles, papers, themes, and verse.

Well-written stories reflect the element of things happening—conflicts, issues, incidents, eventualities. These are factors that maintain and propel reader interest and carry him on to the end. The ever-present human-interest factors help the reader to grasp the social relationships of story heroes as he follows their problems and to reduce human behavior to its elements. In short, when a story makes sense, it keeps the phrase "on with the story" uppermost in the reader's mind. Events that proceed from the beginning to the end unfold in gripping sequence and hold the reader's attention until the climax has been reached.

Pictures vital to the story must be planned and designed to help carry the plot forward and to aid the reader by strengthening, reinforcing, and developing visual images. Pictures help to establish and develop concepts and to heighten the drama and the interest. At no time, however, must the pictures reveal that which is intended to be told in the story. In other words, pictures as well as words provide the medium for telling a story. A good picture is worth a thousand words, but the picture and the story should not use the same thousand words.

DEVELOPING PURPOSES FOR READING

The key step in a Directed Reading-Thinking Activity is developing purposes for reading. As described in Chapter 1, "purposes" or "questions" or "set" represent the directional and motivating influences that get a reader started, keep him on course, and produce the vigor and potency and push to carry him through to the end.

Purposes for reading represent the key element in versatility. The versatile reader adjusts rate of reading according to his purposes for reading and to the nature and difficulty of the material being read. By focusing on purposes for reading from the very beginning of formal instruction, the reader acquires an attitude toward reading and an appreciation of the use and value of purposes for directing the reading act. In the early phases of the instructional program the young reader will not be too articulate about what he is doing and how he is doing it, but by repeated experience he will, as he matures, begin to see how to be deliberate. Of all the reading skills, the one most lacking is that of versatility. The principal reason why students complete high school and college without accomplishing this high-order reading skill reflects the use of inappropriate methodology from the very beginning of reading instruction.

Why Pupil Purposes?

It has been said that to know that you know that you do not know is the beginning of wisdom. Francis Bacon (2) said that an appraisal of one's ignorance is the beginning of wisdom, and John Dewey (7) believed that the crucial problem for the teacher is to utilize the intellectual curiosity of a learner in such a way that the initiative and the questioning attitude lie with the learner. Dewey said also that a question well asked is half an answer. If the beginning of wisdom is an appraisal of one's ignorance, the beginning of reading to seek wisdom is also an appraisal of one's ignorance.

The reading-thinking process begins in the mind of each reader as he experiences a state of doubt or curiosity about what he knows or does not know, and what he thinks will or will not happen. The reader must develop the ability to ask questions while reading fiction as well as nonfiction. The reader's questions must reflect his best use of his experience and knowledge (18).

When pupils have become involved in the dynamics of a purpose-setting session, the self-commitment on an intellectual as well as an emotional level has tremendous motivating force. The power of this force is almost immeasurable as it compels and sustains the reader until he finds an answer. The ideas a pupil declares are *his* ideas; they reflect *his* experience and knowledge, *his* association and projection, *his* ego. He is out to prove himself right or wrong. The self-actualizing tendency of self-declared purposes is enormous.

The reader, having helped to create the reading climate, will strive to maintain it. Its tempo is geared to the finding of answers and to the proving or disproving of conjectures. He will want to move forward to test his ideas, to seek, to reconstruct, to reflect, and to prove. What is most astonishing about all this is the integrity with which the reader operates. He is out to seek the truth, and this is his dedication.

What About Teacher Purposes?

The most mature and the most experienced person in a group is the teacher. The ideal situation is one in which the material being read is absolutely new to both the teacher and the pupils. In such a reading situation, the teacher can without pretense or condescension be an active reading-thinking member of a group.

Since this discussion applies primarily to the use of basic readers, that ideal situation is seldom met. The teacher knows the story or article being read, and the pupils know that she knows it. Any conjecture ventured by a teacher will instantly be viewed by a group as either a tip-off or a gross distortion. On occasion, though, a teacher purpose is acceptable in the over-all training of thinking readers, even though her purposes may be mis-construed.

What Is the Role of the Teacher?

The role of the teacher is of vital importance. As G. Polya says:

One of the most important tasks of the teacher is to help his students. This task is not quite easy; it demands time, practice, devotion, and sound principles.

The student should acquire as much experience of independent work as possible. But if he is left alone with his problem without any help or with insufficient help, he may make no progress at all. If the teacher helps too much, nothing is left to the student. The teacher should help, but not too much and not too little, so that the student shall have a *reasonable share of the work*. [Italics in original.] (15, p. 1.)

The teacher must avoid being the instrument of authoritarian indoc-trination. Her teaching must be such that the group is never intimidated by the tyranny of a right *teacher* answer—one which the group dare not question. Tyranny, if it is to reside anywhere, especially in the use of basic-reader stories and selections, must rest in the text and in the group.

If the teacher is to live up to our affirmation and so direct a reading activity that pupil thinking is both required and honored, she will be in a very important sense emotionally removed from the give and take—the predicting and confirming or rejecting—of the reading-thinking process. Her role is, as one second-grade boy described it, that of an *agitator*—an intellectual agitator. In this capacity she asks and asks again, *What do you think?*, *Why do you think so?*, and *Read the line(s) that proves it*. These directives are sufficiently specific to stir the minds of all school-age children. When the pupils state what they think, express their opinions, and listen to the ideas voiced by others in the group, they will be reading to see who in the group is right and why they are right.

With such motivation the pupils will not be reading to find an answer to satisfy a teacher-asked question. They will not be preoccupied with the fear of being wrong and rousing signs of displeasure in the teacher or a sharp reprimand. Neither will they be preoccupied with currying the teacher's favor. In turn, if they fail to find an answer, the blame of failure will not be projected on the teacher, since it was not a teacher question. This is the degree to which, and the sense in which, the teacher is emo-tionally freed from asserting the tyranny of a right answer. She is not impaled on her own boomerang. The tyranny rests with the pupil (I am right or wrong), the group (we are right or wrong), and the text (I have the answer).

It would be a serious error to think that the skills, abilities, and attitudes essential to functioning as a thinking reader could be accomplished without teacher guidance. To perfect learning—to make the skills, abilities, and attitudes vital and functional parts of children's reading performance—requires constant practice and coaching under the watchful eye of a competent teacher. It is only a result of frequent practice with different materials, handled in different ways, that the art of searching for truth and beauty approaches mastery.

The Role of the Group

H. Gordon Hullfish and Philip G. Smith, in their *Reflective Thinking: The Method of Education,* say, "Certainly, before the child enters kindergarten or the first grade he is already a going concern, a *thinking, knowing, individual person.* John B. Watson once said that by this time the child was a graduate student in learned responses" (13, p. 72). The impact of the interaction of a group of thinking, knowing, *individual* persons dealing with the same story or material sparks the resolving of the problematic aspects of a situation. Emphasis on personal interest or purpose, on the creative element of inferences, maintains the personal integrity of each member of the group. It is the development of thinking on the part of all students that provides the thread that unites the group.

In turn, all members of the group are involved in the act of creating hypotheses, conjectures, purposes, using them to guide their reading, and reading to test their significance. It is here that the adequacy of reading and of meaning is tested in the context of the group. It is the group that demands that individual predictions, to be acknowledged, must be warranted on the basis of available evidence. The group sits as auditors, authorized to examine the evidence, verify the questions and answers, and state the results.

The Role of the Story

The story, especially at the primary level, provides the substance—the matter—for cognition. The story has a title, a plot development, and an ending. The story is told by means of pictures and language conjoined in such a way that both elements help develop the plot.

Title Clues. A story title can be the equivalent of a central theme. It has an over-all, encompassing value. It suggests the plot setting, possible story trends, and possible outcomes. It plays a unifying role. By way of illustration, the title of a story in a so-called first reader is "A One-Time Magic Garden" (21, pp. 101–106). At once, such a title can set in motion creative, divergent thinking. It suggests many ideas that are plausible within the limits of the information available.

Three concepts are given in this title, each within the grasp (experience and knowledge) of six-year-olds. *One-time* is an idea all youngsters have experienced. A one-time visit to a zoo, a one-time ride in an airplane, a one-time fall from a jungle-gym, a one-time contact with measles, and so on. *Magic* is a word that really sets their imaginations spinning—drawing out, winding, and twisting ideas into the most exciting of yarns. *Garden* is a fairly common concept that has some meaning for most children.

One group of six-year-olds, asked what they thought this story would be about, said: "Maybe it's about a magic hat." "It might be a magic hat that shoots cannon balls like in the cartoons." "Maybe it's about a magic pumpkin that grows very big in a day." "Maybe a fairy turns the garden into gold and does it only once." These are speculations typical of six-year-olds. Adults are seldom able to match the predictions of children, for they think on another level—less imaginatively and more realistically—and often with fewer variations in their speculations.

First-Picture Clues. The picture below introduces the characters in the story, an animal, and—what is most likely a central prop—a huge cornstalk. The stalk is so tall its top is out of sight. The clues a first picture can provide are just these: characters, setting, time.

The six-year-olds referred to earlier turned to this picture. A first and spontaneous reaction was, "Oh, Jack and the Beanstalk!" Others quickly picked this up and agreed. Other comments were, "I think now it's not about a magic pumpkin but about a magic beanstalk." "It may still be about a magic hat." "Maybe one of the boys will climb the beanstalk and find a magic hat." "Maybe all the children will climb up and see a giant." "Maybe they'll climb up and see Jack and the giant." "Maybe they'll climb up and see all kinds of things."

Titles and Subtitles. In another D-R-T-A session, the group was asked to read the first two and a half pages (or one-fourth) of a particular story. The pupils were like detectives who had been given one-fourth of the clues to examine. With this much information in their possession, how did they examine the evidence and weigh the clues? What conjectures did they make concerning the second quarter of the story?

Pupils performing as thinking readers will analyze and synthesize the ideas as they search for plot clues. They will not memorize the story. The group mentioned above first examined the title and subtitle. "Washington's Scout" (the title of the story) (25, p. 83–94) could refer to George Washington and the struggle for independence. "Maybe he is a Revolutionary War scout." "Maybe he does something that saves the day for the Continental Army." "Maybe he is a Boy Scout from Washington, D.C., who saves the day on the Deering Farm." ("Deering Farm" was a subtitle of the story.) "Maybe Washington's headquarters are on the Deering Farm." "Perhaps the Deering Farm is an ideal hideout for one of Washington's scouts." These are just

A One-Time Magic Garden

"This must be magic," said Bill.
"Dad just put it in this morning.
Then it was little, but see it now."

"I can see it go," said Cooky.
"It is going up as fast as a bird.
I wish I could go up on it."

"You can," said one of the twins.
"I will show you how."

101

some of the ideas the pupils had as they reflected over the title and subtitle to this story.

Picture Clues. After examining the title and subtitle, some pupils studied the two pictures on the pages they were permitted to see. The pictures—a small farmhouse and barn with a log-cabin-type annex located in a meadow and nestled among rolling hills—give clues to the geographical or spatial setting of the story. They also give useful time clues: the farmhouse and barn, the dress of the men, the kind of gun used all suggest colonial days. These same pictures also suggest such aesthetic concepts as color, dress, and architecture, as well as certain social concepts: Washington's scout, who is he? Does he operate alone? Does he meet with Washington? Whom is he scouting?

As a reader matures chronologically, intellectually, socially, emotionally, experientially, and scholastically, he realizes more and more the importance of pictures as source material. He studies pictures to obtain all the clues he can that will be helpful in following the plot development. To him a picture may, depending on its quality, be worth a hundred words, five hundred words, or maybe the proverbial thousand words! Experience in reflective reading and thinking teaches this student to seek facts as evidence with which to develop and test his hypothesis, rather than to fear the tyranny of facts dealt with on a *memoriter* basis. This kind of reader will never say, as one boy did who took the "memorize-all, parrot-all, forget-all approach," "Nothing but one damned fact after another."

Language Clues. To the reader schooled in the reading-thinking philosophy, the examination of clues—title, subtitle, and pictures—takes but a few seconds. Words and pictures trigger his thinking, and ideas course through his mind with astonishing rapidity.

Now, primed to deal with the language part of the plot development, he reads on, ever alert to clues to support or reject his conjectures and to facts that suggest new hypotheses. Reading is a continuous process of searching, examining, weighing, changing, adjusting, creating, and testing meanings. The reader finds out that the story is about one of George Washington's scouts, that he is taking a message through the British lines commanded by General Howe, that he does so at midnight, that he is aided by Jack France, a lad not old enough to be in the army, and that the Deerings are friendly to the British. By the time he has finished reading to the end of the assigned passage, he is prepared to offer conjectures about events to follow, how they may develop, why things may go one way or another. Jack has shown himself to be a loyal and resourceful American patriot, ready to render courageous services and to give up his favorite horse if Washington needs him. He is ready to spy on the Deerings, to do so at night, and to make the long ride alone. Apparently what he is doing meets with his mother's approval. Washington's situation is rather desperate. How will Jack fare? Ask some young reader, and he will give you an answer that sparks with emotion and high spirit and that reflects the rebellious and defiant bravado of the developing story. In many instances, girls, even more than boys, speak with zest as they become imbued with the spirit of the occasion and espouse the cause of freedom.

Maps, Graphs, and Charts. Unschooled readers—and this includes many college-level adults—have a strong tendency to skip maps, graphs, and charts. Even at the graduate level, students tested on information presented in graphic media frequently fail because of their inattentiveness to information of this type. Sound reading habits acquired early in the learning-to-read program can overcome such major delinquencies.

The following illustration is the second page of a four-page article entitled "Catch That Airplane." The story appears in a basic reader (27) designed for use at the sixth-grade level.

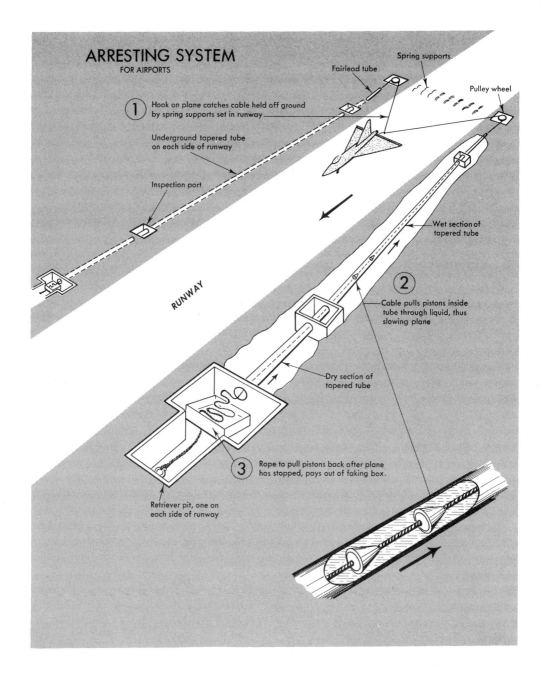

ARRESTING SYSTEM
FOR AIRPORTS

1. Hook on plane catches cable held off ground by spring supports set in runway

Fairlead tube

Spring supports

Pulley wheel

Underground tapered tube on each side of runway

Inspection port

Wet section of tapered tube

RUNWAY

2. Cable pulls pistons inside tube through liquid, thus slowing plane

Dry section of tapered tube

3. Rope to pull pistons back after plane has stopped, pays out of faking box.

Retriever pit, one on each side of runway

It is recommended that the group be asked to study the illustration and to speculate concerning the meaning of the title and the process used to catch the airplane.

Pupils trained to examine such diagrams will look first for the diagram label: "Arresting System for Airports." Speculation about the meaning of the word *arresting* may require some thought-provoking questioning on the part of the teacher, or a quick check by the pupils in a dictionary for different meanings of the word, or both. Other labels are studied: tapered tube, pistons, retriever pit, and so on, as the details illustrated are examined.

Typical conjectures obtained are: "The article will tell how this system works." "Maybe it tells how it is built." "Probably it tells why it is needed, since planes can stop on their own." "If the system stopped a plane too quickly, what would happen to the passengers and the crew?" Thus armed, the readers are ready to study carefully the body of the article. Discursive material demands that the reader approach the reading with a questioning mind. This is not the time to memorize isolated and discrete facts. Now it is all the more urgent that creative reading of a scientific nature be done so that meaning may be obtained.

This approach to the use of a diagram is only one of a number of approaches that may be used to teach pupils why and how to read graphic aids. Asking pupils to study the diagram first should help them make a quick appraisal of what they know and do not know and of what to look for when they read the article. The teacher might have discussed first each item in the diagram in detail, but this would have resulted largely in teacher-telling. On the next page of the book, this article has another illustration and a photograph. Pupils turning to these two pages are asked to read ahead on their own. No group study of the two illustrations is done first. Each pupil is being required now to make his own analysis or to do his own reading. If lack of skill is revealed, subsequent training can be provided. At a later point there is presented in greater detail a discussion on this topic.

The Reader's Background

The reader's background of experience, intellect, language facility, interests, and needs determines his ability to examine sets of reading circumstances like those described in "The One-Time Magic Garden," "Washington's Scout," and "Catch That Airplane" and to make conjectures about either plot development or selection content. This is true at all levels.

It must be kept in mind constantly that a Directed Reading-Thinking Activity in which basic readers are used represents to a large degree a captive-audience-type situation. The selection or story to be read depends on the book being used. The opposite circumstance occurs in an individualized program (see Chapter 5) in which the materials to be read are self-selected. A half-way position between these two extremes—teacher-selected materials, and pupil-selected materials—might be the circumstance in which a student searches for more information as a result of some class activity in science, social studies, or arithmetic. Under these conditions the pupil has some choice about materials to be used, even though his choice is limited by a predetermined bibliography.

On occasion, even staunch advocates of the use of basic-reader teacher's manuals question the lack of freedom of choice imposed on pupils when manuals are used exclusively. Some teachers say they allow the pupils themselves to select the next story to be read in a basic reader. This is a weak defense that deceives no one, least of all the pupils. They know what story is the "next story." Other teachers say they do not follow the sequence of stories as they appear in the reader but "skip around." This gives readers some choice, but the choice is very limited and is restricted to one particular book. Furthermore, teachers who "skip around" are violating the sequences set up by the authors of the basic-reader series. It is difficult to understand why these teachers defend a basic reader so vehemently on the one hand and on the other hand violate one of the sacred doctrines of a basic series— sequentially prepared content. In short, these arguments add up to not much more than idle chatter.

Readiness to read a basic-reader story is usually spoken of in hushed voices, because it, too, represents a basic-reader sacred cow. It is not that the doctrine of readiness is being questioned; rather, it is the way in which it is practiced. Let us examine a typical readiness directive that represents an adaptation of a set of instructions appearing in a recently revised series of readers. The instructions accompany a story appearing in a reader planned for use at a third-grade level.

Explain: Our story for today is about a hungry mother lion and two hungry cubs. They went searching for food in the jungle. Look at the pictures in the story. See if you can tell what they found. What have the lions found in the first picture? Do you think the berries will be a treat for the lion? The first part of the story tells that they also found juicy bugs. Why do you think the lion cubs are standing up and sniffing? Let's look at the next picture. What has the mother lion found? Explain that the story answers this last question. Suggest: I think you'll have fun reading the story to find out.

Why explain all this to the children before they read? Why "tell" the children this much about the story? For what kind of children is this pablum intended? Are teachers this incompetent? Why must the children be reassured that they will have "fun" reading the story? It sounds like a "you had better have fun or else" command. Can't the children for whom this is intended *think*? Can't the teachers for whom this is intended *teach*?

On occasion, one of the best ways to motivate interest is to read part of a story to a group. This is a top-flight way to arouse their curiosity—to whet their reading appetites. However, the directives used above are not of this variety and, furthermore, are not being used "on occasion" only.

Again, staunch advocates of an all-out basic-reader approach say in defense, "Maybe this kind of readiness is not the best, especially for pupils able to read at a third-reader level. However, it is necessary at the first-grade level." This, too, is an indefensible position. Such pablum is no more needed for six-year-olds than it is for eight- or twelve-year-olds.

Still others defend such practices by saying that they are needed to build a background of experience or to build concepts. Will talking about a hungry mother lion, a merry-go-round, a farm, a zoo, a circus, or an Indian build concepts? Even if pictures are introduced during this so-called readiness period, will they suffice? If they will suffice, then why not incorporate them in the story?

The sixty-four-dollar answer that the basic-reader devotees give is that this kind of readiness promotes "language" readiness for the reading of the story, particularly for the so-called new words introduced in a story. In the case cited, the teacher did most of the talking. She first used such key words as *hungry, lion, jungle, berries, bugs, juicy, cubs, sniffing,* and so on. How did this teacher know that these words were not already a part of the children's oral-language vocabulary? True, the pupils were asked to respond to certain elements in the pictures. But why be this specific in obtaining pupil response? The responses given by six-year-olds when they reacted to the title and first picture in "The One-Time Magic Garden" stand in sharp contrast to what is described here.

Oral-language usage of key words in a story prior to the reading and during the reading of a story is of much importance and not to be underestimated. What is questioned is the way it is done. Chapter 3 in this book provides ample illustration of preferred methods.

Just one more thought will be raised about this kind of readiness and its liabilities. Basic-reader stories are planned and prepared to reflect pupil interests, language development, experience, and maturity. This being the case, the stories should, if well chosen, be within the range of most children, insofar as these controls are concerned. Why, then, these elaborate readiness recommendations? Why? Why? Why?

The Group's Background

A group is made up of individuals, and the total backgrounds of the individuals comprise the sum and substance of the group's background. It is the *sum* of the experiences, intellects, language facility, interests, and needs that warrants the following discussion. When directing a so-called low group of second-grade-level children as they read a second-reader-level story, the following incident occurred. The first picture in the story showed a man and woman—perhaps a father and mother—in a living room of a house. The room was stripped; boxes and packages were on the floor, items of furniture were grouped together, and the two seemed to be busy packing. One boy in this group of five said he thought the parents were wrapping packages, but he did not know why. Another said they might be wrapping gifts, perhaps for a party. Two had no ideas to offer. The fifth pupil said she believed the family was going to move. When asked why she thought so, she answered: "We have moved, and that is how we got ready to move."

None of the other children had ever moved, but they thought Mary Ann's idea a good one. Subsequent reading showed Mary Ann to be right. It was a story about a family that was moving from a city to the country. Certainly Mary Ann was pleased to have been right. It was not necessary to ask her about this. The moment she read the lines about the family moving, her face lit up with the satisfaction one experiences with having made a right deduction. No, the other children were not depressed and unhappy at having been wrong. On the contrary, they seemed happy in Mary Ann's behalf. At the same time, their experiences were being extended, their concept of *moving* was refined, and their picture-examination skills were sharpened. Granted that this was a vicarious extension of experiences and concepts; yet it was a practical one.

The sum of the group's experiences permitted this learning to occur. Even though this story dealt with "moving"—a concept common to almost all children in one form or another—the particular concept of moving used here was not that common. This was true even though it is reported that approximately 30 percent of the population in the United States changes residence on an average of once a year. In this group of five, only one of the children had had this experience.

Think how unfortunate it would have been if this teacher had been instructed to develop readiness for the reading of this story by saying: "Listen. Today's story is about a family that moves from the city to the country. Look at the first picture and tell me what you think Father and Mother are doing here. Now look at the next picture, and the next. The children are concerned about whether or not they will find suitable playmates in the country. You will have fun finding out if they will or will not." This kind of pablum would never liberate the individual or permit him to use the richness of his experiences, limited as they may be, or expose him to the exciting and illuminating ideas induced by a *"process in which he could gain the techniques of controlling them."* [Italics in original.] (13, p. 9.)

Directing a reading-thinking activity is best accomplished in the dynamics of a group situation. This is especially true when material is structured for basic reading instruction, as are most basic readers. The fertile and varied experiences, interests, and needs of a group are very apt to be productive.

The Content

The content of basic readers, or of any books for that matter, consists of concepts or mental constructs. Concepts are the "characteristics common to certain objects, attributes, or ideas, so that those objects, attributes, or ideas having elements in common may be grouped into a separate category or class" (14, p. 468). This recent definition of *concept* is as concise as any. Chapter 10, "Concept Development," will discuss different phases of conceptualization in greater detail.

Concepts are cognitive structures. As such, they link an individual's present perceptions and learnings to his previous experience and knowledge (31). In Chapter 1, the words *mental construct* were used synonymously with the words *concept* and *cognitive structures*. The words *mental construct* are preferred here, because they seem to be more definitive. Concepts are of the mind—cognitive structures—and are mental. Concepts are constructs in that they are built from or emerge from "such materials as perceptual experiences, memories, images, and the products of imaginative thinking" (16, p. 118). While it may be true that many concepts are arrived at fortuitously, it is also true that the objective of acquiring knowledge (the sole objective of education) demands a planned and systematic approach to the construction of concepts. Mental construction work, or the building of concepts, is the primary task of the learner and, to be accomplished effectively, requires the direction of a skilled teacher.

John Dewey (7) refers again and again to the need for examined experience. Socrates said that the unexamined life is not worth living. Both philosophers, representing the present and the past, were right. Mental constructs must be based on examined discriminations and on wise generalizations.

As stated earlier, the semantic triangle illustrates in a most effective way the fundamentals of conceptualization. Needed are referents, or experiences and symbols. Use of the word *symbol* indicates clearly that the individual may use both verbal and nonverbal symbols, or words and signs, or graphic aids.

Stories in basic readers involve concepts of time, place, number, people, animals, aesthetics, humor, and so on. Children come to school with many concepts ranging from concrete-perceptual to abstract-conceptual. Many of their concepts are sound and accurate, especially those of the concrete variety. Abstract concepts, while formed early, are not as accurate and adequate.

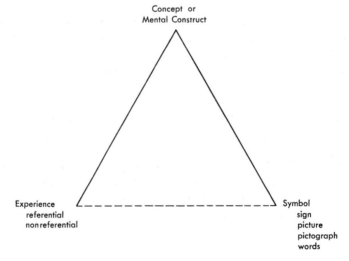

Concept or
Mental Construct

Experience
referential
nonreferential

Symbol
sign
picture
pictograph
words

At the primary level in particular, stories are carefully selected and written so as to deal with the common concepts that children bring with them to school. One main reason for such story controls is to free the child learning to read from having to acquire *new* concepts. This is just as important as control of vocabulary. This does not mean that no concept work is done in the primary-level basic-reader program. Rather, the work done is largely that of seeing and grasping and appreciating the different relations that known concepts may have as they appear and reappear in different plots, actions, suspenses, surprises, novelties, and outcomes.

As the content of the basic readers change to keep up with the maturing individuals, the concepts introduced also change, and the teaching of concepts becomes the primary function. Children must be taught how to acquire new concepts, what to do when they meet a new concept, and what to do when they meet a word that is used in a new way and represents a modification and extension of meaning; in short, they must be taught how to discriminate and generalize.

In "The One-Time Magic Garden," the key concepts are substantially known to most six-year-olds: one-time, magic, garden, big, little, fast, going up, uncle, give away, toys, coat, hide, find. In "Washington's Scout" many of the concepts are common, but some are not. Some, the word *scout,* for instance, and its use in the story to mean to go about to explore a region, to obtain information of the movements and plans of an enemy, must be understood clearly in order to grasp the plot. Other key ideas are: messages, delay, horses, friendly, enemies, and so on. Others—sandy path, saddle, wrapped box, Howe, army, and the like—while important, are not as essential. In fact, in the minds of children these concepts may not be totally accurate, but this will not stop them from grasping the nuances, intensities, and effects of the plot. The adequacy and clarity of these mental constructs should be determined by the teacher, but it is more important for her to check on key concepts than to spend an inordinate amount of time on concepts of secondary value to the purpose.

In addition, at this level the pupils should be introduced to a glossary or dictionary, for they now need to know how this source of information can be used to obtain meaning. Here words are used to define words, illustrations frequently are provided, and illustrative sentences are given.

In the story "Catch That Airplane" (27), the concept burden is considerable, but it is not out of keeping with the expectancies one might rightly have for students competent to read and to be instructed at this level. At this stage of progress or of reading maturity, some of the concepts may be completely new to the students. This being the case, it is of utmost importance that the students know how to acquire mental constructs built on vicarious experience. A useful means of contrasting the circumstances that tend to distinguish concept differences at the primary level from those that exist at the intermediate level and at increasing frequency beyond is as follows.

Primary Level

known: word meaning (experience)
known: oral language usage (speaking)
unknown: printed language (reading)

Intermediate Level

unknown: word meaning (experience)
unknown: oral language usage (speaking)
unknown: printed language (reading)

At the intermediate level, for sound instructional purposes, the *unknown* concept burden may not be too great. It must be controlled so that pupils may be taught how to deal with such demands without being overwhelmed and frustrated. This is as essential as the rate of new-word introduction is at the primary level.

One might draw a line to illustrate how the concept burden shifts from the primary level forward. At one end would be the conventional concepts known to so many children: house, dog, tree, and so on. For these concepts the children have quite adequate concept content. They can pronounce the word and, when circumstances require, can remember the right word, produce it orally, and, in some instances, write it. At the other end of the continuum are concepts that are completely unknown. In the middle one might find words that are partially known. If someone speaks a word, a child may recognize it. However, the child may not be sufficiently familiar with it to produce it on his own.

At the intermediate level, then, some of the words will be recognized because the author used them in the material. Others, though, may go unrecognized, even though they are presented in a context. This is when the use of a glossary becomes more and more important. In addition, since all of the words that might need to be defined cannot and should not be given in a basic-reader glossary, it now becomes essential that pupils learn to check them in an appropriate dictionary. Therefore, at this level it would be helpful if each pupil could be supplied with a desk dictionary. If this is not possible, such dictionaries should be readily available in the room.

The words *tapered* and *pendant* occur in the glossary of "Catch That Airplane." Other key words may need to be located in a dictionary: *pulley, arresting, piston,* and *retriever.*

A question frequently asked is when to teach new concepts—before the reading is done or during and after. The answer is critical. In basic readers that use controls and are designed for developing basic reading skills, the concepts should not be "taught" in advance of the reading. To do so is to vitiate the glossary.

Word-attack skills are taught from the very beginning of a basic-reader program. Throughout the primary level these skills are mainly those of structural, phonetic, and context analysis. At the intermediate level the glossary and dictionary provide meaning and pronunciation help. The structural and phonetic skills taught at the primary level lay the ground-work for the use of the phonetic guide, which usually appears at the bottom of a dictionary page, the phonetic respellings, the syllabifications, and the diacritical and accent marks. Training in the use of context clues started at the primary level provides essential preparation in the use of dictionary definitions and in selecting a meaning that fits a context.

All a basic-reader program can do is simulate typical reading circum-stances. In a library or in the privacy of his home, the reader needs to be self-reliant and resourceful, for at such times there is usually no one avail-able to provide word-recognition aid. A pupil meeting a word he does not know or a concept he does not grasp must be trained to cope with his need.

GUIDING THE ADJUSTMENT OF RATE

The psychological and pedagogical principles on which this book is based might well be summed up in one concept: *versatility*. Versatile ad-justment is emphatically and truly the act of an efficient reader searching for meaning. In form and in substance, versatility emanates from cogni-tion.

To read is to comprehend, and the principal determiner of what is comprehended is the reader's purpose. In turn, achievement of purpose is much influenced by the reader's experience (examined) and knowledge, and by the nature and readability of the context.

All that has been said thus far regarding purposes for reading in general and pupil purposes in particular is brought to fruition when adjustment of rate, or versatility, is defined. Purpose not only is the principal deter-miner of what is apprehended; it is also the principal determiner of rate. This being the case, it is paramount that the reader learn first how to declare his own purposes for reading and learn second how to adjust his rate of reading accordingly.

There are four general categories of rate adjustment: skimming, scan-ning, survey reading, and study-type reading. Skimming may be defined as the ability to read swiftly and lightly to locate bits of information. If the reader's purpose is to locate literal and brief answers or if he wishes to gather facts and ideas piecemeal, he should skim his text. This performance can be called superficial only if he fails to skim properly.

Scanning may be defined as the ability to read along at a good rate on a point-by-point basis to locate literal information. This performance differs from skimming in that the answer to a question may be located in differ-ent parts of the text, thus requiring the reader to do more than garner a single fact or a series of isolated facts. Furthermore, the facts needed to answer scanning-type purposes may be of a qualifying nature and may require the reader to do a certain amount of discrimination. Again, this performance can be called superficial only if the reader fails to scan properly.

Survey reading may be defined as the ability to move along at a good rate so as to get an idea or picture of a story or article as a whole. This may be a loose, point-to-point survey as one may do with a newspaper, or it may be a more careful observation to determine the nature or inward design of a text or to pass a general judgment on it. It is in this panoramic sense that survey reading differs clearly from scanning and skimming.

Study-type reading may be defined as the ability to read carefully and reflectively for the purpose of passing judgment. Such reading requires more than the grasping of literal information. A reader must be able to read critically, to read between the lines, and to weigh ideas not only against personal experience but also on an acceptable yardstick.

Each of these techniques for rate adjustment represents a practical and useful way to permit a reader to be versatile. At the primary level the reader acquires the attitude and habit of reading with a purpose. He learns to do this largely with story-type material. To some degree, too, he learns to change his pace of reading. In "The One-Time Magic Garden," a reader may set as his purpose to find out who the man in green is. This being a purpose that fits the *skim* category—to locate a piece of information literally stated—he may find himself moving along faster than usual. Gradually, with repeated experiences of this kind, he begins to note the differences among the various kinds of reading and becomes more deliberate.

When rereading material to locate a word, a phrase, or a sentence so as to prove a point, the reader may move swiftly and lightly, skimming the page until he finds the desired answer. This is a type of reading performance that should be done over and over again at the primary level and beyond, for reading to prove a point not only develops foundation knowledge for adjusting rate to purpose, but it also helps develop the attitude and practice of "proving," or "putting to the test."

At the intermediate level, systematic instruction should be initiated to train pupils to be versatile. Now is the time to capitalize on all the experience acquired at the primary level. Now, too, is the time to so train the pupil that he can be deliberate and articulate about rate adjustment. This training must be done in different materials: science, history, geography, biography, and the arts, as well as in story-type selections.

OBSERVING THE READING

The "big moment" in the Directed Reading-Thinking Activity, is when the pupils are actually reading. This is the teacher's best opportunity to see how the pupils perform. She will want to be at hand to watch what they do.

How are they holding their books? Do they move their heads? Is there any lip movement, finger pointing, head nodding, and so on?

Adjusting Rate

At the primary level a good time to note rate adjustment occurs during the rereading-to-prove-points time. The rereading should be done faster for at least two good reasons. First, the pupil is about to prove or disprove, and the impetus derived from the desire to do so sends him along in haste. Second, the pupil has already read the material and is familiar with it.

On some occasions pupil purposes will present an opportunity for skimming or scanning, as, for instance, if they want to answer such questions as, To what place will the family move? In what places will they search for the lost toy?

A feature of the D-R-T-A skill-training programs is to stop the reader at different points of the reading. The purpose of these stops is primarily to ascertain what use the reader will make of the information obtained up to a certain point or points. At times pupils may be asked to read a first page and stop, or one-third of the story, or one-half of the story, or two-thirds of the story, or everything except the last page. The alert teacher notes whether or not each reading performance is done at varied rates or at the same rate.

At the intermediate level the same practices occur. However, at this level a major difference should also be taking place. Now pupils should be taught how to be deliberate in adjusting rate to purpose (s) and how to adjust rate to the nature and readability of materials. Even though the pupils become increasingly more self-reliant and independent, they still need the basic training essential to becoming versatile readers. Such training is best accomplished under the careful direction of a teacher.

Providing Help in Comprehension

When will pupils ask for help? The answer is, when they are encouraged to do so. But that is only half the story. When will pupils realize that they should ask for teacher help? When they are encouraged to do so and have been taught to be intellectually honest readers. Honest readers are always intent on seeking meaning and therefore usually recognize when they are not obtaining it.

All this adds up to a simple story. Pupils will acquire the habit of ferreting out meaning even if this involves seeking teacher help, and they will do so with the passion of a scholar, *if* this is the aim taken seriously in each classroom. Where this is so, teachers may discover that there are far more sensitive and eager readers among their pupils than they had dreamed possible.

The psychology of learning has shown that habitual use of a practice (s) tends to give it the stamp of certainty. This being the case, we want the habit of searching for meaning to become so firmly established that it takes on the air of certainty—the certainty that whenever one reads he searches diligently for meaning. The varied demands made by different reader purposes and different materials at different levels of readability provide all the assurance needed that the habit of searching for meaning will be that of a habit as an instrument and not a habit as a master. Searching for meaning or discovery in reading is a means of gaining reader freedom—freedom from bias, prejudice, and fear—that results when the habit is under control and is used deliberately as an instrument.

Clarifying Purposes

A pupil who discovers as he reads that the purpose(s) he had declared are not appropriate to the story facts being revealed should, if he seems at a loss, feel free to turn to the teacher for help. A few well-chosen questions on the part of the teacher will soon have him reading again. For example, the teacher may ask, "Now that you have read so far, what do you think will follow, or happen next?" "Why do you think so?" "Why not read on and see if your new predictions are right?" Pupils facing such circumstances are learning four important skills on the road to reading-thinking maturity: first, that reading *is* a continuous process; second, that a wrong estimate of facts and the resultant wrong prediction is not a calamity, for within the limits of the facts available the prediction may have been legitimate in that it did fall in the realm of possibility; third, that a good reader adjusts and readjusts his sights as new information is obtained; and fourth, that it is better to seek the teacher's advice than to be stymied.

Clarifying Concepts

"Empty heads console with empty sounds," said Alexander Pope. Teachers satisfied with empty sounds foster empty-headed pupils. The art of verbalism beguiles the human mind. A teacher indifferent to the correctness of pupil concepts traffics in deception and superficiality. Words, words, words, empty words sound good and often are deceptively convincing. If parroted words are the coin of the classroom realm, pupils soon learn to render unto that teacher the things that she accepts. The following story told by William James illustrates this point well:

A friend of mine, visiting a school, was asked to examine a young class in geography. Glancing at the book she said: "Suppose you should dig a hole in the ground, hundreds of feet deep, how should you find it at the bottom—warmer or colder than on top?" None of the class replying, the teacher said: "I am sure they know, but I think you don't ask the question quite rightly. Let me try." So, taking the book, she asked: "In what condition is the interior of the globe?" and received the immediate answer from half of the class at once: "The interior of the globe is in a condition of igneous fusion." (4, p. 36.)

Pupils must be taught to respect accurate concepts in the same way that they are taught to respect people, and they should be taught early, so that the attitude can pervade the thousands of situations that will require them as readers to meet new concepts courageously and even to take joy in the difficulty. This ability is of greater general usefulness to pupils than any other skill a Directed Reading-Thinking Program has to offer. It will lead them to understand that things are connected and not isolated as they learn to mount the ladder of abstractions.

At the primary level requests for help with concepts may be infrequent. As already said, at this level effort has been made to control concepts so that children can give fuller attention to learning to recognize words. Even so, concepts that are not truly common to all children will begin to appear in stories. For instance, a second-reader-level story ("The Lucky One," 28, pp. 6–11) is about a lad named Ted who meets a boy named Jack. Jack lives on a houseboat, and now Ted longs to have the same kind of life. Ted's father suggests that he invite Jack to visit in their apartment home. As a result Jack helps Ted see many advantages of apartment living and in turn gain a different appreciation for houseboat living. The concept *houseboat* may not be clearly grasped by many pupils, even though one of the pictures provides some help. All will have good understanding for the word *house* and at least some ideas about *boat*. By connecting these ideas, pupils will have sufficient grasp of *houseboat* to read and understand the story. After the story has been read, the concept of *houseboat* can be sharpened and refined. This is a good time to do so, because certain pupils will have "discovered" that they do not know very much about a houseboat. Again, what may appear to be a small point is actually one of great moment. The teacher did not "introduce" this story by telling pupils that they would read about a houseboat and that she was going to show pictures of a houseboat and tell them all about it. The former is the approach of discovery; the latter that of rote indoctrination.

In reading the story, if a pupil asks for teacher help with the meaning of *houseboat,* a good first step would be to refer to the illustration. Attention could be given to the boat elements apparent and to the house elements apparent, as well as to the dock and the river. Pictures can provide an excellent source of specifics for mental constructs.

At the intermediate level, the number, difficulty, and remoteness of concepts increases. At this level, however, basic readers introduce glossaries—a quasi-dictionary giving explanations of words. Pupils have been and are continuing to be taught dictionary-usage skills. At this level, then, when word meaning or concept difficulty is experienced, pupils should be trained to seek all the help they can get from a glossary or dictionary before turning to the teacher. Until pupils are self-sufficient in this respect, any request for teacher word-meaning help should be met with the question, "Have you checked in the glossary or dictionary?" At the primary level the teacher would ask, "Did you read to the end of the sentence and also look for picture clues?"

A pupil encountering the words *conveyor belt*, in the story "The Railroad Cat" (25, pp. 6–13), turned to the glossary. There he found "con vey' or belt, 7. See *belt*." Puzzled, he sought teacher help. In this instance the teacher pointed to the words, "See *belt*" and asked, "Did you turn to the word *belt*?" "Is that what is meant by "see *belt*"?, he asked. Then he turned to *belt* and found three definitions. The third definition was, "3. An endless, moving band on which things can be moved; a conveyor belt. Picture on page 6." He turned to page 6 of the story and re-examined the picture, either more carefully or in a way different from his first examination. "Do you understand?," inquired the teacher. The boy merely nodded his head; he was already reading on.

Another pupil, reading the selection "Arts: Modern and Centuries Old" (26, pp. 171–177), came upon the word *mosaic*. Even after he had read the following paragraph and studied the three pictures, he was puzzled.

> A very popular use for clay as an art material is making mosaics. Not only can you make your very own mosaic, but you can make the materials for the mosaic. First, roll the clay on an even surface with a rolling pin. Then brush the surface of the clay with glazes of different colors. (26, p. 173.)

Rather than read on, this pupil felt the scholar's obligation to turn to the glossary, where he found the following definition:

> mo-sa-ic (mō-zā′ -ik), 173. A design made of small pieces of varicolored glass, stone, or the like, inlaid in some other material; also, a piece of work so made. (26, p. 296.)

Still uncertain, he sought teacher help. The teacher, seeing that he had stopped reading on page 173, suggested that he read on. The next page provided the following additional text about mosaics and two more illustrations.

> As soon as the glaze is dry, cut the clay into strips. Then cut the strips into squares. Once the clay has hardened, you can begin the design of your mosaic. It is like arranging the pieces of a puzzle.
>
> Recently, in the last few years, scientists have discovered some very old mosaics in Italy. The mosaics of bright glazed colors had been laid in floors. These recently discovered mosaic floors show both humans and animals alive with natural movement. People who visit Italy today can walk on mosaics more than 1600 years old. (26, pp. 173–174.)

"So that's how a mosaic is put together! That's what *inlaid* means!" said the pupil. The teacher nodded approval, but she could not be certain that the pupil really understood. After he finished the article she followed the suggestion in the "Additional Activities" section of the teachers edition, which recommended that pupils make a mosaic.

Rereading

Rereading can serve many purposes, but one that is especially worthwhile is to seek clarity. When a teacher recommends *rereading* to a pupil, this is generally the reason. A pupil asked for teacher help with the word *swap* in the sentence, "We like to swap things" (28, p. 54). He could pronounce the word when asked to do so but was uncertain about the meaning. Next the teacher asked him to reread the previous sentence, "I gave my new glove to Donald, and he gave me his whistle." Then the teacher asked, "If you and I swap pencils, what do we do?" "I see," replied the boy. "You give me your pencil and I give you mine. Is that right?"

Another pupil asked for help with the word *corral* appearing in the sentence, "Rabbit paths nearly always ended at a corral where some rancher fenced his cattle" (25, p. 104). When the teacher stopped by, the girl seeking help reread the sentence orally and then asked the teacher if this meant that a corral was like a fenced-in pen where horses might be kept. The teacher nod of approval was all that was needed.

In yet another instance a pupil asked for teacher help with the words *grieving* and *grieved*. The teacher reread the lines aloud, while the girl listened:

> Then began a battle to save Jenny's life. Again she lost all interest in everything. For hours she stood without moving, her small eyes looking off into space. She was grieving for Albert.
> He had been such a care to her and, now, she missed him. She wouldn't eat. She couldn't be worked. She just grieved. (26, p. 74.)

Then the teacher asked, "How do you think Jenny felt?" She had helped the pupil understand the meaning of the word *grieving* by reading aloud the facts that Jenny "stood without moving," "eyes looking off into space," "she missed him," "she wouldn't eat," and "she couldn't be worked."

Giving Help in Word Recognition

To teach children to become thinking readers and to acquire skills that will permit them to read independently is a goal of the highest order. This is true in the area of word recognition as well as in comprehension.

At the primary level a child learning to read has to acquire ways and means for recognizing words. Materials in primary-level basic-reader programs are planned to take advantage of pupils' oral-language facility. This is done by capitalizing on what they already know. Words introduced in a basic-reader primary-level program are usually chosen so that the following conditions are true:

known: the meaning of the word
known: the speaking of the word
unknown: the printed form of the word

Words introduced at the primary level (grades one to three) are to a large degree words that occur frequently in the speaking vocabularies of most six- to eight-year-olds. In addition, almost all basic readers use some set of rules to regulate the introduction of words. One reader used the following set of rules (28, p. 238):

No more than two *new words* are introduced on a page. No words are introduced in a story or unit title. Each new word is used five times or more in the story in which it is introduced and in the following story. At least one of these five uses is in the second of the two stories. The new words are maintained by being used a minimum of nine times in the book.

All variant forms of known words are counted as new except: possessives; compounds made from two known words, and words taken from known compounds; inflectional variants formed by adding -s, -d, -ed, -es, -ing; inflectional variants formed by doubling the final consonant and adding -ed or -ing; words formed by adding -ly. (Also, if a word has been introduced in any of the above variant forms, the base word is not considered new.)

In addition, the following forms of known words are used in *People on Parade,* after the pages indicated, without being considered new: page 28, contractions in which one or two letters have been dropped; page 53, words to which a beginning a- has been added; page 65, words formed by adding -er and -est; page 76, inflectional variants formed by dropping the final e and adding -ing. (Also, if a word has been introduced with any of the above affixes or inflectional endings, these may be dropped without reintroducing the word.)

The concept *new word* needs clarification. The words introduced in basic readers at the primary level are all among those common to children's oral-language vocabulary. They are known words in the sense that children can think of them and speak them in a given set of circumstances. For example, they can speak the word *ball* when they see one and can ask for a ball if this is what they want, even when they do not see a ball. Basic-reader authors have made every effort to be sure that the words introduced on children's meaning-speaking level are "old words."

These "old words" become "new words" when they are reproduced in print. In a basic-reader series, a "new word" is one presented in print for the first time in that particular series. For example, in a first-reader-level story (21, pp. 54–59), the words introduced as "new" are penny, luck, bag, happy, please, and hot, all of which are known by all six-year-olds. Words introduced in a fifth-reader-level story (26, pp. 255–257) are tunnel, soil, liquid, container, capsule, stiff, and shade. Some of these words may be only partially "known" or "old," and some of them may be "unknown" and therefore "new" to some children.

Each basic-reader series also presents a comprehensive and sequentially organized program designed to teach word-attack skills. One series, by way of illustration, presents 88 activities in two readiness books and 131 activities in three studybooks planned for use at the first-grade level alone. The teacher manuals contain an additional 180 activities.

All these controls are observed and all the skill-developing activities are presented to teach children how to recognize words on their own. In an all-inclusive reading program, only basic readers provide the kinds of controls described here. Basic readers offer unique source material in which children can try the word-attack skills they have been taught without feeling overwhelmed and frustrated by the demands on them.

It follows, then, that, if children are taught to apply word-attack skills when they meet a word they do not recognize at sight, they should try the skills first in material especially designed for the purpose—*basic readers*. When children use a library as their source of reading matter, they will encounter materials in which controls of only the loosest sort have been used. A child reading a trade book or a magazine, even those designed for children, may meet as many as five new words in a single paragraph. If he has good command of word-attack skills, he may go on; if not, he is very apt to put the book aside, especially if no teacher or other person is present to help him with the words. The end result is the fostering of an intellectual and emotional attitude toward reading that can be summed up in one word—rejection. This is why it is so important that words presented as "new words" in a basic-reader series *not* be taught in advance of reading the story or article. A more detailed discussion of this principle occurs in Chapter 9, "Developing Skill in Word Recognition."

Language Context. When, during the reading of a basic-reader story at the primary level a child asks for help with a word, the teacher should check first to find out whether or not he has read to the end of the sentence. The child is not being taught to "skip" words, as some uninformed individuals would say; rather, he is being taught to get the "sense" of the word through meaning. The teacher might ask, "Did you read to the end of the sentence to see if you can get an idea of the word?"

At the first-grade level pupils may need more help than this, for some do not understand what is meant by an "idea of the word." A good procedure here is for the teacher to read the sentence or sentences orally, leaving out the word in question. The oral reading by the teacher—her voice, her intonation, her interpretation, and the language rhythm—help pupils get a feel for the reading-for-meaning idea.

In the following lines the word being introduced is *family*.

Dad said, "We have Bill.
We have Nancy and Susan.
This is a big family." (22, p. 16.)

This language context provides helpful clues to the meaning of the word *family*. In fact, the clues might almost add up to a definition clue. Dad is speaking, and he names three members of the family. All four have been appearing in stories in the series, starting with the Readiness materials. Most likely the word *family* has been used innumerable times in oral discussions concerning this group. So, the great amount of oral-language "readiness" plus the rich written-langage context permits most children to come up with the word *family*.

Picture Context. Another important "context" aid to meaning is provided through carefully planned pictures in basic readers. As already described, pictures are an integral part of a story context and help carry a plot forward. Pictures can and should do more than that though, if they are wisely planned. They can supply an excellent graphic aid to support words, or ideas, or concepts. The picture on page 16 (22) shows the entire family with Mother and the three children seated around a circular lawn table and Father about to sit at the table.

Context clues should, wherever possible, include both language clues and picture clues. Both are useful and conventional symbol systems, with the picture symbol being less abstract than the word symbol.

Phonetic and Structure Clues. If language and picture clues are not sufficient, two other supporting word-recognition skills are available. Prior to reading the story in which they meet the word *family*, the pupils have been taught phonetic and word-structure clues. They have had work in visual discrimination of word forms, discrimination of capitals and small letters, auditory discrimination of beginning and ending sounds, and visual and auditory discrimination of initial sounds. The teacher might, therefore, alert the pupils to the beginning sound of the first pronunciation unit *fam* in *family* and so on to the *i* and the *ly*. By knowing the sounds represented by the beginning letters and by having some knowledge of the sounds represented by the vowels, the child may get sufficient sound clues to conclude that the word is *family*.

The Fertile Guess

In each of the circumstances described—language context, picture context (meaning), phonetic context (sound), and structure context (sight) —the pupil needed to make an intelligent guess. He needed the learning opportunity to put two and two together and come up with the right word.

Jerome S. Bruner put it this way (5, p. 14): "The shrewd guess, the fertile hypothesis, the courageous leap to a tentative conclusion—these are the most valuable coin of the thinker at work, whatever his line of work." This is a statement with which almost all teachers would agree. Furthermore, all would most likely answer Yes to the question Bruner raises, "Can school children be led to master this gift?" School children *can* be taught to be self-reliant, skilled performers.

In *Democracy and Education* (6, p. 164), John Dewey wrote, "To 'learn from experience' is to make a backward and forward connection between what we do to things and what we enjoy or suffer from things in consequence. Under such conditions, doing becomes a trying; an experiment with the world to find out what it is like; the undergoing becomes instruction—discovery of the connection of things." In the instances described in which the teacher gave help when help was sought by the pupils during the reading of a story, the pupils were being shown how to take a backward look at skills already learned or being learned and make a forward connection through application. They were asked to try their skills, to experiment and see how they worked, and to make the *discovery* of connecting things. In short, they were being asked to learn from an educative experience. At the intermediate level, requests for help are met in a similar manner, but one important condition alters the circumstances, for now the pupils have access to a glossary and a dictionary. Before they seek teacher help, they should have made full use of these sources of help.

The same conditions apply concerning the "new words" introduced in a basic reader. Again, *none* of the new words should be pretaught or predigested for the students. Such overindulgence sets up an attitude of dependence, and pupils soon learn to lean on the teacher who caters to their incompetencies.

Of the seven words introduced in "An Underground Helper" (26, p. 296), three appear in the glossary: *liquid, container, capsule.* The pupil who is qualified to be instructed at this level is mature enough to turn to a glossary on his own and get the help he needs. With the word *liquid,* he may need both pronunciation help and meaning help, and the glossary provides both: liquid (lĭk′ wĭd), 256. 1. not solid; freely flowing. 2. a *liquid* substance." If, after consulting the glossary, a pupil does not understand, he can now seek teacher help. When he does so, he knows *why* he needs help, and this is an important part of the learning process.

The other two words in the glossary are: "container (kŏn-tān′ ēr), 256. Something in which goods are kept or shipped" and "capsule (kăp′ sōol), 256. 1. a seedcase which breaks open when ripe. 2. a skinlike sac enclosing some part or organ of the body." (26, pp. 292, 293.) In addition, the context provides both language and picture aid. The language context is (26, p. 256):

> First it had to make a container for its eggs. It took some of the liquid out of a little pocket in one of the middle parts of its body. This liquid formed a kind of capsule around the earthworm's body. This capsule hardened quickly. It looked like a small container made of stiff, greenish-brown paper. It was fat in the middle and had a narrow neck.

The picture shows a cross section of land, with a worm in a worm tunnel. The capsule is separated from the worm and looks like a small container.

If the teacher had put these words on the chalkboard and discussed them prior to the reading of the selection, she would have denied her pupils the opportunity to try their skills, to experiment with their know-how about glossary usage, and to discover that they could obtain meaning on their own. How could any teacher act in this way? How can any basic-reader series endorse such a procedure? To do so is not only to deny the learner the opportunity to learn, but also to refute one of the main reasons for constructing basic-reader materials.

DEVELOPING COMPREHENSION

In discussing "speed reading," Miles A. Tinker (30) said the phrase was misleading. He preferred the label "rate of comprehension," because he says, there is no reading without comprehension. Similarly, in a directed reading-thinking activity, there is no reading without comprehension.

Producing and Reproducing Content

There exists, however, polar differences between methods of teaching for and checking comprehension. At one extreme or pole is the comprehension check best described by the word *reproduce*. At the other extreme is the comprehension check best described by the word *produce*. If reading is taught as a thinking process, the comprehension checks will be largely on the *produce* side of the bipolar arrangement.

reproduce *————————————————————————* produce
　　　　　　　parrots　　　　　　　　　　　　thinkers

Pupils asked to do their own prereading and thinking and to set their own purposes should be asked to defend or refute their purposes. This means that after they have done some reading they should be required either to prove they were right or wrong, or to give reasons why they should alter their conjectures. To do so will require that they *produce* evidence from the material read. This children can do; furthermore, they thrill to the intellectual challenge. To produce evidence is the task of the detective and the lawyer as well as the scientist. Readers required to perform in a similar manner acquire enduring attitudes that will render them eager for and comparatively competent in situations requiring effort and perseverance, thought and proof, all through life.

To produce evidence means to produce facts. The realm of fact is distinct from fancy. Speculations advanced must now be supported by the facts. The person who produces facts must be an alert person. No fact must be left unturned. This places a considerable responsibility upon the producer. The six-year-old described on page 3 had started out on the road to being a producer of facts. "I've found my answer and can read the line that proves it," she said.

Pupils asked to prove their points are far more attentive to facts than those who are not asked to do so. They seek out all the evidence and do so on a selective basis. On the other hand, pupils asked to reproduce facts may tell back a story and do so in excellent sequence, making their recitals with considerable enthusiasm. If this is the kind of "reverence" the teacher is seeking, the pupils are sure to recognize her desire and to play their roles accordingly. They will bow and scrape upon the stage of idolatrous recital as long as the teacher audience applauds—either with both hands, a smile, a look of satisfaction, a nod of the head, or an *A*. Not once are these pupils concerned with selecting facts to prove, with searching for the relevant, or with the consequences of the sequence of a story plot or a scientific report.

When reading is directed as a thinking process, the teacher is concerned with how pupils produce facts to prove or disprove their conjectures. She is also interested, of course, in sequence, but only as the consequences of a certain order help confirm or deny a conjecture.

Checking Purposes

"Honor pupil purposes!" After the reading has been done, an easy way to honor the pupils' prereading thinking is to ask, "Did *you* find the answer to *your* question?" "Were *you* right about what *you* thought would happen?" Open-ended questions of this kind will get things started, if this is necessary. Teachers soon discover that, once pupils understand that their thinking and their producing of evidence is being honored, even a teacher question to get started is not needed. As soon as *all* the pupils have finished reading, they will voluntarily offer to prove that they were either right or wrong. In fact, on many occasions the teacher will need to restrain the enthusiasm. This is a far cry from the situation in which teacher coercion—by fear, by sugar-coated threats, or by vacuous inquiry—is employed.

A degree of cogency, arising from evidence, convinces the mind of any truth or fact and produces belief. "Read the line(s) that proves it" is a request consonant with the laws of proof. What could be more timely in this age of science than to foster in our children the attitude of demanding and providing proof, and to do so from the very beginning of their school days?

At times all members of a group may have declared individual purposes. This is especially true when purpose-setting has been done on a limited-clue basis, such as predicting from a title only, a title and first picture only, or a title, first picture, and first page only. This is the time when divergent thinking is most likely to occur. As J. P. Guilford has defined it, divergent production is the ability "to produce a variety of ideas, all of which are logically possible in view of the given information" (10, p. 177). Pupils reacting to the story title "The Wish That Came True" (20, pp. 65–70) all had individual ideas, each of which was logically possible in view of the given information.

In other situations or those of convergent production when "at least there is a recognized best or conventional conclusion" (10, p. 177), all pupils in a group may agree on a single prediction. As the facts in a plot are uncovered, weighed, and integrated, all reading detectives may see all signs pointing one way. In "The Eight O'clock Surprise" (20, pp. 52–58), one teacher directed the reading of the story in such a way that a final purpose-setting session occurred after six of the seven pages in the story had been read. At this point all the pupils predicted that the "eight o'clock surprise" would be an 8 P.M. birthday surprise party, even though in previous years the party had always been in the afternoon. A reading of the last page of the story provided the needed proof.

Redefining Purposes

Reading is a continuous process and, as such, subjects the reader's mind continuously to new information requiring him to adjust his thinking. Thus the reader's progress through a story is marked by continuously changing ideas. Each word, each fact, each concept, each line and sentence requires the reader to react, accept, reject, associate, and assimilate. To the degree that he can deal with the barrage of information will he be an *able* reader.

Put differently, the reader is asked constantly to suspend judgment. Many readers suspend judgment without ever fully realizing it. If more did realize it, there would be fewer people jumping to conclusions until all the evidence was in and more people realizing that they were doing so if they did reach a conclusion on limited evidence.

Why, then, do so few people suspend judgment? In the final analysis, faulty attitudes and methods are the culprit. Although all agree that meaning is the desired outcome of reading, not all agree that a glib recital of story facts represents meaning. Neither do all agree that children must be motivated to read by being told in advance what a story is about, by being asked to find answers to teacher questions, or by having so-called new words predigested for them.

When reading is taught as a thinking process, pupils discover early in their reading careers that predictions based on limited clues are subject to change. They also discover that predictions based on nine-tenths of the clues available are also subject to change. The pupils who made different and individual predictions in response to the title "The Wish That Came True" discovered at once when they saw the first picture of the story that most of their predictions needed to be changed or modified. The picture showed a log cabin, a stream, a rail fence, a clearing, and wooded land. Predictions were quickly adjusted in keeping with the new information. This occurred without some teacher saying, "Today, boys and girls, we will read a story about early settlers in America." The children could make this analysis on their own, given the opportunity.

Information gained on the first page helped them focus in on the facts that the story occurred about a hundred years ago in West Virginia, a part of the country where Indians once hunted and fished. White people had moved into the area, among them the Barto family. Predictions at this point changed to involve the Barto family, the time and the setting, and the wishes the family may have had.

Whenever predictions had to be readjusted, the children did so readily. No child sulked because his first prediction was wrong. None was embarrassed. Neither did any feel that at this point in the story he could predict the final outcome. Pupils were appropriately modest, yet ready to venture conjectures. There were no false conceits, for they had learned through repeated experience not to be know it alls on such limited evidence. At the same time, they were quite tolerant of each other's thinking and conjecturing. A scholarly atmosphere prevailed.

Recognizing the Need for Other Source Material

The recognition of need for other source material becomes more evident as the content of the basic reader changes and as pupils are required to deal with ideas and events beyond their immediate experience. At the primary level there is little need to go beyond the stories presented. If pupils want to go to a library for such a purpose, most basic readers recommend stories that will get them started and help them satisfy their desire. For example, the following suggestion accompanies the story "The Wish That Came True" (29, p. 124):

LITERARY APPRECIATION
There is suspense and adventure in store for children who read *Hoot-Owl*, by Mable G. LaRue; and *First Adventure*, by Elizabeth Coatsworth. In each book a pioneer boy is lost in the woods and found by Indians.

At the intermediate level, where some basic readers provide materials typical of different content areas, pupils are more apt to recognize the need for more information. Such a need is in many ways quite different from the desire to read more stories of the same kind. It tends to be representative of the need of a scholar in quest of more knowledge—the scholar, for instance, who realizes that a single history text is but a bare outline of historical events and their significance and wants to read original sources.

After reading the article "Americans Move With Their Bridges" (23, pp. 47–53), students knew the locations of the suspension bridges with the longest spans, details of the size and cost of the Golden Gate, Mackinac, and Transbay bridges, materials used in bridge construction, different uses of bridges, and some facts about the role of bridges in the growth of the United States. Now some pupils wanted to know more about how people pay for bridges, why some are toll bridges and others not. Others wanted to know more about the geographic characteristics of the locations of bridges, large or small. Some wanted to locate other notable bridges in the United States.

This provided an excellent opportunity for pupils to discover, if they did not already know, that dictionaries, particularly unabridged dictionaries, usually provide illustrations and additional information. *The World Almanac and Book of Facts* (32) is an excellent source of information. It provides facts about notable bridges in the United States, the year they were built, their location, the length of their main span, and their type—suspension, cantilever, steel arch, and so on.

In addition, the manual directions accompanying this selection have the following to say about additional reading (24, p. 72):

Bridges and Their Builders by Steinman and Watson (New York: Dover Publications, Inc., 1937), describes the ideas behind bridge engineering, the men who built bridges, and the history of great bridges throughout the world. The late Dr. Steinman, from whose article in *The Scientific Monthly* this picture-essay was adapted, is considered to have been the world's foremost bridge designer and engineer. Other very worthwhile related reading includes Adele Nathan's *The Building of the First Transcontinental Railroad* (New York: Random House, 1950) and *Wheels* by Edwin Tunis (Cleveland: World, 1955).

When materials of this kind have been used, teachers have reported keen interest on the part of pupils. Young people are ready and eager to respond to the intellectual challenge of expanding horizons, and they rise to the occasion with astonishing vigor and curiosity.

Developing Concepts

In the discussion on clarifying concepts, stress was placed on the importance of concepts and how concepts provide the fabric—the framework and structural plan—of, by, and through which information is organized. The discussion was concerned with how pupils meet immediate reader needs when they encounter words or concepts that are either not clear or are unknown and how a teacher can help the reader proceed when he asks for teacher help while reading. Obviously that was not the time to stop and make a thorough study of a concept, but now, when the object is to develop comprehension, the circumstances are different. Now the reader has dealt with the material and is ready to give attention to other intellectual opportunities associated with the materials. Of course, not all comprehension checks occur at the end of a story. Each stop made in the process of accomplishing different schemes in a Directed Reading-Thinking Activity sets in motion the predicting-reading-proving cycle.

Pupils capable of reading a third-reader-level story such as "Danger on the Cliff" (19, pp. 93–97) may, when the first stop is made to check on purposes and comprehension, have questions about Lookout Mountain. If so, a quick look at a map to locate Lookout Mountain, Tennessee, is in order before reading on. Similarly, questions about a bobcat may be dealt with by a quick check in a dictionary or encyclopedia. At this point, the most important thing is to get on with the story, but even so attention should be given to checking concepts. Questions of clarity result from the discussion and may reflect a group need rather than an individual need. At the end of the story, there is time for a more careful check on Lookout Mountain, on the bobcat, or on Mr. Stover's decision about the mutt. Pupils native to the area may be especially interested and may wish to check more carefully on Lookout Mountain and the animals that do or did inhabit it.

At the intermediate level, pupils reading, say, "Handy Sandy" (26, pp. 15–24) may at the first stop have questions about shells and how cannon-ball shells were used. Some may not be clear on the meaning of *foundry* and may wish to check what they gleaned from the context and the glossary against what others in the group gleaned. This is a good time for the teacher not only to note the needs voiced, but also to so direct pupils' thinking as to add some clarity to their notion of *foundry*. The paragraphs in the story describing the foundry might be reread. After the story has been read, such ideas as "Sandy was his father's name" and "a chip off the old block" may be clarified immediately, as may the term *head cracker*.

FUNDAMENTAL SKILL-TRAINING ACTIVITIES

Only *one* phase of a total Directed Reading-Thinking Activity has been accomplished when a basic-reader story has been read. What is done after a story has been read is equally as important. This is the time when skill training of a different kind is accomplished. Now special attention is given to developing such skills as firming up and refining word-attack skills, clarifying and developing concepts, increasing powers of observation and reflection, and developing adeptness in the use of semantic analysis.

While reading the basic-reader story, pupils were learning how to make educated guesses, how to be reading detectives, how to deal selectively with facts, how to adjust rate to purpose and materials while under the pressure of a reading act performed in a reading group, how to prove or refute conjectures, how to apply word-attack skills already learned, how to deal with unknown words, and how to acquire concepts. Even though all these actions may be in progress in any one directed reading-thinking session, the time required for a D-R-T-A should not be unusual.

A question frequently asked by teachers unschooled in teaching reading as a thinking process is "How much time will a D-R-T-A consume?" To those experienced in the art, the question seems unnecessary. Children, even six-year-olds, are quick to respond to the challenges of a D-R-T-A. They are quick to size up a situation, to make conjectures, to read, to prove, and to get on with the story. At the first-reader level, for example, a typical seven-page story can be dealt with as prescribed in ten minutes.

True, the inexperienced teacher and the untrained pupils may, as they get started, require twice as much time, but this is no reflection on the approach. In almost any circumstance in which skills are acquired, the neophyte requires more time than the experienced person.

How long will it take a six-year-old who is instructional at a first-reader level to read a five- to seven-page story? The five-page story "Two In One" (21, pp. 21–25) has five pictures, one on each page, and consumes slightly more than two full pages. This leaves the equivalent of slightly fewer than 3 pages of language, or a total of 335 words. Of this number, 84 are different words, which means there are 251 repeats. Even so, only 8 of the 84 different words are used 10 times or more. Of the 84 words, 7 are introduced in this story.

A seven-page story, "Happy Again" (21, pp. 171–177), has seven pictures, one on each page. These seven pictures consume the space of about two full pages. This allows about five full pages of language context for a total of 654 running words. Of this number, 161 are different words, which means 493 words are repeated. Only 13 of 161 different words are repeated 10 or more times. In addition, only 4 of the 161 words are introduced in this story.

Neither story makes excessive word-recognition demands. The 161 different words in "Happy Again" represent more than 56 percent of all the words introduced as new in the materials designed for use at the first-grade level in this series. If the pupils read through either story without a stop, the total reading time would be quite short, ranging most likely from two to five minutes.

Similar word-recognition demands are made at subsequent levels. A third-reader-level story entitled "The Red Arrowhead" (19, pp. 200–206) is seven pages long. It has six pictures consuming the space of slightly fewer than two full pages. The total number of running words is approximately 700. Four new words are introduced.

The method for handling each story varies, which means that the number of stops made (to check comprehension, to set or reset purposes) varies. In some stories there may be as many as four stops, whereas in others there may be only one. This variance influences time consumed. In addition, some groups are more responsive or quicker than others. Also, a particular group's performance will vary from day to day.

In short, when a Directed Reading-Thinking Activity is well handled there should be ample time to devote to fundamental skill training.

An investigation of different basic-reader series reveals that they contain only a few skill-type activities. Where are the skill-building activities to be found in a basic-reader series? The answer is easy. Skill-building activities are located in the teacher's manuals and in the studybooks or skillbooks that accompany each basic reader. In all instances, studybooks are an integral part of a basic series. The studybooks and manuals together with the basic reader form the one-two punch needed for effective instruction.

Basic readers should not present skill-training activities. Basic readers present stories and articles to be read and enjoyed and, in the case of articles, to be studied. The attitude required to read a story and enjoy its progress and outcome or to follow an article is quite different from the attitude needed to acquire a skill. When pupils read a basic-reader story or selection, they do so to seek answers to pupil questions or purposes. They do the conjecturing and seeking and proceed as reading detectives trying to unravel the uncertainty of the unknown.

When pupils approach a studybook activity, they must pursue carefully defined purposes and follow detailed instructions. This task should be approached with the attitude that *work* is to be done. The business at hand is serious; it requires full attention and effort. The students' interest and enthusiasm are governed by the attitudes and habits appropriate to the business of learning and mastering a skill. In short, the approach to the studybooks and skillbooks is to be businesslike.

SUMMARY

The essential difference between teaching reading as a thinking process and ordinary catechetical methods is that the students think. In the latter method, the main lines of communication are between the teacher and the pupil, and the pupil is not encouraged to think. In many cases, the pupil is intimidated by the tyranny of a right answer. In a Directed Reading-Thinking Activity, on the other hand, the emphasis is on pupil thinking. Pupils are being taught to examine, to hypothesize, to find proof, to suspend judgment, and to make decisions. They learn to do this in terms of their experience and knowledge.

In a Directed Reading-Thinking Activity it soon becomes clear that it is the pupil who must extract the information; he must comprehend and assimilate. If he repeats the thoughts of others, he does so not as a parrot but to supply evidence either to refute or substantiate a claim. If he accepts the purposes of others, he does so because he has examined them carefully and decided that these purposes are acceptable in light of the circumstances, and that they represent his interest and ambition. In these situations, if the pupil worries at all he does so because he discovers he has made a faulty examination of the evidence, cannot find the lines to prove his point, needs to extrapolate on limited grounds, or does not know where to go next to find proof.

In our democratic culture, we cannot afford for one moment to become careless on this score. Pupils free to think and to evaluate are also responsible for proof and sound decisions. A Directed Reading-Thinking Activity in a group situation provides the conditions from which may emerge scholars who understand what it means to think, to learn, and to test.

Furthermore, it is from such a setting that they will learn to have the strength of their convictions and the courage to deal with ideas. They will not be fearful but courageous; not blind, but discerning; not hasty, but deliberate; not deceitful, but honest; not muddled, but articulate; not acquiescent, but aggressive; not conceited, but modest; not imitative, but original.

REFERENCES

1. Adler, Mortimer J., *What Man Has Made of Man*, New York, Ungar, 1937.
2. Bacon, Francis, *Bacon's Essays*, New York, Macmillan, 1930.
3. Betts, Emmett, A., *Foundations of Reading Instruction*, New York, American Book, 1946.
4. Brownell, William A., and Verner M. Sims, "The Nature of Understanding," *The Measurement of Understanding*, Forty-fifth Yearbook of the National Society for the Study of Education, Part I, Chicago, University of Chicago Press, 1946.
5. Bruner, Jerome S., *The Process of Education*, Cambridge, Mass., Harvard University Press, 1960.
6. Dewey, John, *Democracy and Education*, New York, Macmillan, 1916.
7. Dewey, John, *How We Think*, New York, Heath, 1933.
8. Gray, William S., "The Nature and Organization of Basic Instruction in Reading," *The Teaching of Reading: A Second Report*, Thirty-sixth Yearbook of the National Society for the Study of Education, Part I, Bloomington, Ill., Public School Publishing Co., 1937.
9. Gray, William S., "The Nature and Types of Reading," *The Teaching of Reading: A Second Report*, Thirty-sixth Yearbook of the National Society for the Study of Education, Part I, Bloomington, Ill., Public School Publishing Co., 1937.
10. Guilford, J. P., "Frontiers in Thinking That Teachers Should Know About," *The Reading Teacher, 13* (February, 1960), 176–182.
11. Harris, Albert J., *Effective Teaching of Reading*, New York, McKay, 1962.
12. Herrick, Virgil E., *et al.*, "Basal Instructional Materials in Reading," *Development In and Through Reading*, Sixtieth Yearbook of the National Society for the Study of Education, Part I, Chicago, University of Chicago Press, 1961.
13. Hullfish, H. Gordon, and Philip G. Smith, *Reflective Thinking: The Method of Education*, New York, Dodd, Mead, 1961.
14. Johnson, Ronald C., "Linguistic Structure as Related to Concept Formation and to Concept Content," *Psychological Bulletin, 59* (November, 1962), 468–476.
15. Polya, G., *How to Solve It*, Princeton, N.J., Princeton University Press, 1948.
16. Russell, David H., *Children's Thinking*, Boston, Ginn, 1956.
17. Russell, David H., "Continuity in the Reading Program," *Development in and Through Reading*, Sixtieth Yearbook of the National Society for the Study of Education, Part I, Chicago, University of Chicago Press, 1961.
18. Stauffer, Russell G., "Productive Reading-Thinking at the First Grade Level," *The Reading Teacher, 13* (February, 1960), 183–187.
19. Stauffer, Russell G., Alvina Treut Burrows, and Millard H. Black, *Across the Valley*, New York, Holt, Rinehart and Winston, 1960.
20. Stauffer, Russell G., Alvina Treut Burrows, and Millard H. Black, *Into the Wind*, New York, Holt, Rinehart and Winston, 1960.
21. Stauffer, Russell G., Alvina Treut Burrows, Millard H. Black, and Evelyn Rezen Spencer, *Away We Go*, New York, Holt, Rinehart and Winston, 1960.
22. Stauffer, Russell G., Alvina Treut Burrows, Millard H. Black, and Miriam Mason Swain, *Come With Me*, New York, Holt, Rinehart and Winston, 1960.
23. Stauffer, Russell G., Alvina Treut Burrows, and Thomas D. Horn, *Above the Clouds*, New York, Holt, Rinehart and Winston, 1961.

24. Stauffer, Russell G., Alvina Treut Burrows, and Thomas D. Horn, *Teachers' Edition for Above the Clouds,* New York, Holt, Rinehart and Winston, 1962.
25. Stauffer, Russell G., Alvina Treut Burrows, and Thomas D. Horn, *Around the Bend,* New York, Holt, Rinehart and Winston, 1961.
26. Stauffer, Russell G., Alvina Treut Burrows, and Thomas D. Horn, *Through the Years,* New York, Holt, Rinehart and Winston, 1961.
27. Stauffer, Russell G., Alvina Treut Burrows, and Dilys M. Jones, *Skyways to Tomorrow,* New York, Holt, Rinehart and Winston, 1961.
28. Stauffer, Russell G., Alvina Treut Burrows, and Evelyn Rezen Spencer, *People on Parade,* New York, Holt, Rinehart and Winston, 1960.
29. Stauffer, Russell G., Alvina Treut Burrows, and Mary Sue White, *Teachers' Edition for Into the Wind,* New York, Holt, Rinehart and Winston, 1960.
30. Tinker, Miles A., "Recent Studies of Eye Movements in Reading," *Psychological Bulletin,* 55 (July, 1958), 215–231.
31. Vinacke, W. Edgar, "The Investigation of Concept Formation," *Psychological Bulletin,* 48 (January, 1951), 1–31.
32. *The World Almanac and Book of Facts,* Harry Hanson, ed., New York, Newspaper Enterprise Association, 1963.

Chapter 3 ⚜️⚜️⚜️⚜️⚜️ Directed Reading-Thinking Activity Illustrations ⚜️⚜️⚜️⚜️⚜️⚜️⚜️⚜️

The aim of a Group Directed Reading-Thinking Activity is twofold. The first aim is to teach children how to extract information of predictive value from a given context, either fiction or nonfiction. The information each pupil extracts depends on how it fits into his store of experience and knowledge. At times the ideas or assumptions called into use interact with each other freely; sometimes, they interact less freely. The likelihood of extracting information of good predictive value is increased if the ideas and assumptions are flexibly related to each other. When this is the case, various combinations can be examined and their usefulness tested as the material is read.

To accomplish effective utilization of this skill in different content areas it is necessary that D-R-T-A training be given using materials in different areas of interest in both fiction and nonfiction. If the skill is accomplished first on fiction, its transfer to other materials is not necessarily automatic. Pupils must see the relevance of the reading-thinking process in all areas. This way they can continuously relate what is learned in reading class to the job of being a student and to the reading of everyday life. They can make use of their new skill immediately in a practical way.

The second aim is to provide, through the group medium, ways of behaving like a thinking reader that would be useful to pupils when reading on their own. In a group situation whose aim is to encourage pupil thinking, each pupil's fund of experience and knowledge can become clearer. What a pupil "sees" in a story or article, a title or subtitle, a picture or illustration, depends on the way he has perceived and organized previous information of a related nature. He is the one who must see how things are alike in some respects and different in others.

If the earlier-received information is too generalized, too close to the nonverbal level, too dependent on haphazard concrete-perceptual experiences, the pupil may become aware of these inadequacies in the group situation. Otherwise, left on his own—or educated in the nonthinking, parrot-like tradition—he may never learn to question the validity of his notions and concepts. He operates in an uncultured way using his loosely structured concepts inappropriately and failing, therefore, to extract information of predictive value from what he reads. So he continues to perpetuate his blunders and his shortcomings. Persistent and intelligent effort is required; otherwise the new constructs a pupil makes will be fabricated at the same low level as the constructs he has already made.

How can a student become aware of his own conceptual resources and limitations in a group-directed reading situation? As already described in brief in Chapter 2, the role of the group can provide the milieu conducive to sound mental construction work rather than compounding wrong concepts. The favorable conditions are as follows:

First, all in the group are examining the same material.

Second, each pupil reacts in terms of his own private stock of experiences and knowledge.

Third, because pupils share ideas, the spirit is competitive and fosters the will to do; it *motivates*.

Fourth, the information extracted and the assumptions made are compared and contrasted, and likenesses and differences are noted.

Fifth, the activity itself provides the *means* for the creative use of ideas.

Sixth, each pupil's personal integrity is at stake.

Seventh, each pupil will need to defend his "educated guesses." They must be proved or disproved.

Eighth, available evidence will need to be presented to the group for acceptance or rejection. The group is the auditor, the jury, and the judge.

Ninth, pupils learn to have the strength of their convictions and not to be dominated by the loud verbalizer.

Tenth, pupils learn to respect the thinking of others, to study how they examine evidence and how they prove points.

Eleventh, pupils learn to temper their emotions in the crucible of group interaction, to be enthusiastic without being obnoxious, to rejoice without being offensive, to accept mistakes without being stifled.

Twelfth, all this is done under the direction of the teacher. She knows the content, knows the important concepts to be attained, and knows how to promote thinking on the part of others without putting words in their mouths. She knows the *effect* desired.

If children can interact intellectually as described, they can investigate the hidden processes of their own and other people's thinking. Then they can avoid being too docile or unimaginative or stereotyped in their thinking. Furthermore, the authority-dependency relationship orients toward the text and the group, rather than toward the teacher. A quotation from M. L. J. Abercrombie on free-group discussions is apropos at this point (1, p. 75):

Perhaps from the educational point of view the most important feature is the wide range of behavior which is useful; in different ways it is as useful to listen as to talk; to agree as to disagree; to criticize as to approve. The topics covered are so varied that no one person can for long retain a dominant position as the most knowledgeable or the most clear-headed. Sooner or later even the cleverest finds himself in a web of confusion out of which he is helped maybe by the most inarticulate. Often indeed it is the academically weak student who can offer a direct common-sense way out of the maze in which they all are stuck. Any one student may be at one moment the teacher, at another the pupil, and the tact, patience and skill which students severally or jointly may command when they undertake to teach another are worth seeing.

Those who are skilled in the business of teacher education will recognize at once that the pursuit of such purposes is primarily a matter of outlook and philosophy. The ends described can be accomplished in almost any kind of learning situation. The child acquires from repeated experience the attitude that he can think and that he can find out what he wants to know. He acquires a craftsmanship and an artistry. The wonder of knowledge becomes as intriguing as a great adventure.

A FIRST-READER-LEVEL D-R-T-A

In Chapter 2, a Directed Reading-Thinking Activity was outlined and discussed, and certain basic principles and assumptions underlying the development of an effective group D-R-T-A were described, as were practices in each of the five basic steps. It was pointed out that in essence a D-R-T-A had two parts—a process and a product. The first four steps—identifying purposes, guiding adjustment of rate to purposes and materials, observing the reading, and developing comprehension—comprised a process cycle. Each stop made during a D-R-T-A sets the cycle in motion: check comprehension, reset purposes, adjust rate, read. In fact, each time a reader stops to reflect, even in the middle of a sentence, he sets a similar cycle in motion. He pauses to check his understanding, decides to proceed with the same or different purpose(s), quickly adjusts rate, and then reads on. The product phase of the D-R-T-A is the *extending and refining* stage. This is the time when, by direct attack, attempt is made to increase powers of observation, of reflection, of word recognition, and of conceptualization.

It was also maintained in Chapter 2 that basic readers were especially adaptable to the fundamental purposes of a Directed Reading-Thinking Activity in a group situation. Controls of vocabulary, concepts, interests, illustrations, and story length make this true. The rate of new-word and new-concept introduction is controlled, and pupils are permitted to try their new comprehension skills without being frustrated by various demands. At the primary level, the stories and selections are about events or ideas within the scope of children's experience. Gradually the content reaches out beyond their experiences—socially, historically, numerically, geographically, aesthetically, scientifically, and humorously—but it does so at a pace that should not overwhelm them. The length of the selections is such that the material can readily be read in the time limits imposed by the demands of the total curriculum.

In this chapter, procedures of a D-R-T-A will be discussed in detail, using typical stories and articles selected at different levels. The interacting processes of pupil-teacher, pupil-pupil, and pupil-content will then be carefully examined.

The first story described in detail is a first-reader-level story called "A Newspaper Helps" (12, pp. 119–124). In this basic-reader series, if only the preceding books in the series had been dealt with (it is hoped that this would not be the case), the pupils would have been introduced to 139 words in three preprimers and a primer. Since the story occurs in the fourth unit of this first reader, pupils will have been introduced to 96 more words, making a total of 235 words. If the skill-training program prescribed in the studybooks has been followed, the pupils will have dealt with 114 word-attack skill activities and 103 comprehension activities up to this point. If the manual activities have also been used as described, the number of activities will be sizable. There are about twice as many manual activities as there are studybook activities, or 229 word-attack activities and 206 comprehension activities. This could make a total of 342 word-attack activities, and 309 comprehension activities. The word-attack skills supposedly acquired include visual and auditory discrimination of beginning and ending letters, consonant substitution, inflectional changes, compound words, and so on. Also, the children will have had, in this book alone, the experience of twenty D-R-T-A sessions.

New Words

Six new words are introduced in the six pages of "A Newspaper Helps":

New Words			
dog	page 119	lives	page 120
where	page 119	other	page 122
found	page 120	trick	page 123

There are two pages (121 and 124) on which no new words appear. Note that page 121 is the middle page of the story while page 124 is the last page. This means that the reader has two complete pages (including the all-important climax page) on which no new words appear.

In addition, each new word is reused in the story, as follows.

New Words	PAGES						
	119	120	121	122	123	124	Total
dog	2*	3	2	2	2	4	15
where	2	1	1			1	5
found		1	1	1	1		4
lives		1	1			2	4
other				1	2	1	4
trick					3	1	4

* Number of times word is used on page.

The frequency with which the student meets new words is vital for retention. As any experienced first-grade teacher can confirm and as any new teacher soon learns, one or two contacts with a word are not enough to effect retention, even among bright children. They can also confirm that presenting words in isolation by rote drill, in order to get needed recontact with a word, seldom does the trick. Flash cards misused are the shackle of the learner, the despair of the naïve teacher, and the frustration of the well-meaning parent.

The above table indicates how vocabulary usage is governed in basic readers. From a strictly mechanics-of-reading point of view, the repetition of new words within the story is good. Each new word is used a minimum of four times in the story. The psychology of learning has for years been clear about the efficacy of meaningful repetition or recontact with what is to be learned. J. B. Stroud puts it this way (14, p. 373):

> The two great expediencies used to insure retention are thorough initial learning and subsequent practice or review. No matter how thorough the initial learning is, forgetting is to be expected in time unless subsequent practice is engaged in. Such practice may take several forms, as in rereading material previously studied, using the material in different contexts, engaging in symbolical practice by direct recall, [and] class discussion. . . .

Further analysis of the new words in the story is interesting and illuminating. Compare the new words with the number of different words and the number of running words (total number of words) in the story:

Number of new words in story	6
Number of different words	126
Number of running words	441

This means that the ratio of new words to different words is 1:21; the ratio of new words to running words is 1:73. Both of these ratios are remarkable in that they so clearly indicate how very low the new-word burden is.

In addition, of the 240 words introduced in the three preprimers, the primer, and up to page 124 in the first reader, 126 have been reused in this one story. This respresents a reuse of 53 percent of all the words in one story.

Far more important, though, is that words are introduced meaningfully and appropriately according to the natural communication demands of the context and the concepts. The context provides two sources: the language context and the picture context.

Examining the language context on page 119 of this story for the introduction, or first use, of *dog* and *where,* the following reproduction is illustrative:

"Cooky," said Ned.
"Do you know this little *dog?*
He has played with us all day. . . ."
                         and
"No one on our street has a dog like this," said Cooky.
"*Where* did he come from?"

Ample language clues are provided in both instances. This is especially true for the introduction of the word *where.*

In addition, the picture provides clues that help cinch the usage in the language context. The picture shows Ned, Ted, and Cooky examining a dog without a tag. This confirms the use of the word *dog* (dog in picture) and *where* (without a tag, where is he *from?*).

Page 119 provides the basis for the semantic concept triangle.

The story provides the correct *language* or word, and the picture provides *experience.* When the two ingredients are joined in the mind of the reader, a *concept* or idea is fashioned. This is the third side of the triangle and ensures its apex, the peak of attainment or conceptualization.

Similar conditions are true for each of the other four words introduced in this story: *found, lives, other, trick.* All are presented in a natural, logical, and correct language-experience situation.

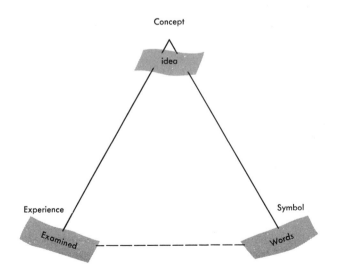

Since these words are used in a conventional way, agreed upon and accepted by our society, the children who are to read this story should meet these words in the story context. *The words should not be presented first in isolation.* Because of the appropriate and timely use of the new words and because the children will be intent on reading for meaning, the likelihood of their recognizing the words on their own is high. When the pupils wish to use any of the six words introduced here, they need no one to stand by and prompt them. The words and their meanings are now familiar. Similarly, the teacher should not need to stand by when the children read these words used appropriately in a meaningful setting.

Carefully structured materials are prepared so that children learning to read may recognize new words on their own in the context in which the words are presented. If the context does not suffice, the pupils should have the opportunity of using, again on their own, the phonetic clues or structure clues they have learned.

In situations where the teacher writes all new words on the chalkboard and tells the children what the words are, or helps them analyze the words before they meet them in context, the pupils do not have an opportunity to use their skills. The teacher short-circuits their learning.

Basic-reader materials contain such vocabulary controls as spaced introduction of new words, natural and meaningful introduction of words through picture and language contexts, meaningful reusage in the same and similar contexts, and frequent reusage to facilitate recall and recognition.

Experiences and Concepts

Identifying lost dogs, lost and found ads, evening paper, pet tricks, and dog show are the experiences and concepts developed in "A Newspaper Helps." The story begins by introducing the problem of what to do with a stray dog. Then the reader is given clues that indicate how the owners may be found and where the dog might have come from. The solution, however, is not wholly apparent until the last page of the story. Pupils will most likely be stimulated to suggest their own solutions to the problem.

Here, then, is a real opportunity for creative reading—deciding what to do about a realistic problem and comparing personal ideas with story events. The teacher is provided with lists of experiences and concepts to help her quickly single out the key ideas involved in the story. This does not mean that all the children must have had experience with all the concepts listed in order to read. Rereading can, even at this level, extend children's concepts, and the teacher needs to be alert to all the opportunities for extending them as well as for refining them.

For example, many children may not know about lost-and-found ads and how to identify lost dogs. When they read this story, they will learn about this as they follow the actions of the boys. They will do as adults do—learn by reading about events. Thus it would be extremely unwise to explain lost-and-found ads or to describe how to identify lost dogs before they read the story. After the children have read the story, certain basic ideas can be extended by referring to local newspapers. This is an excellent next step.

It is common knowledge that "experience is the best teacher," particularly, let us add, if it is second-hand. Life is filled with second-hand experiences. In fact, much of what we learn is gained through second-hand experiences. One need not jump off a bridge to understand the danger involved or lose a dog to discover how to find him. Reading is a rich, indispensable, and dynamically vital source for gaining experience. It is paramount, therefore, that from the very beginning children be taught to read in such a way that they acquire this attitude. As early as possible, children need to become sensitive to the fact that reading can give them new ideas and change old ones. Most important in all this is that the teacher's attitude toward reading be such that it will foster a reading-to-learn attitude.

Directing the Reading-Thinking Activity

One way to segment "A Newspaper Helps" for the purpose of providing training in the process portion (examining, predicting, proving) of the D-R-T-A is as follows:

1. Speculate using only information obtained from the title.
2. Check the predictive value of these conjectures by examining the first picture and readjusting speculations.
3. Read page 119; check predictive value of conjectures; adjust speculations.
4. Examine pictures on pages 120–121; check speculations; adjust speculations.
5. Read pages 120–121; check predictive value of conjectures; adjust speculations.
6. Read pages 122–123; check predictive value of speculations; adjust speculations.
7. Examine picture on page 124; check speculations; adjust speculations.
8. Read page 124; check predictive value of speculations.

If this kind of segmented treatment were given *each* six-page story, one would soon defeat the purpose of a D-R-T-A, for the process would soon become as stultifying as the recommended practice in so many other instances: readiness—teacher tells, teacher asks questions; guided silent reading—teacher watches pupils read; comprehension check—pupils answer teacher questions and tell back the story; oral reading—pupils read page orally taking turns and following in book to detect pupil errors. This procedure is usually labeled *introductory reading of the whole story* or *first silent reading*. The labels sound good enough, but the practices prescribed belie the labels. In addition, it is usually recommended, particularly at the first-grade level, that this cycle be accomplished on a page-by-page basis. If this is done, the number of stops, the length of the stops, and the monotony of the daily routine serve but one purpose—to banish a love for reading forever.

At a later point in this chapter many ways will be described for segmenting a story so as to train thinking readers. At this point, remember that the purpose of dealing with various amounts of information is to teach children to be reading detectives. They must see for themselves the predictive value of the clues in one-sixth of a story, one-fourth, one-half, two-thirds, or five-sixths. That this kind of thinking-reading performance can be initiated at a first-grade level is easy to prove.

Title Clues, Step 1.   Have the pupils find the story in the Table of Contents. Note, please, that *this is not to be done* with each story. It would be ridiculous to start each D-R-T-A by turning to the story title in the Table of Contents. Other ways of starting are described in subsequent examples.

If the book is being used as directed, the children will have a very good idea which story comes next. They do not need to turn to the Table of Contents to locate either the title of the story or the page where it begins. If this practice is indulged in in every D-R-T-A, it makes a sham of a skill that is of much use to an able reader—locating information.

Why then turn to the Table of Contents as recommended in this particular D-R-T-A plan? Even though the pupils know quite definitely which story comes next, now they will learn the exact title of the story. It is nonsense to think that pupils who had dealt with this book on at least twenty previous D-R-T-A occasions would not have seen the title to this story. There should be no pretense about the reason for turning to the Table of Contents: The reason is to get the exact wording of the title and then to see what information of predictive value can be deduced from it.

A title carefully chosen serves many purposes. It can be the equivalent of a central theme and have an over-all encompassing value. In "A Newspaper Helps," the title is highly suggestive as to the possible outcome of the story, and the able reader will keep this in mind throughout. All clues, all items of information, must be oriented around these ideas. The title gives direction and focus and is in a sense an all-encompassing clue.

The title permits and encourages the use of *divergent* thinking. This means, as J. P. Guilford (8) has said, producing a diversity of ideas that are logically probable, that are reasonable or credible within the limitations of the facts available. Divergent thinking prompts *creative* thinking. In the words of E. Paul Torrance (15, pp. 62–63),

the creative reader sensitizes himself to problems, gaps in knowledge, missing elements, something incorrect. This calls for the formation of new relationships and combinations, synthesizing relatively unrelated elements into a coherent whole, redefining or transforming certain elements to discover new uses, and building onto what is known. In this search for solutions, there is the operation of ideational fluency (the production of a large number of possibilities).

Before reading on, stop and list as many ideas as you can think of that are suggested by the title "A Newspaper Helps." This will permit you to judge the ideational fluency of typical six-year-olds.

a. Pupil Predictions. All ten pupils in a group of first graders had already opened their books to the Table of Contents and read the title silently. There was no need to read the title aloud. All had books, all could read, so why read the three words aloud? Silly to do so, is it not?

No new words were introduced in the title, precluding the remote likelihood that some pupil might be puzzled by a new word. All words had been introduced at the primer level and earlier and had been repeated many times since. This kind of control of new-word introduction permits pupils to concentrate on using the title and not on new-word analysis. Furthermore, a title just does not provide enough context clues to new-word recognition and therefore denies the reader access to one of the most important clue sources to word recognition.

On occasion, teachers defend the oral reading of a title by saying that is how they can be sure that all "know" what the title is. Explanations of this kind are extremely weak and reflect more on the teacher than on the pupils or the text. Are the pupils so poorly trained that they cannot read three words silently and think about them? If this is the case, it is a sad, sad commentary on the type of teaching that has been taking place. If a pupil is having difficulty with a word, he should use his own word-attack skills; if these are not adequate, he should seek teacher help. But of most significance is the fact that, if a child misreads or misunderstands, his conjectures or predictions will reflect this. When he tests his ideas against those offered by others in the group, he will soon realize that he is wrong. He will *discover* the need for more careful reading. The teacher will not have told him.

After all pupils have read the title, the teacher asks them to close their books. This is done so that full attention can be given to the use of the title for predicting purposes. Pupils will not be distracted by picture clues or other titles in the Table of Contents. Attention is focused on the task at hand.

The teacher initiated the purpose-setting session of "A Newspaper Helps" by asking her group of ten first graders: "What do *you think* a story with a title like this will be about?" In most instances this question is enough to get things going. On occasion, though, and particularly in the earlier D-R-T-A sessions, it may be helpful to rephrase the question and ask, "What do you think might happen in this story?"

"It might be about a family that is going to move," said one boy. "We moved to Newark and looked in the paper to find a house." "Maybe it's about training a dog," said another. "Why do you say that?" asked the teacher. "We rolled up a newspaper and made a paddle to help train our dog," he replied. A girl said, "It might be about garbage. We roll up our garbage in newspaper before we put it in the garbage can." Another pupil said, "It might be about a dog who helps deliver newspapers." A girl said, "Maybe they will paint some things and put newspapers on the floor so they won't get paint all about."

b. Pupil Experiences. Note how each of these conjectures is within the realm of possibility. Note especially, though, how each reflects the experience and knowledge of the pupil making the prediction. Ben Jonson is reputed to have said, "Speak that I may judge thee." That is exactly what can be done in every instance in which pupils express their ideas. How ridiculous it would have been for this teacher to have *told* the boys and girls that the story was about a lost dog and how three boys locate its owner by putting an ad in the paper. Such tripe would yield nothing, and it never could.

Children know about newspapers. They know what it means to help someone or how a newspaper might help. So, why tell them? The author purposely selected material of a kind that would be within the experience and interest range of the children.

Even though an interest inventory was not made, a background account was obtained by permitting each child to draw from his experiences. If the teacher did not previously know that the boy who first reacted to the title had moved to Newark, she now learned that this was the case. Equally as important is the way she found out. The stimulus "A Newspaper Helps" evoked the response about moving. This boy made the association with moving on his own; he recalled his earlier experience, sensed a relationship, and spoke up. He was operating in a free group situation; he knew that his thinking was being invited and would be wholesomely received by the group as well as by the teacher. He also knew that he should explain why he thought as he did, and therefore he offered a reason immediately. Here, in a setting of democratic culture, a child is being prepared for a future role as an active, independent citizen.

Apparently the second boy had experience with training dogs. Perhaps he had helped train a puppy of his own or that of a relative or neighbor. Regardless, he had the experience, recalled it, made the association, spoke up, and explained why he thought so.

The girl's "garbage" association is an interesting one and reflects her experiences. Her association is credible and clearly in the realm of possibility.

The next idea about the dog helping to deliver newspapers both is and is not reasonable. Even so, it is the boy's association, and it reflects his experience. Perhaps he meant to say that the boy who delivers newspapers will be helped by both the dog and the newspaper.

The fifth pupil made a very plausible projection. Newspapers are often used to cover or protect. Her experience included using them to protect the floor while painting. One might deduct that she enjoyed a variety of experiences in her home life.

Five of the ten children made proposals. This is an excellent percentage. At times all ten may offer a different conjecture. At other times, only one may be offered. At all times the teacher must be ready and willing to accept whatever response develops. If only one response is made or even no response, the teacher must exercise a good deal of restraint. It is tempting to step in and offer ideas, and this might be done on rare occasions. But it is far better to try to discover what kinds of information are needed to arouse response and to determine later why the title clues did not suffice. If this kind of teacher reserve is exercised and if alertness to additional clues is maintained, the children may gain in thinking power and assurance. They are the ones who must experience the difficulty and discover how to cope with it. This is certainly not the time for teacher barricades against learning.

Before going on, the teacher asked the other five which one of the ideas they thought would be the right one. Three thought the story would be about the paper-paint idea; one thought it would be about moving; and one thought it would be about training a dog. All had done some thinking, and all had made a decision without teacher coercion.

First-Picture Clues, Step 2.   Pupils schooled in the art of purpose setting would most likely, as they did in the situation on which this discussion is based, offer their conjectures in the time that it takes five different people to say the few words that each said. Six-year-olds are impatient, even though they are usually careful about observing the rights of others. They could not all speak at once, but they came as close to doing so as circumstances permitted. Yet, at the same time, they listened to each other. Pupil reactions to ideas offered were immediate and almost of the standard adult variety: smiles, eyes aglow, head nodding, frowns, ohs, and ahs. It was easy to tell when an idea was warmly received.

Time is important; about this there is no quarrel. But time does not determine quality, though it may reflect quality indirectly as a symptom. In this situation, the pupils were preoccupied with ideas, not time.

Next the teacher directed the group to turn to the first picture on page 119. "Study it carefully to see which of your ideas seems right," she said. "Then close your books." In a second all had turned to the page and were poring over the picture. The pupils were engrossed, their attention monopolized by the force of a purpose and an eager interest.

To a good degree, the dynamics of the group situation spurred them on. Each had declared himself in the presence of the group, and each was driven by an impulse to prove himself right. Each sought the satisfaction of achievement.

Books closed quickly. Eager faces turned toward the teacher. Almost before she could say, "What do you think now?," the boy who had predicted the story might be about a dog helping to deliver newspapers spoke up. "I might be right," he said. "Maybe the dog in the picture helps deliver papers."

"I might be right, too," said the lad who spoke about training a dog. "The boys look sad or something. I think this dog wants to follow them wherever

A Newspaper Helps

"Cooky," said Ned.

"Do you know this little dog?

He has played with us all day.

No one has come after him,

and now he will not go home."

"No one on our street has a dog

like this," said Cooky.

"Where did he come from?"

"We do not know where he came from.

We saw him in the field

when we were playing ball," said Ted.

119

they go, and they want him to stay home. Maybe they will train him with a newspaper."

"I think he's a lost dog," said a girl. "He looks unhappy, and the boys don't know what to do or where to go."

"I think the boys want to play ball and the dog gets in their way," said another. "They will find a place where he can play."

Again it was hardly necessary for the teacher to ask, "How can we find out?" because all in the group knew what to do. In this instance she received almost a shouted "Read!" from the group. They knew what it meant to "read to find out."

"Read to the bottom of page 119, and then close your books," said the teacher.

Children must be trained to be independent and to recognize a need and know what to do about it. Just before the first reading, pupils need to review briefly what to do if they encounter a word they do not know. The steps are:

1. Read to the end of the sentence.
2. Look for picture clues.
3. Sound it out.
4. Ask for teacher help.

Certainly, to know that they do not know a particular word, the children will first have to "see" the word. Visual discrimination is their first reaction—noting likenesses and differences of structure. Undoubtedly, too, they will then try to sound it out. Now, failing to recognize it, they will use context clues.

However, in reviewing the steps, context clues or meaning clues should always be listed first. The potency of meaning is so great and the idea of reading for meaning is so important that meaning should always take precedence. Also, once pupils have an idea as to what the word might be, the skills of phonics and structure become more functional.

As soon as the group knew how far they were to read, they "took off."

The first picture helped focus in on the nature of the plot and its direction. Now all knew that, at least for the present, three boys and a dog seemed involved. All in the group knew the boys from previous stories as Ned, Ted, and Cooky. The dog, however, had not appeared before.

The pupils who found their predictions were wrong were not distressed. They had done good thinking. They readjusted their thinking according to the predictability value of the new information. They knew from experience that circumstances like these required flexibility of adjustment. They were developing emotional stability and maturity as well.

Page 119 contains only sixty-seven running words. Pupils instructional at this level will read a page like this in a minute or less. If the "slow" group in a second or third grade is instructional at this level, they, too, will read along at a good pace. Pupils instructional at these levels should not be reading with obvious lip movement. Such pupils are experiencing other kinds of difficulty.

The words introduced on this page, *dog* and *where,* were used repeatedly by the children when they were predicting. Note how naturally they were used. Note, too, that they were not "dragged" into the discussion by a well-intentioned teacher poorly advised. The circumstances stimulated the oral usage of *dog* and *where* and provided readiness for recognition of these words when they occurred in print. Of course, the likelihood is considerable that all in the group already knew the words. (See Part IV, "Beginning Reading Instruction.")

First-Page Clues, Step 3.   Silent-reading time may be the most important period in the entire word-recognition training program (see pp. 45–50). All reading teachers agree that the object of instruction is to develop self-reliant, independent, discriminating readers. All agree, too, that it is the teacher who sets the climate of a D-R-T-A by words, tone of voice, manner, and skill-training facility. If children are to be self-reliant in their use of word-attack skills, it is the teacher who must direct experiences that will foster such an attitude.

A first step on the road to word-recognition independence is to foster an attitude of "try it yourself first, and then get help if you need it." One of the major advantages of structured basic-reader material is that new words can be so presented as to encourage the reader to try the word on his own before seeking help. This is done by controlling the number of new words on a page, the ratio of new words to running words, or old known words, and the relationship of new words to picture content.

This is only half the process, though. If the child is to try out his fund of word-attack skills, *he must be given the opportunity.* The best opportunity for the child who is learning to read is to meet new words for the first time in a story context. It follows from this that the teacher must not present the new words in isolation in a mistaken notion that she is preparing the child to read, for all she is actually doing is preparing him for a kind of mental servitude—one in which he lacks the freedom and ability to determine his own word-recognition-skill acumen.

Next in importance is the pupil's willingness to ask for help. Teachers sometimes parry by saying that children will not ask for help. This, of course, is true—in a situation where pupils are deprived of the normal, healthy give and take of the discovery approach to learning. In such instances the teacher should examine her own behavior as a part of the child's learning environment. Where the teaching environment is open, accepting, warm, and understanding, pupils will know that they do not know and will ask for help.

Some child might ask for help with the word *where*. Occasionally children at this early stage of progress experience difficulty with *wh* words and the like. The first recommendation—to have the children read the whole paragraph—is sound because it alerts them to the value of the total context and to the value of meaning clues. Because of the nonphonetic nature of the word *where,* not much would be gained by alerting pupils to its sound-clue elements. This gives added significance to the value of meaning clues.

Sometimes receiving help with a troublesome word is not enough to fix it. So, when the pupil meets it a second time, he may request help again. Do not be concerned; this is not at all unusual. Suggest to the pupil that he turn back to the first appearance of the word. Interestingly enough, seeing the word again in its first setting is frequently enough to help him recall it. If the pupil does not recognize the word, the teacher should tell him what it is and make a note of his need, so that she can give him additional help during the fundamental skill-training period.

When all books are closed, the comprehension check can be started by a number of teacher questions. The teacher might ask, "What do you think now?" or "Were you right?" or "What do you think will happen next?" Each question serves a particular purpose.

"What do you think now?" and "What do you think will happen next?" set in motion very similar lines of thought. The second question invites anticipation and speculation about events to come and calls into play ideas garnered thus far. To make educated guesses, pupils will need to put to work ideas obtained on page 119. They will have to screen and evaluate ideas and make decisions about events to come in the light of events thus far. The first question does almost the same thing, but it lets the pupils decide that "what next" ideas are in order. In other words, "What do you think now?" is somewhat less directive than "What do you think will happen next?"

The question "Were you right?" focuses on set purposes and an evaluation of *right, wrong,* or *partially* right. This is a good approach and meets with favorable pupil response. They know whether or not what they had pre-dicted actually occurred. They know, too, that the test of their decision will be to read the lines that prove, disprove, or partially support it. The ques-tion "Were you right?" focuses on proof.

Pupils schooled in the D-R-T-A method will hardly wait for a teacher question. They know that, when their books are closed, their comprehension will be checked and evaluated.

When the teacher in this instance asked, "Well, were any of you right?," the girl who had spoken about a lost dog immediately replied, "I was right, it is a lost dog." "Read the lines that told you the dog was lost," the teacher said. The girl opened her book and proceeded down the page eagerly. (All other books stayed closed.) She reached the bottom of the page, paused, and started down again from the top. This time her expression was one of concern, rather than of open-faced eagerness. This time, too, her rate down the page was slower, more cautious, more reflective. Finally, she looked up and said, "It doesn't say he was lost but it says they don't know where he came from." Then she read aloud the lines: " 'We do not know where he came from. We saw him in the field when we were playing ball,' said Ted." The teacher turned to the group and asked, "Do any of you agree with Janet?" A number of hands went up. Then one boy read the lines, "No one has come after him, and now he will not go home." Another read the lines, " 'No one on our street has a dog like this,' said Cooky. 'Where did he come from?' " All agreed that no one had proved the dog was lost, but all thought that this was the case.

Janet was learning an invaluable lesson in her second rereading of page 119. She was strongly influenced by the purpose she had declared—that the dog was lost. When she first read the page, all the clues seemed to confirm her expectancy. Janet was finding what Janet was looking for—ideas to support her preconceived notions. Research shows that a reader's emotional status, attitudes, interests, and purposes influence what he reads. (4, 7, 11.) Of special interest is the report by Anne S. McKillop supporting the idea that answers to questions of fact are not so apt to be influenced by attitudes and beliefs as are answers that require value judgments and evaluative conclusions. Janet was looking for facts so eagerly that she was unaware of the fact that the conclusion she reached was based on inconclusive evidence.

Janet was so certain she was right that she turned to page 119 and skimmed down the page looking for a specific or literally stated fact. When she did not find the fact, her attitudes and beliefs were sharply influenced. How could she have been so wrong? She started down the page again—this time doing a study-type reading. Reflective thinking made her stop and weigh more carefully the information given. This required an adjustment of reading pace to purpose and material and provided training in versatility. What she did not realize at this stage on her road to reading maturity was the fact that she was dealing with inferences or implied information. The three comments about the dog suggested that the dog was lost. Repeated practical experience of this type would provide the substance for training in how to evaluate implied information. Repeated experience would also teach Janet the difference between skimming for literal information and skimming for implied information. This situation provided the teacher with an opportunity also. Skimming skills need to be adapted to different materials, and such adaptations need to be taught. A pupil might have similar experiences frequently and yet never be able to make the proper deductions and become articulate and deliberate in applying the skill.

Even though the other members of the group were not required to make the same kinds of decisions as was Janet, they could see how she was adjusting. Some were attentive enough and recalled the plot sequence well enough to know that other lines could be read in support of the "lost dog" idea.

The *oral rereading* to prove a point was done in each instance with a considerable degree of smoothness and expression. These folks were out to prove a point, and this was their preoccupation—not the saying of words. None read on a stilted word-by-word basis. None read with sing-song, high-pitched voices. The reason is obvious: these children were providing evidence in defense of a point, not evidence that they could "say" words.

The *oral rereading* was *not* motivated by purposes different from the purposes that motivated the original reading. Such notions apply only in situations where the pupils reread a story orally after it has been read silently.

Even then the purposes are usually trumped-up teacher purposes that do neither motivate the children nor deceive them. They soon realize that all the teacher wants is a routinized pronouncing of the words. In a D-R-T-A the oral rereading is motivated by the purposes that initiated the silent reading. This is as it should be. Now is the time to read to prove or disprove.

In this situation none of the children asked for help with either of the two new words, *dog* and *where*. Neither did they ask for help with any of the old words. In the oral reading, the pupils knew the words well enough to read them smoothly. The teacher had ample evidence at this point that the new words were being recognized and put to work. Even so, as will be explained later, she made a double check on the words.

When the lines were read orally, the other members of the group kept their books closed. This required them to listen to the lines being read. Not only did they need to listen, but they needed to listen discriminately. They needed to decide whether or not the lines being read were correct and proved the point being defended. This kind of training in listening is of a high order because it requires discerning attentiveness, and these six-year-olds were attentive.

Most in the group thought the dog was lost. Two thought he was a dog without an owner. One of the more alert pupils felt this could not be, because the dog was wearing a collar. "If the dog is lost, what do you think the boys will do?," asked the teacher. One boy said, "I think they'll go around in the neighborhood and see if they can find where he lives." Another said: "I think they'll ask their parents about what to do." A third said: "I think they'll ask people on the street."

Picture Clues, Step 4. "Take a look at the next two pictures and see what clues you can find there," said the teacher. The boy who had said they would check with their parents spoke up. "I was right," he said. "They are checking with Cooky's mother."

At once the first lad cut in: "I think the lady is a neighbor."

"She is Cooky's mother," the other replied. "See, she has red hair like Cooky has." All the group accepted this idea as the most likely.

"I think they are looking in the newspaper to find out if the owner is asking people to look for his dog," was another conjecture.

"I think the boys put a notice in the paper," said another. "They want to find out where he lives."

"Read pages 120 and 121 and see who is right," said the teacher.

The teacher might have probed for more conjectures, but she sensed that all were sufficiently questioning in attitude to go on. A most important skill for teachers to grasp in such situations is to know when to step in and have the pupils read on. No one could spell out all such circumstances, nor would one want to. Each situation varies, and the teacher must, to a degree, "play it by ear."

Note how objective children can be in seeing and using ideas. Many adults overlook the fact that the lady in the picture has red hair as does Cooky. Adults usually predict that the woman is a mother because she is wearing an apron and has a mop in her hand. These are symbols that are frequently associated with a stereotype of mother.

The questions now before the group are, Is the dog lost? Is the woman Cooky's mother? Is she a neighbor? Did the boys put an ad in the paper telling about the dog? Did the owner of the dog put an ad in the paper? This is an excellent set of questions. They are better than any textbook author or teacher could dream up.

So, on with the story!

The boys went to Cooky's house and took the dog with them. Cooky's mother was standing inside the house.

Cooky said, "Look, Mother! The twins found this dog in a field. What can we do with him? I wish he could stay at our house."

Mother said, "He may stay here now but not all the time. He must have a home, too. We will find out where he lives. I will call Mr. Jack so he can put news of the dog in the paper."

The next morning the twins went to Cooky's house.

They ran as fast as they could. "Here is last night's paper," said Cooky. "I will read what Mr. Jack has put in it."

Found: Little Black Dog in field on Penny Street. Call 8-4886

"Now we can find out where our little dog lives," said Ted. "We may stay here and play with you. Mother said we could."

Reading for Information, Step 5. This time the teacher did not remind the children how to handle word-recognition needs. They knew what to do. More important, they knew they could ask for help and receive help without dissatisfaction on the part of the teacher or scorn on the part of the group. The learning climate was good. To know that you do not know may be the beginning of wisdom, but it is equally important to know what to do about what you do not know.

Two new words are introduced on page 120 but none on page 121. Both words are in a meaningful language context. Picture (experience clues) aid is also provided. Pupils should be able to handle both words phonetically and structurally for pronunciation-recognition purposes by means of skills already taught such as consonant substitution—new word *found,* old words, *round* and *fun;* new word *lives,* old words, *give* and *look*—and inflectional changes—*lives* and *live.*

One child asked for help with the word *lives.* The first thing the teacher asked was, "What do you think it is?" This is a timely question. The teacher knows that the pupil had already tried his word-attack skills. It may be that all he needs is the teacher's reassurance that his decision about the word is correct. "Is it *lives?*," the boy asked. "Read the sentence to me and see if it fits," said the teacher. The boy reread the line to the teacher in an audible whisper: "We will find out where he *lives.*" The word fitted. It made sense in this context. So, the boy read on.

Throughout this silent-reading session the teacher stayed alert not only for requests for help but also to observe the pupils' reading performance. She watched for good reading posture, lip movement, finger pointing, facial reactions to the plot development, and rate of reading. Not all pupils closed their books at the same time, so she took advantage of these seconds by carrying on a person-to-person private conversation with a pupil or two. She asked, in a low whisper, "Was it Cooky's mother?" and "Did you find out why the boys were reading the newspaper?" Children respond especially well to these brief sessions. They welcome the personal attention. Furthermore, it serves as a comprehension double check for the teacher. A pupil reluctant to speak up may be drawn into active participation in this way.

When all books were closed the comprehension check started at once. All the teacher said was, "Well?," in an invitation-to-respond way. In rapid order, now, they read orally lines to prove it was Cooky's mother, to help confirm the lost-dog idea, and to show that the boys had actually put the news about the dog in the paper. One boy argued that it was Mr. Jack who had put the ad in the paper, but a girl said that Mother had called him and told him to do so. Reading the lines that proved this developed into an interesting point. First the girl read the line, "I will call Mr. Jack so he can put news of the dog in the paper." When the teacher asked her, "Who is the I?," the pupil needed to go back four lines to find the antecedent for *I:* "Mother said."

"Look there," said Cooky.

"The ball went into our garden."

"I found the ball," said Ted.

"Now I am looking for my hat.

It came off when I ran for the ball."

"Look! Look!" called Ned.

"See how fast the dog can run.

Is he going to jump?"

The little dog did jump.

He went up on one side of the bat

and came down on the other side.

This surprised the three boys.

122

At this point the group was almost equally divided as to what would happen next. Some felt very sure that the owner would show up; others did not. As one boy said, "If they put an ad in the *Newark Post* [a weekly], the man might not see it." "Read two more pages and see who is right," said the teacher.

Note how the number of conjectures has narrowed to two. This is to be

Cooky went into the house
and found some clean yellow paper.
"Our dog did a trick with the bat,"
he said.
"I will see what other tricks he knows."

"Run and jump," Ned called.
"Make a hole in the paper."

The dog did make a big hole in it.
Then he did other tricks.
He sat up and asked for cake.
He jumped up, standing upside down.
Again and again he surprised the boys.

123

expected. As evidence accumulates, the plot ideas converge. Now a recognized best or conventional conclusion is beginning to emerge.

Reading for Information, Step 6. This time pupils are responsible
for "reading" both the pictures and the text. The most obvious source of
information is the two pictures. At this stage, pupils should be schooled to
turn first to the pictures. Note, too, how throughout this story, the pictures

have helped to carry the plot forward. In this instance, pupils are primed to see "owners" come into the story. Both pictures provide no such evidence. In addition, both provide information but raise such questions in the reader's mind as, What is Ted looking for? Is Cooky pointing to a lost object? Were the boys playing ball? Will the dog find the ball? Why the large yellow paper? What is the dog doing? Is he jumping up at the paper? Or is he going to jump through the paper? Answers to these questions can be found only in the text.

Note, too, how the two facing pages reproduced on pp. 81–82 help carry the plot forward. The ideas presented are not what the children had expected. Yet they are plausible and "fit" the plot. The content does not sound contrived. The owners did not show up immediately, and the boys could be playing with the dog. This surprise element in the plot holds the reader's attention and keeps him involved in unraveling the story. This is as it should be. A good deal of careful planning, writing, and arranging is required to set up a series of basic-reader stories designed to be useful in the teaching of reading as a thinking process.

Again the teacher observes reading performance. Again she makes short but very timely person-to-person visits to keep the readers focused on finding meaning. Such visits and appropriate teacher questions help foster the attitude paramount to successful reading—reading for meaning. Certainly attention is and has been given to recognizing words, but the reason words are to be recognized is so that the plot can be comprehended.

Two new words are presented on these two pages: *other* on page 122, and *trick* on page 123. Again, both words are embedded in excellent language and picture contexts: "Up on one side, down on the _____" (other); and "our dog did a _____" (trick). Both words could most likely be supplied if a closure test were used.

When all books were closed, the comprehension check got under way at once. "The owner didn't come but he will," said one lad with a great deal of assurance. "Why are you so sure?," asked the teacher. "This is a dog who can do tricks and they will want him back," was the reply. "Yes," said a girl, "he can do many tricks. Maybe he is a circus dog."

"How many think the owner will show up?," asked the teacher. All hands went up. "Then, take a quick look at the last picture and close your books."

Study Last Picture, Step 7. The look at the picture on page 124 was a quick one. The moment the pupils saw the two strangers they were sure the owners had called. The comprehension check showed this to be the case.

"It's the owners," said one. "The dog knows the lady."

"Yes," said another, "and the man is rewarding the boys."

"I don't think it's the owner," said one boy. "The man is giving the

boys some paper, not some money. Money would be green and this is white."

All books flew open almost instantly. Yes, the paper was white. Maybe the folks were not the owners. Maybe this was Mr. and Mrs. Jack from the newspaper.

"Read and find out," said the teacher.

All too often last pictures in materials designed for this level "give away" the story ending, and there is no need to read. In this instance, the picture seemed to give the obvious, yet it proved to be puzzling. The pupils needed to read to find out, and the teacher knew this.

Reading for Information, Step 8. Almost before the teacher could look around, the books were closed again. It was obvious by the "ohs" and "ahs" that the pupils had reached the end. All knew the owners had come. During the discussion that followed the teacher asked a girl to read the line that proved the man was giving the boys tickets.

"It doesn't really say tickets," said the girl, "but that's what I think it is." Then she read: " 'The man said, 'Take this and come to see our dog show.' " During the span of this one Directed Reading-Thinking Activity this girl had acquired caution about interpreting inferences as information.

All in the group agreed that the man was giving the boys tickets. The teacher agreed that this might be the case, and that ended the story.

Before dismissing the group, the teacher printed the six new words on the chalkboard. Then she asked different pupils to pronounce a word. She made it a point to ask the boy who had inquired about *lives* to read it.

A lady called and talked to Mother.

Then the lady and a man came

to the house.

"This is the first time our dog

did this trick," said the lady.

"We did not know where to look."

The man said, "Take this

and come to see our dog show.

Many other dogs live with us.

We go from town to town,

and next we will live in your town.

Then you can see our dog again."

124

After he had pronounced the word, the teacher asked: "How did you get the word?" "It seemed to fit," the boy said.

Next the teacher had all the children turn to pages 120 and 121 and count the number of times the word *lives* appears on these two pages. This required some rapid skim rereading, and the answer was soon found: two times.

Reading the new words in isolation represents a good check. First, the words were met and dealt with in context. Now the double check occurs in isolation. If the boy had not recognized *lives* in isolation, the teacher could have asked him to turn to the story and use context clues to recognition.

Throughout this D-R-T-A much thinking was going on. Purposes were set and altered as new information was supplied. Pictures as well as text were read. Ideas were compared. Pupils used their experiences and interests and knowledge fruitfully. They made decisions. They reread orally to prove points. They met and dealt with new words. Pupils participated eagerly on a give-and-take basis. The teacher did not tell the story or any part of it. She did not dominate the reading-thinking act; she directed it. Pupils read to find answers to their conjectures, not to the teacher's questions. This teacher did ask questions, but of the kind that stimulated thinking and kept the process moving ahead. She made important decisions essential to directing reading as a thinking process.

Given next is a transcribed tape recording of a D-R-T-A in which the story "A Newspaper Helps" was used. This verbatim reproduction provides a good idea of the give and take of a reading session. Note how the teacher directs the thinking. Note, too, how the different experiences of pupils were tapped: a lost dog, a chained dog, a lost cat, a newspaper helping, valuable things, diamonds, a doctor who dies, a dog chasing a cat, a dog running loose, cornfields, ringing doorbells, feeding the dog, telling parents, Mother, dog owners, a runaway dog, a dog catcher, a circus dog, tickets, circus people, and so on. All this was done without telling the pupils what the story would be about, without giving the story away by talking about newspaper ads and lost-and-found columns, without talking about a dog show. The story was designed to be within the experience range and plot-grasping ability of most six-year-olds, and that is what proved to be the case.

In the following D-R-T-A transcription, the letter T stands for teacher, the letter P for pupil(s).

T. Open the book to the Table of Contents and turn to the next story. Find the name of the story, then close the book.

T. Now what do you think a story with a name like this will be about?

P. If somebody loses a dog they could put it in the newpaper and the people who read about it might find the dog and turn it in.

T. What makes you think somebody might lose a dog?

P. They might forget to chain him up.

T. I see. That's a good idea. We have one good idea. Who has another? Lee?

P. Someone might lose their cat.

T. Might be a cat, too. . . . Right? Might lose a cat, hmm? How would a newspaper help them?

P. Well they could put it in the newspaper and tell what street it is if they found a dog and . . .

T. Yes. . . . What do you think, Eric?

P. Maybe they lost some good thing—some valuable thing.

T. What do you mean by some valuable thing? What kind of thing might they have lost?

P. Maybe a diamond.

T. Oh yes, and then how would the newspaper help?

P. They would put it in the newspaper probably and then if anybody found it they would give it back.

T. All right. Do we have any other ideas?

P. Somebody might ah—, ah—, ah—die and he might be a doctor and let the people whose doctor that is know that the doctor is dead.

T. I see. In other words, the doctor might die and they might put a notice in the newspaper that the doctor has died.

T. Now we have four ideas. One about the doctor, the lost dog, the lost cat, and the lost diamond. Let's turn to page 119. Take a good look at the picture on page 119 and then close your books. Which of the four ideas do you think is the right one?

P. Pat's.

T. Pat's—about what?

P. Somebody lost a dog.

T. You think it's about a lost dog?

T. What do you think, Susie?

P. Oh, it's a dog.

T. A dog. What do you think now, Nancy?

P. Pat is right.

T. What do you think? (turning to another pupil)

P. Pat's right.

T. You think Patsy's right?

P. I have another idea . . .

T. Good.

P. Maybe they left the dog at the house and he went home and he forgot to take the dog home and they had to go somewhere.

T. To get the dog?

P. No, to go somewhere else.

T. They had to go somewhere else.

P. They left the dog at home and they forgot him and they had to go somewhere.

T. That's a good idea. . . . Does somebody have another idea?

P. Maybe the dog chases a cat and the cat gets lost.

T. What do you think now, Nancy?

P. Maybe those boys found the dog running around loose.

T. I see. Now which one of these ideas do you think is good? One idea is that they found the dog running around loose. You think that he is a lost dog; you think that perhaps they forgot the dog; you think the dog may be chasing a cat. How about you, Eric?

P. Maybe a dog ran off and got lost in the cornfields.

T. All right. How can we find out which idea is right? Lee?

P. Read the story . . .

T. Yes. Read the first page and see which idea was right. [They read the first page.]

T. Which idea was right?

P. Not exactly right.

T. Not exactly? How were they right?

P. Well, I found Pat was right in a way, that the dog got lost.

T. He did get lost? Go ahead—what else were you going to say?

P. I was right in a way because they were playing ball in a field.

T. You were right in a way, too, weren't you?

T. Now who will read the line that proves that he is a lost dog? Do you have it, Lee?

P. Yes.

T. The rest of you will close your books and see if Lee will read the right line. Go ahead, Lee.

P. "Do you know this little dog?"

T. Does that prove that he is lost? How many would read the same line? Who would read a different line? Eric, what line would you read? Close your books again.

P. "We don't know where he came from."

T. Why do you read that line?

P. Because it says they don't know where it came from.

T. Does it say that the dog is lost? They just don't know where he came from, is that right? Okay? Now, what do you think is going to happen next? Susie?

P. Maybe they might go to the newspaper; they might go to the newspaper, and uh, tell them to put it in the paper. . . .

T. You mean the boys might go to a newspaper and tell them to put it in the paper that they found a dog? That's a good idea. What do you think, Eric?

P. Maybe owners come and say it's their dog.

T. There's another good idea. What's yours, Nancy?

P. They might go around and see, and ring doorbells and see if it is a neighbor's dog.

T. Oh, that's a good idea. You mean go around in the neighborhood and ring doorbells; a very good idea. Pat?

P. They might keep him and try to find—and like keep him and feed him until they find the—his owner.

T. How do you think they will find the owner?

P. They might put it in the paper.

T. Like Susie said? Uhuh. Lee?

P. They will tell their parents about it and their parents will put it in the paper.

T. You think the parents will do it, not the boys? What do you think, Susie? Will the boys put it in the paper or the parents?

P. I think the parents.

T. The parents. You agree with Lee that the parents will do it. What do you think, Kathy?

P. The parents will.

T. Now, let's turn the page and take a look at the next two pictures. Let's see which of your ideas is right. [They look at the pictures.] Now which idea do you think was right?

P. Lee's.

T. Why was he right?

P. Because it shows on the pictures that the boys were—that they went in to their mother and they told their mother about it.

T. You think that's the mother? [Head nodding.] Do the rest of you think that's Mother? How many think it is Mother? Oh? Why are you so sure it's Mother, Nancy?

P. Because they went to the door to tell some—to tell the mother and on the other page it shows that it is in the paper.

T. But why are you so sure that is Mother?

P. Because when she put it in the paper, newspaper.

T. She probably put it in the newspaper. You think that Lee was right. But why are you so sure that this lady is Mother? Could it be some other lady?

P. They might go to somebody's house asking if they found—if they lost a dog.

T. They might go to somebody else's house—how many think this is Mother? How many think maybe this is a neighbor lady? Pat, what do you think?

P. I don't know.

T. And who do you think put the notice in the newspaper? The boys, the lady, or the owner?

P. The lady.

T. You think the lady did? What do you think?

P. Maybe the owners.

T. Maybe the owners. Ah, here's a new idea. Maybe the owners put it in. How can we find out which is right? Go ahead. Read two more pages. [They read.]

T. Who was right this time? Eric?

P. All of them.

T. What do you mean "all of them" were right? How were they right?

P. Well, they went to Cooky's mother and she put it in the paper.

T. Right. And who had you thought it was?

P. Mother.

T. Who can read the line that proves that the boys put the notice in the newspaper.

P. "I will read what Mr. Jack has put in it."

T. Kathy, what line would you read?

P. "I will call Mr. Jack so he can put news of the dog in the paper."

T. Good for you, and who is it that's talking? Who said that?

P. Mother.

T. Right—Mother. Now what do you think is going to happen? Nancy?

P. Um, they found, find the owners to the dog.

T. You think the owner will show up? Do you think he'll come, Susie?

P. Yes.

T. What do you think, Pat?

P. The dog might run away, back to the house.

T. Oh. . . . The dog might run away before the owner comes. Do you think Nancy is right that the owner will come?

P. Yes.

T. You do? Or do you think Patty is right that the dog might run away again? Do you think the owner will come?

P. Yes.

T. Eric, what do you think?

P. Maybe while the owner's coming the dog will run away.

T. You think that perhaps Pat is right—that the dog might run away. Lee, what do you think?

P. I think the owner will show up.

T. You think the owner will show up? How many think the owner will show up? What did you want to say, Pat?

P. Um, I forget now.

T. What did you want to say, Kathy?

P. I, um, maybe they, um, they didn't know that the owner was coming and they might let the dog loose. And the dog catcher might find the dog and take him away.

T. Now that's a good idea. How many think the dog catcher might get this dog? Let me see your hands again. How many think the owners will come?

How many think the dog might run away again? Let's read two more pages. [They read.]

T. Did the owner come like you thought? Did he come, Lee?

P. No.

T. No? Do you think he will come?

P. Yes, maybe.

T. Maybe? Why do you think he will come if he didn't show up so far?

P. Maybe he didn't get the paper yet.

T. Maybe he didn't. Do you think the dog owner will show up? Why? Pat?

P. I have another idea. The dog might belong to a circus.

T. A circus dog? What makes you think he might be a circus dog?

P. Because he did some tricks.

T. Do you think they will come then and get him?

P. I don't know.

T. Do you think the circus would want him back? What do you think, Lee?

P. Yes.

T. You think they would want him back?

P. Yes.

T. How many think he might be a circus dog? You all do? And you think they will come for him, therefore? Are you sure, do you really think they'll come for him?

P. Yes.

T. Do you think the circus people will come for him now?

P. No.

T. You don't think they'll come? What are they going to do with the dog if they don't come?

P. Maybe they could give it to the dog catcher.

T. They could give the dog to the dog catcher.

P. No, the mother.

T. Oh, the mother would. You think the mother doesn't want the dog around?

P. Uhuh.

T. How many think Mother will give the dog to the dog catcher? Only Kathy. All right, how many think the circus owners will come? How many think this is not a circus dog? All right, let's take a look at the next picture. Take a good look. Now close your book. [Children groan.] Now what do you think? Nancy?

P. He belongs to some parents.

T. Not a circus dog? Why do you say some parents?

P. Because. . . .

T. Go ahead.

P. Because they're just some parents.

T. How many think they're just parents? Why do you think they're just parents? Why do you think so, Eric?

P. Because in the picture it showed two people.

T. But you don't think they're circus people?

P. It looks like he handed something . . . looked like he was giving the boys a reward for the dog and those two people might be the owners of the circus.

T. What do you think those papers might be? What?

P. Tickets?

T. Tickets—do you really? Well, if they wanted to give them a reward. . . . Yes, Kathy.

P. I have another idea. . . .

T. Good.

P. Maybe they were some parents and the father was a circus man and he gave them a re— some money for catching the dog.

T. You think he is giving them some money? How many think that is money? Do you think that is money, Susie?

P. No, I think he may be giving them. . . . I don't think it is money, but I think he may be giving them some money to buy some tickets.

T. How many think that is money in the picture?

P. Tickets. . . .

T. Tickets? Why do you say it is not money?

P. Because it looks like . . . it's all like paper.

T. What do you think now, Nancy?

P. They might be some men and they come to get the dog and they didn't want the tickets because they didn't want to leave their dog again and they gave them to the three boys.

T. Oh, you mean parents who had tickets and now they give them to the boys because they don't want to lose their dog again. . . . That's a good idea.

P. *Uh* . . . they might . . . they might be giving the boys some tickets and, and they might give them another reward, too.

T. Another kind of reward, too? What other kind of reward might they give?

P. They might give them another puppy just like him.

T. That's a good thought; maybe they'll give him another puppy. You have another idea, Eric?

P. Maybe they're going, they're going to give tickets and let them have the dog, too.

T. And let them have this dog, too? Yes, Kathy?

P. Maybe he is giving them some money to buy another dog.

T. That might be. Let's read and see which one of these ideas is right. [They read.]

T. Lee, which idea was right?

P. Nancy's.

T. Nancy's? What was Nancy's idea?

P. They were parents.

T. Uhuh—they are parents. How many agree with Lee? Are these parents? What do you think, Pat?

P. They might be. They said in the story they, they were members of a dog show.

T. Oh, then they're not parents? You don't think . . .

P. They could be parents. . . .

T. But you think they're also owners of a dog show? Would you read the line that proves that they're the owners of a dog show? Susie, read the line. . . . Oh, wait a minute! The rest of us close our books.

P. "The man said, 'Take this and come and see our dog show.'"

T. Would you have read the same line, Lee?

P. Uhuh.

T. So they're going to see the dog show?

P. Yes.

T. Were you surprised at the way it ended?

P. Yes.

T. Were you? What did you expect, really?

P. They, some, some circus people might come along. . . .

P. That there would be. . . .

P. They would be some circus folks and they might give them some tickets to the circus.

T. How would you think they would be dressed if they were circus people? Kathy?

P. In a clown suit.

T. Were you all looking for clown suits? Were you looking for a clown suit, Eric?

P. I don't know.

T. How did you expect them to be dressed?

P. In just, not in really good clothes.

T. Oh, because circus people might not be in good clothes, is that it?

P. Especially in the circus with a dog. . . .

A FOURTH-READER-LEVEL D-R-T-A

"A Newspaper Helps" was based on story-type material. As such it is typical of materials to be found in primary-level basic-reader programs. In *Webster's Dictionary of Synonyms* (16), we read that a story, narrative, tale, anecdote, and yarn are very much alike. A story may be actual or fictitious, in prose or verse, designed to inform or to entertain, and usually treats of a connected series of events or incidents.

Stories have been the grist for the reading-thinking mill of the readers. The stories have varied in style and content, but each of the synonyms for *story* could be used to define one or another of the materials. Many of the stories were fiction; a few were nonfiction.

Stories provide the appropriate organization of events useful in developing thinking and reading skills. Using stories, children can be taught to examine evidence, to declare knowns and unknowns, to conjecture or hypothesize, to seek answers through their own reading discoveries, to change conjectures as new evidence is presented, to suspend judgment, to evaluate, to associate, to accept or reject, and to conclude.

Much of the material presented in the primary level has been within the pupils' everyday experience range—people, animals, friends, neighbors, heroes—or within their imaginative range. As pupils learn to read, they begin to range far and wide in their reading selections, often move into the world of nonfiction. Curriculum changes, as they progress through the primary grades and into the intermediate level, lead them into an ever-widening circle of interests. In basic-reader series this reaching out can be initiated through biographical material that is informational in nature, yet packed with human interest.

It is necessary that pupils instructional at a fourth-reader level receive training in how to deal with nonfictional discursive material: biography, social science, biological science, natural science, and mathematics. Any well-stocked library for children has a wide variety of informational material, including encyclopedias, dictionaries, periodicals, digests, and newspapers. These materials are filled with facts.

The article selected for use here is representative of materials that should be used starting at the fourth-grade level or even lower. "Of Plows and Plowing" (13, pp. 42–45) is an informational-type article of a picture-essay variety, the kind that pupils will encounter in encyclopedias and periodicals. Pupils should receive training not only with materials in different interest areas (science, history, geography, astronomy, music, sports, and arts), but also with materials presenting information in different ways: new stories, picture essays, editorials, descriptions, narration, digests, documents, sketches, and so on. Pupils must be able to deal with such material accurately and efficiently, and they must be able to interpret graphic arts. Reading photographs, illustrations, maps, charts, and graphs takes on increasing importance in the fourth grade.

The article on plows is an historical piece sketching the development of plows across the centuries in a time-order account. The history of plows is told through pictures and text. It describes man's early plows, no more than large sticks, which were used virtually unchanged from before the time of Christ until the early 1600s, when the moldboard was introduced. In 1785, cast-iron shares were invented. Then, in 1800, John Deere and James Oliver came up with innovations still in use today. In addition to the pictured history of plows, information is given regarding the contribution plows have made to farm production, and, in turn, to our growing population and to urbanization.

The art of reading material filled with information is one that all pupils need to learn. Although students can be trained for such reading, in, say, their social-studies classes, this training can be initiated and refined in a reading class, where preoccupation with reading skills is paramount. In a social-studies class, this is not so.

New words are introduced in special articles in the same manner and on the same basis as in stories. The eleven words in the list below are

New words

during	page 42	James Oliver	page 43
*moldboard	page 42	*gang	page 44
*cast-iron	page 43	steam	page 44
*furrow	page 43	*diesel	page 45
Deere	page 43		

introduced in the article on plows. The ratio of new words to running words is low: 1 to 52. Even though excellent, this is not as good as the ratio for the story, "A Train Races an Airplane," 1 to 102. This is so because picture essays use fewer words. The four pages contain nine

Of Plows and Plowing

Many tools have been used by man through the ages. Of all the tools, the plow is perhaps the oldest and most useful.

Although the oldest of man's many tools, early plows didn't turn up much ground at all. Very poor plows were used in the days before the birth of Christ. Even during the time of Christ, the plows used did not do a very good job. They hardly cut into the ground.

moldboard lifted and turned the ground, something the early plows could not do. Now a better job of farming could be done.

John Deere

The first plows were little more than large sticks pulled by men. For many hundreds of years the stick plow was the only plow known. Even today, some countries use sticks for plowing.

The first real change in plows came in the early 1600's. Dutch farmers, among others, began making wooden moldboard plows. The

The first moldboard plows were usually pulled by oxen. Early settlers in the United States used large, heavy moldboard plows. Sometimes as many as eight oxen

Moldboard   Share

John Deere

42

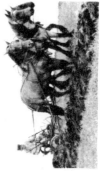

thought that iron was bad for the ground and would not use cast-iron moldboards. But in time, these early complaints against cast-iron plows were overcome.

Great leaders like Washington and Franklin were interested in the plow. They knew very well that life depended upon food, and that getting food depended upon the plow.

By 1785, cast-iron shares came into use. The share is the part of the plow which cuts the furrow loose from the ground. A little later an American farmer made a cast-iron moldboard, too. This should have been a great day for farming, but it wasn't. Many farmers

were needed for pulling the great moldboard plows through stony ground. With such use the settlers' wooden plows did not last long.

Soon after 1800, men who are now quite well known became interested in making plows and other farm tools. Two of these men, John Deere and James Oliver, had clever ideas. In fact, steel plows based on John Deere's and James Oliver's ideas are still used today.

Little by little, other changes were made. Instead of walking behind a plow, men now rode on the plow. The old one-share walking

43

plows gave way to two-bottom gang plows pulled by horses. A two-bottom gang plow had two shares and moldboards placed side by side. This let the plow turn two furrows at a time instead of just one furrow.

→

John Deere

As more bottoms were added to plows, more horses were needed to pull them. By the late 1800's riding plows were often pulled by six- or eight-horse hitches.

↓

John Deere

Steam engines also came into use. Run by steam engines, gang plows with as many as ten bottoms were used to furrow the earth. In this way, a ten-bottom gang plow could do ten times the work of a plow with only one share and moldboard.

→

Great heavy tractors appeared in this country around 1920. Many were run on gas as they are today. These very large tractors were soon replaced by smaller, better running tractors with rubber tires.

↓

Station WHO, Des Moines, Iowa

In the last few years, tractors with diesel engines have been used to pull gang plows. Usually, gang plows pulled by a powerful diesel tractor turn four or five furrows at a time.

↑

John Deere

John Deere

Though steam or diesel tractors may be used for power, the plow stays pretty much the same. Cast-iron or steel shares and moldboards are still the base for turning a fur-row.

↓

45

pictures. Pictures provide context clues to meaning that are far less abstract than language-context clues.

A special article dealing with a factual subject requires use of a special vocabulary. Just as guns have their nomenclature (barrel, hammer, trigger, sight, chamber), so do plows (moldboard, share, beam, jointer, gauge wheel, gang plow). As the areas of interest dealt with become more diversified, and as an area is dealt with in more detail and scope, the need for specialized or technical vocabulary increases.

Five of the words—*moldboard, cast-iron, furrow, gang,* and *diesel*—appear in the glossary. The language and picture contexts provide the reader with specific clues to the meaning of *moldboard* and *furrow*. Context clues also give some meaning to the words *cast-iron, diesel,* and *gang*.

As stated earlier, concepts are the essentials of a thinking reader's mental storehouse. They are obtained, refined, and extended by noting specifics or attributes, noting different uses or category classifications, and noting figurative-usage possibilities. Also, as stated earlier, in basic-reader instruction, concepts are not to be taught in advance of reading a selection, for to do so denies the reader-learner the opportunity to discover the concepts on his own, make his own analysis and association, and reach his own conclusions. The art of discovery, backed up by a teacher who checks on the discovery, is still the crux of learning.

Directing the Reading Process

It is important always to have pupils read with specific purposes in mind, especially when they are reading discursive or content-type material. In the content areas, assimilation, retention, and use of ideas are prime objectives.

For this first picture essay, a good procedure will be to have two purpose-setting sessions. In the first, use the title and the five pictures on pages 42 and 43. In the second, set purposes for reading the rest of the article after making a comprehension check of pages 42 and 43.

Making Predictions, Step 1. A thinking reader proceeds in almost the same way when reading nonfiction as when reading fiction. In fact, it is even more important that when dealing with nonfiction he do his own prereading thinking. Now he has a double obligation—to retain and to use ideas.

As he progresses through the grades, the pupil is more and more often required to deal with subject matter he knows little about. As a result, it becomes exceedingly important that his purposeful reading be fruitful. How to set good purposes and ask insightful questions is of great importance at this point. With these kinds of reading demands, the idea that "a good question is half an answer" is axiomatic. How to do divergent thinking, how to be creative is a real challenge.

This is not the time, though, to fall back on either a routinized what, when, where, why, and how approach to question asking, nor to be dependent on teacher questions. A reader must learn how to proceed on his own. D-R-T-A procedures when reading nonfiction must be just as sound and thorough as they are when reading fiction.

The reader must learn to take full advantage of all clue sources. He must study title and subtitles and pictures and other graphic aids carefully. He must deal with content in such a way as to tease out all information of predictive value. Listening to the predictions of others is crucial. If they are equally as ignorant, the pupil should realize that little is to be gained by an exchange of ignorance. If, though, some are more informed than others, their use of evidence and their conjectures take on significance. Or, if the teacher offers a directional clue, this, too, can be valuable.

Now is the time when it becomes tempting to teach by telling. Why take time and energy and skill to show the blind how to see? Now more than ever, however, the teacher must be vigilant and resourceful and patient. Above all, she must resist the temptation to take the easy road. Her determination can make the difference between future scholars and future pedants.

Now is the time to direct pupils to locate this selection in the book, read the title, and examine the pictures on pages 42 and 43. By this time, pupils trained to be thinking readers will be quite skilled in the use of picture clues. Even so, since this is the first selection of this type, it may be helpful to alert the pupils to the need for a careful examination of the pictures. Do no more, though. This is not the time to lecture pupils about the difference between illustrations that accompany narrative material and the kind that accompany nonfiction. Pupils must discover the differences for themselves. So be sure to allow this period of discovery to occur.

Be especially careful not to call the pupils' attention to the labels on the third illustration: *moldboard* and *share*. These are the kinds of "aids to concept development" pupils must learn to discover and value. During the first comprehension check there will be time to find out what the pupils "saw" when they "looked" at the illustrations.

With books closed then, encourage pupils to speculate about the article and its content. Predictions that may be made are: "This article may be about how plows were first used and developed." A pupil may support this conjecture by referring both to the title and to specifics in pictures. Another pupil may predict that the item is about "how plows helped America grow."

"Maybe at one time people used sticks to plow," another may comment. "But how could they get oxen to pull such a plow?"

"People pulled them," another may venture. To which the former may reply: "I don't believe people can pull a plow."

a. Channelizing Thinking. Most likely, all pupils will agree that the selection has something to do with the history of plows. If this is the case, encourage them to hypothesize about how plows may have changed and how they have helped man. Ask them to speculate about such matters as the date when the plow was first used, how long man plowed with a stick, and who the people were who improved plows.

With material like this, one way to direct the reading-thinking act is to help channelize pupils' thinking. This must be done without giving away answers. In this selection, the pupils' thinking has been channelized along time or history lines, production or economic lines, social or human lines, and space or geography lines, with the predominant emphasis on time or history. If pupil speculation should fail to touch on one of these areas, it is now appropriate to alert them. For instance, they may not associate space problems with plows until prompted. Questions such as "How might the improvement of plows influence geography?" and "How may geography have influenced the development of plows?" will set them thinking.

The art of discovery must always be the principal idea insofar as learning and teaching are concerned. With the reading of nonfiction, this becomes even more crucial than with the reading of fiction. In fiction, the plot helps carry the reader forward as it unfolds its mysteries and perplexities. The straightforward exposition of informative material places on the reader a greater responsibility to initiate and maintain interest, to identify and assemble relevant ideas, and to associate, evaluate, and digest them.

It would be simple, but incorrect for the teacher to tell the pupil that the labeled illustration of the plow merits careful analysis because it supplies specifics that will help him attain a more accurate concept of plow. It will require considerable restraint and knowledge about the art of learning for the teacher to take the course that will lead the pupils to attain calculated, penetrating, and judicious thinking on their own through discovery. These are learning occasions that provide the tangibles that can be grasped by the mind and appraised with reasonable accuracy— the tangibles that furnish access to knowledge.

b. The Glossary. The basic reader has a glossary with phonetic respellings and a pronunciation key. This means that pupils are being supplied with all the word-recognition aids needed for independence in pronunciation. The dictionary is the ultimate source of pronunciation help for most people.

If the teaching of reading has been accomplished by means of group Directed Reading-Thinking Activities using basic readers and individualized Directed Reading-Thinking Activities using libraries, there is considerable likelihood that the pupils have on many occasions used dictionaries for pronunciation purposes. This being the case, pupils will welcome the handy glossary.

Some pupils need more learning opportunity than others. Some may be new to the school and may not have had systematic instruction in dictionary usage. Some may not have had an opportunity to experience Directed Reading-Thinking Activities in an individualized reading situation and may never have faced the need to refer to a dictionary. Some children may have been taught in one of the basic-reader systems that advocate the teaching of new words before a story is read and thus may not have experienced the true need to refer to a glossary.

The purpose of a glossary is to provide the pupils with a ready tool for unlocking words, either for pronunciation or meaning. During primary-level D-R-T-A's, pupils turn to the teacher when they meet words they cannot recognize after using any or all of their phonetic and structural-analysis skills. At the intermediate level, pupils consult the glossary before finally turning to the teacher.

A pupil should proceed as follows when he meets a word he does not recognize at sight:

Step 1. Context Clues
   a. Language clues (found in the sentence or paragraph)
   b. Picture clues
Step 2. Structural and Phonetic Clues
   a. Prefixes and suffixes
   b. Syllables
   c. Sounds represented by letters and different letter combinations
Step 3. The Glossary
   a. The syllabified word entries
   b. The definitions
Step 4. Teacher help

To become self-reliant and efficient readers, the pupils must be trained to be resourceful. It is of utmost importance that, from the beginning, they be alerted to the value of the glossary and be trained to use it.

Words in the glossary should not be taught before a story is read. To do so violates the purpose of the glossary as an aid to independent word recognition. If pupils are taught the glossary words before they read, they have no need to refer to the glossary while reading. Such practices deny pupils the opportunity to learn to be resourceful.

An important factor in the psychology of learning is how much initiative should rest with the learner. If it is accepted that the function of a teacher is to help students discover and use means of satisfying their needs, then it will be understood why pupils must learn to use a glossary. Command of this skill will help them be more independent and self-reliant students. This is why skill training in the use of a glossary is essential and why basic-reader glossary training is provided. At no time should pupils be denied the opportunity to put their skill knowledge to work by wrongly teaching in advance words introduced in a basic-reader glossary.

In addition, the psychology of learning has indicated quite clearly through the years that any skill that is to be mastered needs to occupy the center of attention for a time. We have also known that a skill may first be needed in a broad context and that attention must then be shifted to it for intensive work. Also, we know that skill usage must be checked and corrected so that correct usage may be reinforced and remembered. All of this stresses once again the importance of an active, problem-solving attitude on the part of the learner and the value of a conscious purpose. Finally, it reconfirms the efficacy of introducing a skill in the context in which it will be used so as to provide meaning, and then momentarily lifting it from that context to concentrate on it.

c. Observing Reading. To read a picture essay such as the one about plows may require more time than might be needed to read only expository material. Since a picture may equal a thousand words, note to what degree pupils examine the pictures. Note also that girls frequently hurry over the pictures. The pupils will go back and forth from pictures to text. The good readers will check one against the other.

The reader bent on obtaining understanding will most likely use the glossary to confirm or sharpen his concepts. Although the illustration of a moldboard may be helpful, the glossary definition may be needed for full clarity. On pages 42 and 43, three new words are presented, which are also in the glossary—*moldboard, cast-iron,* and *furrow.* When a pupil turns to the glossary, the teacher can stop at his deck to see how he is doing. "Why did you turn to the glossary?," she may ask. (Pupil: "To check on *furrow.*") "Have you found the word?" (Pupil: "Yes.") "Did you get enough help? Do you understand?" (Pupil: "Yes, I know now what it means 'to cut a furrow'.")

Once again, pupil performance while reading provides an excellent opportunity to study the reader in action. The reader truly bent on understanding will use every available clue—especially picture clues and glossary clues.

Appraisal and Readjustment, Step 2. When all books are closed, comprehension can be checked by a teacher question: "Were you right about what you thought would be told in this article?"

"It did tell about how plows were first used and how they changed," said one pupil.

"People did use stick plows and pull them, too," said another. "But it didn't say whether oxen pulled stick plows."

"Oxen pulled wooden moldboard plows," said a boy.

"What are wooden moldboard plows?" asked the teacher.

"A moldboard is a part of a plow," was the reply.

"What part?" asked the teacher. "A top part," came the reply.

"Who can be clearer about a moldboard?" asked the teacher.

"It's the part that turns the ground," said another boy.

"Did anyone check this word in the glossary?" was the next question, and two hands went up.

"Why didn't the rest of you check in the glossary?" asked the teacher.

"I got enough help in the picture and the story," said a girl. "The story said that a moldboard lifted and turned the ground. The picture showed the moldboard."

"Did the glossary give any more help?," asked the teacher.

"Yes," replied one of the boys. "It said it also breaks up the ground."

At this point the teacher wrote the word *moldboard* on the chalkboard. Under it she listed the three things it did. This writing and organizing of the attributes of the concept helped pupils understand and remember it.

Moldboard

1. lifts
2. turns
3. breaks

"The story told about the history of plows," said one pupil. "The first wooden plow was made in 1600 by Dutch farmers."

The teacher wrote this date and event on the board.

"Washington and Franklin made the cast-iron plow," said a girl.

"They were only interested in plows," commented another. To which the former replied, "It said the men are famous and well-known today."

"Let's all turn to the article and see who is right," said the teacher.

By means of this silent rereading, the group determined that Washington and Franklin were interested in plows. Since all books were open, there was no need for oral reading. No one needed to listen to the lines read orally because each could read in his own text.

Now the teacher listed *1785* and *cast-iron shares* on the chalkboard under the heading *1600*. Then she turned to the group and inquired about the meaning of *cast-iron* and *share*.

A number of hands went up, but the teacher called on a girl who did not raise her hand. "I looked up *cast-iron* but not *share*," she said. "The story said the *share* is the part that cuts the ground." "Cast-iron is iron that is melted and run into a mold," she went on. "Is the mold like something we need to make candles?"

The teacher nodded to the latter question and then asked a girl to read orally the lines that defined *share*.

The girl opened the book and read aloud, "The share is the part of the plow which cuts the furrow loose from the ground." (All other books stayed closed.)

The group agreed that the line defined the word. At this point, the boy referred to earlier who had checked *furrow* in the glossary raised his hand to define it.

"Are there any other dates and changes to record?," asked the teacher. Then *1800* and *steel plows* were added to the list.

"How many had noticed the words *moldboard* and *share* in the picture?," the teacher asked. Only two hands went up.

"I didn't see the words until after I had looked for the word *moldboard* in the glossary," said one.

"The plow helped our early settlers and they needed more land to plow," said a boy.

"There are three more pages in this article," said the teacher. "What do you think you'll learn there?"

"Other changes in the plow since 1800," said one.

"What kind of changes might there be?" asked the teacher.

"I have no idea," she replied. "I guess they don't use horses any more. Maybe they now have an electronic plow."

A boy said: "It may tell more about steel plows and how they are used."

"Maybe it will tell about tractors," said another boy. "Tractors are used on farms."

"It might tell more about how much food is being raised," said another girl. "That is why Washington and Franklin were interested in plows. People needed food."

"Read on to the end," said the teacher. "Before you do, though, what will you do about the pictures?"

"Look at them carefully," came a reply. "I can't see how I missed the words *moldboard* and *plowshare.*"

There are a number of marked differences in both pupil and teacher roles between this D-R-T-A on plows and the earlier one about the newspaper story. First, the teacher channelized thinking in the prereading purpose-setting period. The human and social elements in stories makes it possible for children to make predictions. Even though human factors may be presented in an informational article, they most likely will not help the reader conjecture about the facts in the article. If pupils lack experience in the area with which the article deals, it is necessary to guide their thinking.

In the D-R-T-A account on plows, the pupil responses were obtained in a classroom in a suburban area of a sizable East Coast city. The same story was used experimentally in a rural area in Maryland, where the children knew much about plows and farming but nothing about the history of plows. The rural children knew the word *furrow,* but not *moldboard* and *share.* In both kinds of circumstances, the teacher has to channel thinking.

This teacher invited the group to think along historical or time lines and geographical or space lines. She gave no answers, revealed none of the content, but she encouraged thinking in a fruitful direction by means of a leading question.

Second, during the comprehension check the teacher made direct inquiries about the concepts *moldboard, cast-iron,* and *share.* She recorded ideas defining *moldboard* on the board. This helped call attention to the concept. She started a list of chronological changes in the history of the plow. She inquired about pupil picture-study and alerted them to the value of pictures. She also inquired about their use of the glossary and/or a dictionary. In other words, this teacher realized that she had an obligation to fulfill in her fourth-level reading-thinking skill-training program different from her obligation at the primary level. In the content areas, the teacher must plan for, supply training in, and require a more thorough comprehension of subject matter. To do this she must see that the reading purposes grow out of the experience and knowledge of the reader, and that the purposes lead the reader to make an active quest for information and new ideas.

Observing Reading. Again the teacher will observe the reading act. That teacher observation was important at the primary level would be questioned by no one. That it is doubly important at this level, when informative material is being read, should be questioned by no one. Now the emphasis is so completely on understanding—or the assimilation and use of ideas—that an all-out effort must be made to see that the needed comprehension skills are acquired.

In the D-R-T-A previously described, a hand went up almost instantly when the pupils started their silent reading. "What does *two-bottom* mean?," asked the girl. (The old one-share walking plows gave way to two-bottom gang plows pulled by horses.)

"Did you read to the end of the paragraph?," asked the teacher. The pupil had not done so, but did so at once. She also checked to see if the phrase was in the glossary.

"What do you think now?," asked the teacher.

"I think it means two furrows," was the reply.

"You are close enough in meaning to read on," said the teacher. "We'll check more carefully later."

Then the teacher saw a boy using the glossary and went to see how and why. He was looking up the word *gang*. He knew what a gang was, but he was not sure about a gang plow. The third meaning in the glossary gave him the help he sought. A number of pupils checked on the word *diesel* in the glossary. Two pupils checked for pronunciation as well as meaning.

Comprehension Check. When all books were closed, pupils began to share ideas immediately. Other changes of the plow were reported and recorded on the chalkboard. Some of the pupils had counted the number of furrows being turned by the plows shown in the different pictures.

The word *bottom* entered into the discussion and the girl who had inquired about *two-bottom* reported what she thought. One lad thought *bottom* referred to the plow, and he read the following lines in support: "A two-bottom gang plow had two shares and moldboards placed side by side. This let the plow turn two furrows at a time instead of just one furrow." To this another boy added the line: "As more bottoms were added to plows, more horses were needed to pull them." The group was puzzled, and so an unabridged dictionary was consulted. The boys were right. *Diesel* also came in for some discussion, and the idea that a diesel engine runs on air and oil was investigated. Pupils spoke about diesel trucks and diesel engines.

"Do you see now what we owe the plow?," asked the teacher. "Oh, yes," came a quick reply. "It helped our country grow. Without the plow big cities like Philadelphia and Wilmington might not have grown. People wouldn't have had enough food."

A quick double check and review of the facts on the board was done. Then the group was ready to deal with what might be considered by many the most important phase of a D-R-T-A: extending and refining. (This phase is discussed in the next chapter.)

The second half of the D-R-T-A becomes more and more important at the intermediate level, because of the growing concern with vocabulary, concepts, and organization of ideas.

Again, it is apparent that at the intermediate level the reading-learning skill requirements make different demands on the teacher. It is not that these demands are more numerous or more critical in the total reading-to-learn process, but that they represent a change in reading behavior. More and more, reading is done to learn, understand, assimilate, retain, and use. When stories alone comprise the major type of material being used to direct reading as a thinking process, it is not necessary that pupils deal with the plot information as they would when dealing with the order of ideas in an article about science. There is no need to remember the details of the numerous stories read, nor is there any need to assimilate the points in a plot for future use. The points do not represent basic knowledge essential to the understanding of more advanced ideas.

Harl R. Douglass and Herbert F. Spitzer point out that "the school has not always given understanding its due emphasis" and add that too often "the learning [is] a learning of words" (6, p. 8). This kind of learning is superficial, artificial, and relatively useless. They say:

> In reading, learners were required to pronounce words as given on the printed page with what passed for appropriate inflection, tempo, and emphasis. Reading was not viewed as a thought-getting process. Rather, the aim seemed to be the development of mechanical proficiency in the recognition of the printed word, and it was assumed that this proficiency would operate satisfactorily however and whenever reading was engaged in. As a consequence, too few children acquired the techniques (or even realized the necessity) of understanding what they read, together with its meanings, its significance, and its potential applications to life experiences. (6, pp. 9–10.)

There is some danger that, once informational material is introduced in basic readers, the story content is dealt with lightly. The concept of reading must always be that of as a thought-getting process. The nuances of plots give pupils numerous opportunities, as William A. Brownell and Verner M. Sims says (2, p. 28), "to act, feel, or think intelligently with respect to a situation." Situations as plots are infinite in their variety, with differences in complexity, in urgency, in familiarity, and in kind. Many pupils capable of reading with understanding fail to do so because they have not been trained to analyze situations that confront them (such as a story plot), to identify the elements that are relevant, and to channelize their thinking on a convergent basis. Story plots at all levels can provide excellent grist for the thinking mill and will help readers develop habits of analysis that will be useful in all reading situations.

Pauses to Reflect. The art of extracting information of predictive value is interestingly exemplified by an incident that occurs in A. Conan Doyle's *Sign of the Four* and is related by Hullfish and Smith (10) in their discussion of abductive inference. In the anecdote, Watson decides to test the powers of Sherlock Holmes. He says to him (10, pp. 118–119):

I have heard you say that it is difficult for a man to have any object in his daily use without leaving the impress of his individuality upon it in such a way that a trained observer might read it. Now, I have here a watch which has recently come into my possession. Would you have the kindness to let me have an opinion upon the character or habits of the late owner?

Thereupon Watson handed Holmes the watch. Holmes examined it carefully, opened the back, looked at it with a lense, and otherwise examined it. He then returned the watch and amazed Watson with the following remarks.

There are hardly any data. The watch has been recently cleaned which robs me of my most suggestive facts. . . . Though unsatisfactory, my research has not been entirely barren. . . . I should judge that the watch belonged to your elder brother, who inherited it from your father. . . . He (your brother) was a man of untidy habits—very untidy and careless. He was left with good prospects, but he threw away his chances, lived for some time in poverty, with occasional short intervals of prosperity, and finally, taking to drink, he died. That is all that I can gather. Watson confirmed Holmes' judgment in every detail but had difficulty in believing that Holmes was able to surmise all this from his brief examination of the watch. Holmes explained in these words:

What seems strange to you is only so because you do not follow my train of thought or observe the small facts upon which large inferences may depend. . . . [The initials H. W. were on the back of the watch.] The W suggests your own name. The date of the watch is nearly fifty years back, and the initials are as old as the watch; so it was made for the last generation. Jewelry usually descends to the eldest son, and he is most likely to have the same name as his father. Your father has, if I remember rightly, been dead many years. It has, therefore, been in the hands of your eldest brother.

When you observe the lower part of that watch case you notice that it is not only dented in two places, but is cut and marked all over from the habit of keeping other hard objects, such as coins or keys, in the same pocket. Surely it is no great feat to assume that a man who treats a fifty-guinea watch so cavalierly must be a careless man. Neither is it a farfetched inference that a man who inherits one article of such value is pretty well provided for in other respects.

It is very customary for pawnbrokers in England, when they take a watch, to scratch the number of the ticket with a pin point upon the inside of the case. . . . There are no less than four such numbers visible to my lens on the inside of this case. Inference—that your brother was often at low water. Secondary inference— that he had occasional bursts of prosperity or he could not have redeemed the pledge. Finally, I ask you to look at the inner plate which contains the keyhole. Look at the thousands of scratches all around the hole—marks where the key has slipped. What sober man's key could have scratched those grooves? But you will never see a drunkard's watch without them. He winds it at night, and he leaves these traces of his unsteady hand. Where is the mystery in all this?

As Holmes indicates, a trained observer notes the facts upon which inferences may depend, and there is no mystery in that. Similarly in reading, the reading detective observes the small facts, makes his inferences, and then reads to check whether or not his deductions were right. There is no mystery in that, either.

Also, as in the Holmes case, the information each pupil extracts even as a trained reader depends on his pre-existing store of experience and knowledge. If a particular pupil has had numerous examined experiences, and if his knowledge is primarily functional rather than canned, the likelihood of his extracting information of good predictive value is increased. This is especially true if the ideas and assumptions are flexibly related to each other. Then, various combinations can be examined and their usefulness tested as material is being read. It is the purpose of this section of the chapter to describe various combinations and their usefulness in training reflective reading detectives.

The "pause that refreshes" has become one of the best-known phrases in our country. Its self-evident truth is being applied in many situations: a coffee break, a cigarette, a Coca Cola, a nap, a stretch, and so on. Children grasp the significance of the "pause" at an early age and experience its use on many occasions and in many circumstances. The basic meaning remains relatively constant from context to context.

How significant it would be if the phrase could become equally as commonplace among readers! The "pause" in reading can be applied in all materials and at different places for different purposes. The intellectual significance of a pause to reflect can be understood on the ground of experience. Then the main task, to develop the capacity to read with critical discrimination and ability to reason, can be accomplished. This will give the children sure anchorage in their intellectual life and will not leave them at the mercy of every slippery half-truth. As Hullfish and Smith put it (10, p. 142):

> There is a clue for the teacher here. Students should be encouraged to play with ideas, not in order to live in a realm of fantasy where exact knowledge is irrelevant but, rather, to gain a feeling for the way in which the projected hypothetical idea, when tested against what one knows, opens the way to new knowledge, to continued transformation of the human scene. . . . It is in the relentless effort to see beyond the immediate and the actual, coupled with the responsible checking out of ideas that emerge, that the creative work of the world is done.

They add the further idea, relevant at this point, that "the life of the free man is a life of making choices. . . . And the wise choice always means a delay in action until the alternatives confronted can be imaginatively explored and their consequences forecast." (10, p. 142.)

These considerations bring to the fore a number of points that teachers should remember. First, education, and therefore reading, is the reconstruction of experience and knowledge in such a way as to add to the meaning of both and increase the ability to direct the course of subsequent experience. (5) Second, children bring with them to school, even at age six, a considerable backlog of experiences and knowledge loosely organized but relatively functional, and these mental constructs can be used as a basis on which to build wisely and soundly. Third, patterns of organization and reconstruction can be changed or extended in many ways by reflective activity. Fourth, children can be *trained* in such a way that they will acquire the right attitudes and be the directing agents for habits of reflective reading. Fifth, the training process is in the hands of those who control the Directed Reading-Thinking Activities, whether they be in a group reading situation or an individualized reading situation.

THE USE OF HINDSIGHT IN LEARNING

Basic-reader stories should not be just stories. Plot developments should not occur by chance. Plan and design can go a long way toward making basic-reader material truly functional.

A set of teaching-learning patterns fits into the backward-look idea. As all educators know, more seems to be learned by hindsight than by foresight. This, in brief, is the philosophy of the backward look. There are two main approaches to a backward look. A first approach is accomplished by taking a backward look at a story that has been dealt with on a D-R-T-A basis, using one of the patterns described. "A Newspaper Helps" will be used to illustrate, for the reader should now be quite familiar with this story and its order of events. The teacher makes a record of all predictions. Then, when the story has been read, the predictions are dealt with in the order of their relevancy. She lists first the predictions made after the study of the title only; these she places side by side across the top of the chalkboard or across a large sheet of newsprint.

At the first-grade level not too much can be expected from so detailed a tracking of clues. Yet it is astonishing how many six-year-olds catch on to the idea of how a conjecture gets started and stays relevant throughout the story. They also see how other conjectures need to be dropped because subsequent evidence makes them implausible. In addition, some pupils begin to see how they might have made better judgments by using clues more wisely. They see situations and the interaction of ideas more clearly, and they understand the need for adaptability.

Note that the lost-dog idea occurred to one six-year-old after he had examined only the story title and the first picture. The lost-dog thread continued throughout the discussion and led to two related questions: How will the owner be located? Will the owner show up? Some ideas appear relevant for a page or two and then prove untenable. A plot change anywhere may result in divergent-type thinking. The dead-ending of ideas as new evidence is presented does not by any means prove frustrating to the

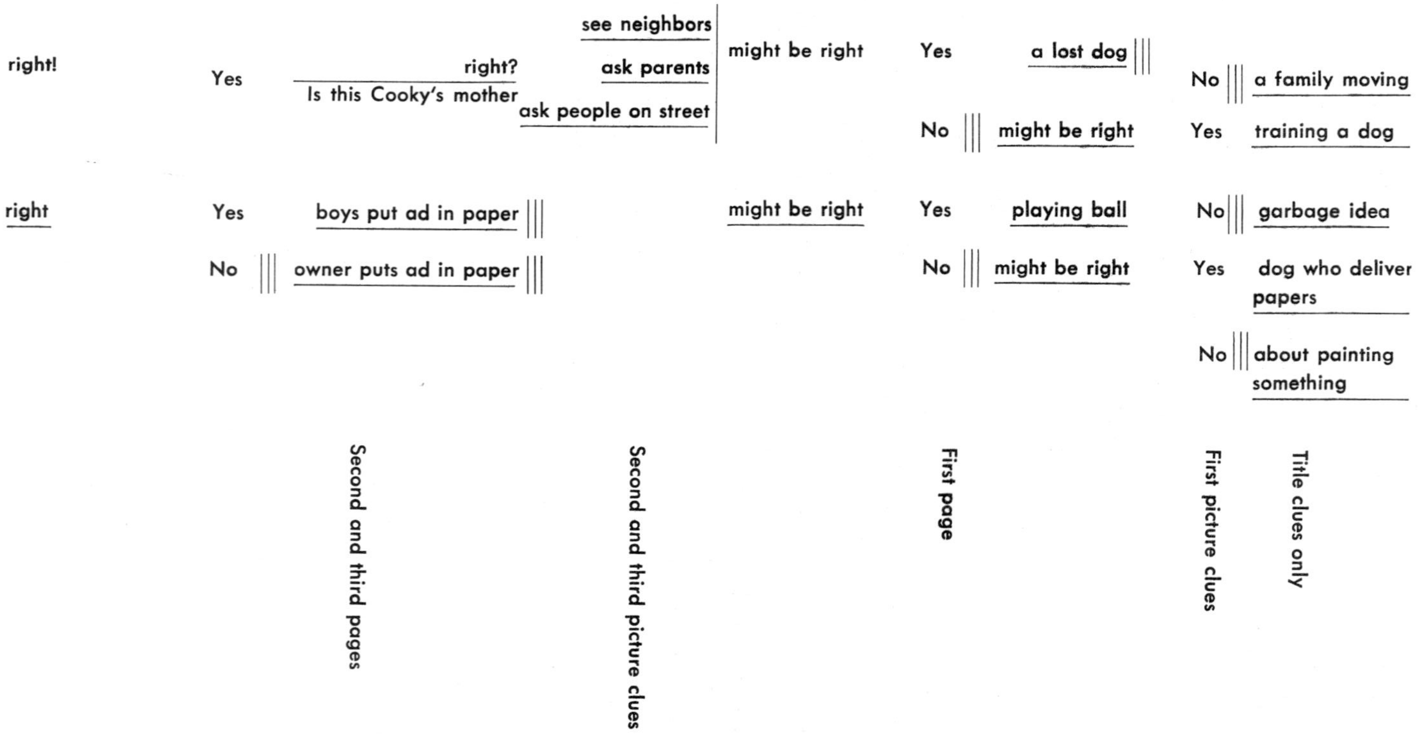

Title clues only

- No — a family moving
- Yes — training a dog
- No — garbage idea
- Yes — dog who deliver papers
- No — about painting something

First picture clues

- Yes — a lost dog
- No — might be right
- Yes — playing ball
- No — might be right

First page

- might be right

Second and third picture clues

- see neighbors
- ask parents
- ask people on street
- right? — Is this Cooky's mother
- might be right
- Yes — boys put ad in paper
- No — owner puts ad in paper

Second and third pages

- right!
- right

tickets

Yes rewarding boys
money
paper
Yes

might be owners
might not be
Yes
Yes

might
might not
Yes
Yes

owner shows up
owner doesn't
right
right

Fourth and fifth pages

Last picture

Last page

children. They realize this and deal with it as a concomitant of thinking, conjecturing, and testing. There is no cringing before the tyranny of a right teacher answer. On the contrary, devotion to seeking the truth fosters the spirit and confidence of a steadfast scholar.

Eight- and nine-year-olds love the backward-look idea and begin to see the light. They comment often, "Oh, now I see." "I thought that might be right but I didn't say so." "I didn't know about horses, but now I see." It proves helpful not only to "conjecture-diagram" stories at their level, but also to use stories from an earlier level. The plot structure tends to be more elementary and in many ways more suggestive. With practice, the children learn to use clues that they formerly overlooked or ignored. As their alertness increases, so does their creative ability to use the facts. Items that had been mentally invisible are now seen, and old patterns take on different relevancies. Inventiveness or imaginative use of information is the key to discoveries and inventions as well as to mature reading. Initiating training in the art of discovery from the very beginning of a basic-reader program helps children break the grip of the conventional, the traditional, and the stereotyped relationships. Furthermore, these people will not some day go to college and expect magic results from a course in reading and thinking.

The second pattern for a backward look is hindsight. From time to time even a basic-reader story should be read for purpose setting without any interruptions. Let pupils identify the story and read it through. All the conditions for good reading practices should operate: pupils know what to do with word-recognition difficulties, and the teacher is readily available to give help as requested.

The comprehension-check session, when all have finished reading, can become an ideal testing ground. The group shares ideas, reactions, feelings, and opinions about the story in a free group discussion. Here the pupils talk to each other while the teacher plays the role of listener. Her primary task is to make it possible for the pupils to compare and contrast their reactions. The freedom and spontaneity of the ensuing discussion may get out of hand, but the principal concern of the teacher should be to avoid inhibiting thinking and sharing.

The problem of intellectual organization *can* be worked out. Motives, attitudes, and thoughts can be examined on both a discrete and a continuous basis when students are encouraged to see the relation of consequence to means and the way things interact with one another to produce certain effects.

SUMMARY

Only the teacher who believes that children can be taught to read as scientific readers can handle the dynamics of teaching reading as a thinking process, for the teacher's attitude and skill make the difference between a class in which there is freedom and spontaneity of thinking and discussion and one in which there is not. Freedom resides in the intelligent observation of suggestions and opportunities and in the making of such judgments that sound purposes may be developed. Spontaneity suggests the unstudied naturalness of young minds and an agreeable freshness. As Ernst Horn pointed out (9, pp. 388–389), "In reading, as well as in objective experiences, selection, organization, and interpretation are all governed by purpose. It is purpose that guides the construction of ideas and holds them together." Pupils must be required time and again to exercise to the full their intellectual powers so that, as Jerome S. Bruner says (3, p. 50), "they may discover the pleasure of full and effective functioning. Good teachers know the power of this lure." Students should realize what it means to use their own experiences, their knowledge, and their creative powers so as to become absorbed in seeking solutions. The effect of this approach is such that the child generates his own discoveries.

In the 1930s, it was said that on the social-moral-political front we had nothing to fear but fear itself. Today the most widespread fear is the fear of making decisions. In the 1930s, reading was still being taught as it had been for decades—on an oral-recital level. "Speak the words so that I can hear you read" was the test to pass. "Recite the facts, word by word, and prove that you have read" was the measure of comprehension. Pupils learned this kind of reading at home and daily passed in oral review before the teacher. It was a review regimented and circumscribed by the open-booked, open-eared teacher. The use of the mind to search, to discover, to hypothesize, to prove was second to the power of elocution. Sound, not sense, acquitted the scholar. "Don't think; recite" was the motto.

All this was going on in spite of the brilliance, perception, and wisdom of Francis Bacon, Jean Jacques Rosseau, Johann F. Herbart, Horace Mann, and John Dewey, who urged that brain-stretching creativity take the place of memorization. With eloquence and resolution, these thinkers finally closed the Pandora's Box of ignorance and dogma. At the same time they gradually forced open the lid of a new box, releasing the method of learning by discovery, searching, weighing, and decision-making. Just as surely as there can be only one straight line between two points, there can be only one straight line between thinking and learning.

The older ways of memorizing and reciting are collapsing. The security of a parroted text and a teacher's daily log of recitations is disappearing. The uncharted seas of discovery demand a different kind of confidence, a different kind of cognition, a more comprehensive grasp of freedom and responsibility. Change is the order of the day: yesterday, Charles Lindbergh; today, John Glenn; tomorrow, who knows? Today, the 1969 model car, tomorrow, the 1970, and the 1971, and the 1972. Yesterday, the trail and the crossroads; today, the freeway and the interchange. Change,

change, change; decisions, decisions, decisions! This is the challenge that confronts the "lost generation" of the 1930s. We must face up to these conditions not only to keep pace with the world in our time but more essentially to educate the youth of our land who are brought up on the doctrine of change and discovery. Their's is a ready acceptance. They will make the decisions—and right ones, too. It is up to us to set in motion the ferment of creativity and discovery and ideas.

The milieu of a directed reading-thinking session beckons us on. Here, all other things can be held constant while we observe pupils using their experience and knowledge, wisdom and ingenuity, resolution and faith. We can ban our fear of information explosion by using these attributes and categories in the service of structured patterns and productive thinking.

REFERENCES

1. Abercrombie, M. L. Johnson, *The Anatomy of Judgment*, New York, Basic Books, 1960.
2. Brownell, William A., and Verner M. Sims, "The Nature of Understanding," *The Measurement of Understanding*, Forty-fifth Yearbook of the National Society for the Study of Education, Part I, Chicago, University of Chicago Press, 1946.
3. Bruner, Jerome S., *The Process of Education*, Cambridge, Mass., Harvard University Press, 1960.
4. Crossen, Helen J., "Effects of the Attitudes of the Reader Upon Critical Reading Ability," *Journal of Educational Research, 42* (1948), 289–298.
5. Dewey, John, *Democracy and Education*, New York, Macmillan, 1916.
6. Douglass, Harl R., and Herbert E. Spitzer, "The Importance of Teaching for Understanding," *The Measurement of Understanding*, Forty-fifth Yearbook of the National Society for the Study of Education, Part I, Chicago, University of Chicago Press, 1946.
7. Groff, P. J., "Children's Attitudes Toward Reading and Their Critical Reading Abilities in Four Content-Type Materials," unpublished Doctoral dissertation, University of California, Berkeley, 1955.
8. Guillford, J. P., "Frontiers in Thinking That Teachers Should Know About," *The Reading Teacher, 13* (February, 1960), 176–182.
9. Horn, Ernest, "Language and Meaning," *The Psychology of Learning*, Forty-first Yearbook of the National Society for the Study of Education, Part II, Chicago, University of Chicago Press, 1942.
10. Hullfish, H. Gordon, and Philip G. Smith, *Reflective Thinking*, New York, Dodd, Mead, 1961.
11. McKillop, Anne S., *The Relationship Between the Reader's Attitude and Certain Types of Reading Responses*, New York, Teachers College, Columbia University, 1952.
12. Stauffer, Russell G., Alvina Treut Burrows, Mary Elisabeth Coleman, and Evelyn Rezen Spencer, *Away We Go*, New York, Holt, Rinehart and Winston, 1960.
13. Stauffer, Russell G., Alvina Treut Burrows, and Thomas D. Horn, *Above the Clouds*, New York, Holt, Rinehart and Winston, 1960.
14. Stroud, J. B., "The Role of Practice in Learning," *The Psychology of Learning*, Forty-first Yearbook of the National Society for the Study of Education, Part II, Chicago, University of Chicago Press, 1942.
15. Torrance, E. Paul, "Developing Creative Readers," *Dimensions of Critical Reading*, Russell G. Stauffer, compiler, Proceedings of the Annual Education and Reading Conferences, 1963 and 1964, Newark, Del., University of Delaware, 1964.
16. *Webster's Dictionary of Synonyms*. Springfield, Mass., Merriam, 1942.

Chapter 4 ❧❧❧❧❧❧❧ Directed Reading-Thinking Activities: Extending and Refining ❧❧❧

The destiny of civilization demands that reading and thinking habits and listening and thinking habits be geared to the processes of constructive change, for civilization is premised on change, as is every reading-thinking act. The reader—to achieve effectively—must perform with an open mind, with judgment suspended, and with a readiness to accept conclusions supported by evidence.

THE DISCIPLINE OF ACCURACY

Change is a direct result of an organized performance motivated by a mind geared to a free-enterprise way of thinking and learning. At the heart of this free-enterprise system are two powerful forces: the hope of discovery, and the discipline of accuracy. The hope of discovery is the mainspring of constructive change. Accuracy is the governing force that transforms ideas into soluble experiences. Whether the first steps of a reading-thinking performance be big or little, the pressure of discovery and accuracy results in a creative and critical performance. These processes are chain reactions. The tremendous potency of discovery and accuracy works for the good of the reader as a whole, and their contributions to learning are as important as the system that stimulated them.

No other system has so successfully turned each man's natural interest toward his own advancement and that of society's, for no other system has held out such great potential rewards to the successful scholar. The free-enterprise system of reading and thinking encourages enlightened self-interest as well as the acquisition of functional knowledge in its most useful form.

113

The phrase "potential rewards to the successful scholar" raises a fundamental point: the dynamics of constructive change are not possible without the risk of tentative hypotheses and extrapolations. The process of change is the process of the educated guess. Before new ideas can stand the test of accuracy and find their way to the market place, an investment of time, effort, and reflective thought is required. Often the investment in all three is large. The formulation of the theory of relativity—the grasping of time-space relations—represented the time, effort, and thought of many scholars and, at the apex, the dedicated culminating accomplishment of Albert Einstein. Yet, for every concept that finds its way to the market place, many are tested and cast aside.

Thus, while the hope of discovery and the discipline of accuracy ensure the spread of change, it is usefulness—the potential reward—that leads to the speculation that makes change and growth possible. Our civilization's great potential for growth can be realized only if students are taught the disciplines of discovery and accuracy.

This is the contribution that sound training in reading and thinking can and must make to ensure dynamic growth. It is, moreover, a challenge that all nations and all teachers face if persons who are learning to read and think are to become productive citizens. Students trained in the discipline of accuracy must be taught to examine ideas systematically and must learn skills by means of frequent practice and review so that they can form and apply mature concepts. The competent reader is able to transfer to whatever he is reading at the moment the experience and knowledge acquired in similar situations in the past. If this kind of transfer does not occur, teaching has failed, and pupils have not learned. This process of transferral depends not only upon the similarity of situations but also on the nature and usefulness of the generalizations involved.

The Second Half of a Directed Reading-Thinking Activity

As stated in Chapter 2, reading a basic-reader story represents only half of the teaching-learning activity. Equally as important is the "extending and refining" process when specifics are isolated for attention. The basic-reader story provides the context in which the specific learning is introduced. Needs are identified or recognized during the actual reading of a story or article and then singled out for specific attention during the extending and refining session. Skills developed in these semi-isolated circumstances can be put to use in subsequent reading situations. The two form an interacting learning cycle. As principles and skills and concepts are identified and acquired, they can be put to use. This meaningful association of logically learned skills presented and applied in familiar contexts is the key to retention. Learning then becomes a relatively permanent behavior change through the restructuring of experience accomplished on an active, problem-solving basis. These two phases—the predicting-reading-proving phase and the extending and refining phase—form the one-two punch of a Directed Reading-Thinking Activity.

False practices and notions have produced in many classrooms across the country a strange paradox. Somehow, over the years, each basic-reader story came to be handled in the same time-consuming way. First came the readiness period when the group was prepared and oriented for reading the story. These "readiness" sessions became longer and longer. More and more *telling* was done about the story, about teacher experiences related to the story, about pupil experiences, and about the "new" words the story contained. The readiness session frequently consumed the whole reading period. This, then, meant that either the pupils read the story on their own while the teacher "readied" another group, or the books were put aside until the next day. The former was the practice that seemed to be followed most frequently. The guided silent reading never really came off because the teacher was busy elsewhere.

The next day the class discussed the story. The teacher asked questions to see how carefully the pupils had read. The questions were usually about particular facts or events. The pupils, knowing this, read and reread the story to prepare themselves for any teacher question. To a degree the pupils enjoyed the story. A standard teacher question at the end of each session was: "Did you like the story?"; the expected answer was, of course, a chorus of oh's and ah's.

After checking pupil knowledge about story facts, the teacher initiated an oral reading of the story for purposes different, it was said, from those of the silent reading. The oral reading was done to help each pupil pronounce the words, speak clearly, read with expression, follow in the book while someone else read, and to stay alert in case he was asked to read next. There must be *no stumbling over unknown words*. This reading was to be done for "enjoyment," as well as to "express the thought." The purpose of the third reading was to intrepret the author's meaning even though the mechanics of oral reading received much of the attention. To get all this done without many traumas required a day and usually two days.

Three days were thus devoted to one story. The first day was for readiness, the second day for silent reading, and the third day for oral reading. This left no time for follow-up, so exercises in the studybooks and skillbooks had to be done by pupils largely on their own. This was not too bad because teachers could "grade" the studybooks after school. It was a terrible way to treat a studybook, but after the way in which the basic-reader story had been mutilated and disfigured, it was mild by comparison. After a period of time, a feeling of immunity set in, and the pupils started to accept and like the three-day cycle. Interestingly enough, people in concentration camps also report some feelings of immunity and security.

Another aspect of this paradox was the need for grouping within a room. As long as all the pupils in a room could use one self-contained basic reader and be kept in one reading group, the mutilating cycle could be accomplished without too much difficulty. Some odd schemes have been developed at places on the national scene in an effort to maintain a one-group, one-room, one-basic-reader arrangement. In fact, in some schools eleven-year-olds are grouped with seven-year-olds so that the fiction of a homogeneous reading-level group might be attained. But gradually, as the three-groups-in-a-room idea became accepted, teachers became increasingly frustrated, for it became virtually impossible to do all the things recommended and to do them with the three groups. Studybooks now served a new purpose. Children in Groups I and II could be doing studybook activities, while Group III was being directed through the mutilating cycle. Deplorably, though, studybooks became busybooks, and atrophy set in. The waste and degeneration that followed grew to such proportions that the odor spread to the administrative offices, whence came the order, No more funds for studybooks. This lack of systematic skill-teaching shackled many children and brought down the wrath of an angered nation on reading instruction in general and basic readers in particular; it also gave rise to a wave of phoneticism. Panaceas mushroomed. Everybody had a phonic system. Sideshow medicine men of the early twentieth century with their fanfare and ready-packaged cure-alls were amateurs in comparison with the "experts" whose mulish, bemuddled, multifarious remedies, so prodigal of counsel, swept the country in the 1950s.

The same administrators who refused funds for basic-reader skillbooks now spent even larger sums for the panaceas. Teachers grasped at them eagerly and stick-plowed their way along. With tremendous effort and time, they dogmatically produced results. They proved that when children are given instruction over and over and over again, they will learn how to *say* words. If anything, we owe a considerable debt of gratitude to the phoneticists, for they showed that regular effort and time will produce results. If teachers had used the studybooks and skillbooks as directed, however, they would have obtained far better results with much less time and effort.

These strange paradoxes have been dealt with at some length here to support the point being advanced in this chapter: the second half of a D-R-T-A is a must. Extending and refining activities must be taught.

A FIRST-READER-LEVEL ILLUSTRATION

Sequence of Ideas. Careful examination of basic-reader stories designed to be used for directed reading-thinking purposes will reveal the attributes they have that are intended to develop discrimination and skill. In "A Newspaper Helps," events follow in order, and the shift of action as a meaningful set of different events is introduced is easily noted. The pupils, after reading the first three pages, were quite certain the owner would show up and that the next events in the story would prove this true. Instead, other events—plausible in the same context—followed. The owner did not show up immediately as expected. While the three boys waited, they played with the dog and discovered that the dog did tricks. He was not an ordinary dog but a carefully trained dog. The pupils used this information, as it was hoped they would, by seeing its relevance in the possible plot outcome. A trained dog would certainly be sought by his owner.

Another look at the sequence of ideas in this story seems timely, therefore. The pupils may be asked either to recall the events as they occurred or to turn to the story and note them. Either way, the teacher can then list on the chalkboard the events as reported.

1. Boys played ball and saw dog.
2. No one came for dog.
3. Dog would not go home.
4. Dog was not seen on street before.
5. Boys turn to Cooky's mother for help.
6. Cooky wants to keep dog at his house.
7. Mother suggests putting ad in paper.
8. Boys read ad Mr. Jack published.
9. Twins stay and play with Cooky.

The events may not be given in such detail by the children; but again, they might. This listing represents what one group did.

As each event is listed, one pupil could read the supporting line orally to the teacher. She is serving as recording secretary, and the oral reading will prove helpful to her in many ways.

Now events on the next two pages can be recorded. The two sets might be separated by the prediction that the owner will show up.

10. Boys lose ball in garden.
11. Ted looks for hat.
12. Dog jumps over bat.
13. Dog jumps through paper.
14. Dog sat up and begged for cake.
15. Dog walked on front feet.

Again, list prediction: Owner will surely show up. Dog is a trained dog.

16. A lady called Mother on phone.
17. A lady and man came to house.
18. Dog belongs to them.
19. Lady and man run a dog show.
20. They go from town to town.
21. Next, will be in boys' town.
22. Give boys tickets to see show.

Here are the facts and two of the predictions or deductions. It may be that this detailed listing will help pupils see that they overlooked a cue that could have proved rather significant. The last lines on page 121 in the "Newspaper" story are: "We may stay here and play with you. Mother said we could." This could have indicated that the boys would play together while waiting for the owner to show up. Now predictions may be solicited from the group relevant to this point, predictions such as, maybe the boys will play and the dog will help; maybe the dog gets in their way and then runs off; maybe the dog saves one of the boys by hurrying to Cooky's house for help.

Listing events is useful: it alerts the pupils to the value of noting order for predictive purposes, a skill that may prove very helpful when at a later point these same pupils are asked to deal with historical, political, or scientific material. The ability to order events so that their consequences become discernible is a skill serviceable in all areas of the curriculum and in almost all phases of life. Training should be initiated early and adjusted at different levels by the demands of a more complex cognitive structure.

Another thing that can be done with a list of ordered events is to invite the pupils to structure a different order. This is the idea behind encouraging pupils to write a different ending to a story. What is suggested here, though, is to proceed with the objective of seeing sequence in the light of consequence.

One six-year-old structured the fourth and fifth pages of the story as follows:

1. The boys play ball.
2. The dog chases after the balls.
3. The ball is lost.
4. The ball is found lying near a poisonous snake.
5. The dog warns them and saves them.

A girl structured events in this way:

1. The boys play war.
2. One boy is the U.N. observer.
3. The dog helps the observer.

When pupils are encouraged to think and be original, it is astonishing how they recall and use experiences and knowledge. What adult, given this freedom to create, would have thought either of the snake episode or particularly of the U.N.-observer episode? Pupils' unstudied naturalness and agreeable freshness can be profoundly astonishing.

Substituting Final Consonants. Teaching word-attack skills is as important as teaching comprehension skills. If these skills are taught regularly and systematically in a functional context, pupils will learn how and when to use them.

The substituting skill recommended here is one of the most useful to acquire. Knowledge of the substitution of sounds serves the reader not only at the learning-to-read stage but throughout school and life. Every time a person turns to a dictionary to get pronunciation help, he puts to work his knowledge of sound substitutions and blending of sounds.

It must be kept in mind that word-attack skills other than substituting final consonants were previously taught. Skills very closely linked with this skill are auditory discrimination by rhyming, auditory discrimination of ending sounds appearing in a pronunciation unit (a syllable or word), visual discrimination of words, visual discrimination of letters and letter combinations that represent different sounds in known common words, and the blending of sounds and the saying of words. The auditory facet of these skills is strategic. The foundation of phonetics is *sound*. The better a pupil hears sounds—their likenesses and differences—the better he will be able to use sounds in attacking a word.

In this basic reader, manual instructions to the teacher are as follows[1]:

Print the following sentences on the board or on chart paper:

Bill put out his bat and hit the ball.
Ted saw ten little dogs at the dog show.
How many holes did Red dig in the garden?
Ned sat by a big boy named Sam.

Beside these sentences, print: cat, bag, him, soon.
Have the first sentence read silently and ask whether anyone needs help with the new word. If he does, ask these questions: "What word in the sentence is like this word except for the last letter? What word at the side ends like this word? If I take the t from cat and put it in place of the s in his, what word will I have? Now who can read the sentence aloud?"
Direct the reading of the other sentences similarly.

Note that the sound elements used always appear in a sound context or unit. The sound that a letter represents is pretty much determined by the sound context in which it appears. For instance, the sound the letter t represents varies according to its position in a sound context and the neighboring letters: hit, the, paint, part, tree, stop, strike, and so on. To say to a child: "Tell me the sound of this letter (t)" is as meaningless as the question, What is your speed of reading? Pupils trained in the art of phonetics should reply, "I don't know. The letter must be in a sound context."

In this activity each sound that could be used appears in a known context. For the new word *hit* (the word may not be new for any of the children), the pupil is supplied with his and cat; for ten, with Ted and soon; for dig, with did and bag; and for Sam, with sat and him.

The difficulty pupils experience in learning the skill of consonant

---

[1] This and similar instructions to teachers in this chapter are quoted from the *Teachers' Editions of the Winston Basic Reader Series* (New York: Holt, Rinehart & Winston, 1960).

substitution is that of either locating known words like his and cat somewhere in the printed context of a story, or in remembering useful key words. It is better at first to ask pupils to locate useful words in the story. The unaided-recall approach, if introduced too early, produces a spelling approach to word recall. So, learning to locate another key word on a page is an excellent procedure.

This represents only half the story, though. Blending the sounds together proves to be more difficult for some than locating or recalling a key word. An excellent way to facilitate blending-skill development is to use meaning clues as is done in this activity. A child may reach the hi-t level and be saying the two elements almost as discrete sounds. This hi-t level along with the language context helps the pupil recognize that the sounds, if blended together properly, yield the word hit and that the word means "to hit a ball."

The range of individual differences in learning word-attack skills is considerable. Some people acquire mental skills almost as easily as they acquire motor skills. Some do not. Some people learn to swim easily; others need some training and, interestingly enough, they need the training while they are in water. This is true about acquiring proficiency with mental skills such as the phonetic skill or sound skill of consonant substitution. Those who experience difficulty need repeated opportunities to learn not only under the supervision of a coach or teacher but also in a natural-language context (swimmer in water) rather than in isolation.

Meeting Individual Needs

Individual differences are both the boon and the bonds of classroom instruction. The range of differences in capacity, creativity, curiosity, social and emotional adjustment, physical stamina, and experience and knowledge is what makes the wheels of society go around. These are the differences that make a classroom a vital, exciting, and stimulating environment. These are the differences that make a D-R-T-A so functional and profitable. This is why John B. Watson said that by the time children go to school they are graduate students in terms of learned responses. Each pupil represents a tremendous reservoir of potential that can be put to good use by any teacher. Thank goodness for individual differences.

The bonds are largely of our making. We are the cruel robbers who make of learning a Procrustean bed. We try to rob the children of their tremendous wealth, and to a good degree we succeed. Procrustes shortened or stretched the legs of his victims until all were a uniform length and all were dead. All too often, reading is taught in the Procrustean tradition, so that a love for and a use of reading are equally short and equally dead. John I. Goodlad and Robert H. Anderson say (10, p. 1):

Certain time-honored practices of pupil classification, while perhaps not lethal, trap school-age travelers in much the same fashion as Procrustes' bed trapped the unwary. These practices are concomitants of our graded system of school organization. First, a certain amount of progress is held to be standard for a year's work. Then, the content of the work is laid out within the grade, to be "covered" and, to a degree, "mastered." The slow are pulled and stretched to fit the grade. Sometimes, because their God-given limbs lack enough elasticity, they are "non-promoted"—left behind, where presumably another year of stretching will do the trick. The quick are compressed and contracted to fit the grade. In time, they learn to adapt to a pace that is slower than their natural one.

Some pupils will not need additional skill practice; some will need a little; some will need a great deal. The best single determiner is the performance of the pupils. Requiring uniform skill practice can be just as Procustean as any other phase of instruction. Sometimes those who do not understand individual differences justify equal amounts of practice by claiming that it will produce uniformly good or well-trained students. One condition that seems to be true as evidenced by pure research and action research is that equal amount of practice increases rather than decreases performance. The generalization that can be made is that the better the teaching, the greater are individual differences likely to be.

If, for instance, while reading "A Newspaper Helps" a pupil had experienced difficulty with the new word *other* on page 122, the teacher might have referred the pupil to the word *mother* on page 121. This might not have been sufficient, and a quick writing or printing of the words might have helped: M̲other.
 other

It may be that this pupil's request for help is indicative of a need for more practice in initial-consonant substitution. Similar requests for help by this pupil may confirm this. It may be that when the word is reused on page 123, he may seek help again. Or, the reader may ask this pupil to read aloud another sentence containing the word o̲t̲h̲e̲r̲. This will provide additional evidence of the pupil's ability to recall a̲n̲d̲ recognize. It will also offer some evidence of the efficacy of frequent recontact with the word in different functional contexts.

The teacher makes note of this request for help and of others like it during the D-R-T-A. At a later person-to-person confrontation, she and the pupil proceed as follows. First, she writes the word o̲t̲h̲e̲r̲ on a piece of paper and presents it to the child for recognition. If h̲e̲ recognizes it instantly, the teacher asks him to review the help given during the silent-reading session. If the pupil can repeat the M̲o̲t̲h̲e̲r̲-o̲t̲h̲e̲r̲ aid, she may then write a̲n̲o̲t̲h̲e̲r̲ and b̲r̲o̲t̲h̲e̲r̲ so that the pupil can t̲r̲y̲ his skill on similar words.

If, though, the pupil does not recognize the word in isolation (o̲t̲h̲e̲r̲), the teacher asks the pupil to turn to page 122 and read orally the l̲i̲n̲e̲ in which the word first occurs. For some children just seeing the page on which the word in question is introduced triggers the recall. For most others, seeing the word in the sentence in which it first occurred or the setting in which the difficulty was met is enough to accomplish recall.

If one or two other children had difficulty with the same word, she calls them together in a group and proceeds in the same way. It is important to note, though, that the individualized help is given to those who need it, not to the whole group under the false pretext that "it won't hurt them." Such corruption of sound teaching practices sabotages the self-reliance of many scholars, some of whom never recover.

The next day, the teacher re-presents the word other to the one(s) who had difficulty. Again, she follows the same steps: word in isolation, review learning steps, word in story context, other similar words. The psychology of learning has shown that a good way to facilitate recall and recognition is to review that which is to be learned and to do so on a short time-interval basis. The frequent reinforcement will promote retention. In this example the time spans were (1) meeting the same word five sentences later, (2) meeting it nine sentences later, (3) meeting it twenty-one lines later, (4) meeting it during oral rereading to prove a point, (5) meeting it during individualized help time, and (6) meeting it the next day. The time intervals were approximately twenty seconds, thirty seconds, eighty seconds, five minutes, ten minutes, and twenty-four hours.

The efficacy of meaning, of context clues, of thinking by relating ideas, and of frequent recontact cannot be overestimated. The potency of meaning and purposeful thinking has no bounds. It is undoubtedly the best memory adhesive available. The laws of learning have shown this to be true. Furthermore, this knowledge about learning and retention takes on even greater significance when applied to a skill such as phonetic analysis. All too often phonics is taught by rote *memoriter* methods and as a result becomes largely nonserviceable.

Studybook Activities

Basic readers contain few if any, skill-building activities. Basic readers are bound with hard covers. This means they are nonconsumable. Should a skill exercise be presented in a hard-bound, nonconsumable basic reader, it could not be a writing activity, for if it were, the pupil would need to copy the material, and this would be an endless, time-wasting task.

Studybooks, on the other hand, are consumable material, bound with soft covers. The exercises frequently require writing. Usually each page in a studybook presents a different exercise. Some are as long as two pages. The exercise deals with one specific skill or one aspect of a skill so that the pupil(s) can concentrate on the task at hand. Unfortunately, and very unfortunately indeed, some skillbooks are so loosely structured that a single activity is designed to teach six different skills. If those preparing the materials did not know what skill they were teaching, the teacher cannot be expected to know, much less the children.

Studybooks should present sound (professionally correct), carefully structured (each page clearly designed and produced), and sequentially organized (skills programmed) materials. To ensure student retention, skills should be reinforced periodically, that is, similar skill activities should be presented at intervals.

One of the principal values of a studybook activity is that it helps pupils *follow* directions. To do a studybook activity, the pupils must know the directions they are to follow. Either they can read the directions on their own, or they can be told what to do. Obviously the former is desired. If pupils must be told what to do, teaching again becomes telling, and self-reliance becomes teacher-reliance.

Directions on how to complete an activity should be so explicit and so worded that the children can read them and follow them. At the first-reader level this may not always be possible, but beyond that point it should be. Studybook activities should be so directed that pupils are required to read the directions and do the activity and ask for help if they do not understand. Here, as in any other learning situation, pupils should be required to say that they do not know, if and whenever they do not. As stated so often already, *intellectual honesty* is the first prerequisite in a learner's repertory. A pupil cannot learn if he cheats himself. Teachers should take every precaution to avoid making intellectual cheats out of their students. Studybooks provide one of the best means for doing this—by providing pupils with opportunities to follow directions.

All this means, of course, that a studybook page has to be so presented that a pupil—even a six-year-old—can find the directions and read them. Print size must be easily readable. Directions should be placed on the page so that the pupils can readily move from them to the activity. Directions awkwardly placed produce awkward results.

Learning to follow directions is of the highest importance. It is a skill used over and over again throughout school and throughout life. Ability to follow directions is often of vital importance: reading directions on a medicine bottle, a household appliance, a dangerous tool, highway signs. Ability to follow directions is one of the best measures of an independent, self-assured, self-reliant, self-sufficient, and self-controlled scholar.

At the first-grade level, reading the directions should be a co-reading job. Pupil(s) read orally all words they know, and the teacher supplies immediately those they do not know. Then she stands by to see how well they follow directions. She watches especially to see how well they do the first part of an activity. If all seems satisfactory, the pupils proceed on their own. By careful observation the pupil can learn, by a steady pace of increasing responsibility, to proceed on his own. The teacher should proceed from the beginning with this objective in mind. The pupils will sense the teaching climate and fall in with it.

Not all studybook pages need to be taught to all students. "Pages can be skipped," say some authorities. "This makes studybooks adaptable to individual differences." This is a most unfortunate position to take. People who endorse such a policy are compromising the learning act in behalf of expediency. These same authorities also endorse testing, and claim that testing is not being done often enough.

A well-constructed studybook activity can be used on a teach-test basis, a test-teach basis, or on a test-attain basis. This allows for considerable latitude insofar as adapting instruction to individual needs is concerned. If education is a process that seeks to change the behavior of students and if testing is the process of appraising these changes, methods of evaluation should include any valid way of securing evidence as to whether or not pupils are attaining objectives. So, if studybook materials appropriate to a pupil's instructional level are being used, all pupils should deal with the different activities on one basis or the other—teach-test, test-teach, or test-attain.

In the teach-test approach the pupils are required to read the directions and seek help whenever needed. The teacher stands close by to give help as requested and to watch how the pupils proceed. Results may indicate a need for more teaching, in which case manual activities or similar teacher-constructed activities can be used.

In the test-teach approach the pupils are largely on their own. They read the directions and do the activity in the quickest and most efficient way. Rate of performance becomes a measure of skill control as well as accuracy. If further teaching is needed, manual activities or teacher-prepared activities can be used.

In the test-attain approach the procedure is much the same as for the test-teach approach. Rate of performance should be very good; accuracy, of course, should be 100 percent. These pupils are out to prove that they know the skill and that they know it so well that they can perform with ease.

In each of these situations the children are performing as in a problem-solving situation. The pupil sees the problem—the skill being developed on a particular page. He does not know what to do until he reads the directions, so he is experiencing perplexity. He does not panic or experience utter confusion, because the demands are at his level of understanding. He proceeds with the activity as directed, reorganizing and restructuring his own experience, bringing insight and achieving a solution. For the test-attain pupils the problem is a very familiar and understandable situation so that now efficiency of performance is a good part of the problem. This is not to imply that efficiency is unimportant to the teach-test and test-teach pupils; rather it indicates that rate of performance is most likely the highest measure of efficiency. In all instances, the problem or activity involves meaningful relations that are to be solved by discovery and utilization of those relationships. These are not to be chance successes but are to reflect progressive growth in understanding.

At times, the teach-test pupils may devote an entire period to studybook and manual activities. After all, this is the practice session to help the reader acquire a skill.

Activities in studybooks should be sequential or *programmed* in nature. This means, of course, that the person(s) preparing the program should possess a thorough knowledge of the skills to be developed—their structure and sequence. The skills presented should be continuously and directly controlled so that the pupil may proceed on a step-by-step basis. He must be able to see and understand the order of events.

Unfortunately, many studybooks are so organized that pupils as well as teachers find it difficult to follow a sequence and see relationships on a step-by-step basis. Phonetic activities are scattered throughout a skillbook and usually in random order. Some "reading lessons" will include phonetic

Studybook Page 31

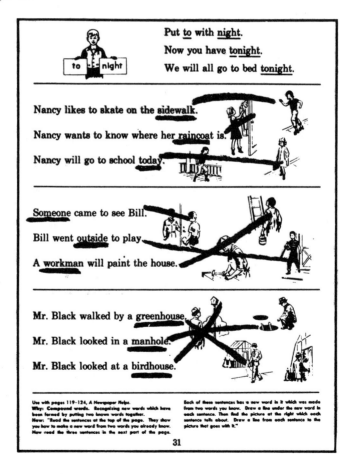

skill-building activities and some will not, resulting in both a knowledge gap and a time gap.

In those studybooks in which all the word-attack skill activities appear together, both pupils and teacher can see the sequence and the system of skill development. As a result, the teacher is better able to determine the level at which a child is performing and, therefore, teach at his instructional level; she can provide the specific instruction needed to move the pupil along to the next skill; and if a child forgets a skill or needs more practice, she can go back to the specific skill that is lacking, reteach it, and then proceed. There is no substitute for individualized skill instruction.

The studybook page shown is one of three recommended for use as a part of the total D-R-T-A "A Newspaper Helps."

The studybook activity shown above is concerned with the recognition of compound words. At the bottom of the page are the directions—the *why*

Studybook Page 79

A New Trick

Cooky and the twins went to the dog show. They wanted to see the dog they had found.

Ned said, "This is good. The dogs put out a fire."

"I see our dog," said Ted. "He is going up the side of the house. He will help the baby dog."

Just then the big dog looked up. "He is looking at us!" said Cooky. "He did not forget what we did for him."

As Cooky talked, the dog jumped down and ran to the boys. He ran and jumped up on Cooky.

The other dogs were surprised. They did not go on with the show, and the fire was not put out.

The boys went to the dog show to see the dog. / to put out a fire.

Ted thought the big dog was going to sit down and look. / to help the baby dog.

The big dog jumped up on Cooky. / up on Ted.

All the dogs were surprised to see the fire put out. / to see the big dog run and jump.

Use with pages 119 124, A Newspaper Helps.
Why: Reading for detail. Reading a story and completing sentences about facts in the story.

How: "Read the story and the sentences below it. In each sentence below, there are two endings where one belongs. Draw a line under the ending which makes the sentence right."

79

and *how* of the activity. The *how* part gives the directions to be followed in doing the activity. The first part of the activity illustrates how two words are put together to form a new word.

Those pupils who will do this page on a teach-test basis may need careful teacher supervision through the part requiring the drawing of lines. Then they may be able to proceed on their own as they complete the next two parts. *Specific purposes* are of crucial importance in the reading of a story, but they are even more crucial, if that can be, in the problem-solving atmosphere of a studybook activity.

For the most part, the pupils should help correct their own papers. This can be done on a whole-group basis or by teaming up pupils or by complete self-correction. In the whole-group procedure, all follow the teacher as she checks through each item on her copy or a master copy. Errors are discussed immediately. In the team approach, two pupils exchange papers and

Studybook Page 80

Things to Live In			Things to Read		
rabbit hole	bag	car	Grandmother	book	dog
umbrella	house	street	newspaper	ice	bag

Things for School			Things to Play With		
paint	skates	paper	jacks	skates	ice
fire	house	book	bat	cooky	ball

Things for Picnics			Things for Rain		
lemons	milk	cake	bat	umbrella	hat
garden	ice	bed	parade	cake	raincoat

What a Baby Can Do			What Birds Can Do		
big	ride	fly	stand	talk	walk
laugh	read	play	read	fly	look

What Children Can Do			What Dogs Can Do		
tricks	hide	drink	eat	talk	fly
fly	laugh	walk	run	laugh	jump

Use with pages 119-124, A Newspaper Helps.

Why: Classifying Ideas. Classifying objects according to use and according to the action of a doer.

How: "Read the title in the first block. Then read the other words in the block. Draw a line under each word that goes with the title.
"Do the same thing with the words in the other blocks."

80

check the accuracy of each under the watchful eye of the teacher. This is a good approach since it requires a good second look or re-examination by each pupil operating under different motivation. In the third approach, each pupil checks his own work against a master copy and seeks teacher help as needed. This approach promotes self-reliance and self-knowledge in a better way than either of the other two.

Pupils should be discouraged from regarding such activities as grim and unpleasant. As they participate in the checking and the adjusting they should be interested, alert, and active.

The activity shown on p. 125 is the thirty-first word-recognition activity in the studybook from which it was taken. In all, there are forty-eight such activities in this one book. The first forty-nine pages are devoted to word-recognition skill training.

The two activities shown on pp. 126 and 127, recommended for use with this D-R-T-A session, are concerned with specifics of comprehension.

Now is the time to alert pupils to story details as required by this exercise. The facts are not to be used to predict or to determine consequences; they are just to be identified. It is hoped, of course, that in the reading-thinking process of a D-R-T-A the reader will use his skill in locating and recalling facts and select those facts that lead to fruitful predictions.

The thinking reader is always classifying ideas or identifying attributes and noting categories. A next activity is concerned with classifying objects according to use and according to the action of the door. As educators are beginning to realize, children are capable of learning much that at one time was thought to be beyond their capacities. This activity requires the child to classify by discrimination and discovery. The pupil must construct his own conceptual grouping by processing and organizing the information given. The decisions required may cause him to see new relationships and to remake and extend concepts to accommodate the classification requested. He has to develop a strategy for organizing facts into a category.

Pupils may actually discover the relationships among the different concepts and understand how these relationships are caused. The experiences are organized around selected instances and are sufficient to produce a category generalization.

An adult might read into the words to be classified experiences and ideas not relevant to the scheme of things as perceived by children. A child, for instance, might list *car* as a thing to live in. Noting attributes and fixing class or category membership is geared to the experience and semantic level of pupils—not of adults. Children, like adults, are constantly putting ideas together. They note little details and group them. Almost the moment something new is presented we ask: What is it? What does it do? We seek for understanding usually by searching our experience for related ideas or events. Immediately we seek some organization, some intellectual unity. In the "Classifying Ideas" activity the pupils' thinking was directed to suggested meanings for the sake of experimenting with them. The ideas used—bag, car, umbrella—are very familiar and would, in isolation, be recognized quickly without much thought. Now, though, because they appear in this grouping, and reclassification is required, they give rise to a problem. Recognition is no longer automatic. Mental effort is required to group them and understand the grouping. Old attributes are examined in a different way; new ones are sought. When the classification is established the items become things understood—things with a meaning. The better we see a thing or event in relation to other things, the better we grasp its meaning.

Making some sort of association is a natural for most people. They do it instantly and spontaneously. And here is the rub: in all too many instances the associations made do not reflect studied judgment. Some factor of almost no value may be used. For example, almost everyone has had the experience of trying to remember a particular book he has read. All that could be recalled was that the book had a red jacket and was somewhere on the right side of the room. Associations such as these are useless.

This skill activity, then, represents just one step in the direction toward habits of sound thinking via better discrimination and classification. It requires pupils to decide that objects belong under a certain classification according to use and according to the action of the doer.

Additional Activities

The activities outlined below are in addition to those in the studybook and those already defined as basic-book activities. It is readily apparent that each activity involves other facets of the language arts, especially the newspaper-ad activity. It is obvious, too, that all aspects of language power develop together: reading and writing, speaking and listening.

DIRECTED OBSERVATION.   Pupils have seen how a newspaper can help to find the owner of a lost pet. They may now get some satisfaction from discovering some real Lost and Found ads.

Have the children bring in copies of the newspapers they get at home. Show them the part of the paper that contains Lost-and-Found notices. Invite them to find the ads for themselves by looking for the word *Found.*

Then read one or two of the ads aloud and have pupils tell why each bit of information was included.

DICTATING A LOST AND FOUND AD.   In any primary classroom there are frequent occasions when a child loses something or finds an article that is not his. When this happens, get pupils to make up a Lost and Found ad. Print the ad on chart paper. Have it read orally to all the children. Then place the ad where everyone can easily see it.

Now that the pupils have had this "Newspaper Helps" experience, turning to the Lost and Found section of a newspaper will have meaning. They have not done the exercise in advance of reading the story, and reasons for turning to the Lost and Found section have not been trumped up. Each pupil knew why he was turning to that part of the paper. They all had a common experience to which they could relate. For each, a series of "knowns" in terms of experience was grouped into a new pattern. Most children know dogs or about them; they know what it means to lose something or to find something; they know about turning to parents or other appropriate persons for help; they know about newspapers, about tricks, about rewards, about dog shows. Few, if any, may have had experience with Lost and Found ads in newspapers. Now, though, all these resources of the pupils have been brought to bear upon a new "resource" by the way they have been combined. Pupils' personal experiences have been extended—vicariously extended.

Thus, at this early stage of the learning process pupils are gaining possession of the means of still further extending their knowledge and "experience." Now they have moved only slightly beyond their experience, but they are able to store up what they have learned by actually examining newspaper ads. Through history and geography, they will be able to include experiences far remote from them in time and space. Now a newspaper ad, then the landing of the Pilgrims; now the school and community, then Troy and the Trojans; now a teacher and a school principal, then the soldiers and General Washington at Valley Forge.

It is not easy to grasp the fact that concepts cannot be foisted on children. Only by entering into a context of use, by bringing help and enjoyment, by arousing curiosity through bafflement, by directing inquiry and examination, by structuring and restructuring experiences—only thus can meaning be acquired, extended, and refined. "A Newspaper Helps" set up conditions by means of which a set of consequences were brought to pass (lost dog, ad, owner, reward). These consequences called out the inventiveness and ingenuity of pupils in examining story clues and obtaining predictive information (purposes and conjectures), and they provided the means by which the predictions could be confirmed or rejected. This performance did not call for simple mechanical dexterity, but rather for a set of circumstances requiring reflection to see what consequences could follow.

Once the story has been read, the groundwork of experience is initiated, and the newspaper-ad concept can be extended through related schoolroom ads. This personalizes and socializes the extension. Better yet, it makes the *means-consequence* factor dominant. As the schoolroom ads are developed, the whole concept of Lost and Found ads gains meaning because the ads are used to bring about a consequence. As John Dewey says, this is "the center and heart of all understanding" (7, p. 146).

Children love to bring to school newspapers that their parents read. They seem to gain special delight from examining different sections of the newspaper. This activity can be one of the most interesting and may engender a considerable amount of enthusiasm. Do not be concerned about the fact that they cannot read most of the ads. The pupils will be satisfied to have you read certain ads to them. Then, too, they may by chance and on their own locate a lost-dog ad. Composing ads about things they have lost provides the personal touch that will help children remember the purpose of ads.

CLASSIFYING. Help pupils classify ideas which answer questions *When? How?* or *Where?* First print the three questions on the board as column headings. Then say the following words and phrases and have the children tell which fits each column:

last night	like magic	next Sunday
in the house	by the skates	as fast as she could
today	in the garden	this morning
faster and faster	on a truck	with a ball and bat
at school	soon	at first

Print the words and phrases under the headings the children select. Then ask a child to read each column aloud. Have the others listen and decide whether each word or phrase is correctly placed.

RECALLING OPPOSITES. Print the following words, one per card, on 3 by 5 inch index cards: *white, black, night, morning, off, on, sit, stand, hot, cold, give, take, last, first, old, new, girl, boy, yes, no, stop, go.* Distribute the word cards one to a child. Ask each pupil to find a partner by discovering who has a word opposite in meaning to his.

Then have each pair of partners make pictures to illustrate their opposite words. Later let them show the pictures and ask the other children to guess what the words are.

One of the basic notions supporting *knowing* or comprehending is that the attributes of various circumstances or events must be grasped in their relations to one another and/or in categories. Whenever conditions permit or whenever they can be contrived, children should be required to group and regroup and to structure and restructure information and to classify it. In this activity, the judgments required to rearrange the different concepts will facilitate recall and use in new situations. The actual process that takes place on a pyschological level is much more apt to be orderly and logical than random and disorderly. It should lead to planned scholarly acting and behaving and help students resolve the problems structured via a school curriculum and those encountered in life. The acquisition of such logical processes are not foreign to the minds of children and are not by any means wholly dependent on formally structured learning situations. Children come to school with many functional concepts. Survival circumstances tend to promote logical, reflective qualities that for some result in quite sound logical habits.

Dealing with opposite ideas is one form of classification. It is one that focuses sharply on likenesses and differences. "You can't appreciate heat until you've really been cold" is a common adage. Asking pupils to group opposites as is suggested here makes for an attitude of alert, cautious, and thorough inquiry.

Most likely the pupils already assembled the opposites listed here and did so on their own. Doing it here, though, may cause them to give the groupings a more careful examination. This kind of attention will help them make more penetrating classifications and help combat habits of vagueness and incoherence.

A FOURTH-READER-LEVEL ILLUSTRATION

The effect of overindulging a child can be most damaging. This is true not only with respect to social and emotional adjustment but also with respect to language development and verbalism. Pupils who are overindulged in language development sometimes demand that those listening to them and those who read what they write make "the big effort" and try to understand them. As speakers or writers, they feel little, if any, responsibility to communicate precisely. They seek out situations that enable them to communicate without effort or perseverance.

Overindulgence in language is usually started in the home. All too often slovenly habits of word usage are permitted and encouraged by parents. "Baby talk" can be amusing and cute, but it frequently sets the attitude and habits of language usage at a very low plane. Later, parents accept such phrases as, "you know what I mean," "that thing," "it," "that," and "oh, you know," rather than giving help in or requiring correct labeling or language usage. These language habits spill over into the classroom and set up an aversion for and an immunity to the demands of correct usage.

Children can say and use words correctly. At a surprisingly early age they can name the different models of planes both private and commercial, and they do so easily and correctly. Note how readily they speak of astronauts, spaceships, nylon, teflon, radioactivity, and so on.

It is the business of a teacher to check on and require the use of words that are correctly spoken and used. Pupils should not be permitted to fall back on shrug-of-the-shoulder and the you-know-what-I-mean approaches. Failure to direct correct vocabulary usage represents disloyalty to the principle of education.

Teachers unfaithful in this regard usually are, in addition, ready to accept the parroting or reciting of a text as evidence of knowing. Such loose use of words is just as damaging as the use of the shoulder-shrug and the you-know-what-I-mean approach. When these habits are endorsed over a period of eight to twelve years and more, they become extremely hard to break.

Such acceptance of ignorance on an exchange-of-ignorance altar centers, as Ernest Horn says (13, p. 141), "chiefly upon words rather than upon the ordering and authenticating of meanings, and either fails completely to give the student ideas of any sort or leads to ideas that are not sufficiently accurate or complete to be of use." We must be eternally vigilant against the habit of memorizing empty words if we wish to check the verbalism that we loathe.

Vocabulary

At the primary level most of the words introduced in basic readers are *known words* for most of the pupils. The meanings have been related to spoken symbols or oral language. The nouns are largely of a concrete variety and the verbs name actions. For the pupils all that is needed is to relate the meanings to the printed symbols. This is a relatively easy task.

At the intermediate level, however, the number of words introduced that are new or unknown to the pupils increases, and many known words are used in new ways. It is, in fact, these semantic inconsistencies that may prove more challenging to pupils and more demanding of teacher attention than new words. Children tend to develop firm, and temporarily reliable, notions about the semantics of words they know. These notions may be only partially right and of little predictive value. Any error, bias, or inadequacy of this kind must be apprehended if the students are to form sound and functional ideas. The full significance of these facts must be appreciated if reading is to be taught as a thinking process.

Classroom "boners" or "howlers" are the staple of many a comedian's repertory and the light moment of teachers' meetings. Amusing as they may be, however, they represent cause for serious concern. Uncorrected, they symbolize a shocking travesty of education. One of the earliest and most extensive investigations of pupils' erroneous ideas was made by Joseph C. Dewey. Ernest Horn (13, p. 187) reports that in Dewey's study pupils asked to explain the word *primitive* as used in the clause "the most primitive way of starting a fire" offered, *the only way, the easiest way, the most important way . . . the usual way, the most dangerous way,*" and so on. John Dewey had this to say about vagueness (7, p. 160): "It is the aboriginal logical sin—the source from which flow most bad intellectual consequences."

Under the chairmanship of J. Conrad Seegers, a committee of the National Conference of Research in English prepared a bulletin entitled *Vocabulary Problems in the Elementary School*. In the summarizing statement they made the following recommendations with reference to developing vocabulary, most of which are as applicable today as they were in the late 1930s.

D. With reference to developing vocabulary we have a right to believe:
1. That one cannot depend upon word lists to state all of the words children can, will, or should use, or to provide an index of difficulty; that many of the lists are manifestly paradoxical in minor details—for example, excluding words often used by children but not found as often in writing or in adult usage.

2. That richness and variety of the vocabulary used depends largely upon the variety of stimuli employed.

3. That real, concrete experiences not only extend vocabulary, but make meaningful the words already at one's command, and that such media are used too infrequently.

4. That unless the use of the dictionary is taught, limited results are obtained.

5. That word study is probably productive, but the type and degree most useful for certain grades or mental ages have not been determined.

6. That inflectional and semantic variations constitute great, but not insurmountable problems, and *thought,* rather than *simple recognition,* requires emphasis.

7. That original expression is more effective than mere reproduction, natural experiences are more effective than books alone, that spontaneous interests should be supplemented, that telling and context methods of presenting words are superior to the dictionary method as the dictionary is ordinarily used. Of course this does not imply that the less effective methods are useless.

8. That the attention of children should be focused upon words; that vocabulary notebooks, individual lists, and methods designed to vary expression are helpful.

9. That sometimes words are best taught in isolation, especially when logical resemblances to other words and word forms can be emphasized. This needs to be studied further, with attention to related problems of mental age, reading age, and I.Q.

10. That oral language needs more exact attention than it often has received.

11. That vocabulary improvement should be planned for, not left to chance. (19, pp. 36–37.)

At the intermediate level it is essential that the extending and refining phase of a Directed Reading-Thinking Activity focus sharply and clearly and continuously on vocabulary development. Pupils must be made word conscious. They must learn to question their own knowledge of a word and face up to their own weaknesses. This they learn during the process part of a D-R-T-A. By so doing pupils learn that, if they identify a word in the context in which it appears, they can at the same time identify the meaning to be stressed. In the same way they learn to understand why the drilling of words out of context is ineffective.

In Chapter 3 the discussion of the first half of the D-R-T-A on "Of Plows and Plowing" describes in some detail how to deal with new vocabulary. The new words were not introduced to the pupils prior to the reading of the selection. This practice was recommended because it best teaches pupils how to become self-reliant, independent readers, how to read for meaning, to be intellectually honest, to use context clues, to use a glossary, to fuse ideas. Even so, vocabulary development is of such importance that it needs to be singled out for special attention during the extending and refining period.

In many instances, pupils reading "Of Plows and Plowing" will have spotted all of the key words on their own and thus will have provided the opening for a teacher double-check. Even if this natural scholarly opening is not provided, the teacher should make a double-check on vocabulary by initiating the inquiry. In the "Of Plows and Plowing" instance, the following procedure is recommended in the manual.

Key words associated with plows, such as *moldboard* and *share,* warrant discussion since they represent correct nomenclature. And to a considerable degree, the pictures and the texts here presented provide enough specifics to allow pupils to use the labels correctly. This is a good way to combat verbalism.

Different meanings for the word *furrow* may be reviewed. Pupils might explain how they would "furrow" a garden or study a "furrowed" face.

Phrases such as *before the birth of Christ* and *B.C.* and *A.D.* might be discussed. Others to note are: *getting food, depended on plows,* and *present way of life.*

It may well be that for most of the pupils this look at *moldboard, share,* and *furrow* will be a second look (see Chapter 3, pp. 93–103) and will constitute a review. Even if this is the case, the review will be worthwhile. Meaningful repetition tends to result in mental fixation and recall. Pointed teacher questions may cause the pupils to note differences, to make comparisons, and to catch the little details that would escape a more casual observer. A pastry board or sculptor's board could be compared with a moldboard. Molds of clay, mud, and sand could be compared with cookies, doughnuts, and candy. This kind of analysis would help pupils grasp the specifics of mold: to shape, pat, whittle, fashion. This in turn could lead to further inquiry into the history of and diversified use of molds and molding. It could also result in some examination of other meanings of *mold*: decay or a kind of loose, rich soil. The word *share* may be analyzed similarly. Some pupils may be familiar with the terms *share of stock* and *shareholder*; others may know something about *sharecropper.* All will have experience with sharing of one kind or another.

The interim report on *Children's Knowledge of Words* by Edgar Dale and Gerhard Eicholz (6) indicates, for example, that three meanings of the word *mold* are generally known by sixth-grade-level pupils: mold (growth on bread), mold (to shape things), mold (hollow form). This suggests that teaching of the type recommended here is very much in order at the fourth- and fifth-grade levels.

Misconceptions about *time* are as common as those reported by Harry A. Greene (11) in "Geography." While time relationships cannot be dealt with in as graphic a manner as longitude and latitude, pupils can be made increasingly aware of time-event relationships. Fourth-grade-level pupils asked to date the birth of Christ have said: one hundred years ago, three hundred years ago, a thousand years ago. Invariably, though, some fourth-grade-level child will date the birth of Christ correctly.

The psychology of learning has shown that, while repetition is important, the number of different meaningful associations made is equally as influential in promoting fixation and recall. In vocabulary development this means that the more experience a pupil has with a word and the better he grasps likenesses and differences, or synonyms and antonyms, the better he is apt to remember and use the words. Direct instruction is effective, but it has its limitations. Recall and use of the words is much dependent on each pupil's facility with words, his intelligence, his experience, and his motivation.

Vocabulary Notebooks

A tried-and-true method for encouraging vocabulary growth is the every-pupil vocabulary notebook. This is especially true if the number of entries is not too large and if the complexity of the constructs is not too great. Ernest Horn put it this way (12, p. 385): "The first step in establishing more favorable conditions for understanding is to drastically decrease, at each grade level, the number, difficulty, and remoteness of the problems which pupils are required to attack." Horn also referred to a study by Olive P. Ritter (22) on the technical, difficult, and unusual terms in an introductory book in geography designed for use in fourth grade. There were so many such words that pupils were required to learn on an average of more than ten per day. Geography, is only one of the curricular fields that fourth-grade pupils study. If they are required to learn ten words per day in each of the fields, the number of words they were expected to learn each day could easily be overwhelming.

In connection with the article on "Of Plows and Plowing," five words appeared in the glossary, and some or all might be added to the pupils' vocabulary notebooks. Not all five words will be new words, and some pupils may know one or more meanings of such terms as *furrow* and *gang*.

If the notebook entry is well supported with illustrations, word retention will be greatly facilitated. Early in their vocabulary-notebook experience, pupils should be made cognizant of the value of illustrations as used in dictionaries. Wherever possible, pictures should be used in their notebooks just as they are in dictionaries. The pictures should be labeled and accompanied by an explanation. Pupils find labeling and writing explanations interesting and enlightening. Pictures may be obtained from many sources: catalogs, periodicals, newspapers, old texts, and so on. In addition, dictionaries frequently use quotations to illustrate how other people have used the word in question. Pupils might be encouraged to find illustrations of this sort and add them to their notebooks. They might copy sentences from the basic reader, or each pupil might write an illustrative sentence or two of his own.

Vocabulary Tests

All too often pupils obtain lower scores on vocabulary tests than on tests of reading comprehension. One explanation is that vocabulary tests require that the pupil have a fairly accurate word knowledge. Specific words have specific meanings. To understand and remember such specifics requires the diligent and deliberate kind of attention described thus far. Tests of reading comprehensions, on the other hand, provide a context that must be sufficiently clear and comprehensive to permit the pupil to read and understand.

It is apparent that vocabulary development must be ardently pursued. Words must be singled out for elaboration and study. The number and complexity of the words to be studied should be controlled so that they can be assimilated and used rather than merely verbalized. It is apparent, too, that the teacher's role in vocabulary building is crucial. If she knows what she is about, appreciates individual-learner differences, is versatile in her approach, systematic in her teaching, and demanding of accuracy, she will see noteworthy progress.

Concepts

As David H. Russell (23) points out, children's knowledge of concepts and vocabulary are closely related but not identical. The distinction often made between concepts and vocabulary (4, 5, 18) is based on the nature of the tests used. Russell says that: "When vocabulary tests develop more as tests of depth, breadth, precision, and application, they should come still closer to being tests of concepts understood by the child" (23, p. 124). Dale and Eicholz commented on the validity and reliability of their multiple-choice word-knowledge tests (6, pp. 3–4):

How Valid and Reliable Are These Findings?

1. Multiple choice tests have been found to be valid measures of word knowledge. The three-choice test, according to our study, provided data with no significant differences in means from four-choice tests.

2. Every test was expertly constructed according to a set of rules and was reviewed by two or three persons before testing was begun. These rules related to the nature of distractors, avoidance of spelling confusions, etc. The choices were phrased in the idiom of children.

3. Test data were carefully inspected by experienced teachers, and when scores seemed inaccurate, samples were hand-checked for scoring accuracy and the alternate choices carefully scrutinized. In cases of doubt, words were retested. Only rarely did these retests change results significantly.

4. At least 200 children were tested on each word in each grade. On the basis of twenty "control words" used on each 12th grade test, thereby increasing the sample to over 2800 students per test, we found that the scores were not altered by more than a −5% or +2%. Therefore, we assumed that a sample of 200 students per test was adequate to meet the desired accuracy and the practical demands of time and money.

5. The reliability of a series of tests was determined by the split-half technique. The results ranged between .68 and .80.

6. The tests themselves had "face" validity in that the instructions were simply to select the best of three definitions for a given word. Content validity was achieved by using the Winston Dictionary for Schools as a basis for definition. The validity of multiple choice tests is excellent when compared with other means of testing vocabulary, such as matching and identification tests, either written or oral.

7. Although we supervised some of the testing in its early phases, most of the later testing was administered by classroom teachers. We have every reason to believe that it was seriously done.

8. These scores may be accepted as national averages. Although many of the later tests were given in Ohio, at least 100 students in each sample of 200 were from other states. There are slight regional differences, but these are usually not statistically significant.

Roger Brown (2) reports a meager but suggestive study of the vocabulary of preschool children. His impression is that the nouns and verbs of the children "were more nearly consistent with the usual semantic definitions than the nouns and verbs of adults" (2, p. 247). He also compared the nouns and verbs found among the first thousand for adults but not for children using the Thorndike-Lorge list for adult usage and the Rinsland list for children. For children he found that the nouns had more "thing" character and were more "concrete" in the sense of naming narrow categories that had characteristic visual contour and size. There were a much larger percentage of action verbs in the children's list than in the adults'. In addition, Brown reported that:

> The children made correct use of a subclass of nouns—the mass nouns. These are words like *dirt, snow, milk,* and *rice* which are given different grammatical treatment from such particular nouns as *barn, house,* and *dog.* While we say *a barn,* for instance, we do not ordinarily speak of *a rice* but rather of *some rice.* The semantic difference between the two classes of nouns is suggested by the designations "mass" and "particular." Mass nouns usually name extended substances having no characteristic size or shape while particular nouns name objects having size and shape. (2, p. 250.)

Vocabulary vs. Concepts. It might be concluded that one of the subtle differences between a person's vocabulary and his stock of concepts is a semantic difference as exemplified by the differences noted by Brown between children's vocabularies and adults. Not only is there a "concrete-abstract" difference but also a "superordinate-subordinate" difference. As Ernest Horn (12) points out, to acquire constructs such as the Industrial Revolution or the effect of the sun position upon temperature presupposes the making of many subordinate constructs.

In addition to the "concrete" and "subordinate" character, vocabulary might be distinguished from a stock of concepts by the commonality of a word's semantic dimensions. A car may be distinguished from a truck on such a basis much more readily than subclasses of Chevrolets. A car and a truck have certain similar attributes such as wheels, motor, and radiator, but they also have others that are on a form-class level and are readily distinguishable, such as their size and shape and the number of wheels. To distinguish between an Impala sedan and a Belair sedan, however, requires recognition of more subtle differences. There are, of course, cases in which the category-attribute semantic commonality is not preserved. Still another difference between vocabulary and concepts could be reflected in the statement made by Russell after his review of concepts and vocabulary studies (23, p. 122): "Often such [vocabulary] knowledge is tested only by superficial recognition of the nearest synonym in a multiple-choice situation." From this it might be inferred that vocabulary can be measured by a check on a person's ability to note the more obvious likenesses and differences and produce a synonym or antonym. This knowledge is superficial when compared with a knowledge of concepts that discriminates carefully among synonyms, that can be supported by clear comparisons between words of a common denotation, and that distinguishes the differences in implications. *Webster's Dictionary of Synonyms* (24), which provides discriminating groups of words and three types of auxiliary information—analogous words, antonyms, and contrasted words—represents to a good degree a dictionary of "word concepts."

One more distinction may account for the difference between vocabulary and concepts. Vocabulary is usually described as being a composite of four vocabularies: hearing, speaking, reading, and writing vocabularies. The hearing vocabulary is for most people a first vocabulary. It is acquired first and is the largest vocabulary a pupil possesses until he reaches a reading facility comparable with so-called sixth-reader-level reading ability. Then the reading vocabulary tends to exceed the former. Hearing and reading vocabularies may be classified as receptor- or response-type vocabularies. The listener or reader needs only to recognize or respond to a spoken or printed word. He does not have to produce the word as he does when he speaks or writes. The hearing and reading vocabularies of most people are accordingly larger than their speaking and writing vocabularies.

Basic to each of these sensory vocabularies is the notion of an "understanding" vocabulary. The "understanding" vocabulary might be thought of as a fifth vocabulary. It represents the number of words that a person fully understands from the total that he hears, reads, speaks, or writes. It is the ratio of Understanding Vocabulary (U.V.) to Listening Vocabulary (L.V.) to Reading Vocabulary (R.V.) to Speaking Vocabulary (S.V.) and to Writing Vocabulary (W.V.) that is important. For Shakespeare the ratio may very well have approached 100 (U.V., L.V., R.V., S.V., W.V.). Unfortunately the widespread prevalence of verbalism most likely reduces this ratio for most pupils to 20 or less.

Vocabulary building is a must in any teaching circumstance, especially in a D-R-T-A. This is predominantly true because D-R-T-A's can from the very beginning of a pupil's reading study life foster attitudes favorable to vocabulary development and can produce habits of correct usage.

Words are the coins of the concept realm. They represent a first step in the hierarchy of concept attainment. Words are also the principal medium of thought and the tactical instrument of instruction. It behooves us, then, to make our word-teaching strategies sound, thorough, and orderly, since words are requisite to all learning and communication.

Development of Concepts

If words represent a first essential in conceptualization, it is apparent that concepts go well beyond vocabulary per se. On page 35 of Chapter 2, there is a definition of concepts by Ronald C. Johnson. At this point it seems appropriate to add the operational definition of a concept developed by Jerome S. Bruner *et al.* in their experimental work with strategies of concept attainment. They regard a concept as

a network of sign-significate inferences by which one goes beyond a set of *observed* criterial properties exhibited by an object or event to the class identity of the object or event in question, and thence to additional inferences about other *unobserved* properties of the object or event. We see an object that is red, shiny, and roundish and infer that it is an apple; we are then enabled to infer further that "if it is an apple, it is also edible, juicy, will rot if left unrefrigerated, etc." The working definition of a concept is the network of inferences that are or may be set into play by an act of categorization. (3, p. 244.)

To this they add that "Concept attainment is, to be sure, an aspect of what is conventionally called thinking. . . . But we have also urged a broader view: that virtually all cognitive activity involves and is dependent on the process of categorizing" (3, p. 246).

The critical factor in concept attainment, and this is especially significant to the classroom teacher, is *each pupil's capacity to infer* from experiences or environmental phenomena, to note likenesses and differences between and among them, and to classify or categorize the likenesses as belonging to the same class or kind.

The pupil who sees that the items in the chart below are all leaves has attained a *class* category. Most likely the attributes used to infer the category *leaves* are shape, color, and general appearance. The pupil who can identify certain of the leaves as *pinnate* is making inferences from other significates or grasping another network of sign-significate inferences. This pupil may at first select only leaves like the oak, the birch, and the elm. When he becomes more discriminate he may add to the pinnate group leaves like the ash, the sumac, the locust. Now he sees that a pinnate leaf is not only featherlike but also may have leaflets or primary divisions arranged on both sides of a common petiole or stalk by which a leaf is attached to the stem. Similarly, attributes must be identified to make sign-significate inferences about *palmate* leaves—the maple, the sycamore, the tulip, the aspen.

To go beyond this and make inferences using the more capricious attributes that lead to designating the oak as *venerable* and the willow as *gossamer* requires a considerable capacity to infer and to use various clues.

A concept, then, may often be represented in a word or in other symbols as in arithmetic and science. According to Bruner *et al.* (3, p. 245), "categorizing serves to cut down the diversity of objects and events that must be dealt with uniquely by an organism of limited capacities and that makes

LEAVES

Black Gum

American Elm   White Ash

        Dogwood

Black Willow

American Sycamore   Aspen

                                              Persimmon

Sumac Species

        American Beech

                                              Black Cherry

                                              Tulip Tree

Basswood

                                              Black Oak

White Oak   Pin Oak

                                              Sweet Birch

Chestnut Oak   River Birch

        Gray Birch

                                              Yellow Birch

Scarlet Oak   Red Maple   Sugar Maple

                                              Hickory

possible the sorting of functionally significant groupings in the world." A person of limited capacities may deal quite adequately with certain botanical elements in his environment if he knows only the general designate *leaves*. Others may need to make a much more functional sorting into *pinnate* or *palmate,* or into *broadleaf, conifer,* and *palm.*

The building of mental constructs is an arduous task that must be assiduously pursued and cannot be left to chance. Again the teacher is the principal catalyst in the learning situation. Much depends on her method of instruction. Much depends, too, on her capacity to infer and to categorize.

Manual Suggestions

The suggestions for concept development in the manual accompanying "Of Plows and Plowing" are as follows:

CONCEPTS

Early tools of man: The use of stick plows for so long a time can be used to alert pupils to the long period when man used tools before he knew how to make them. Sticks and stones of various kinds, sizes, and shapes were used to cut, to hammer, to wedge, and to lift. The Stone Age marks the time when man began to put handles on hammers and the like. In other words, he learned to join sticks and stones for more effective use. This, too, will be a good time to check on when man first used saws and shears.

Growing plants: While it is true that not everything a farmer grows needs to be started from seed each year (grapes, fruits, nuts), most of the things grown are started that way. It is true, too, that, while there are many different ways of raising plants, there are some things that are alike about farming. The concept of the cycle of *preparing the soil, planting the seed, cultivating, harvesting,* and *marketing* can be developed.

Corn: It appears quite certain that corn was not known in ancient times in the Old World. There is no reference to corn in the Bible. Yet in the New World, all the kinds of corn used today were already known when the first explorers arrived. Scientists found evidence supporting the idea that corn had existed in the New World as much as 4000 years ago. This is unusual when one considers the fact that corn could not take care of itself or could not grow wild. How corn influenced American history makes an interesting story as do such items as: *hot cornbread, hoe cake, corn pone,* and *corndodgers.*

The three general categories listed are but a few of those that might have been selected. The three, however, are of considerable consequence in this context of plows and plowing. As has been noted before, it is professionally sound to deal selectively with ideas rather than to overwhelm and negate by trying to develop many ideas. Quality should always take precedence, as should its attributes—thoroughness, integrity, frugality, and fruitfulness. In this instance, it is better to deal with the few specifics as recommended: sticks and stones (early tools of man), soil and plants (growing plants), and corn and man (corn).

Each of these concepts might be approached by turning to an encyclopedia such as *Compton's* or *World Book* or *Britannica.* There pupils will find information of the kind given in the manual for the teacher. Other material may be available in the form of books or pamphlets or periodicals. The amount and quality of the reading may be determined primarily by the pupils' interest, capacity, and motivation.

This kind of reading may very well be designated as research-type reading. To add to one's store of knowledge depends to a good degree on one's willingness and capacity to search for knowledge. Important at this level is the fact that attitudes and habits of research through reading are being established. Fourth-grade-level pupils are beginning to acquire skills that will be useful throughout school and throughout life.

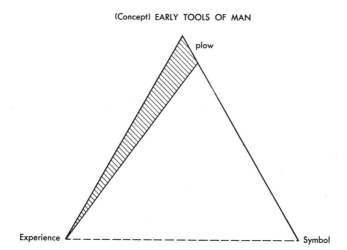

Figure 1

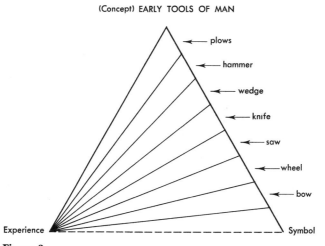

Figure 2

The early-tools-of-man concept might be illustrated by means of the semantic triangle. There it can be noted again that there is no direct connection between a symbol and an experience (see the dotted base line of the triangle below). The connection culminates at the apex of the triangle. The quality of the mental construction is determined by the nature of the work accomplished as the attributes of the early tools are determined, categorized, and labeled.

In Figure 1, the mental construct *early tools of man* is limited to plows. This pupil's semantic structure may be supported only by facts from the article "Of Plows and Plowing." Then again, it may be a rich and full concept of plows as shown by the number of crosslines and may reflect firsthand experience with plows on a farm, in a museum, or in models.

On the other hand, the concept *early tools of man* may be semantically triangled as shown in Figure 2.

In Figure 2 the mental construct *early tools of man* extends over a period of historical time and a goodly number of tools. While many tools are known, none is so thoroughly known as *plow* was for the pupil represented in Figure 1. Yet knowledge about each of the seven tools seems to be more than superficial, and, in the case of plows, knives, and wheels, it appears to be quite extensive.

In either case the triangle is not filled. The breadth and depth of knowledge about the early tools of man is far from exhausted. In fact, to *know all* might require the effort of a lifetime. As is true of so much in teaching and learning, the degree of thoroughness of learning is an arbitrary matter. Much depends on the teacher's skill, the pupil's interest and capacity, and the school's curriculum.

Organization of Ideas. In his article, "Do You Really Understand Brainstorming?," Sidney J. Parnes (21) describes the "kaleidoscopic" mind. This analogy of the kaleidoscope is a most fitting way to enlarge on the concept of the organization of ideas.

A kaleidoscope is a cylindrical device fitted at one end with pieces of crystal of different color and design. At the other end is a peephole through which the pieces of glass may be observed as they fall into various patterns. By manipulating the cylinder, the viewer can see countless patterns. If a new piece of crystal is added to the kaleidoscope, a slightly different pattern appears, and if the cylinder with the new crystal is manipulated a large number of new possible patterns can be seen.

The brain operates in a similar way. It stores millions of crystals of knowledge and experience. If one manipulates these crystals by turning on the brain with a stimulus, one can get countless patterns. The word *dog* can evoke countless numbers of dogs in the mind of a pupil listener. If the pupil is introduced to the concept of *pedigree* and *mongrel* many new combinations and arrangements can be obtained.

The teacher can, by adding new "crystals" to the mind and by manipulating or turning the kaleidoscopic mind's arrangement of the crystals, cause pupils to see countless new combinations. At first the judicial powers of the teacher are required to screen and develop the most likely ideas. However, in due time and with proper direction the young minds should learn to be selective.

Things and events tend to have a certain amount of organizational coherence. They have a harmony and a logic. It is the wise teacher who helps her pupils sense the harmony and grasp the logic of ideas. She can best give meaning to the definition of education drafted by O. Hobart Mowrer. Education, he says (17, p. 675), "is a means whereby one person (usually through language) helps another solve some problem more quickly than he himself could do on an unaided (trial-and-error) basis."

An isolated fact is of little if any value. Yet one of the most frequently voiced criticisms of education is that it involves too much parroting of undigested facts. Teachers deny this vehemently. Yet, as Dressel points out (9, p. 3), "Someone wisely remarked that we judge others by their words and deeds; ourselves by our thoughts and our intentions." Undoubtedly it is not the intent of teachers to require their pupils to parrot facts either orally or in written examinations. Furthermore, most teachers would readily agree with the Committee for the Yearbook, *The Integration of Educational Experiences* (20), that the integration or the organization of ideas is the central problem of education. And they would agree that the task is not that of teaching all patterns of organized knowledge but to develop students who will seek to do this for themselves.

This does not mean, of course, that organized experiences or ideas are not used. Rather, it means that their use must be tempered by the wise use of organizing ideas. If one is told to look at organized labor, one is apt to look at the who and what of organized labor. If, on the other hand, one is asked to see how labor is organizing, one looks to the process—the why and the when (timing) and the where (location) of things. Similarly, if asked to look at a picture of a gyroplane, one expects to see a plane; but, if one is told that the picture shows gyroplaning, one expects to see the process. Organized ideas are ideas that have been organized for one. Organizing ideas suggests that one does it oneself.

In teaching the organization of ideas and the organizing of ideas, it is the thinking of the student that is of chief concern. The teaching must be done in such a way that the student himself pulls the ideas together. This way, learning effectiveness can be improved. Studies of remembering and forgetting and of learning curves provide much evidence concerning the effect of organized ideas, particularly logical organized ideas, on retention. (1, 14.) Not only can organized material be better remembered and used, but also more can be remembered for a longer period of time. David R. Krathwohl (15, pp. 47–48), in reviewing George A. Miller's (16) analysis of the operation of memory in terms of information theory, points out that one can carry more wealth in a purse filled with dimes than in one filled with pennies. Similarly, pupils can use their memories to better advantage if they stock them with information that is organized and scaled according to complexity.

Some of the reasons cited for excessive verbalism in teaching in the 1940s are as true today as they were then (8, p. 11):

1. The prevailing psychology of learning, with its emphasis upon isolated units or items rather than upon wholes and relationships.

2. The rather general dependence upon textbooks which frequently are little more than compendia of detailed facts and of generalized summaries.

3. Overconfidence in teaching by telling, and in learning by memorizing what has been heard or read.

4. The rapidly expanding content of the curriculum, which encouraged teachers to attempt the impossible.

5. The poor quality of teacher-preparation and the limited experiential backgrounds of teachers.

6. The wasteful practice of individual recitations as contrasted with cooperative group activity.

7. The tendency to make of schooling an artificial thing by divorcing it from the activities of ordinary life.

After pointing out these negative aspects of the educational scene, the authors defined positive considerations to give evidence of the contribution that understanding (in good part obtained through the organizing of ideas) makes to learning. Learning with understanding, they said, is economical, relatively permanent, cumulative, and functional.

The manual recommendations dealing with the organizing of ideas are as follows:

Retention and use of ideas are greatly facilitated by organization. Order is a first law among thinkers and scholars. This picture-essay offers a number of organized ways for presenting information: by picture, by language, and by number.

1. The chronological order of plow changes is clearly illustrated. If the pictures were arranged in tight sequence, the observer could readily study the changes that occur and could compare each change. A topflight way to remember and understand is to note likenesses and differences. Here this can be done by a careful reexamination of the picture sequence.

2. The details provided by the language give the reader many opportunities for making meaningful associations. Linking the stick plow with the years before the time of Christ and the years after gives pupils a vivid associational clue. The deeds of the Dutch farmers of the seventeenth century can add much to aid retention if pupils make a brief study of the Dutch people of the time. This study can show the link between wooden moldboard plows and wind mills and ice skating without promoting the stereotype so odious to the Dutch of wooden shoes and the boy with his finger in the dyke.

3. A listing of dates or numbers found in the article provides another organizational structure. Remembering dates is easier to do when they are linked with the drama of many contemporary items. Here we have, in order, the time of Christ, 1600, 1785, 1800, late 1800s, 1920, 1948, 1956.

Here are three ways of establishing order and making relevant associations. Each puts information of a kind into perspective. Step by step, the ideas related to plows are programmed.

One of the best illustrative devices for dealing with ideas is a continuum. A common illustration is a hot-cold continuum—a line showing different degrees of variance from hot to cold.

In the article on plows a useful and graphic continuum or time-line can be made.

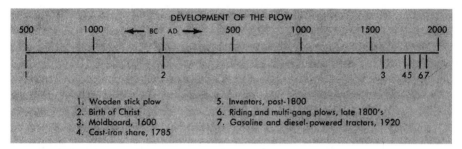

DEVELOPMENT OF THE PLOW

1. Wooden stick plow
2. Birth of Christ
3. Moldboard, 1600
4. Cast-iron share, 1785
5. Inventors, post-1800
6. Riding and multi-gang plows, late 1800's
7. Gasoline and diesel-powered tractors, 1920

To help pupils gain some appreciation for the time factor, the A.D. part of the line can be marked for each 100 years. The pupils can be asked to count each hundred as a mark is made on the line. For instance, start with the year 100 and proceed by having the pupils give the century number.

B.C.	A.D.							
5000 B.C.	100	200	300	400	500	1000	1500	1966

The length of the counting session plus the increase in the numbers seems to make a rather vivid impression on pupils. Even though their appreciation of the passing of centuries will not be as profound as it will be when they are nineteen, it will be better than would be true otherwise. Pupils will better grasp the idea that man as a toolmaker has made most of his progress during the last two centuries. Continuum-type organizing of ideas helps illustrate how gradations of learning are accomplished from abecedarian memory through relatively elemental understanding to a degree of mastery approaching maximum knowledge. It should be clear that the organizing of ideas and the resultant knowledge gained may vary greatly in breadth and richness, in subtlety and complexity, in remoteness, or in the intellectual and social distance pupils may be called upon to span in their thinking and evaluating. It should be clear also that instruction must be planned with full awareness of this variability and directed toward appropriate levels.

Additional Reading. Teachers may be astonished by the eagerness and zest with which pupils read articles like "Of Plows and Plowing" in a so-called reading period. By the time they reach fourth-reader-level competency they will welcome a reading diet that is varied and rich and challenging. While it is true that narrative material or stories can be varied in style and nature, it is also true that they represent one type of material. As the world around them comes into increasing perspective, as the past unfolds with greater clarity, as the future in space, medicine, and science comes into credulous focus, nine-year-olds demand and will respond to informational material.

Teachers unskilled in the art of individualized reading instruction may be even more astonished by the desire of nine-year-olds to read other similar materials. Teachers who are skilled in this art have clearly witnessed the power and sustained drive of personal interests and motivation, and they recognize "wide reading" as the outcome of reading instruction.

The following recommendations are given for extending and refining the ideas in "Of Plows and Plowing":

Additional Reading. Children's understanding of time spans may be enhanced by White's *Prehistoric America* and Herman and Nina Schneider's *Rocks, Rivers and the Changing Earth* (New York: William R. Scott, 1952). *Dustbowl: The Story of Man on the Great Plains* (New York: Coward-McCann, 1958), by Patricia Lauber, provides information about the results of overplowing and other misuses of land in the plains area.

The three books mentioned are but a small sample of the kinds of books available and the kinds of pupil interests that may be awakened. These books may be used by the teacher to spark the wide-reading flame into a roaring fire. This is especially apt to happen if an attractive, well-stocked library is the hub of the school. It is comforting to note that today many of the newer schools place the library in the center, so that it becomes the structural as well as the educational hub of the building. No longer is the cafeteria the place of central prominence. All corridors funnel into the library. Food for the mind has come into its own and, insofar as schools are concerned, is replacing in importance food for the body.

SUMMARY

Improving a program of reading instruction usually involves changes in practice. The implementation of such changes and practices is in good part the responsibility of authorities in the field of reading. One of the best ways for authorities to effect changes is to set forth specific recommendations of methodology and practices with sufficient abundance and clarity that all who wish to may understand them and use them. The production of a basic series of readers provides authorities with an excellent opportunity to give teachers the kind of help they need.

A professional book on teaching reading, like this book, cannot discuss all the ideas and specifics encompassed in a basic-reader series. It can, though, in a very practical way present both theory and principle along with certain illustrative practices. When this is done there should be no difference between the psychology of reading instruction and the pedagogical practices. In this chapter, extending and refining were discussed in an attempt to link theory and practice. One of the chief reasons why reading instruction at the high school and college levels is recommended is to extend and refine ideas in keeping with the increased maturity and experience of the students. This being the case, all the practices recommended in this chapter should be used and should be fruitful.

A common complaint among teachers is what to do with Groups II and III while Group I is being directed in a reading-thinking activity. Teachers who see the value of extending and refining activities and follow practices such as those recommended will not ask such a question. On the contrary, they are apt to complain about the shortness of the school day and the many demands of the rest of the school curriculum. In addition, teachers who use such manual instructions as those described in this chapter will maintain such a busy classroom and make such wise use of the basic readers and the library that none of the pupils will be able to finish the materials geared for his level.

The emphasis on meanings and relationships and activities can contribute greatly to an individual's learning. Children can be led to seek greater breadth and depth of knowledge if learning is based on their experiences.

The specific directions and suggestions contribute to skill development. Weaknesses or deficiencies noted during the process part of the D-R-T-A can be corrected and developed into sound reading habits conducive to efficient learning. In all this the role of the teacher is crucial. Skill development, extending and refining of concepts, acquiring interests and attitudes, and, above all, self-reliance cannot be left to chance. The extending and refining time of a D-R-T-A is teaching time.

REFERENCES

1. Bartlett, F. C. *Remembering*, London, Cambridge University Press, 1932.
2. Brown, Roger, *Words and Things*, New York, The Free Press, 1958.
3. Bruner, Jerome S., Jacqueline J. Goodnow, and George A. Austin, *A Study of Thinking*, New York, Wiley, 1956.
4. Cronbach, L. J., "Analysis of Techniques for Diagnostic Vocabulary Testing," *Journal of Educational Research, 36* (1942), 206–217.
5. Cronbach, L. J., "Measuring Knowledge of Precise Word Meaning," *Journal of Educational Research, 36* (1943), 528–534.
6. Dale, Edgar, and Gerhard Eicholz, *Children's Knowledge of Words*, Columbus, Ohio, Ohio State University, 1961.
7. Dewey, John, *How We Think*, New York, Heath, 1933.
8. Douglass, Harl R., and Herbert F. Spitzer, "The Importance of Teaching for Understanding," *The Measurement of Understanding*, Forty-fifth Yearbook of the National Society for the Study of Education, Part I, Chicago, University of Chicago Press, 1946.

9. Dressel, Paul L., "The Meaning and Significance of Integration," *The Integration of Educational Experiences,* Fifty-seventh Yearbook of the National Society for the Study of Education, Part III, Chicago, University of Chicago Press, 1958.

10. Goodlad, John I., and Robert H. Anderson, *The Nongraded Elementary School,* New York, Harcourt, Brace & World, 1959.

11. Greene, Harry A., "Measuring Comprehension of Content Material," *Report of the Society's Committee on Silent Reading,* Twentieth Yearbook of the National Society for the Study of Education, Part II, Chicago: University of Chicago Press, 1921.

12. Horn, Ernest, "Language and Meaning," *The Psychology of Learning,* Forty-first Yearbook of the National Society for the Study of Education, Part II, Chicago, University of Chicago Press, 1942.

13. Horn, Ernest, *Methods of Instruction in the Social Studies.* New York, Scribner's 1937.

14. Katona, George, *Organizing and Memorizing,* New York, Columbia University Press, 1940.

15. Krathwohl, David R., "The Psychological Bases for Integration," *The Integration of Educational Experiences,* Fifty-seventh Yearbook of the National Society for the Study of Education, Part III, Chicago, University of Chicago Press, 1958.

16. Miller, George A., "Information and Memory," *Scientific American,* CXCV (1956), 42–57.

17. Mowrer, O. Hobart, "The Psychologist Looks at Language," *The American Psychologist, 9* (November, 1954), 660–694.

18. National Conference on Research in English, *Child Development and the Language Arts,* prepared by an NCRE committee, David Russell, Chaiman, Champaign, Ill., National Council of Teachers of English, 1953.

19. National Conference on Research in English, *Vocabulary Problems in the Elementary School,* prepared by an NCRE committee, J. Conrad Seegers, Chairman, Chicago, Scott, Foresman, 1939.

20. National Society for the Study of Education, *The Integration of Educational Experiences,* Fifty-seventh Yearbook of the National Society for the Study of Education, Part III, Chicago, University of Chicago Press, 1958.

21. Parnes, Sidney J., "Do You Really Understand Brainstorming?," *A Source Book for Creative Thinking,* Sidney J. Parnes and Harold F. Harding, eds., New York, Scribner's, 1962.

22. Ritter, Olive P., *Repetition, Spread, and Meanings of Unusual, Difficult, and Technical Terms in Fourth-Grade Geography Texts,* Doctoral dissertation, Iowa City, Iowa, University of Iowa, 1941.

23. Russell, David H., *Children's Thinking,* Boston, Ginn, 1956.

24. *Webster's Dictionary of Synonyms,* Springfield, Mass., Merriam, 1942.

PART III
INDIVIDUALIZED
INSTRUCTION

Chapter 5 Individualized Reading Instruction

How to direct a reading-thinking activity in a group situation through the use of a basic-reader program is described at length in Chapters 2, 3, and 4. The decision to discuss the "group" approach first is based on instructional practices across the country. The vast majority of schools use basic readers as a primary source of materials for reading-instruction purposes. And, in the vast majority of classrooms, basic-reading instruction is accomplished by organizing classes into groups.

Well-constructed basic readers can be ideal for the purpose of teaching reading as a thinking process. In Chapter 2, the continuity, content, graphic aids, readability controls, and skill-development potentials of basic readers are discussed, and it is pointed out that basic readers that reflect high standards of structure lend themselves well to the purpose of teaching reading. Materials are paced so as to permit a teacher to use them to develop thinking readers. While this primary purpose of reading instruction is being accomplished, the pupils are also learning word-attack skills, dictionary skills, and perception skills. These skills are important, but they play a secondary role in the total reading process, and no amount of rationalization should ever be allowed to obscure this fact. Statements such as, "We believe in reading for meaning, too, but . . ." should tip off the alert reader. There are no *if's* and *but's* about reading; it is a communication skill and this is how it should be taught and used.

Basic readers as a source of materials play a significant role in teaching reading as a thinking process. However, it is the *dynamics of the group* that makes the real difference. Insofar as materials are concerned, the one condition that needs to be met in a group-Directed Reading-Thinking Activity is that all in the group read and examine the *same* material at the *same* time. This means that almost any book—history, science, arithmetic, geography, or fiction—can be used as long as all in the group have a copy. For example, a D-R-T-A could be accomplished if all in a group were reading *Charlotte's Web* or a story in *Jack and Jill* or an item in *My Weekly Reader*.

The principal pedagogical difference is between *group* instruction and *individualized* instruction, *not* between basic readers and a library. If this distinction is kept in mind, the value of the two approaches can be kept in proper focus, and the wild charges and countercharges of extremists in both camps can be shown to be no more than that.

This is not to imply that many of the charges leveled at the misuse of basic readers by the all-out advocates of individualized instruction are not merited. The practices endorsed by many basic-reader programs are in direct violation of sound reading-thinking processes. By way of illustration, one of the practices advocated that is almost unbelievable is concerned with vocabulary controls and the teaching of so-called new words prior to the reading of a basic-reader story. Why, for so many years, have people spent endless hours writing basic-reader materials using such vocabulary controls as (1) introducing only two new words on a page, (2) separating each new word introduction by at least twenty running words, (3) reusing the words a minimum number of times throughout a basic reader, (4) doing extensive vocabulary studies to be sure the words used are the most common words in children's speaking-meaning vocabulary, and (5) using picture clues to support new words wherever possible? Anyone who has tried his hand at preparing basic-reader materials that meet these criteria knows what a demanding task it is.

In addition, each basic-reader system presents a carefully developed word-recognition training program. Word-attack skills have been studied and restudied by basic-reader authors and organized and reorganized in an effort to teach the skills in a "logical" order. Studybooks, skillbooks, and special booklets have been developed to teach the skills. Invariably, basic-reader teachers' manuals supply additional word-attack skill exercises to supplement the studybooks. All this is done to teach children how to attack words and how to do so on their own (11). The objective is praiseworthy— to develop independent readers. Why, then, after taking all these precautions, are the teaching practices in direct contradiction to the theory? Why? The facts in the case lead to only one verdict: Guilty. Vocabulary controls are used so that the number of "new" words introduced in story context will not overwhelm or swamp the neophyte reader. Word-attack skills are "logically" organized and taught on a regular and continuous basis so that the reader can attack words on his own. Why, then, teach these few carefully selected and introduced words in advance of the reading of a story to pupils who are being trained to attack words on their own?

Another equally damaging practice that merits all the outrage heaped upon most basic readers is that of "teacher-question–pupil-parrot," a practice that denies pupils the opportunity to think, to weigh evidence, to make educated assumptions, and to prove or disprove.

Mary Austin and Coleman Morrison (4) have shown that most of the teachers graduating from teacher-training schools are not adequately prepared to teach reading. This being the case, the new teachers lean heavily on teachers' manuals for guidance and know-how. As a result, the bad practices referred to are perpetuated, and they are uprooted only in those situations where wise supervision is available or where expert reading-consultant services are obtained.

Both procedures—group-type D-R-T-A and individualized D-R-T-A—have a rightful place in a sound reading program. In the group situation each member of the group deals with the same material at the same time, whereas in the individualized activity each pupil may be reading a different kind of material.

BOUNDARIES OF A GROUP D-R-T-A

What are the boundaries of the group-type and the individualized approaches? It seems best to review the boundaries of the group activity again so that they may be contrasted with the individually directed activities.

1. Pupils are grouped for instruction on the basis of reading appraisals that have placed them at about the same instructional level. Both informal procedures and standardized test results may be used. There are, generally speaking, two kinds of informal inventory procedures. First, each group-directed D-R-T-A provides the medium for appraising the reading performance of each member of the group. One of the most common rules-of-thumb in teaching is that "all teaching is diagnostic." This may be adapted to a D-R-T-A: each group-directed reading-thinking activity is diagnostic. The concept is easy to understand. The teacher is in a position to observe each member of the group in his ability to set purposes, to adjust rate to purposes, to attack words and to use a glossary, and to read orally to prove or disprove. Furthermore, this inventory can be made again and again as each successive D-R-T-A is accomplished. As any statistician will confirm, a "truer" norm can be determined, the larger the number of instances used. (See Chapter 11, "Evaluation.") In other words, the D-R-T-A inventories are not of the "one-time magic garden" variety.

A more "formal" Informal Reading Inventory can be used to help place those few pupils who seem to defy placement analysis through the group D-R-T-A situations. An Informal Reading Inventory (IRI) (5, pp. 438–487) is designed for use on an individual basis. It consists of short selections usually chosen from a basic-reader series. Two selections at a level are used: one to be read silently, one orally. A set of questions to check comprehension is used following the reading of each selection. The practice is to start a pupil at a level at which he can read and have him proceed from level to level until he is frustrated. Informal inventories of the type referred to can be prepared by a teacher. In essence, such inventories are "homemade" versions of the *Durrell-Sullivan Reading Capacity Test.*[1] Standardized test scores may be used if a single score is not interpreted as an exact indication of reading level (8). Of the three procedures, the "diagnostic" aspect of each D-R-T-A provides the most useful information. It best takes into account the changes and the progress made during the school year, and it does this because of the frequency of observation.

2. Group size varies from situation to situation, but it is commonly accepted that, in order that each pupil may participate actively, the group number no more than ten or twelve.

As was evident in the reports on D-R-T-A's in Chapter 3, participation in the "predicting-reading-proving" cycles is vital to successful instruction and learning. Each pupil needs to become involved as the cycle recurs during the reading session. Pupils participate actively throughout the proving process. One factor that obviously can limit pupil participation is group size.

3. All pupils in the group read the same material (basic-reader story) at the same time and do so under teacher direction. This is one of the cardinal virtues of a group D-R-T-A. It allows pupils to compare, contrast, collate, balance, liken, match, and rivet their personal stock of experiences and knowledge. Each member of a group can compare his predictions with those of others to see how different members manipulated story information, to compare his conclusions with those reached by others, to evaluate the skills he has used and note whether or not others used the same skills and why, and to scrutinize the way others extended and refined concepts and generalizations gained through the reading. Furthermore, in a group where all deal with the same material, authority for the acceptance of proof rests with the group as well as with the teacher. Each member serves as an auditor, examining and weighing proofs and conclusions presented—frequently by oral rereading.

4. Purposes for reading are declared by the pupils. At times all may read to accomplish the same purpose. At times each may have an individual purpose. At times two or three in the group may have the same purpose. The authority to comment on each pupil's conjectures by referring to the facts at hand rests with the group. Each pupil is encouraged to have the strength of his convictions until proved right or wrong.

At every step in the D-R-T-A, the reader has to take into account the content—its parts, its problems, its perplexities—and adjust his purposes accordingly. Habits of thoughtfulness, carefulness, and thoroughness need to be established early so that they become deep-seated and persistent.

The teacher takes full advantage of the content, whether fiction or non-

[1] Published by World Book Publishing Co., Yonkers-on-Hudson, New York, 1937.

fiction, to stir pupil thinking: to get it going, to arouse intellectual excitement, and to give it a momentum that will maintain the readers to the end. All this is best accomplished in the lively give and take of a group situation. Then the ideas, experiences, and information of the members of the group spark the reading, dominate the questioning attitude and the searching, and end in understanding.

5. Answers found are reported to and discussed with the group. Again, the authority to accept or reject rests in the group. Lines in the story may be read orally to the group to prove points.

Interestingly enough, the intellectual responsibility afforded the children by this method produces an astonishing amount of integrity. Seldom do the conjectures voiced or the conclusions reached venture beyond the evidence. There are few wild, irrelevant hypotheses or conclusions—only what might be termed "educated guesses" and "educated conclusions." This is true largely because the reading is aimed at the discovery of facts or ideas that will serve their purposes, and because the group, as well as the content, serves as the monitor for each member's thinking.

6. The teacher directs the reading-thinking process with such provocative queries as, "What do you think? Why do you think so? What do you think will happen next?" She stands by during the silent reading to give help as requested with word-attack needs and in clarifying meanings. She does not teach so-called new words or concepts in isolation before a story is read. Since she is using material that is structured according to controls of vocabulary, new concepts, and interests, she allows her pupils to put their word-attack skills and comprehension skills to work. One of the chief reasons why basic readers are so carefully structured is to permit pupils to use the skills they have learned.

7. Fundamental skill training in word attack and in comprehension is provided as prepared in a systematized studybook program. Some pupils do all of the activities; some do most of them; some do only a few.

8. Additional skill activities are suggested in an accompanying teachers' edition. In addition, the teachers' edition defines a variety of methods for directing the reading-thinking process for each story and each article.

9. Related activities are recommended in the teachers' edition as follow-up work subsequent to the reading of a story or article.

10. Other materials are recommended to be read either in school or at home.

Items 3 through 6 differ sharply from those commonly practiced where basic readers are used. During the past three decades many teachers have been encouraged in such malpractices as motivating the reading of a story by telling part of the story, explaining to pupils that the story to be read is a surprise story, asking pupils to read to see what Tom or Dick or Harry said, saying that the first sentence on the next page will tell what happened and when it happened, and telling children what the story is about.

These malpractices resulted in teaching and reading that became, in the words of Laura Zerbes (33), "uncreative by responding to requirements, following directions, and waiting to be told what to do." This kind of intellectual stripping down in the erroneous belief that children cannot think foisted on teachers and in turn on children a "waiting to be told" and a "rote parroting" attitude and performance. Creative teaching of reading, on the other hand, is intended to direct children to think about implications, to consider their ideas and test them as they read and think, and to realize that reading is a continuous and creative process (25).

BOUNDARIES OF AN INDIVIDUALIZED D-R-T-A

It should be apparent that *boundary* as used here does not mean limits so clearly ascertained and charted that one may not stray across them. Rather, the boundaries represent arbitrarily stated requisites prescribed so as to give explicit directions or clear guidance to those who accept them. The intent is to prevent confusion, conflict, and even overlapping.

The boundaries of an individualized D-R-T-A are as follows:

1. Pupils are not placed in traditional groups. Each pupil is free to work without interruption in order to pursue an interest. At times two, three, or more may work together to pursue the same interest. At other times one or all may work alone.

2. The materials read are in a large measure self-selected by the pupil(s). Included for selection are textbooks in other curriculum areas, trade books, basic readers, newspapers, and magazines—material of different degrees of complexity and covering a wide range of interests.

3. Purposes for reading are largely self-declared and reflect each pupil's interests, abilities, and needs. Purposes may vary from vague, undefined desires for reading fiction to specifically declared goals requiring versatility in rate adjustment such as when reading to skim, to scan, or to study.

4. The self-reliance and responsibility essential to self-declared purposes for reading are equally as essential in dealing with *answers*. A completely self-contained pupil, sufficient unto himself, would certainly be a rare person. Individuals are social-minded. They want to discuss what they read and profit by the discussion; they want to *share* with others. An ability to share with others requires use of and control over two other facets of the language arts—speaking and writing. Preparing and presenting reports is no easy task. Many skills are involved and need to be learned.

5. The teacher is constantly available to give help as requested in comprehension and in attacking words not recognized on sight.

6. Skill training is provided as needed in word recognition, in comprehension, and in concept development. The materials used for specific skill training may be either teacher-prepared or studybook-designed as part of a basic-reader program or of other commercial workbooks.

Short, private sessions with pupils are held to clear up immediate needs.

These sessions are either requested by the pupil or are initiated by the teacher in teacher-check periods. These short sessions help fix or clarify a skill, but they serve chiefly as a means for identifying skill shortcomings that will require systematic instruction to overcome. The systematic instruction may be done either individually or in small groups made up of pupils with similar needs.

7. Pupil as well as teacher records are kept of reading done, purposes accomplished, and needs declared and resolved. Pupil schedules are maintained.

8. Teacher pacing is necessary to direct each child to locate materials in keeping with his interests and skills, to develop purposes that are clearly defined, to organize knowledge gained, to appraise understandings, to share adequately with others, to provide needed skill training, and to foster interests in wide reading. Teacher pacing proceeds at a tempo that will assure a maximum amount of success and a minimum amount of frustration for each pupil.

9. Communication skills are refined as pupils learn to listen attentively to reports or audience reading and to ask intelligent questions about what they heard. Writing skills are similarly refined as pupils learn to prepare reports and to keep records. Speaking skills are also refined as studied reports are presented by oral reading or from memory, as extemporaneous speeches are given from outlines or notes, as impromptu talks are delivered, or as creative dramatic presentations are improvised.

Even this specific defining of boundaries shows that there is a great deal of overlap between the two approaches. The group program includes a great deal of individual thinking, reading, and reasoning, and the individualized program includes much group work.

It should be apparent, too, that both approaches are essential to a well-rounded reading program. The group-training sessions, using basic-reader material, provide fundamental skill training in reading and thinking and help prepare each pupil to operate individually. A group provides one kind of medium in which an individual can discover the effectiveness of his thinking and reading. Pupils can learn that it is almost as useful to listen to others making predictions or hypotheses as it is to make their own. It is equally as useful to learn when to agree and when to disagree, when to criticize and when to approve, when to prove and when to disprove. An aim of group reading and thinking is for the individual to learn ways of acting (reading-thinking) that will be useful to him when he is on his own.

TEACHER'S ATTITUDE

Most essential to the successful use of individualized instruction is the teacher's attitude. It must be favorable and reflect understanding of the following:

1. Children can and will select material in which they are interested.

They can assess materials and decide what will fit their likes and their abilities. They do this in terms of their own interests, attitudes, experiences, and concepts.

2. Children will read to understand, and they will enjoy the material they select to satisfy their curiosities. As in the group-directed reading-thinking sessions, the pupils will have purposes to accomplish, even though they may not be forged and patented through the group-thinking process.

3. Interest in self-selection and the reading of materials selected will vary from individual to individual, just as the individuals themselves may vary from day to day. Performance will be no more uniform than it is when other methods are used.

4. Pupils will want to share what they have read. In situations where children are encouraged to do their own thinking, reading, and reflecting, they are eager to share with their peers and with others.

5. Teacher pacing is needed by all pupils—the bright as well as the slow. The teacher needs to provide materials and, to whatever degree possible, experiences in keeping with each child's level of maturity. In short, actual teaching is done.

Some teachers may question the efficiency of basic readers, and some may even feel incompetent to conduct individualized instruction. Such feelings of incompetency may be experienced as a sense of guilt. The feelings should be recognized as stemming from a misuse of basic readers. During the process of reconstructing reading-thinking standards, the abandoning of long-established basic-reader codes may cause some anxiety. But change and reconstruction usually involve some danger. The great danger, however, is to deny individuals the opportunity to develop the ability and inclination to read and to think.

KNOW CHILD GROWTH AND DEVELOPMENT

The teacher must know as much as possible about the growth patterns, social and personal, of each child. But this is not enough, because, if the pacing of each pupil's progress is to be governed by his maturity, the teacher needs some maturity yardstick. Each pupil encouraged to do so will explore his environment and seek experiences that fit his maturity. For the teacher to provide materials and experiences in keeping with pupil's maturity and at a pace that will assure success, she must make decisions not only about what to offer but also when, how much, and how soon. To do this she must be informed about the development of children and the diversity of their interests and needs.

Directing reading activities is not a matter of external imposition but a freeing of each child's curiosity, creativity, and interests so that each may achieve his own most adequate fulfillment. Study should reveal that the learnings and achievements of children are fluid and moving, changing from day to day and from hour to hour. For years children suffered from an invidious comparison with adults—they are not little adults! It is equally as harmful to assume that a child of a given age has certain purposes and interests that can be cultivated just as they stand (9, p. 15). Rather, the interests and tastes must be viewed in the light of larger, more encompassing growth processes. John I. Goodlad and Robert H. Anderson put it this way (10, p. 3):

> The realities of child development defy the rigorous ordering of children's abilities and attainments into conventional graded structure. For example, in the average first grade there is a spread of four years in pupil readiness to learn as suggested by mental age data. As the pupils progress through the grades, the span in readiness widens. Furthermore, a single child does not progress all of a piece. . . .

They conclude their chapter on "The Child and Procrustean Standards" with certain generalizations that are relevant here in this effort to convince teachers that individualized instruction in reading has advantages that no basic-reader series has if differences among children are appreciated. They say (10, pp. 27–28):

> 3. The achievement range among pupils begins to approximate the range in intellectual readiness to learn soon after first-grade children are exposed to reasonably normal school instruction.
> 4. Differing abilities, interests, and opportunities among children cause the range in certain specific attainments to surpass the range in general achievement.
> 5. Individual children's achievement patterns differ markedly from learning area to learning area.
> 6. By the time children reach the intermediate elementary grades, the range in intellectual readiness to learn and in most areas of achievement is as great as or greater than the number designating the grade level.

Garrett Hardin quotes Elbert Hubbard as saying that (13, p. 22): "An opportunist is a man who takes the lemons that fate has handed him and opens up a lemonade stand." The philosophy suggested by this remark could effect a system of reading instruction that, insofar as human variability is concerned, might reach a very high level, for the range of intelligence and achievement of the "lemons" is considerable.

The ultimate in instruction is to so fit to each individual the curriculum, the learning time, and the teaching methods that his unique aptitudes, abilities, and interests are best realized. This kind of utopia seems beyond attainment. As a result we continue to face the need for *standards,* and we risk interpreting norms as standards. By adapting standards, we in turn give up some variety and have to contend with academic failure, frustration, misery, truancy, and delinquency. These conditions are especially true in the content areas—arithmetic, science, social science, geography—which represent subjects and bodies of knowledge that are organized and systematized in structure from simple to complex.

Reading, however, is not a subject. To be able to read at even the most mature level is to have command over skills and abilities that enable one to proceed, as William S. Gray and Bernice Rogers state (12, p. 236), "with reasonable ease and understanding in grasping and interpreting meanings, in reacting rationally to the ideas apprehended, and in applying his ideas with sound judgment and reasoning." Reading instruction is in the unique position of lending itself to individualized instruction, for the standards to be attained are clearly paced by each pupil's own resources and limitations, or as Horn states (14, p. 383), "the student's 'funds'—his interest and mind set, experience, language abilities, and habits of work."

PROVIDE BOOKS AND MORE BOOKS

If children are to seek and select, they must have books and materials among which to seek and from which to select. Textbooks, story books, encyclopedias, magazines, and newspapers at many levels of difficulty are required.

With the advent of paperbound books and the organization of book clubs for children, it is not uncommon to find a goodly number of books for children in home libraries. It has been found that a good practice, useful in promoting wide reading, is to invite children to bring to school books from their home libraries so that others may share what they have enjoyed.

Even though the number of librarians is on the increase, selecting materials continues to be a responsibility of teachers. Where librarians are available, the selecting process is enhanced. Librarians are quite intimately familiar with standards of selection. The American Association of School Librarians recommended that specific criteria for selection of materials be established in each school. Miriam Peterson suggested that the following factors be considered when selecting a book (22, p. 68): "literary quality; scope and content; character portrayal and plot construction of fiction; accuracy of fact and organization of material in nonfiction; freedom from bias; physical format including print, paper, and illustrations; suitability of style and presentation; appeal; and curricular and personal value."

Nancy Larrick presents an interesting discussion on the need to measure books objectively for literary and artistic merit when selecting books for children. She also selected two quotations from Paul Hazard's *Books, Children and Men* that warrant repeating, because the book is one of those rare treasures that appear on the literary scene so infrequently (16, p. 197):

"I like books," he says, ". . . that offer to children an intuitive and direct way of knowledge, a simple beauty capable of being perceived immediately, arousing in their souls a vibration which will endure all their lives."
And again, "I like books that set in action truths worthy of lasting forever, and of inspiring one's whole inner life. . . ."

When funds are limited, the problem of providing material can be quite challenging. In fact, even when funds are almost unlimited there is now such an abundance of material that the problem of selection is a thorny one. Since 1935 the *Library Journal* has tried to examine every children's book published and to give each a professional appraisal. Periodically, the *Journal* publishes a special listing of books with complete reviews. Copies of this list can be obtained for fifty cents each, net postpaid, by writing to *Library Journal,* 62 West 45th Street, New York, N.Y. 10036. Since 1938, the American Library Association (1) has published a "Subject Index to Books for Primary Grades," which is periodically revised and expanded. In 1960 the National Council of Teachers of English (20) published a bulletin called *The Use of Paperbound Books.*

The *Combined Book Exhibit* (7) list including the recent books of forty-seven publishers on "Learning to Live" is an excellent source of selected, classified, graded, annotated, and indexed materials. The Madison Public Schools Curriculum Department (19) has published a bulletin on *Magazines for Elementary Grades.* This bulletin also has a section listing comic magazines as entertaining, informational, super-thrilling, and undesirable. Certain school systems publish lists of books for use by teachers who are teaching reading on an individualized basis. An excellent example of such work is that made available by the Board of Education of the City of New York (21): *Books for Children to Read.* Not to be overlooked are lists made available by publishing houses, Chambers of Commerce, State Departments of Public Relations, industry, and so on. All usually can be obtained for the asking.

KNOW BOOKS AND MATERIALS

"Love for reading is not taught, it is created; not required, but inspired; not demanded, but exemplified; not exacted, but quickened; not solicited, but activated" (26, p. 4). To do this, the teacher must know materials. She must have read most of the material herself and enjoyed reading to the point where she is enthusiastic about what she has read and knows to whom to recommend what.

A pupil's interest will vary and fluctuate: today, a book about shells; tomorrow, one about the moon; the day after, Olivia E. Coolidge's *The Wings of Icarus;* next week, Ferdinand C. Lane's *All About the Sea.*

On the other hand, as children are maturing in reading ability and in interests, they are also maturing in their willingness to pursue one interest or hobby. An area of interest may then occupy them for weeks as they read and learn and read some more.

It has been estimated that there should be available in the classroom a minimum of five books per child, and that this supply should be replenished on a rotation basis. Periodicals such as *Children's Digest, Highlights for Children,* and *Geographic School Bulletins* should also be on hand. One or two sets of a scholarly encyclopedia are essential, as are anthologies of poetry and folk tales, newspapers like *My Weekly Reader,* a local paper, and periodicals like *Life, Look, National Geographic,* and *Nature Magazine.* A good way to supplement the classroom library is to buy a hundred post cards and write to various publishing houses, museums, industries, Chambers of Commerce, Departments of Health, Education, and so on, for free materials.

While teachers are not amateur psychiatrists, they learn many things about children's needs and may want to recommend specific books such as *Lassie Come Home* by Eric Knight or *Silk and Satin Lane* by Esther Wood. Children have sufficient insight to appreciate how others meet and resolve problems similar to theirs. They realize full well that they do not have to dash in front of a moving car to know the consequences. Learning through the experiences of others is not new to them, nor is learning through books and stories. Hardly a child enters school who has not heard, read, or been told some stories.

In "When Teachers Read, Children Read" May Hill Arbuthnot says (2, p. 82): "Whatever we enjoy we feel others should enjoy also. Whether it is books, art, music, or baseball, we feel the urge to share our enthusiasm. So the teacher who likes to read spreads a contagious liking for books among her children." The author goes on to make a strong plea for teacher "reading aloud" as one of the best ways to spread enthusiasm for books. This is one of the tried and true methods, as almost any teacher will confirm, to charm and attract pupils to books.

While "to charm and attract" may be the primary reason for a teacher's oral reading of Ellis Credle's *Down, Down the Mountain* or *Henry Huggins* by Beverly Cleary or E. B. White's *Charlotte's Web* or Joseph Krumgold's *Onion John,* other reasons are almost equally important. It helps fill the gap between a pupil's reading ability and his level of understanding and enjoyment, it helps him to enjoy a book he might otherwise miss, and it stirs in him a strong receptive feeling to hear someone read aloud with warmth and zest. May Hill Arbuthnot also makes a timely plea in behalf of the bookish teacher who brings to school the adult books she is reading and shares her enthusiasm about the books with her students. Children are inspired to reach out and grow into reading. As Thoreau put it so wisely: "You will find at the inn in Trochate excellent bread, meat, and wine, provided you bring them with you."

According to Paul Witty, "More than two hundred studies of the reading interests of children and youth have been made from 1893, when M. B. C. True reported 'What My Pupils Read', to the present time. . . ." (31, p. 134). The studies show that factors such as age, health, home training, sex, and mental capacity influence the type and amount of reading boys and girls do. A recent study on "Boys' Reading Interests" reported by the Committee on Research Studies of the Los Angeles City School Districts is illustrative. The study was conducted to discover the present (1961) reading interests of elementary school boys in grades four, six, and eight in relationship to the grade-level reading achievement. Among the recommendations made, the following seem particularly relevant and illustrative (17, p. 4):

1. An essential part of the elementary school program should be one of becoming increasingly aware of reading problems at the third and fourth grades and of beginning a concentrated program to analyze deficiencies and develop reading skills.

2. Classroom teachers should demonstrate their own reading orientation and build upon the boys' attitudes by talking about interesting books, by reading fascinating books aloud, and by advertising challenging books on the bulletin boards.

3. Books in the classrooms have to compete for children's interests in a world where mass communication media strive incessantly to capture attention. Teachers and librarians should choose carefully to meet this competition. . . .

5. Schools should make available reading materials to satisfy varied interests. A well-stocked school library containing a balanced collection of materials is essential.

6. There is an urgent need for easy-to-read books for poor readers. These should be made available.

7. Teachers and librarians should take note of the importance of sex differences in reading interests and compile separate reading lists. A comparative study should be made of the reading interests of girls.

8. Teachers are not fully aware of their key position in molding children's reading interests. Help from librarians, annotated book lists for both sexes, and in-service training would help the classroom situation.

"At last reading is fun" seems to be the pupil comment most frequently voiced by teachers who have not only tried individualized reading instruction but have made it *the* program. The choice of the word *fun* is a pupil choice, and if they were more articulate in expressing their feelings they would probably say *pleasant, gratifying, rewarding,* and perhaps *beguiling.* That pupils should voice such sentiments at all is a tremendous reflection on and damaging charge against the misuse of basic readers. One child is quoted by Picozzi as saying (23, p. 304): "We don't have to study the story. We can read faster and more books." Children encouraged and permitted to express their feelings about the way so many basic-reader stories are mutilated are very apt to speak this way, even when they do not have a basis for comparison with a better way of learning to read. Or, as Jeanette Veatch put it (28, p. 68):

Free-choice reading (or, as we shall call it, individualized reading) can change children's attitudes toward reading; ease the problem of dealing with a great range of reading abilities in one classroom; take the drudgery out of the reading period; challenge the brilliant child without discouraging the slow child; increase the number of books read; and most of all, make school happier for everybody concerned.

Paul Witty (31) cites two studies—one made in San Francisco (24) and the other at Northwestern University (27)—that estimate the amount of reading done by elementary school pupils. Results in both studies were similar: (1) The amount of book reading increases from first grade through sixth. (2) Girls read more than boys. (3) The average student, once he has learned to read, averages about a book per month during the school year. (4) Book titles listed showed a spread of reading preferences rather than a concentration. (5) Most of the books reported were fiction. (6) Little time is spent on books outside the school. (7) Stories of famous people were the favorite nonfiction stories. (8) Poetry, essays, and drama were read less often than fiction. (9) As compared with television, reading has little appeal.

The last point is not a reflection on television, for similar circumstances existed before the TV age (32). It is a reflection, though, on attitudes about reading acquired in schools in which the principal source material for reading instruction is basic readers. Either basic readers are not measuring up to the task, or they are being misused. On the other hand, all reports on individualized reading indicate that more reading is being done and done selectively. Even the comparative studies made indicate this, in spite of the fact that standardized test scores do not reflect it—and how could they? Add to this the fact that, as Robert Karlin points out (15, p. 81), "library circulation figures are at best a very rough measure of library-book reading."

Unfortunately, too, many teachers are not reading. Alvina Treut Burrows conducted a questionnaire and interview study to find out whether teachers read. She reported as follows (6, p. 254):

> If less than 20 percent of our general population are likely to read from a book on any given day, and only about one-third of the college-educated citizenry is involved daily with books, it follows that many children have little close association with books and with people who use books spontaneously. Fortunately, these indicated attitudes-in-action prevail in only about one-third of our school leadership. And even more fortunately, the segment of rather inactive readers is balanced by one of similar size who apparently live with books as part of normal life affairs. But it is also obvious immediately that teachers as a group are not outstandingly active in the wider reaches of literate pursuits. The old question of learning by precept or percept again intrudes. . . .

Couple with this the fact that adults are not reading, and the "everyone is guilty" cycle is completed. Lester Asheim states in his summary of adult reading interests (3, p. 22) that "there seems to be an over-all pattern which cannot be lightly brushed aside. That pattern reveals that there are very few adults in the United States today who do much reading of a purely voluntary sort." This comment might have been made by Douglas Waples and Ralph W. Tyler (29) in 1931.

The need to instill good attitudes and habits of reading is urgent. Apparently basic-reader regimentation has failed. This means that if a program of individualized instruction can do anything to change the "nonreading" picture, the action and practices should be pursued ardently.

SKILLS

Just as it is a half-truth to say that skills are the province of basic-reader instruction, so is it a half-truth to say that reading (wide reading) is the province of individualized reading instruction. Such statements distort the circumstances and reflect jaundiced opinions.

Similarly, it is a distortion of the circumstances to say that individualized reading instruction results only in "incidental learning," whereas basic-reader group instruction results in "learning." Incidental learning is defined by John A. McGeoch and Arthur D. Irion as *"learning which apparently takes place without a specific motive or a specific formal instruction and set to learn the activity or material in question"* (18, p. 210). The same authors define learning as *"a change in performance which occurs under the conditions of practice"* [italics in original] (18, p. 5). While practice is not synonymous with learning, it does embrace all of the techniques of learning: to see and grasp the meaning of causal relationships, to reach sound conclusions through reflective thinking, and to acquire habits and skills through reinforcement.

Basic readers, because of their packaged effect, tend to create the aura of systematized practice opportunities; on the other hand, no such giant-economy-size package exists or can exist for individualized reading instruction. As has already been shown, basic-reader texts, like libraries, present only materials to be read. Primary-level basic-reader materials are structured with vocabulary controls to facilitate word recognition and concept development. These skills, though, are presented in manuals and skill-books. For individualized instruction, many books at various readability and interest levels are available, and they provide to a degree comparable materials for individualized reading instruction. Both approaches can and do make use of other commercially prepared and teacher-prepared skill-building activities.

The post-Sputnik days seem to have given the word *skills* a front and center position on the learning stage. The simultaneous advent of machine learning provided new focus. As a result, the charlatan as well as the authority cries "skills" and makes claims and counterclaims. All this is fine insofar as the objective observer is concerned, but it is damaging in the hands of the subjective observers and the deliberate distorters of the truth.

To be proficient in the exercise or practical application of technical knowledge is a valuable skill. A habit is a way of acting, thinking, or behaving that has become so natural through repetition or practice that one does it without premeditation (30). Many of the reading-thinking skills essential to efficient reading have already been defined. As indicated, most of this technical knowledge can be developed in *any* area of the curriculum requiring reading and thinking, and with *any* materials. It is not the materials that counts, but rather what is done with the materials.

The major point about reading skills is that a basic-reader program and an individualized program of instruction both have distinct and different contributions to make to developing the all-around skills of an efficient reader. In the basic-reader group approach, all read the same teacher-selected material at the same time; in an individualized program all pupils may be reading different material that each selected on his own.

Reading skills that are most effectively taught in an individualized reading program premised on self-selection are as follows:

1. Locating materials. Pupils need to learn where different materials are kept and how they can be obtained. This is a many-faceted skill requiring a technical knowledge of libraries (a room library, a school library, a community library, specialized libraries). To use a library effectively and expertly, pupils must know the layout of libraries, how to use indexes, how to follow cross-references, and how to obtain materials from a librarian. At certain levels they need to know how to locate materials in newspaper files, police files, court records, and museums. None of this can be done within the confines of any basic-reader program.

2. Selecting materials. Once materials have been located comes the equally important job of selecting them. How does one survey a book, an encyclopedia, or a book shelf to select what he wants? Little if any of this skill can be acquired within the confines of a basic-reader series.

3. Using materials. When does one read an entire book or merely a portion of a book? When does one quote or paraphrase? When does one withdraw a book for use outside the library? None of this can be learned from a basic-reader.

4. Searching persistently. Pupils learn to pursue an interest or a question until they find an answer. This skill can be acquired within the confines of a basic-reader selection, but only to a very limited degree.

5. Being resourceful. Pupils learn to know when they have what they need to satisfy their curiosity and when to look further. This is done only to a very minor degree in a basic-reader.

6. Identifying personal interests. In the wide world of books and materials, an individual cannot read all that is available, even if he has the capacity and inclination to do so. As a result the availability of so much material forces the reader to examine closely his likes and dislikes. Only to a very limited degree can a pupil become proficient at identifying his interests within the limiting confines of a basic reader.

7. Identifying purposes for reading. In an individualized situation the reader is, so to speak, on his own. He has to decide what he wants to read and why. He can to some extent check his purposes for reading against those of others, but not nearly so often as he could in a basic-reader group situation.

8. Reading extensively. The student with a whole library at his disposal will find his reading limited only by his own purposes, capacity, and level of aspiration. Extensive reading habits and skills cannot be acquired within the bounds of a basic reader.

9. Reading intensively. To read and reflect and read again for thorough understanding is more apt to take place in an individualized reading situation in accordance with the practical aspects and demands of a school curriculum. True, a basic-reader series can give training in intensive reading, but only if it offers more than fiction and does so on a scale sufficiently large to develop initial skills.

10. Assembling information. To make a thorough study or an extensive study, the reader must learn to assemble relevant material. This means reading selectively, accepting that which fits the requirements of the purpose and rejecting that which does not. Only in part can this skill be developed in a basic-reader series.

11. Organizing information. Once he has selected his material, the reader is faced with organizing it in a timely and appropriate way. Once again this skill can be developed in only an initial way in a basic-reader series. A start can be made, but only a start.

12. Keeping records. Borrow a book, read it, return it. Do no more and the mind extorts, as a settlement, forgetting. Borrow many books, read them, make endless notes and return the books, and again forgetting will occur. Record keeping must be done selectively, efficiently, and concisely; and it must be done frequently if pupils are to understand the *why* and *how* of records. Obviously this can best be learned in an individualized reading circumstance where there are many books and where it is the rule to have many books. In part, record keeping can be taught within the confines of a single book or a basic reader—but only in part.

13. Learning word-attack skills. If word-attack skills are properly taught in a basic-reader program, individualized reading instruction will help only to reinforce the skills. If anything, the pupil learns to be even more self-reliant. Unfortunately though, too many basic-reading programs present word-attack skills incorrectly. This is why the proponents of individualized instruction claim that, their way, children learn to recognize words on their own. This is why, too, descriptions of individualized instructional programs devote so much space to showing how word-attack skills should be taught.

Children can and should learn all the fundamentals of word-attack skills in a basic-reader program. They can learn to know when to ask for help. Properly taught, they can test their skills in the wide world of many books and many words. This is what an individualized reading program should do. Restated briefly, a basic-reader program can teach pupils to be on their own when using word-attack skills, and an individualized program can provide the best means for refining these skills.

14. Acquiring concepts. As in the case in word-recognition skills, concept development can and should be taught in a basic-reader program and extended and refined in an individualized program. A basic-reader program permits a more careful pacing of concept-development skills because of its concept structuring and pacing. The essential framework is provided for focusing on *how* to do *what* without the risk of either overwhelming the pupil or developing habits of carelessness and indifference. On the other hand, the skills of concept development can be best extended and refined in an individualized reading program.

15. Sharing ideas. All the skills involved in sharing ideas are best ac-accomplished in a program of individualized instruction. Pupils learn the *why* and *how* of sharing in those circumstances in which they have something to share and a reason for sharing. The principal idea supporting this is that all may be reading different materials for different purposes. Sharing is done in a basic-reader program, but it is of a type and for a purpose that is governed by the fact that *all* have read the same material.

16. Listening. A natural sequence of the sharing of ideas is learning to listen and to be attentive. New ideas, presented in different ways, by different people, provide the medium. Not only does a pupil learn to listen selectively and under varied conditions, but also he learns to study these conditions in order that when his turn comes he may hold the attention of his audience. As a matter of fact, it is this type of ego involvement that most likely provides the most effective impetus for the development of scholarly listening.

Also involved is the skill of *how to take notes* when a presentation is being made. The potential for skill training in this respect is tremendous.

17. Asking questions. This might also have been listed as a point subordinate to listening, as was note-taking. However, the asking of questions gets started at an earlier level and is a more active, participating process. The quality of the question is determined by the listener's knowledge and experience as well as his ability to listen. Pupils can learn to ask probing questions to clarify or extend knowledge or to expose prejudices and distortions. They can learn also to ask questions tactfully, to take their turn, to pursue a point. Obviously this is best done in the learning-sharing atmosphere created by a program of individualized instruction.

This is not to suggest that pupils do not learn to ask questions in the dynamics of the purpose-setting and resetting sessions of a group D-R-T-A. It is only to point out that the two settings are different and involve different skills.

18. Reading as fun. The privilege to read and read and read can become an overwhelming responsibility. To be free to go to a book shelf or a library and select again and again can be very demanding. "What to pick now? I've read all about horses" results in a pause to think. "Do I like to read? How much do I want to read? What are others reading? Why?" These are the kinds of self-searching questions that can confront a pupil who is privileged to read. This kind of soul-searching can be of tremendous value and can result in wiser and more deliberate ways of selecting. This is the time when the pupil can examine his preferences while reading to be entertained. This is the time, too, when he can widen his reading-for-fun horizons.

19. Reading to learn. Pupils permitted and encouraged to read widely and given time to do so sooner or later discover that their reading interests go beyond just fun reading. As this occurs and develops, all the conditions described as the circumstances of reading for fun apply as pupils enjoy reading to learn. Pupils learn to examine their likes and dislikes and the likes and dislikes of others and the permanency of these conditions.

Many of the reports on individualized reading instruction tell only about the number of fiction books read. If this is all that is read, the results are disappointing. Children encouraged to read will with steady guidance soon look beyond fiction to fact. And, as a matter of fact, this is a golden opportunity for such a reading program. It can lift readers beyond the reading for vague, emotionalized pleasure to deep-seated enjoyment in reading to know more about the immediate world around them, the world of the past and of the future.

20. Gaining self-respect. The privilege to pick and choose—to do so according to one's likes and dislikes and at one's own pace—is a top-flight way to learn not only to examine oneself but to respect one's judgments. All this occurs when pupils' selections and interests are recognized and honored. All this occurs too in the framework of appropriately declared standards of conduct. Pupils are not just turned loose. As discussed in the section on "discipline," regulations are set up and enforced.

21. Knowing when to get help. At a time when all members of a class are busy on their own, the right to seek teacher help takes on the aura of a privilege. Pupils see more clearly with repeated experience *when* they need help, *why*, and *how* much. Being on your own implies knowing when you are able to achieve and when you are no longer able to achieve and need help.

22. Setting standards. To be your own most severe taskmaster is something to be learned as early in one's education career as possible. "Build for quality not for quantity" may be the standard for many days. For others it may be, "Read for quantity; read, read, read." Setting standards and imposing them on one's own conduct is the crux of the learning circumstance.

Among the important incentives to setting high standards are honors, praise, and rivalry. The strength of the competing conditions and the winning of teacher recognition do much to lower or raise standards. One of the most significant factors operating is the effect of the immediate satisfaction of a job well done. The reward is not as remote as the end of a marking-period grade and, therefore, exerts much influence on standards set and maintained. Meritorious achievement, group sanction and esteem, and personal interest are the noble sources.

23. Reading orally. To read aloud to an audience something they have not heard before and to hold their attention is one of the high aims of audience-type oral reading. Pupils begin to realize this at an early point in an individualized D-R-T-A program. Then they see the need for oral-reading practice and for quality performance.

In audience circumstances other pupils cannot follow in a text. They become listeners. Audience attention is more apt to be focused on content than on word errors, and the situation is more likely to be one in which to learn rather than to find fault.

24. Speaking publicly. To address a class and hold its attention requires the same kind of preparation thoughtfulness that is needed for oral reading. Pupils are made intimately aware of these needs as they deal with the recurring experience of individualized D-R-T-A sessions. Pupils are readily caught up in the *esprit de corps* that becomes a part of a sharing session. This makes for an atmosphere conducive to easy and spontaneous speech. At times the prepared presentations are done on a group basis; at others on a solo basis. The former often proves to be an excellent way to get pupils started on the public-speaking road. This means of overcoming the timidity of the reluctant pupils may be a considerable boon to the whole educational life of such pupils.

25. Appreciating the moment of silence. Step into almost any library, and the busy silence that permeates the atmosphere is immediately manifest. There is a hush and a tranquility as of thinkers at work: quiet work, quiet thoughts, quiet animation. The library silence is an unplanned silence. The librarian does not ring a bell for a moment of silence. Rather, it reflects an attitude of scholarly respect for the rights and privileges of others.

How the students use their time in a library is largely for them to decide. Some are reading, some are searching the files, some are selecting material, some are writing, some are just sitting (thinking, maybe or maybe not), and some may be just nodding. These are the cherished moments.

Many of these same circumstances may exist in the confines of a class-room operating under individualized D-R-T-A conditions. The situation can be such that the character of the arrangements and of the persons involved is advantageous to all and gives security to all.

The pupil, though, who in the midst of this is privileged to just sit and think is enjoying a wonderful freedom. He may be pondering deep thoughts of a scholarly nature or just dreaming idle dreams, or maybe he is nodding with eyes wide open. Regardless, this is a prize of self-selection, self-respect, self-realization and one that all must safeguard.

SUMMARY

Our American heritage—politically, socially, and educationally—is re-plete with evidence of belief in the rights and freedoms and strengths of each individual. Voices resonant with courage and dignity have been raised in behalf of the citizen. All must be educated. Education for the masses, however, has led to mass education. The tradition of indoctrination has kept the masses in intellectual bondage. Only the very bright, the creative, and the curious have been able to rise above these conditions. Yet the arch-indoctrinists, shouting the cult of traditionalism, extort the individual. This is why practices have been running behind theory by at least three generations.

This is the era of change. Technological advances are so rapid and so far-reaching that the "habit" of change is becoming the mark of twentieth-century citizens. The latter half of the century may witness a breakthrough on the educational frontier.

Individualized Directed Reading-Thinking Activities have a definite contribution to make to the total reading-instruction program. As indicated, there are certain skills that can be taught only in an individualized-reading situation, and there are others that can be brought to fruition only in an individualized reading program.

REFERENCES

1. American Library Association, *Subject Index to Books for Primary Grades,* Chicago, American Library Assocation, 1961.
2. Arbuthnot, May Hill, "When Teachers Read, Children Read," *The Instructor* (An Instructor Library Supplement) (November, 1962), pp. 82–84.
3. Asheim, Lester, "What Do Adults Read?," *Adult Reading,* Fifty-fifth Yearbook of the National Society for the Study of Education, Part II, Chicago, University of Chicago Press, 1956.
4. Austin, Mary, and Coleman Morrison, *The Torch Lighters, Tomorrow's Teachers of Reading,* Cambridge, Mass., Harvard University Press, 1961.
5. Betts, Emmett A., *Foundations of Reading Instruction,* New York, American Book, 1946.
6. Burrows, Alvina Treut, "Do Teachers Read?," *The Reading Teacher, 11* (April, 1958), 253–255.
7. *Combined Book Exhibit,* New York [Combined Book Exhibit, 950 University Avenue].
8. DeLong, Arthur, "Toward Improved Accuracy in Test Interpretation," *Merrill-Palmer Quarterly of Behavior and Development,* 7 (1961), 273–285.
9. Dewey, John, *The Child and the Curriculum,* Chicago, University of Chicago Press, 1902.
10. Goodlad, John I., and Robert H. Anderson, *The Nongraded Elementary School,* New York, Harcourt, Brace & World, 1959.
11. Gray, William S., *On Their Own in Reading,* rev. ed., Chicago, Scott, Foresman, 1960.
12. Gray, William S., and Bernice Rogers, *Maturity in Reading,* Chicago, University of Chicago Press, 1956.
13. Hardin, Garrett, "Biology and Individual Differences," *Individualizing Instruction,* Sixty-first Yearbook of the National Society for the Study of Education, Part I, Chicago, University of Chicago Press, 1962.
14. Horn, Ernest, "Language and Meaning," *The Psychology of Learning,* Forty-first Yearbook of the National Society for the Study of Education, Chicago, University of Chicago Press, 1942.
15. Karlin, Robert, "Library-Book Borrowing vs. Library-Book Reading," *The Reading Teacher, 16* (November, 1962), 77–81.

16. Larrick, Nancy, *A Teacher's Guide to Children's Books*, Columbus, Ohio, Merrill, 1960.
17. Los Angeles City School Districts, *Boys' Reading Interests*, Committee on Research Studies, Herbert Popence, Chairman, Research Report No. 86, Los Angeles, December, 1961.
18. McGeoch, John A., and Arthur D. Irion, *The Psychology of Human Learning*, New York, Longmans, Green, 1952.
19. Madison Public Schools, Curriculum Department, *Magazines for Elementary Grades*, Madison, Wis., 1953.
20. National Council of Teachers of English, *The Use of Paperbound Books*, Champaign, Ill., 1960.
21. New York City Board of Education, *Books for Children to Read (Individualized Reading-Book Lists)*, New York, N.Y. Bureau of Educational Research, Board of Education of the City of New York, 1957.
22. Peterson, Miriam, "What Books for the Elementary School Library?," *The Instructor* (An Instructor Library Supplement), (November, 1962), pp. 66–69.
23. Picozzi, Adelaide, "An Approach to Individualized Reading," *Elementary English, 35* (May, 1958), 302–304.
24. *The San Francisco Study of Children and Mass Communication*, Report IV, Stanford, Cal., Stanford Institute for Communication Research, 1939, mimeo.
25. Stauffer, Russell G., "A Directed Reading-Thinking Plan," *Education, 79* (May, 1959), 527–532.
26. Stauffer, Russell G., "The Role of the Teacher," *Reading for Meaning*, Proceedings of the 34th Annual Education Conference, vol. 3, Newark, Del., University of Delaware, 1952.
27. *A Study of the Interests of Children and Youth*, A study made cooperatively by Northwestern University and the Office of Education, U.S. Department of Health, Education and Welfare, Washington, D.C., Government Printing Office, 1960.
28. Veatch, Jeanette, "Individualized Reading—For Success in the Classroom," *The Educational Trend*, Washington, D.C., Croft, 1954.
29. Waples, Douglas, and Ralph W. Tyler, *What People Want To Read About: A Study of Group Interests and a Survey of Problems in Adult Reading*, Chicago, American Library Association and University of Chicago Press, 1931.
30. *Webster's Dictionary of Synonyms*. Springfield, Mass., Merriam, 1942.
31. Witty, Paul, "The Role of Interest," *Development In and Through Reading*, Sixtieth Yearbook of the National Society for the Study of Education, Part I, Chicago: University of Chicago Press, 1961.
32. Witty, Paul, and David Kopel, *Reading and the Educative Process*, Boston, Ginn, 1939.
33. Zerbes, Laura, *Spurs to Creative Teaching*, New York, Putnam's, 1959.

Chapter 6 Individualized Directed Reading-Thinking Activities

A basic-reader series can be kept in perspective if it is contrasted with a library, for both provide resource material useful in reading-instruction purposes. A basic-reader series, however, is at best not even a skeleton of a library. Such a label might be applied to an encyclopedia, but even the contrast between a basic-reader series and an encyclopedia is striking. It is astonishing that basic readers with their dearth of materials should at any time be thought of as *the* reading program.

It is true, of course, that most basic readers provide a guide to related literature. This guide, however, is merely a means of getting pupils out of the basic-reader doldrums—the becalmed, nonreading state of dullness and low spirits—and goes largely unappreciated because of the series' plaintive and pathetic concentration on "saying words" and "knowing" the basic-reader stories. The related-literature approach to wide reading has failed, even though some states imposed a book-a-month requirement on all children.

An individualized reading program can be kept in perspective if individualized instruction is contrasted with group instruction. The reading-thinking skills described in detail in this book are best accomplished in the dynamics of a group and cannot be accomplished in a situation in which each pupil is reading a different book. It is the individual's use of his experience and knowledge, his noting of clues, declaration of hypotheses, weighing evidence, and drawing of conclusions that must be refined in the give and take of a group. The structured materials of a basic reader—if they go beyond vocabulary controls to picture and plot controls and to a diversity of fiction and nonfiction—allow pupils to concentrate on the reading-thinking process. Reading to learn can be kept in focus while learning to read.

It is true, of course, that many books that are purported to use read-ability controls much like those in basic readers are flooding the market. These books, however, do not measure up to the claims made for them (7). The materials are interesting, cleverly constructed, and attention getting, but they cannot replace well-structured basic-reader materials. Although a group might read *The Cat in the Hat* at the same time in an effort to ac-complish reading-thinking skills, this is a bizarre imitation of a Directed Reading-Thinking Activity and a ludicrous use of the story.

A basic-reader series might be thought of as the launching pad from which each pupil departs into his individualized reading orbit. The series provides the rocket and the gentry; the pupil's interest, aptitude, and motivation provide the propellant; the teacher starts the countdown, does the firing, and sees the pupils soar into the wide, wide universe of books. How high they go, the spread of their apogee and perigee, depends on each pupil's potential.

Thus far in this book the point has been advanced that reading-instruc-tion time should *at a minimum* be equally divided between (basic reader) group-type Directed Reading-Thinking Activities and individualized (many books) Directed Reading-Thinking Activities. *At a maximum* the time should be divided on a two-thirds, one-third basis; two-thirds of the reading-instruction time to be devoted to individualized reading instruc-tion and one-third to basic-reader group-type instruction. This will give pupils the opportunity to attain the outcome of all reading instruction—to read widely and selectively for personal entertainment and for knowl-edge.

In the rest of this chapter recommendations are made as to how teachers can break the basic-reader lock step. The teacher willing to try will need courage to break away from basic readers, but once she initiates the program the pupils will help to perpetuate it, and their enthusiasm will carry it through.

BREAKING THE BASIC-READER LOCK STEP

How to individualize instruction at the first-grade level is discussed in Chapter 8, "The Langage-Experience Approach." The suggestions that follow are adapted to a fourth-grade level, but they could readily be adapted to any grade level.

Most teachers who are reluctant to put aside basic readers and try a session of individualized reading instruction feel this way because they are uncertain about how to proceed. This is a natural concern and not a reflec-tion on either the teacher's willingness to try to teach reading more appropriately or on her competency as a teacher. While it is true that "a well-prepared teacher is the crucial factor in individualizing instruction" (2, p. 208), it is also true that a well-prepared teacher is the crucial factor in a program built exclusively on basic readers. As a matter of fact, in the latter circumstances she needs to be more than well prepared because she has to compensate in some way for the shortcomings of the basic-reader program.

In addition, since the records show quite clearly that most beginning teachers are inadequately prepared to teach reading, it is safe to conclude that most experienced teachers felt concern about how to teach reading when they first started to teach. They know, therefore, from personal experience that adjustments can be made and that teaching proficiency can be acquired. They know, too, that competency is not usually acquired after one or two attempts.

Getting Started

One way to make the break is to start with the group that performs at the highest level and is populated by the most alert and self-reliant pupils. Keep in mind, though, that others in the class will be keenly interested and will be quite alert to what is going on. This is a healthy interest and may be used to good advantage at a later date.

It is assumed that this fourth-grade teacher started reading instruction by organizing the class into groups and by using basic readers. When the first unit in the basic reader had been read, the text and the skillbook were put aside. If this was the pupils' first experience with individualized instruction, they will need an explanation of what is to follow. Tell them that (1) for two (maybe three) weeks the basic readers will be closeted; (2) they may select their own reading material; (3) the selecting will be done in the classroom or the school library; (4) how to proceed in selecting and how to conduct themselves; (5) teacher help will be available for word and meaning needs; (6) as the sessions pass, time will be taken to discuss other needs that may develop. Activities that will develop and that need not be discussed at this first session are note taking, sharing, vocabulary lists, listening, sharing preparation, and so on.

It is usually wise to start the first session with a series of props. The props recommended are of two kinds: (1) interests that might have been aroused by the content of the first unit in the basic reader, and (2) the related literature recommended in the basic reader. This way both the pupils and the teacher will feel that the basic-reader prop has been removed slowly and gently.

Now the group can be instructed to go through the first unit of the basic reader and list the interest areas and concepts it deals with. A list such as the following might be obtained (10, pp. 80–81):

A Fight Against Fear

spear fishing	coral
dangers of the sea	sea plants
diving	sharks
clams	Red Sea
fear and bravery	countries around the Red Sea

Young Buffalo Bill

settling the west	Indians
wagon trains	army forts
America during the 1850s	prairie

Away to Happiness

pinto ponies	guitar playing
gypsies	horse racing

The Three-Legged Frog

China today and yesterday	Chinese foods
Chinese courts and gardens	Chinese stories and folk tales

Of Plows and Plowing

early tools of man	feeding America
cast-iron stoves	plowing contests
farms and farming	

Americans Move with Their Bridges

how settlers built bridges	history of Brooklyn Bridge
wooden bridges	bridges in other parts of the world
covered bridges	

Mr. Irons' Misfortune
other court cases
who makes laws
how judges are picked

Editorials

newspapers, magazines	gymnasiums
letters to editor	field days
aluminum	olympics

The range of possibilities is considerable. If pupils are at a loss as to what they might do or what they might read about, this list should be a helpful guide. The entries on the list might be discussed orally without asking any one pupil to make a final choice. Thus the discussion will help pupils identify their interests and prepare them to make their own selections. Such a discussion may be enough to start the group to the library.

The second prop—the recommended related literature (10, pp. 81–82)—may be obtained from the school library or some library unit. If it is the school library, a librarian or an aide may place the books on a cart and wheel them to a specific room. If librarian service is not available, the teacher might locate books and bring them to the room, or the teacher and the group might do so. When the books are in the room, books can be taken from the cart according to the interest area and presented briefly to the group.

Related Literature for Unit I

Call It Courage, Armstrong Sperry, New York: Macmillan, 1941.
Caddie Woodlawn, Carol Ryrie Brink, New York: Macmillan, 1936.

Crazy Horse, Shannon Garst, Boston: Houghton Mifflin, 1950.
Six Feet Six: The Heroic Story of Sam Houston, Marquis and Bessie Rowland James, Indianapolis: Bobbs Merrill, 1931.
Winter Danger, William O. Steele, New York: Harcourt, Brace & World, 1954.
Tree Wagon, Evelyn S. Lampman, New York: Doubleday, 1953.
The Cat Who Went to Heaven, Elizabeth Coatsworth, New York: Macmillan, 1930.
Crow Boy, Taro Yashima, New York: Viking, 1955.
Little Pear, Eleanor Frances Lattimore, New York: Harcourt, Brace & World, 1931.
The Story of Doctor Dolittle, Hugh Lofting, Philadelphia: Lippincott, 1920.
Lassie Come Home, Eric Knight, New York: Holt, Rinehart & Winston, 1940.
Prehistoric America, Anne Terry White, New York: Random House, 1951.
Rocks, Rivers and the Changing Earth, Herman and Nina Schneider, New York: William R. Scott, 1952.
Dust Bowl: The Story of Man on the Great Plains, Patricia Lauber, New York: Coward-McCann, 1958.
The Fair American and Other Stories, Elizabeth Coatsworth, New York: Macmillan, 1940.
Away Goes Sally, Elizabeth Coatsworth, New York: Macmillan, 1934.
Five Bushel Farm, Elizabeth Coatsworth, New York: Macmillan, 1939.
Bridges and Their Builders, David B. Steinman and Sarah Ruth Watson, New York: Dover, 1957.
The Building of the First Transcontinental Railroad, Adele Nathan, New York: Random House, 1950.
Wheels: A Pictorial History, Edwin Tunis, Cleveland: World, 1955.
The Life *Pictorial Atlas of the World,* New York: Time, Inc., and Chicago: Rand McNally, 1961.
The World Almanac, Newspaper Enterprise Association, annual.

Before reading, review with the group a plan for keeping reading records. Cards, either the 3-by-5-inch or the 5-by-8-inch size, or notebooks may be used. The record might show the name of the book, the author, copyright date, the publisher, library-card number, the amount of the book the pupil reads, and pupil comments. This is a good place, too, for the pupils to state why they selected this book, for this helps them see more clearly their purposes for reading.

Now have pupils pick and choose as they wish. If not all interests are satisfied by the selected list, arrange to have the pupils go to a library. Before the reading starts, realert them about what to do if any reading difficulties are encountered:

Word needs

Read the rest of the sentence or paragraph.
Use phonetic-analysis skills.
Use structure-analysis skills.
Use a dictionary for pronunciation and meaning.
Seek teacher help.

Comprehension needs

Read on; maybe help is given in the next paragraph or two.
Study pictures, maps, charts, for clues.
Use a dictionary.
Seek teacher help.

Once again, the pupils are engaged in accomplishing the primary purpose of all reading instruction—to read. This being the case, the teacher has an ideal opportunity to see how they perform. What are the silent-reading habits that are being practiced? Is the posture good? Is rate being adapted? Is there evidence of lip movement and finger pointing? The practices exhibited during the two or three weeks of self-selection time are much more apt to be representative of the practices used outside the classroom than those exhibited during the group-instruction time, so the teacher will want to move about and give help as needed and as requested.

Sit down with different pupils to check progress and performance. Inquire about pupil reading purposes, whether or not the material being read meets their needs, to what degree their needs are being met, whether new material should be sought, and what they plan to do with the material. Check on word-recognition problems and how they have dealt with them. Contact each pupil. This is the time, too, to identify needs and to plan for skill instruction, either individually or in small groups.

Do not make the primary purpose of your pupil-visit the hearing of oral reading. This is not to imply that oral reading is not important, but most reading is silent reading, so if the only measure of appraisal is oral reading, the point is missed, and wrong pupil attitudes are fostered. If a pupil reads a line or two to prove a point or because he finds the passage particularly exciting, this is fine, but start your inquiry as described in the previous paragraph.

Usually, the extreme proponents of individualized reading make strong claims for this kind of oral reading. The oral reading promotes good will between teacher and pupil, but it does little to improve the pupil's oral-reading skill. First, the material is not really read aloud, for to do so would disturb the class. The audible whisper is not a substitute for training in oral reading. Second, the teacher is usually sitting alongside the pupil, not facing him, and this is not a good audience situation. Third, if the pupil looks up at the teacher on occasion, as a reader will do at his audience, he must look sideways. Fourth, usually the teacher is looking over the pupil's shoulder and is more interested in his slips than in his successes.

It is apparent, then, that practices opposite those just described should be used: have the pupil sit facing the teacher; listen to the oral reading; note the oral-reading facility so that if training is needed it can be given at a special skill-building time. If several people need help in oral reading, they can be grouped for this purpose. In other words, when the pupil is reading a favorite passage or the like to the teacher, his enthusiasm should not be stifled by rude interruptions.

After records of pupil-skill needs are obtained, training sessions or skill-developing sessions can be planned. This, as has been said, may be done with pupils in subgroups, the entire group, or singly, depending on the need and who has the need.

As the week or weeks progress, performances will vary. Some pupils will be reading; others preparing reports; others looking for materials; others meeting in teams or groups to plan. This means that the demands for teacher help will be equally as varied. Most of all, it means that, when pupils are working individually, the pace for each is apt to be different. Therefore it would be most unwise to expect that all pupils will be reading at the same time or preparing reports at the same time.

The First Go-Round

In the first go-round with individualized instructors, brief daily sharing sessions help set up the sharing idea. After a few of the short daily sessions, take time out to discuss a sharing session. Keep in mind the following ideas:

1. Provide time for sharing that fits in with the plans of the group.

2. Be sure the reports are ready. Avoid making this a time of discomfort and embarrassment resulting from inadequate preparation or readiness.

3. Provide, or help to provide, props that may be needed: lectern, puppets, tables, flannel board, easel, curtain, projectors.

4. Prepare the group to be good listeners. Review how to be attentive and courteous, how to ask questions and to take notes.

5. Discuss follow-up procedures after reports have been made: more reading, rewriting, visits to other rooms.

When the pupils return to basic-reader group instruction after this first break into individualized instruction, their attitude will most likely have changed. Unless the basic-reader selections and the method for handling the selections is dynamic, pupils will approach the session with a let-down feeling. If the group-instruction sessions do not meet the high standards for materials and Directed Reading-Thinking Activities as defined in this text, the pupils are justified in their reactions. If the standards set for group instruction are being met, the pupils will approach the group sessions in a new way. They will see better than ever before how the group sessions prepare them for the individualized sessions. The meaning of "my-own-purposes" for reading will take on new significance, for they have had a considerable opportunity to set their own purposes with only the limitations of the library to restrain them.

How to deal with word recognition and concept problems will also be seen more clearly in the reflected light of the basic-reader training sessions. The meaning of independence in word recognition will be much clearer because pupil independence was required in a situation in which the pupil was the only member of the group reading a certain piece of material. The word difficulties were more truly his own. He could not wait for the comprehension-check period and listen to someone else deal with the same material.

Comprehension takes on new importance when a pupil needs to understand well enough to share his impressions with others who have not read the same item. For this reason, pupils will participate in the comprehension checks in the group sessions in quite a different way. Standing on their own has taught them what it means to stand together. The evaluating and proving sessions will also take on added significance, because in the individualized sessions no one else had read the material, and the listeners were therefore very much dependent on the sharer's intellectual honesty and skill at interpreting.

Teachers approach the group sessions in a different way. They, too, see more clearly the purpose and value of the group as a means of sharpening reading-thinking skills. Basic-reader materials become the whetstone for individualized reading. The finely structured, compact materials can be used to hone the reading-thinking skills to a razor's edge of sharpness, keenness, and acuteness. These are the qualities of the mind that pupils should manifest when they are reading on their own. Now the group reading-thinking process is much more apt to be characterized by penetrating truthfulness, acute discernment, and a bracing, invigorating terseness.

The Second Go-Round

Once the members of a class or group have learned to love the world of books, they will never completely abandon it. Once they have been given instruction in individualized reading (as recommended after a first unit in a basic reader), they will not abandon the "independent" reading practice. If previous instruction had not already instilled the habit of reading, then the experience of Unit I will have started the venture.

Switching to the individualized instruction period at the end of a second unit will be more readily accomplished because individualized instruction never quite ended. There are many opportunities throughout the school day, the after-school hours, and on weekends to read and read and read. So, students will put aside the basic reader and the skillbook without undue concern about leaving the structured pathways defined by a basic-reader program for the differently structured course offered by self-selected books.

Again, a period of two or three weeks for individualized reading-thinking instruction should be allowed. During this time the basic reader is put aside completely; the library becomes the source of instructional material.

It was suggested that, when the first unit of a basic reader was completed, the teacher begin individualized instruction by turning to the interest areas identifiable in that unit and to the related literature recommended as additional reading. The list of related literature provides the pupils with many ideas and helps them select materials.

In this second experience with individualized instruction, the pupils will be more resourceful and experienced. They now have a good idea how to act. This generally means that they will not need a list of ideas as suggested under Unit I. In fact, during the group sessions they may have kept a personal running list of ideas that they could pursue during the individualized sessions. Pupils showing this kind of resourcefulness could get under way at once. Pupils who did not keep either a written inventory or mental notes of ideas to read about or thoughts to pursue may be grouped temporarily.

This time, it is suggested that two or three "reading clubs" be organized. The areas of interest might be identified through ideas initiated in the second unit of whatever basic reader is used. One club could be a drama club, as suggested by the articles on radio, television, and the movies in the special section of the basic reader. Another could be a history club, thus relating in part to ideas set astir in "Real Adventure . . . A Radio Play" and in "The Ship's Cat." A third could be a fiction club.

A look at history confirms that people are easily led and all too often consent to a restricting conformity. Many people prefer that limits be carefully defined to spare them the trouble of thinking and making decisions. Similar attitudes prevail among children. This means that a wise directing of energies along lines that will lead to self-reliant, resourceful, creative use of ideas is essential. Furthermore, cirumstances of self-selection call for more than fleeting, whimsical picking and choosing. Judgment based on wise reflection, examined interests, and wide experience is necessary.

The three-club idea will increase the need for decision making among the pupils. They will need to decide which club they want to join; then, having joined, they must identify their own drama, history, or fiction interest and the materials they will use. This contrasts sharply with the less demanding, more tightly structured circumstances suggested for the first go-round, yet even that plan encouraged pupils to pick and choose. The three-club idea will also let pupils choose the friends with whom they will read and work. Interests and friends may thus be the deciding criteria, rather than reading achievement or levels.

All too often proponents of the exclusive use of an individualized approach claim that what a pupil needs to do to learn to read is to read. Would that the demanding intellectual reading-thinking skills could be so easily acquired! Unfortunately, this is not the case. It used to be thought that the way to learn to swim was to swim. In fact, in all too many instances the learner was thrown into the water and then allowed to struggle. Today, it is commonly accepted that swimming is learned best if properly taught—in a planned, systematic way.

No one will quarrel with the concept that to read is to read with understanding. Neither does anyone quarrel with the idea that how one reacts to a story is an individual matter. By the same token, no one should quarrel with the idea that to read efficiently—to raise sharp questions, to probe for meaning, to test for accuracy and penetration, and to weigh implications—requires skillful, systematic instruction. This represents an intellectual set of skills that must be taught. They cannot be acquired simply by reading.

The steps that lead to mature, efficient reading-thinking have been declared. The following proposals may be used as steps to accomplish proficiency. When the reading clubs have been formed, have the members meet to declare interests and curiosities. Note the degree to which the pupils raise sharp questions. For example, the history club may raise such questions as, What cargoes did the ships of Captain John Paul Jones' time carry? Why did the Americans want to sink British cargo ships? How big was the English ship *Serapis*? Why did the Americans fight the British instead of having a summit conference? What did the wives of the New England sailors do while their men were away at sea? How long does it take a modern cargo ship to sail from Salem to India? Keep in mind the maxim that the right question is the half of knowledge. Time spent in declaring questions may be of greater importance than time devoted to actual reading.

In the section dealing with critical thinking, it was pointed out how one aspect of critical thinking was for the reader to grasp the function of a "background" purpose. This skill needs to be developed so that the self-reliant, independent reader can know what follows from his purposes. If he is to read with understanding, he must know what evidence will count for or against his purpose, either by direct or implied circumstances.

As in all situations in which skill of comprehension is being developed and especially in an individualized situation, a teacher's first responsibility is to check on the soundness of her pupils' purposes. This may require more restraint and intellectual composure on the second go-round of individualized reading than on the first. Pupils may be so eager to get going that they will want to plunge right in. As any good swimmer knows, one seldom, if ever, plunges into unfamiliar waters without first checking for hidden snares, rocks, and water temperature. So, too, in reading, one seldom, if ever, plunges in before examining his purposes.

A principal liability of candidates for doctoral degrees is their inability to state a thesis topic clearly and concisely. It is difficult to believe that educated men and women could lack a skill that can now be developed early in a reader's training program.

If a pupil decides that he wants to find out all he can about how to improve the school library and has set as his specific purpose to find out how movies are made for school use, he must first clarify his thinking about the terms *improve, school library, movies,* and *made,* for in so doing he may see that his purpose is not specific enough to be tested or clear enough to be applicable. If, on the other hand, he plans to use his father's camera to prepare an 8-millimeter film to show that the propagation of plants is a simple process in which the plants do all the work and the gardener just lends a helping hand, his need for information about how to make movies for school use is specific enough for his purpose.

It might be thought that stating a topic clearly is an aspect of critical reading and thinking in which students seldom err. This is not true. At this level, even in concrete situations, it is easy to go wrong if pupils fail to put questions and answers into the context of situations with purposes.

As the pupils search for materials in which to locate answers, give them a hand where necessary. Help them use an encyclopedia, to follow up a cross-reference, or to locate a special book. Then when materials have been located, move about among the pupils and check. Are they keeping their purposes fixed in mind? Are they finding what they want? Are they checking on ideas that are not clear? Are they using a dictionary? Ask an occasional question that will cause them to stop and reflect. Or, ask a question that will require picture, chart, map, or graph analysis. Sometimes pupils reading on their own become slovenly and overlook some key sources of information. Ask them if the materials they are using actually provide the answers they need. Is enough information given to make an accurate report to a group of listeners? Do all sources used give the same information? What does the teacher of history think about the answer recorded? Are the ideas presented of value to the individual? If so, are they also of value to the group? The question, *what might have happened if . . . ?*, is a good way to get pupils to sense implications. Encourage pupils to think about the information in such a way as to decide whether or not it agrees with what a pupil had thought to be true. In setting realistic purposes, one tends to declare preconceived notions. Note whether or not pupils did this. If they did, note the degree to which they adjusted their thinking.

The role of the teacher in developing pupil skill in raising questions is of the highest importance. When students are trained to ask good questions, their reading comprehension almost always improves.

The sentence "Never in his life will he escape the consequences of his youthful mistakes" might be paraphrased thus: "Never during his reading will a reader escape the consequences of his purposes"; or "Never during a teacher's directing of a total reading-thinking act will the readers escape the consequences of her failure to give proper attention to pupil purposes."

To get this second go-round at individualized reading off the ground, pupils must be doubly alert to the need for purposes sharply stated, and teachers must be doubly alert to offset the students' eagerness to plunge in. The hope of discovery is a powerful force, but it must be tempered with soundness and clarity if the reader is to probe for meaning in such a way that he can test for accuracy.

The Third Go-Round

Before starting the third go-round with directing reading-thinking activities on an individualized basis, it may be wise to review briefly with the pupils the skills discussed and developed in the first two sessions.

The pupils by now are quite well posted regarding procedures to follow during the directed individualized reading-thinking activities period. They know to a good degree the amount of independent action expected and required of them. They see more clearly the advantages of both approaches to reading instruction and the nature and degree of pupil participation and responsibility. Self-reliance, self-responsibility, and self-understanding have taken on new meanings. Action governed by their understanding of "self" has forged a firmer and clearer concept of individualized reading.

A reading period two or three weeks in length will not face the pupils this time as it may have on earlier occasions. Experience has shown them that two or three weeks may pass quickly when appropriate planning and action have occurred. They know now that plans can be made that will cover a three-week period and that such plans differ sharply from those made to cover a day or two. Pupils now recognize that a three-week reading period requires such clearly defined steps as (1) a planning session to set goals through declared interests and purposes; (2) time to select materials or, in many instances, collect materials; (3) reading (usually silent) and studying to understand and organize ideas; (4) preparation-of-reports time; (5) sharing time; and (6) evaluation time.

By now pupils understand, too, that the time allowed is not divided equally between each phase and that these steps are not always accomplished in the order listed. They do understand, however, that there is order and system and that they have a large share of responsibility in determining and accomplishing the plans.

The first go-round leaned heavily on a list of interest areas based on a first unit in a basic reader. This aid helped pupils determine interests and select materials. In the second go-round the pupils received less help in "getting started." The class was organized into reading clubs with different areas of interests, a procedure that increased sharply the pupils' need for making decisions while at the same time providing the security of shared interests and some group thinking for those pupils who did not have self-declared interest areas.

It is proposed that getting-started crutches be kept at a minimium in the third go-round. This time, do not list ideas and materials for class use or organize the class into reading clubs. This time each pupil is on his own. This means he must decide what he wants to read and why, plan his own program, decide what he wants to do about what he has read, and so conduct himself that he does not interfere with the rights and privileges of any other pupil in the room.

As pointed out in Chapter 5, some pupils will get going immediately without much, if any, teacher help. Others will have ideas but may want teacher approval of them. Still others will be puzzled by the freedom accorded them. Stand by, therefore, to give help as needed.

Some pupil may want to team up with another classmate or two to pursue a common interest. Others will undoubtedly prefer to work alone. Do not encourage puzzled pupils to band together. Rather, help them to find themselves. These children may lean more heavily on ideas and interests stemming from the unit just completed. If this happens, as it does frequently, do not deny them the use of this source of help. With experience, they, too will learn to stand on their own feet.

A more detailed analysis of the six steps for directing an individualized reading-thinking situation will help clear up questions that might have occurred to the reader.

A Planning Session. Some pupils will know what they want to do the moment the extended period starts. Usually they have been anticipating this reading time and have been making note of things they want to do. All they need is a brief check of plans and a green light. These pupils usually plan research-type reading. They have interests and problems. They are probing, questioning children who have learned to harness some of their natural curiosity.

Those uncertain about what to do may either meet in small groups or meditate privately. Sometimes a short "idea and plan" session for all pupils, led by the teacher, is in order. The students who are insensitive to the logical qualifiers described at the end of the first go-round and those who do not know whether or not a purpose is specific enough as described at the end of the second go-round will benefit by the teacher's reviewing their ambitions with them, helping them determine a course of action, and helping them get under way.

A course of action is more than a vague, undefined notion to read. Usually it is a fairly clearly stated objective, such as to read other stories about fish, to find out more about gold mining in the early days, to find out how diamonds are mined. If on occasion some pupil prefers to "just read," this should be both his privilege and his responsibility.

Select or Collect Materials. Sometimes teachers expect pupils to finish quickly reading an article that has many pictures. They expect a short reading time because there are not many words to be read. These teachers are being very naïve about the reading performance of a mature reader. A good reader never skips a picture. He gives it thoughtful and careful study, since it may be "worth a thousand words."

Similarly, some teachers tend to be naïve about the time needed to select or collect materials. At times an encyclopedia may provide readily and quickly all that a pupil needs. Often, though, this represents only a starting point. Collecting materials may take even longer than selecting. The pupil who wanted to collect passages that would be illustrative of the language used by the men who manned sailing vessels had a busy collecting time. So did the lad who was interested in automobiles built before 1920. He was busy collecting toy models as well as literature about the cars, which led him to a biographical search of early inventors and manufacturers, and from this to early auto races and racers.

Ideas to be kept in mind when making judgments about the time needed for all this are important. Some may find what they need in a day or so; others may take a week or ten days. Some may be selecting and collecting throughout the entire period, shifting from this to reading, and back again to selecting and collecting. Of special significance, though, is the idea that this part of the total individualized reading session is as important as any other part—and certainly as important as the "reading" time.

Silent Reading. As already pointed out in the discussion of selecting and collecting, silent-reading time may vary considerably. It, too, represents only one part of the six-pronged approach to an individualized reading-thinking session.

Almost every adult has seen a six- or seven-year-old put on a reading act. The child, holding a book, moving his lips, appears to be busy reading. Usually the child puts on his act because he senses warm, perhaps amused, reaction to what he is doing. At the least, he is getting attention. On occasion, eleven- and twelve-year-olds put on similar acts during so-called individualized reading sessions. Be alert to such conduct; it can be adjusted readily by means of a few insightful questions and the giving or denying of attention. Ask pupils who appear to be reading-acting why they chose the material they did, or what they expect to find next, or how much more selecting and reading time they may need.

Regardless, the silent-reading time is the time when the reading is actually being done. In this one sense, it does represent the most important aspect of the total session. Note, therefore, requests for help with word-attack problems. If the request concerns *pronunciation,* check to see if the following steps have already been taken:

1. syllabifying the word
2. sounding the word in parts
3. noting accent possibilities
4. checking the phonetic respelling in
   a. the glosary
   b. a dictionary
5. using the pronunciation key correctly

If the request is a *concept,* or *meaning* problem, check to see if the following steps have been taken:

1. reading the rest of the sentence
2. reading on for a paragraph or two
3. checking for meaning in
   a. the glosary
   b. a dictionary
4. selecting the right meaning and adapting it in the sentence context

Note evidences of versatility in reading performance. Do pupils adjust their rate of reading according to their purposes and the nature and difficulty of the material? If the purposes declared require a *skim* rate, do they proceed rapidly and lightly to locate literal or implied information? If the purposes declared require *scan* reading, do they proceed carefully from point to point? If the purposes declared require *study* reading, do they read and reread, reflecting and evaluating and digesting?

Preparation of Reports. Preparing a report can be time-consuming. All teachers have prepared term papers and reports, and all should understand what will be required of their pupils when they too reach the report-preparing time.

Teacher attitude toward reports is very important; she is director and does the pacing. Some reports are completely oral. Pupils making such reports need to reflect about what they plan to say and then rehearse it once or twice with a classmate or with the teacher as audience-critic. Rehearsal is needed, for it gives pupils an idea as to how much time they will need for their report.

Some oral reports use audio-visual aids. These, too, require rehearsal to coordinate the talk and the aid material. When pupils use audio-visual props, they usually feel more secure and as a result are apt to talk more freely and take more time. These pupils must check their practice session carefully so as to estimate the time they will need.

Written reports that are read orally require careful editing for sequence and structure because the report must be read in such a way as to hold an audience's attention.

Team reports also need rehearsal time, largely to coordinate effort and to estimate the time needed to present them.

Set up a chart, such as the one shown below, describing the type of report and the amount of time needed.

Name	Type Report	Aids	Time
Nancy	oral	none	10 min.
Judy	oral (with outline)	slides	25 min.
Harold, Bill and John	group demonstration	table and science equipment	15 min.

A schedule of this kind points up many things: the need for planning, the amount of time required, the order of importance of presentations, the scheduling of aids.

Sharing Time. How reports are presented and received is of vital importance, and sharing time is pretty much proof-of-the-pudding time. A pupil secretary should be designated to keep pace of things, to note starting and stopping times, to keep things going, and to direct questions.

The teacher may lend a hand if required, but she should do so quietly and unobstrusively. Pupils tend to be excited during report time, and a wise, helping hand may do much to develop confidence and poise. Do not reprimand, or reproach, or correct a speaker openly. Rather, make note of the difficulty and, at a later time, give private help. Remember, the listening group is apt to be a sharp, discriminate, and selective audience. Their reactions may be harshly critical. This will be reproach enough, if reproach is needed, and it will require the tempered influence of a wise teacher.

Evaluating Time. There are three types of evaluations: each person evaluating himself, a preappointed committee evaluating each speaker, or an open-forum group evaluation. It may be that all three approaches are used in one session. Certainly, each person is going to evaluate himself. Help is needed, though, because many people tend to be their own severest critics and readily underrate what they have done.

The group approach is excellent, since it provides a type of therapy and catharsis at the same time. A we're-all-in-this-together feeling permeates the group and helps ease things along.

If a committee is chosen, the members should be carefully picked by the pupils. Then they should be provided with a list of things to look for and how to weigh them. For example, did the speaker talk loudly, clearly, and at a steady pace? Committee reports can be very helpful because they are usually objective.

Word-Attack Time. By now pupils have begun to recognize more clearly that learning how to decipher words is really a minor part of the total act of reading for meaning. This experience helps them put into perspective the need for and use of word-attack skills. It may be assumed, though, that, if the students can sense the role of word-attack skills in the total reading act, they have a better command of these skills than when they do not. Proceed, then, with the total group as though all needed the review and the training.

A good way to start this period of individualized instruction is to ask the following question: "What are the steps a good reader takes when he gets to a word he does not recognize?" Then list the steps in the order taught:

Look for meaning clues.

A. Read the sentence or paragraph in which the word occurs.

B. Look for picture clues.

There is little doubt about the fact that, most likely, the first thing a reader does when he gets to an unknown word is to try to "sound it out." However, at the intermediate level, as pupils meet more and more words that are not in their speaking vocabulary and only partially established in their listening vocabularies, sounding out a word does not render much service. This places a greater premium on meaning.

At the primary level, the following circumstances frequently existed when a word not immediately recognized was met:

Known: meaning
Known: spoken word
Unknown: printed word

At this level, ability to speak the printed word usually resulted in total recognition.

Conditions at the intermediate level are, in many instances, as follows:

Unknown: meaning
Unknown: spoken word
Unknown: printed word

At this stage, sounding out or "unlocking" a word so that it may be spoken contributes very little to the reader. For example, a pupil totally unfamiliar with the word *rind* as used in the story "Queen of the Circus Elephants" (9, pp. 154–160) would have no understanding of the word, even if he did pronounce it correctly. There is considerable likelihood that the pupil would, using phonetic clues correctly, pronounce the word *rĭnd*. This situation would require a look in the glossary and the use of phonetic respelling and the pronunciation key. Even if the pupil said *rĭnd,* this correct pronunciation would not give him any meaning. Such conditions multiply at the intermediate level and make the search for meaning all the more significant.

A look at the context in which *rind* appears (9, p. 154) shows that the alert reader intent on meaning could find excellent clues to its meaning:

> After each show, he watched people crowding out of the big tent. They bought watermelons at the food stands and ate them at nearby tables. Mr. Fields always hired two or three small boys to go around and pick up watermelon rinds after the people finished with them.

So, with meaning accomplished to a good degree, the reader would now be focusing on pronunciation, which he would need in order to discuss the plot orally. He tries his knowledge of phonetics and structure. Usually in a single-syllable word containing only one vowel and ending with a consonant, the vowel is short. The word *rind* is a typical example of the many exceptions to this rule.

Versatility in word attack is a must in the fund of skills of a trained pupil. If the word is totally new, he is beginning to realize that he must check the glossary.

Other words may be unlocked and then recognized because they are actually a part of a pupil's listening-meaning vocabulary. For example, the word *hibernation* may be handled by use of standard word-attack techniques. The syllable breaks follow the "rules," as do the syllable pronunciations (hī bẽr nā′ shun).

As already described, a pupil versatile in word-attack skills would perhaps need to check the word *rind* in the glossary. Similarly, a person not fully certain about *hibernation* should check in the glossary, too. For glossary use, the pupil must know how to deal with phonetic respellings, a pronunciation key, and accent marks. Then finally he must be able to blend sounds together.

Teacher aid may be sought to:

a. confirm context meaning
b. clarify glossary meaning
c. confirm independent use of word-attack skills
d. confirm use of glossary skills
e. tell the word

It is true that not all pupils are equally vigilant and zealous in their dealings with words. A good way to promote intellectual honesty is to seek and encourage it openly. When a pupil asks for teacher help, the assistance should be prompt, courteous, and correct. If this is the practice, pupils will feel that they are in a learning situation that encourages a positive interpretation of freedom.

A safeguard is needed though, regardless. This is achieved by teacher questioning. Go around the room and ask different pupils to pronounce words in the passages they are reading. Any teacher who knows her pupils will have a good idea as to which words they can deal with on their own and which they cannot deal with. Similarly, inquire about word meanings.

Make note of all word-recognition difficulties. Then, at a special time, have those who had similar needs meet together as a group for special instruction. This kind of word-recognition skill training is as much a part of individualized instruction as it is of group instruction. As a matter of fact, it may be even more valuable.

The Fourth Go-Round

By the time this fourth go-round occurs, pupils will be well versed in the idea of individualized self-selection. They will understand what a privilege and opportunity these sessions afford. Primarily, though, they will have learned that the self-selection opportunity results in a good deal of self-study. Likes and dislikes, deep-seated interests and passing fancies, will have crossed their selection guidelines and caused them to take long looks in their own mirrors.

They will also have noted that wide reading, research reading, and sharing preparation does not necessarily end when the individualized reading go-round ends. The continuity of school life bolstered by the continuity of their own interests will have resulted in a continuous seeking, even though basic readers are used during the formal reading instruction time. There are other times in the school day and at home when a pupil can follow up on an interest. Interests are not just turned off and on; they are the ignescent substances that spark the continuity of developing experience and specify the direction that intellectual growth will take.

As already pointed out, the amount and scope of the reading done during the individualized reading sessions takes as its limits the boundary of all knowledge. The total curriculum can and does give latitude to the reading. As a result, pupils soon realize that their interests and tastes, their inclinations and aptitudes go well beyond the bounds of even the best-stocked basic reader. So they will find such other times in the school day and the home-study hours as will allow them to pursue curriculum-based interests. The powers and purposes of the pupils provide in many ways a more important set of conditions for learning than those provided by the educators responsible for the curriculum. Individualized reading sessions can go a long way toward taking the compartmentalization out of a curriculum.

As a matter of fact, a return to the individualized session may result in the group or class starting with a sharing session rather than with a planning session to set goals. The reading, organizing, and preparing of reports was completed as described during the weeks when group sessions were being held. Now that the break-away from basic readers frees reading time for the multipurpose use of the individualized sessions, time will be available for sharing. Starting the individualized session with a sharing period is a gratifying indication that the goals of the two approaches (group and individual) are being attained.

During the 1930s one of the clichés that pedageesed its way back and forth across the national educational flyways was *blocks of time.* There was the so-called language-arts block, the science block, and the arithmetic block. Though the concepts of *blocks* smacked strongly of compartmentalization, it resulted in an integrating of skills, especially in the area of the language arts. Educators knew that listening-speaking-reading-writing were all facets of communication. The core-curriculum idea, which appeared on the pedagogical flyways at about the same time, helped to advance the *block-of-time* notion. Teachers attempted to integrate the language arts, but textbook publishers with their separately packaged reading books, spelling books, handwriting books, and English books blocked the way and continue to block the way today. Teachers unable to break the textbook-imposed lock step continue to hold a spelling class, a handwriting class, an English class, and a reading class; and never the four do meet!

However, teachers who use an individualized approach and do so as defined in this text soon discover that this approach does require use of all the communication skills and integrates the teaching of the skills in a high-order and natural way. This natural integration is an outgrowth of the reading-sharing idea and represents another major contribution of the individualized approach to reading instruction and, in fact, to all instruction.

Furthermore, the teacher sees that not only are all the communication skills being used, but efficiency in the use of the skills is being accomplished at an astonishing rate. Writing and spelling skills are being used and acquired functionally as are listening and speaking skills. This means that the time allotted on the daily schedule for teaching language arts (including spelling and handwriting) can often be used instead for individualized reading-instruction sessions. This leads the teacher to conclude that "individualized reading instruction" is actually a misnomer and that a more apt label would be "individualized instruction in the communication arts."

For this fourth go-round, the pupils should not need any basic-reader props. The momentum provided by identification of interests and freedom of choice should be such that each pupil can sustain himself. Purposes not fully attained may carry over from the previous individual D-R-T-A, as described. Purposes resulting from interests and activities in other areas of the curriculum and at last properly recognized as reading interests may keep the pupils going. Pupils may now begin to understand that every subject is a reading "subject," and that the time designated for directed reading instruction may be an "all subject" time.

This fourth go-round might appropriately be thought of as the time for a creative-reader breakthrough. Creativity, fortunately, is not circumscribed by intelligence, and grouping arrangements based on creative potential are not dictated by intelligence, as are grouping arrangements based on ability. Recent studies on creativity as reported by E. Paul Torrance show that (11, p. 5), "if we were to identify children as gifted on the basis of intelligence tests, we would eliminate from consideration approximately 70 percent of the most creative. This percentage seems to hold fairly well, no matter what measure of intelligence we use and no matter what educational level we study, from kindergarten through graduate school."

The circumstances described thus far that deal with individualized instruction reflect a creative grouping of children. The creative reader may engage in intensive reading or wide exploratory-type reading and enjoy the learning and thinking that result. It is creative reading and thinking that seem to represent the most desirable outcome. Torrance sums this all up extremely well when he says (11, p. 6):

> Instead of trying to cram a lot of facts into the minds of children and make them scientific encyclopedias, we must ask what kind of children they are becoming. What kind of thinking do they do? How resourceful are they? Are they becoming more responsible? Are they learning to give thoughtful explanations of the things they do and see? Do they believe their own ideas to be of value? Can they share ideas and opinions with others? Do they relate similar experiences together in order to draw conclusions? Do they do some thinking for themselves?

These ideas can be readily adapted to the reading situation.

Maintaining Creative-Reading Situations. The pupil who is sufficiently self-reliant to strike out on his own, identify his own purposes for reading, select material himself, and decide whether or not he has found answers is truly an independent person. It is readily understandable that some children cannot break away with as great ease as others from the more conventional group workings. It is so much less demanding to work with the group and let someone else do the thinking and planning and directing than it is to operate on one's own.

Some pupils are concerned, too, that if they work alone too much they may be rejected by the group. One of the best ways to overcome this feeling of rejection is to plan appropriate sharing periods. This is the time when those who operate independently share their knowledge with others and, if they have any doubts about their status, they can see it established or re-established.

Some children may be so concerned about rejection that they will find it quite difficult to work alone. The team approach is an excellent way of showing these people the values of working independently. It is often said among educators that children must learn to compete with themselves in order to improve their own achievement. One of the best ways to realize the value of this approach to learning is to work in an individualized situation. It is here that the feeling of competition with others is more apt to be replaced by competition with one's own achievement.

In situations where group reading is directed on a reading-thinking basis, teachers are frequently astonished by the degree of originality, flexibility, and inventiveness that the children display. Another thing they frequently note is that, even though a pupil is in the slow reading group, he may be as clever and original and inventive as pupils who are in the superior reading group. In fact, in many instances these pupils, who frequently are stifled in a situation in which basic readers are misused, appear to be more creative and flexible than their counterparts. They do well when reading is taught at their level and according to their own flexibility and creativity.

All too often it is assumed that children cannot learn while on their own. This is not true, as any well-planned, carefully directed program of individualized instruction will soon show. When properly motivated and guided, children like to be on their own. They are usually more productive and more original.

Creative readers are much more apt to try out difficult ideas. They are much more apt to go to the library, search diligently for materials, read carefully and critically, and finally prepare a lengthy report. In the process these people learn to deal with failure and frustration. They begin to see better and understand better the value of persistent effort, and they learn how to benefit by their own mistakes. They learn, too, how inadvisable it is to pursue a course that is leading down a blind alley.

E. Paul Torrance makes another very interesting statement (11, p. 117): "Creative children need some purpose which is worthy of the enthusiastic devotion they seem capable of giving."

Throughout this text the words *purpose* and *pupil purpose* have occurred over and over again, and it is relevant that people in the field of creativity, like Torrance, also point out the value of purpose. When students are permitted to declare their purposes, they achieve self-confidence creatively rather than by authority.

By the time of the fourth go-round on individualized instruction, the teacher will have noted how some pupils simply cannot stop reading; for them the individualized reading period never really comes to an end. They seem possessed of the drive so frequently thought of as characteristic of a scientist or an inventor. The fact that the decision to act is so largely their own seems to spur them on.

In situations in which individualized reading instruction occurs on the scale described here, the teacher can maintain a more balanced emotional distance. She is not involved as a coercive, authoritarian influence or as a powerless, inept instructor. The pupils are on their own, working creatively, unimpeded by the strains of a power struggle. The pupil-teacher relationship is open, nonthreatening, and creative.

Viewing this fourth go-round on a creative-reading basis suggests another look at materials. Minimum standards to take into account are: (1) availability of not less than a hundred selected books per class of thirty-five pupils, the books to be maintained on a rotation basis; (2) not less than five periodicals per class, ranging in interest to include, for example, such publications as *Arts and Activities, Children's Digest, Geographic School Bulletins, Highlights for Children,* and *Popular Mechanics;* (3) availability of one set of an encyclopedia per class; (4) availability of at least two anthologies of children's poetry; (5) a local newspaper, if one exists; (6) old copies of pamphlets or magazines such as *National Geographic, Life,* and *Nature Magazine;* (7) supplemental readers: and (8) special award books.

Bring into the classroom the Newbery Medal Award winners, the Caldecott Medal Award winners, and Science Award winners. This would be a good time to have the school librarian or a public-library specialist visit the classroom and discuss with the children some of the award-winning books. All the books are so delightful that it is difficult to suggest here four or five outstanding ones that might receive this special attention. The librarian, however, may do this according to her interest or according to what she has found to be the interest of other children.

Books represent only one of the sources available. At the end of this section there is an annotated list of children's periodicals. Again, it is suggested that a librarian or some other qualified person be invited to the classroom to talk about a number of these periodicals. It is readily evident from this list that there is a wide range of interests represented by periodicals. Some supply useful information; others furnish stories covering a multitude of interests. Some follow particular interest areas such as Scouting, Red Cross, science and aviation, geography, history, sports. Some are of special interest to girls; others to boys. The list mentions a wide range of magazines possessing different degrees of difficulty, ranging from *Wee Wisdom, Jack and Jill,* and *Highlights for Children* to *National Geographic Magazine, Science Digest,* and *Nature Magazine.*

In the last twenty-five years, magazines have grown in prestige and are rapidly being recognized as a primary source in literature. More people read magazines rather than books. The reasons seem to be clearly apparent: (1) magazines deal with a wide range of interests; (2) the stories vary in length; (3) the illustrations and pictures tend to be more varied in style and content; (4) the advertisements are interesting and informative; (5) magazines are easy to handle; (6) stories continued in subsequent issues hold reader interest and encourage recall; (7) many of the activities encourage thinking and doing.

American Childhood. 74 Park Street, Springfield, Massachusetts 01105. (5–9 years.) Educational magazine published for kindergarten and primary grades, 10 months of the year, Sept.–June. 1 year, $4.

American Farm Youth. Jackson at Van Buren, Danville, Illinois 61832. (Boys, 14–24 years.) Published nine months of the year, Sept.–May.

American Girl. 830 Third Avenue, New York, New York 10022. (Girls, 10–16 years, whether they belong to Girl Scouts or not.) Published monthly by the Girl Scouts of America.

American Heritage. 551 Fifth Avenue, New York, New York 10017. Six issues per year. Top flight historical material for superior readers. 1 year, $11.75.

American Junior Red Cross Journal. American National Red Cross, Washington, D.C. 20006. (Junior High and High School.) Published by the American National Red Cross and distributed mainly to schools enrolled in the Junior Red Cross. Subscriptions accepted, but actually publications are designed as program material for the membership.

American Junior Red Cross News. American National Red Cross, Washington, D.C. 20006. Same as *American Junior Red Cross Journal,* but on elementary-school level.

Arts and Activities. 8150 N. Central Park Avenue, Skokie, Illinois 60076. (5–12 years.) Published 10 months of the year.

Audubon Magazine. 1130 Fifth Avenue, New York, New York 10028. (15 years and up.) Published by the National Audubon Society.

Boy's Life. New Brunswick, New Jersey. (Scouts and others. 8–13 years.) Published by the Boy Scouts of America.

Child Life. 3516 College Avenue, Indianapolis, Indiana 46205. (3–10 years.) Published 10 months of the year.

Children's Digest. 52 Vanderbilt Avenue, New York, New York 10017. (7–12 years.)

Children's Play Mate Magazine. 6529 Union Avenue, Cleveland, Ohio 44105. (6–12 years.)

Co-Ed. Scholastic Magazines, 33 W. 42nd Street, New York, New York 10036. (Homemaking classes, grades 7–12.) Teachers ordering 10 or more subscriptions to *Co-Ed* receive a free copy of the teacher's edition.

Current Events. American Education Publications, Education Center, Columbus, Ohio 43216. (Grades 6, 7, and 8.) Eight-page current events paper.

Current Science and Aviation. American Education Publications, Education Center, Columbus, Ohio 43216. (Grades 7–12.) Weekly science newspaper, eight pages.

Every Week. American Education Publications, Education Center, Columbus, Ohio 43216. (Grades 9 and 10.) Especially designed for use in world history, civics, and geography classes.

Explorer. Scholastic Magazines, 33 W. 42nd Street, New York, New York 10036. (Grade 4.) Stories, news, and activities. Published weekly during school year.

Field and Stream. 530 Fifth Avenue, New York, New York 10036. Not intended as a children's magazine, but it is read by many boys, because they find a great deal in each issue that guides them in sportsmanship.

Flying. Ziff-Davis Publishing Company, 1 Park Avenue, New York, New York 10016. Advanced reading level.

Flying Models. 215 Park Avenue South, New York, New York 10003. (12–21 years.) Aimed at model builders of all ages.

Geographic School Bulletins. National Geographic Society, 1146 16th Street, N.W., Washington, D.C. 20006. Weekly bulletin used by children from fifth and sixth grades up through college, but there are more readers in junior and senior high school than in the elementary grades.

Highlights For Children. 2300 West Fifth Avenue, Columbus, Ohio 43216. (2–12 years.) Interesting, meaningful reading and activities for children. $5 a year, but $4 when sent to school or library address.

Humpty Dumpty. 52 Vanderbilt Avenue, New York, New York 10017. (3–7 years.)

Jack and Jill. Curtis Publishing Company, Independence Square, Philadelphia, Pennsylvania 19107. (5–10 years.) Boys and girls of primary and preintermediate grades.

Junior Bazaar for Children. 572 Madison Avenue, New York, New York 10022. *Harper's Junior Bazaar* no longer exists as such, but was incorporated into *Harper's Bazaar.* Consists of fashions for children and appears in alternate months. No fewer than four pages.

Junior Natural History Magazine. American Museum of Natural History, Central Park West at 79th Street, New York, New York 10024. (8–15 years.) Popular introduction to all phases of natural history.

Junior Review. Civic Education Service, 1733 K Street N.W., Washington, D.C. 20006. (Junior High School.) Eight-page paper. Gives students a clear, stimulating introduction to national and world problems.

Literary Cavalcade. Scholastic Magazines, 33 W. 42nd Street, New York, New York 10036. Modern Literature, creative writing for grades 9–12.

Model Airplane News. 551 Fifth Avenue, New York, New York 10017. Junior aviation science. Not a child's publication, but about 30,000 8-12-year-olds read this magazine.

National Geographic Magazine. National Geographic Society, 1146 16th Street, N.W., Washington, D.C. 20006. Monthly.

Natural History Magazine. American Musuem of Natural History, 79th Street and Central Park West, New York, New York 10024. (14 years and older, mostly college and adult.) 10 issues annually.

Newstime. Scholastic Magazine, 33 W. 42nd Street, New York, New York 10036. (Grade 5.) Language Arts, Social Studies, Science.

Popular Mechanics. 200 E. Ontario Street, Chicago, Illinois 60611. Published Monthly. 1 year, $3.50.

Read. American Education Publications, Education Center, Columbus, Ohio 43216. (Grades 6–9.) Balanced variety of the best in current reading for both English and social-studies classes. 32 pages, twice each month.

Scholastic Magazine. *Junior Scholastic* for Junior High School, English and social studies. *Senior Scholastic* for Senior High School, social studies. 33 W. 42nd Street, New York, New York 10036.

Science Digest. 959 Eighth Avenue, New York, New York 10019. Published monthly. 1 year, $3.50.

Seventeen. 320 Park Avenue, New York, New York 10022. (Girls, 13–19 years.)

Sporting News. 2018 Washington Avenue, St. Louis, Missouri 63103. Not intended as children's magazine, but read by many boys. Digest of baseball news, published weekly.

Sports Afield. Hearst Magazines Division of the Hearst Corporation, 959 Eighth Avenue, New York, New York 10019. No fiction. Editorial format designed for hunting, fishing, and boating enthusiasts. Not a child's magazine primarily, but many young people find it interesting and informative.

World Week. 33 W. 42nd Street, New York, New York 10036. (Grades 8–10.) Social studies.

Young Perfectionist, The. *Harper's Junior Bazaar* incorporated into *Harper's Bazaar.* 572 Madison Avenue, New York, New York 10022. Consists of about 10 pages of fashions for the younger set every month.

It must not be thought that the creativity referred to in the fourth go-round evidences itself at this point only. Nothing could be farther from the truth. Many teachers and many, many more pupils take to individualized reading like ducks take to water. So, quite to the contrary, creativity in choice of reading could very well manifest itself on the first go-round.

Neither should it be thought that magazine reading is not stressed until the fourth go-round. This, too, could very easily occur at an earlier stage, depending upon the teacher and her pupils.

It must be kept in mind, therefore, that the careful spelling out of degrees of involvement under each successive go-round are provided primarily for the teacher who is very uncertain about how to proceed. In other words, these details represent a form of teacher pacing. Once a teacher and a class have gained the "degrees of freedom" that experience and knowledge and liberty will foster, they can free-wheel, so to speak. In the process both the teacher and pupils will acquire what John Dewey (3, p. 49) refers to as the most important *attitude* that can be formed—the desire to go on learning. Freed to use their native capacities this way, pupils are prepared to cope with the learning circumstances they will meet in the course of life. What does it avail a pupil if he learns to say words and parrot texts, if in the process he loses his ability to read and think creatively and critically, if he loses all desire to apply what he has learned, and, above all, if he loses a love for reading?

The Fifth Go-Round

Pupil comments recorded in bulletins, periodicals, and books about individualized reading indicate their strong feelings of satisfaction and elation. "Reading is fun now." "I like this." "Oh, see what I found!" "Are there more books like this one?" "I can get it myself." These typical pupil responses represent in many instances initial or early reactions to their new freedom.

Any one method or technique can become just as taxing and boring as any other. This is as true of individualized instruction as it is of group instruction. Of course, where the latter is concerned, it is especially true if basic-reader programs foist improper practices and attitudes on children.

Similarly, malpractices can result in woefully inadequate individualized reading instruction. Most damaging is the lack of directed instruction in *comprehension*. As already stated in the plans for individualized instruction in the second go-round, this is one area that has been left largely to chance by some proponents of individualized reading. A major technique for checking on comprehension, described by many reporters on individualized instruction, is for the teacher to ask a pupil a few questions about what he has read. This is one approach that can be used, but it represents one of the weakest ways of teaching skill in comprehension. Inadequate supplies of books, periodicals, and newspapers can soon leave a class floundering. Lack of planning can quickly result in a disorganized, irresponsible, and frustrating period.

All this points up the need for *pacing*. Teacher pacing must be done to help each child to locate materials in keeping with his interests and skills, to develop purposes that are clearly defined, to organize knowledge gained, to appraise understanding, to share adequately with others, to provide needed skill training, and to foster interest in wide reading. All this must be done at a tempo that will assure a maximum amount of success and a minimum amount of frustration for each pupil.

Other Ideas About Getting Started

A top-flight text on individualized reading is *Helping Children Read* (1) by Peggy Brogan and Lorene K. Fox. The cases they describe of "Miss Meeker" and "Mr. Carlson" illustrate classroom circumstances in which the reading instruction is entirely individualized. Relevant ideas can be gleaned that will have guiding value to the teacher who has a more comprehensive program—one using the advantages of group-directed reading-thinking activities and individualized-directed reading-thinking activities. The reports by Brogran and Fox should be read from this perspective of reading instruction. After reading Chapters 5 and 6 of this book those ideas that are pertinent should be readily identifiable by the reader.

Finally, the ideas of Jeannette Veatch on how to get started and how to share seem timely (12, pp. 48–51):

One-Group-at-a-Time Change-Over

You will take your first steps toward individualizing reading during the regular reading period of the group that you have decided will participate. The rest of the class will continue without change. Independent seatwork will be carried on as usual.

At first, increase the amount of silent reading in the change-over group and decrease the amount of oral reading. Encourage, or at least do not prevent, children reading on ahead of the rest of the group. Give praise and encouragement when you notice children proceeding through their book rapidly and with comprehension.

Work on skills at the end of the period and then deal only with what proved to be most difficult in what was read. Take notes on each child. You may, at first, have everyone work on skills, but try not to have any child wait while you teach a skill that he already knows. Gear each day's skill session more and more to the needs of each pupil until the time comes when each is on the individual plan and the group is disbanded.

As the days pass, encourage each child to come to you when he is ready. As the rest read on silently, have him read a part of the story he has selected—the "best" part, the "funniest" part, etc. Discuss the story with the child, enjoy it with him, ask him to tell you what happens next or what has preceded. In this way you set up a personalized teaching situation and children will come to recognize your genuine interest in what they are doing. . . .

The Individual Conference

If all is running smoothly with each child settled with a book that he likes and can read (and your independent work has been planned), you are ready to retire to your chosen spot with notebook in hand and wait for volunteers. Some teachers put up a list of the names of the children who have already indicated their readiness for their individual conference. Other teachers take volunteers first and organize an "on deck" arrangement so that each will have a fair chance to read. One of the pleasures of individualized reading is to see the eagerness with which children beg for their turn with their teacher. Children will object strongly if they consider they have been unfairly passed over as far as the individual conferences are concerned.

It is interesting that most teachers agree that conferences should be held on a voluntary basis. Having children come by alphabetical order, or by rows or tables, seems to have an immediate inhibiting effect on their interest in their reading. Evidently a child's decision as to when he is ready to come for individual conference is important to his motivation to read.

Should a child come to his conference unprepared, you must gently but firmly send him back. Be sure he knows exactly what is wrong: perhaps he was in too much of a hurry to choose a book, perhaps the book was too hard, etc.

Any alert teacher will follow up a child who does not seem eager to come for his conference. If there is a consistent lack of eagerness, it could be a signal that something is wrong with the motivational sequence. Maybe there are not enough books or not enough *interesting* books. It could be that the individual conference does not seem important to the child. (Perhaps you, yourself, have not emphasized it enough!)

Usually, however, there will be little sign of reticence. As one teacher put it: "They are yanking at my skirts *all* the time. 'Can I read to you now?' 'Can I read to you now, *please?*' And I just have to figure out ways to do it."

There are many other reports on individualized instruction. Those presented here are more or less typical of what is being said. On occasion, a report indicates that the teacher is using basic readers as well as individualized instruction procedures. The account by Maida Wood Sharpe is illustrative (8, pp. 507–508).

A SCHOOL-WIDE APPROACH

Much of the discussion up to this point has dealt with the adapting of instruction in a classroom. Many of the ideas presented implied frequently that the use of individualized instruction and group procedures should be the program for the school. Since the use of both approaches represents the best comprehensive program of reading instruction, the all-school idea is obvious.

Moving into the individualized phase of this dual-track reading program may result in more questions and more hesitancy. It seems timely, therefore, to describe briefly what might be done on a school-wide basis to get started and keep going on a comprehensive program of reading instruction.

To effect a change without violating the integrity of any one teacher can be accomplished if the administrative staff lends its genuine support. This includes the school superintendent, the school principal, the elementary supervisor, and/or the reading supervisor.

Action may fruitfully be initiated from the top or from the bottom. If the administrators initiate the plan, it will be wise to do so by meeting with teachers to define the program and the reasons for the proposed change. Teachers will react in varied ways according to their own understanding of the objectives of sound reading instruction and their facility as teachers. By and large, though, the teachers will lend a receptive ear to proposals that will improve the teaching of reading and the reading competency of their pupils. On the first presentation, time should be allowed for teacher questions.

This first meeting will start teachers talking and thinking. Hardly a school will be without a teacher who has not tried either or both approaches. They will make greater effort to practice the steps, and others will be interested. Of course, hardly a school is without one or two dyed-in-the-wool, all-manual basic-reader miss-useists, but these teachers often develop into assets rather than liabilities to the administrative plan. First, because change is the tempo of these days, their belligerent and defensive attitude will readily be spotted by others. Second, the arguments they will advance will be of the variety already referred to in this text and therefore readily answerable. Third, they seldom want to demonstrate what they are doing. Fourth, when they do understand and develop some confidence in the dual approach, they do a turnabout and become very eager supporters of it.

A teachers' committee could be appointed to study the administrators' proposal, to talk with other teachers informally and, generally, to lay the groundwork. This committee might also single out teachers who are already practicing one or both procedures to serve as spokesmen and, better yet, to demonstrate. A next meeting should then be planned to air further thinking and, perchance, to have teacher demonstrations. If films are available, they should be used. There is no substitute, though, for demonstrations and discussions.

Interclassroom visits might now be planned. Teams might be organized either on a level basis or on a plans basis. A consultant might be invited to meet with the teachers, demonstrate for them, and answer questions. A committee should be appointed to survey the school and its facilities, especially the library, to determine what it needs to operate on the dual plan.

Once the plan is initiated, the teacher get-togethers should continue. This is when the most pertinent questions may be asked. Demonstrations might be continued, as should interclassroom visits. Consultant service should be continued for two or more years, since this is about how long it will take to put a dual program into effect. In the meantime the school administrators will have been eager participants in all of the sessions, even though the responsibility was turned over to a teacher committee.

If, on the other hand, impetus for the changeover comes from the teachers, the rate of progress will be quicker. Now it is the administrative staff that may take convincing. Just as with teachers, administrators have heard about both group-directed reading-thinking activities and individualized-directed reading-thinking activities. Being more answerable in many ways to the public for the achievement of the pupils than teachers are, they are more receptive to ideas that will improve the reading program. Since basic readers are not discarded but used more wisely, they will not feel that the plan is revolutionary. Putting basic readers aside periodically will not be too big a departure. Every teacher has been doing something like this anyway, or has been urged to. Use of the library is a desired goal and one that all administrators want their teachers to seek.

When the plan is teacher initiated, there is some likelihood that teachers opposed to the idea will be more demanding. Some teachers are more resentful of an invasion of their privacy by other teachers than they are by an administrator. This usually, though, is characteristic of their teaching. They dominate the classroom on an assignment-recitation-memorization basis, and they expect the respect of little corporals. In turn, they are ready to obey the captains. A good procedure, though, is to involve these teachers on a team or a committee. Again consultant service may be desirable. Usually the teachers have someone in mind to render such service.

In all of this, whether the plan is initiated by the administrators or the teachers, wise planning of teacher meetings is essential. A teacher's day is long and arduous, and her end-of-the-school-day time should not be imposed upon. So, if meetings are held, demonstrations made, and consultant service obtained, much of this should be planned to occur during the school day. In some instances administrators arrange that half of the meeting time be school time and half be after-school time, a compromise that is well received by many.

INDIVIDUAL DIFFERENCES

Every teacher knows that children are different, that the differences exist before the children come to school, and that good teaching increases pupil differences. Some teachers know that the range of differences among six-year-olds or entering first-graders is a spread of about four to five years and that by the fourth-grade level the spread is about eight years. (See Chapter 5 for quotations in support of this in Goodlad and Anderson, pp. 346 and 347.) Some know, too, as pointed out earlier, that intrapupil variance can be greater than interpupil differences.

Every teacher knows, too, that some pupils learn at a faster rate than others. The rate of intake is influenced considerably by the student's capacity to learn, but attitude, motivation, and social-cultural factors also play a part. Every teacher can conclude that the purpose of individualized instruction is to provide for individual differences. This being the case, to discuss the role of the slow learner or the retarded reader seems like an awkward contradiction of the basic premises of individualized instruction.

If teaching is geared to the level of each pupil, regulated by his interests, tastes, and experiences and his capacity to make decisions about what he "selects" to read, and if it is "paced" by the teacher's knowledge of each pupil and of the materials, each pupil will achieve at his best level (5). It is not a question of the slow learner or the gifted or the average or the retarded. In fact, a basic principle of individualized instruction and of pacing is to adjust pupil expectancy in keeping with the best estimate of pupil capacity.

Accordingly, expectancies for the slow and the gifted must be adjusted. Acquisition of skills must be paced by each pupil's rate of intake. The fast learner will need fewer repetitions, less obvious presentations because of his ability to put two and two together, more material to aid him in his search for more refined meanings, and perhaps less guidance. The slow learner will need easy step-by-step presentations, many repetitions, material at his readability level, and perhaps more guidance. His purposes may be more simple and factual than complex and hypothetical, and his findings will be geared accordingly.

In those situations where these conditions are not fully understood and practices adjusted and paced accordingly, false notions result. One of the most prevalent and frequently quoted is the notion attributed to children that at last they feel more secure in reading class because they are no longer in the "dummy group" or in the "red-bird group." Step into any classroom in which reading instruction is effectively individualized and ask a pupil who is the best reader in the room, and he can quickly name the pupil. Similarly, ask for the name of the poorest reader in the class, and the pupil is readily named. Pupils know each other, their levels and potentials. As a matter of fact, there is less deception on this score than in a regimented "group" situation. Pupils work together in different groups, and many are spontaneously formed by the pupils. Interest groups, skill groups, friendship groups, special-ability groups, and teams all result in a shifting and reshifting of pupils and in pupils knowing each other better. As in sports, any group will be able to name the best all-around athlete in its midst, the best baseball player, and the poorest player.

If pupils know each other so well, why do they make such comments? What is being reflected, of course, is the misuse of basic readers, the misunderstanding of grade norms, and the rigidity of teacher thinking and planning. What is also reflected through the individualized instruction is the increased understanding among pupils—the spirit of working together, the lend-a-helping-hand spirit, and, of course, the better acceptance of pupils by each other. In addition, the steady diet of success breeds success. Pupils work harder, are more friendly and cooperative, and more appreciative of small success. They see more clearly how to win friends and influence people by playing up each other's assets and working cooperatively to overcome each other's liabilities. Team spirit permeates the air.

WHAT ABOUT PARENTS?

Parents will be kept posted officially or unofficially. Children will talk and tell, and they will do so even more readily if they have successes to report. The transition from the "I-tell-you; read; you-tell-me; read-orally" approach to the "I-believe-in-you, so-think-and-predict; read; prove-by-reading-orally" approach will result in enthusiastic tales of successes as all the "private eyes" go home and boast about another case resolved. The seeking, self-selecting, reading, sharing of the individualized sessions will evoke similar enthusiasms and reports at home.

The fact that a basic-reading program is not discontinued and that group instruction is continued leads parents to think that basically the reading program has not been altered. The fact that individualized instruction has been added with the resultant wider reading leads parents to conclude that the basic program, if anything, has been modified in such a way as to result in more and better reading. These are welcome changes and the modification is heralded. Parents do not question practices that are productive. If a child has been experiencing difficulty with reading and has disliked the subject, and now reads more easily and seems to like it, his parent might call to inquire about the reasons and to express gratitude. Similarly, if a superior or a creative child had been stifled prior to the dual approach, a parent may call to express his thanks for the change.

It seems then, as E. W. Dolch (4) has suggested, that it is unnecessary to have a great deal of publicity about the changes that are occurring. Let the success of the "changes" speak for themselves. All this is not to imply that suddenly a magic wand is waved and a panacea found. Much instructional work needs to be done, and much learning effort needs to be made. The wise use of basic readers for group-directed reading-thinking activities and the "easing" of tension that results when individualized reading-thinking activities are used also result in reading performance that are quiet and self-assured.

At a meeting of the P.T.A. or a meeting of homeroom parents a teacher might explain how she is using the basic readers and the library, how she is directing group reading and individualized reading, and how the change in pupil attitude came about. Demonstrations might be made of both approaches. The group method for a D-R-T-A lends itself especially well to demonstration purposes. Children from one of the classes might be used as a demonstration class, or a group of parents might be asked to serve as a class. This latter is an especially good way to demonstrate how reading can be taught as a thinking process. Parents who are active participants in a demonstration soon see what is happening and how it is happening. The ways of learning and thinking are the same at all levels. Or a "sharing" period resulting from an individual D-R-T-A may be planned for a P.T.A. session. This is an excellent time to show parents how much reading is being done and why it is being done. Sometimes an outcome of sharing sessions is a classroom paper or a classroom book. Both can be shared with parents in a very gratifying way.

If a library is in need of more materials, as most of them are, funds raised through P.T.A. activities may be assigned for such a purpose. More books for the home may be bought. Yearly subscriptions to magazines may be paid for by different parents. Or a group of parents may subscribe to a book club and assign the books to the room. Parents with different skills and abilities may agree to come to school and discuss their occupations or their hobbies and answer questions. All in all, the end result can promote top-flight home-school cooperation.

It is far better to operate this way than to set up false expectancies or create unnecessary inquiries about a new program. Neither aspect of the dual approaches is extremist in nature. Combining the two makes for a solid program that not only teaches reading skills but also fosters favorable attitudes toward reading and does so on an individual pupil level.

SUMMARY

It should be apparent that a sound and comprehensive program of reading instruction will include both group-directed reading-thinking activities using basic readers and individualized-directed reading-thinking activities using all kinds of materials. Both phases have distinct contributions to make not only in the area of reading-thinking skills but also in terms of motivation for and attitudes toward reading. Perhaps the most distinctive contribution is the developing of a permanent reading habit.

That "love is not enough" to develop reading skill and the reading habit has been apparent for some time. Children must be given a steady diet of success—merited success—at their level if these objectives are to be attained. What constitutes success is determined by acquisition of skill as much as a steady pacing on an individual level. In a group situation in which the thinking of the children is invited and respected and responsibility for proof rests with the individual, authority is vested in the pupils and the text. Each has a chance to be unique, to be different, to be special. His ideas will be respected; all he needs to do is state them and let them reflect his experience and his knowledge. His chances for status and self-respect are high.

All this regard for himself as a learner is even further enhanced as each pupil moves into the individualized phase of the instructional program. Now it is his decision, his level of aspiration, his self-esteem that set the pace. Both teacher and class recognize his competence. All that is asked of him is that his own interests, tastes, and experiences, his own desires and values be the directing influence. Furthermore, children have an intense desire for honesty and truth—especially the child who has met failure—and both of the approaches to reading instruction are based firmly on each pupil's seeking after honesty and truth. Tyranny resides not in failure but in success; not in teacher questions but in pupil conjectures; not in opinions and notions but in substantiated proof. Pupils are encouraged to think their own thoughts deeply and courageously, to make hypotheses about a set of circumstances that are of their own choosing; and, in short, to be free to be themselves. As William O. Penrose has aptly said, "Freedom is ourselves" (6).

Children taught this dual way are learning a way of thinking, a way of arranging and rearranging facts, a way of searching for and discovering a right structure, a way of getting at the truth. They are acquiring attitudes and actions associated with inquiry, first, in the crucible of a group in which all are seeking after the truth by following the same sequences, and then in the uniquely personal atmosphere of on-your-own self-seeking and of the imposing demands for thoroughness and honesty that the sharing of knowledge imposes on the scholar. Both the group instruction and the individualized instruction utilize a problem-solving approach, whether the problem be one of personal-social escape or an intense desire to see and understand the order of things in science.

The psychology of learning has indicated quite clearly for a long time that pupils will participate actively in learning if their thinking is invited, their ideas respected, and their help sought in the planning. Achievement of a goal—one that is clearly connected with a pupil-stated problem—is its own reward. Even failure to prove a conjecture right, if appropriately recognized, can be rewarding. At least the learner sees where and how he erred. He sees that answers that confirm previous evaluation and speculation are much better retained and of greater use than answers memorized as a result of imposed goals.

In brief, the philosophy, the methods, and the objectives described in Chapters 2 through 6 could best be described as freedom to think, to inquire, and to learn at a pace in keeping with each individual's capacity, interest, experience, and knowledge.

REFERENCES

1. Brogan, Peggy, and Lorene K. Fox, *Helping Children Read*, New York, Holt, Rinehart and Winston, 1961.
2. Cook, Walter W., and Theodore Clymer, "Acceleration and Retardation," *Individualizing Instruction*, Sixty-first Yearbook of the National Society for the Study of Education, Part I, Chicago, University of Chicago Press, 1962.
3. Dewey, John, *Experience and Education*, New York, Macmillan, 1938.
4. Dolch, E.W., "Individualized Reading vs. Group Reading II," *Elementary English*, *39* (January, 1962), 14–21.
5. Olson, Willard C., "Seeking, Self-Selection, and Pacing in the Use of Books by Children," *The Packet* (Boston), 7 (Spring, 1952), 3–10.
6. Penrose, William O., *Freedom Is Ourselves*, University of Delaware Monograph Series, No. 2, Newark, Del., University of Delaware Press, 1952.
7. Russell, David H., "An Evaluation of Some Easy-To-Read Trade Books for Chil-

dren," *Elementary English,* 38 (November, 1961), 475–482.

8. Sharpe, Maida Wood, "An Individualized Reading Program," *Elementary English,* 35 (December, 1958), 507–512.

9. Stauffer, Russell G., Alvina Treut Burrows, and Thomas D. Horn, *Above the Clouds,* New York, Holt, Rinehart and Winston, 1961.

10. Stauffer, Russell G., Alvina Treut Burrows, and Thomas D. Horn, *Teachers' Edition for Above the Clouds,* New York, Holt, Rinehart and Winston, 1962.

11. Torrance, E. Paul, *Guiding Creative Talent,* Englewood Cliffs, N.J., Prentice-Hall, 1962.

12. Veatch, Jeannette, *Individualizing Your Reading Program,* New York, Putnam's, 1959. Reprinted by permission. Copyright © 1959 by G. P. Putnam's Sons.

PART IV ❧❧❧ BEGINNING READING INSTRUCTION

Chapter 7
Readiness for Reading

The term used most commonly to refer to the level of competency required to respond successfully to initial reading instruction is *reading readiness*. The concept signified by this term has a long history imbedded in the concept of *readiness for learning* (32). Over the years scholars like Jean Jacques Rosseau, Johann H. Pestalozzi, Friedrich Froebel, Johann F. Herbart, William James, and John Dewey have declared, modified, and extended the concept of readiness for learning until there was formulated a *readiness* concept as we know it today. Readiness for learning deals with basic ideas of human growth and development—physiological, intellectual, social, and emotional.

Readiness for reading as a concept apparently received sanction on the national scene with the publication of the Twenty-fourth Yearbook of the National Society for the Study of Education (27). Section B of Chapter 3 was devoted to "Experience and Training Which Prepare Pupils for Reading." Section C of this same chapter dealt with "Classification of First-Grade Children." If both of these sections are studied, one can gain a certain perspective on *readiness* as it is used today. The purpose of Section C of the Yearbook was to point out the wide differences among pupils entering the first grade. Those pupils who came fully prepared for instruction in reading were said to come from homes or kindergartens in which they had been prepared. Those who were not adequately prepared for reading instruction needed training similar to that outlined for kindergarten children. This was a training that would "extend their experience, develop habits of good thinking, improve their use of oral English, increase their vocabularies, improve and refine their enunciation and pronunciation, and stimulate keen interest in reading" (27, p. 31). In addition, they also said that "conscious attention at home and in the kindergarten to the six types of training which have been enumerated promotes growth that makes reading a natural and desirable activity in the first grade" (27, p. 27).

Studies on individual differences and human growth and development, along with experience in trying to teach readiness, led educators to see that "home" influence and kindergarten training might make a difference, but they were not a substitute for maturation. Increasing numbers of reading failures continued to occur. Gradually, the concept of *reading readiness* changed to *readiness for reading,* and from *readiness for reading at the beginning reading stages* to *readiness at all levels.* This was the interpretation given by Gray (14) in the Thirty-sixth Yearbook of the National Society for the Study of Education. In essence, this change in interpretation was giving recognition to the principle of continuity and interaction of experience (5, p. 27): "continuity of experience means that every experience both takes up something from those which have gone before and modifies in some way the quality of those which come after"; interaction "assigns equal rights to both factors in experience—objective and internal conditions" (5, pp. 38–39). As a matter of fact, it might be wise to drop the readiness idea and substitute for it the concept of maturity. Maturity in reading, then, implies some basic hypotheses concerning human growth and development and certain assumptions concerning the attitudes, interests, and skills involved in reading (15). Maturity is recognized as a process and not thought of as a level of achievement. William S. Gray and Bernice Rogers discuss the six characteristics of mature citizens in a democracy (15, p. 49): (1) feelings of security and adequacy; (2) understanding of self and others; (3) recognition of democratic values and goals; (4) problem-solving attitudes and methods; (5) self-discipline, responsibility, and freedom; (6) constructive attitudes toward change. If to these characteristics are added "improvement of vocabularies and use of language," then the seven characteristics direct attention to goals to be reached at all stages of progress toward the highest order of *maturity in reading* as well as citizenship. And how interesting it is that with only one modification the six are indicative of a mature reader in a democracy! The maturing citizen as well as the maturing reader is acquiring attitudes that encourage growth and responsibility rather than merely seeking a level. Learning to read is not only accomplished throughout school but also throughout life, and similarly learning to be a citizen is a matter of growth throughout life. Goethe is quoted as saying, "The dear people do not know how long it takes to learn to read. I have been at it all my life and I cannot yet say I have reached the goal" (15, p. 56). Maturity, then, is more an attitude toward reading and a willingness to keep trying than it is a level of competency. It is, in short, an ongoing process.

DEVELOPING MATURITY FOR INITIAL READING SUCCESS

Thus far in this discussion of *readiness for reading* physiological factors have been dealt with only indirectly. While it is true that a person's physical condition can influence his intellectual performance, it is also true that unless a disability is extremely severe it may not have much, if any, retarding influence. All too often, lack of physical fitness is used as an excuse for lack of effort on the part of both the pupil and the teacher. Disabilities of one sort or another, sometimes even the most minor ones, are used as socially acceptable excuses for lack of effort. If a disability exists and if what is considered acceptable development has not occurred, the teacher can render a considerable service by wise counsel and individualized teaching.

Studies of physical maturation indicate a close relationship between growth curves and reading success. Growth curves should, however, be viewed as they are by Willard C. Olson (30), whose concept of "organismic age" was based on the intellectual, social, emotional, and physiological growth and development of children. Where physical growth is studied on a single-aspect basis, the findings cannot be conslusive. Teachers should stay alert to such discernible symptoms as fatigue, hyperactivity, overweight and underweight, frequent illnesses, particularly colds, poor posture, and so on. The proper school authorities and the parents should be alerted when symptoms are noted.

Vision and hearing deficiencies have a rather high incidence. Studies (2, 11, 33) show a significant relationship between hearing and vision acuity and reading success. It is now the practice in most schools to check for visual and auditory defects of entering first graders. Teachers should inquire about each pupil, make adjustments as recommended, and urge parents to follow up on the recommendations. Where such studies are not made, teachers should be alert to such symptoms as the position in which the head is held, requests for repeating of instructions, unnatural tone of voice, incorrect pronunciation, earache, excessive blinking or twitching, frowning, position of book, watery eyes, widely dilated pupils, and red or granulated eyelids.

Even though most first graders are farsighted, extensive television viewing and looking at children's books and comics sometimes influences eye adjustment. In general, books for six-year-olds are printed in a larger type size. Make sure, when writing on a chalkboard, that the words are large enough to be read from the back of the room.

Developing Language Facility

Children, like adults, like to talk about themselves, their possessions, their home, their family, their pets, their friends, their neighbors, their relatives, their trips. Invite them to talk about these subjects and to use whatever props are needed and appropriate: pictures, toys, easels, flannel boards, puppets, pets, and so on.

Invite children to bring to class pictures of themselves or of their families. Pictures may be of occasions such as a family trip, a picnic, a birthday party. Have children who bring such pictures show them to the class and tell about the picture. This is a good time to alert them to details of experiences. Where was the picture taken? Who is in the picture? What did you do after the pictures were taken? Some prodding questions may result in answers; some may not.

Pupils who do not have pictures or who forget to bring them can find ones they like in books, magazines, newspapers. This way they can tell a story about the picture(s) picked or simply discuss the picture. Again, concept-formulating questions can be raised about time, space, number, action, feeling.

A single picture may or may not evoke much response. A lot will depend on its size and its contents. If the pupil who brought the picture is also in the picture, pupil talk is more apt to result. If more than one picture is brought and they are about a particular event, the series of pictures may produce more talk and more language usage. This is good. It is like a series of cartoons in a comic strip or a series of pictures in *Life* magazine. The varied settings and content may result in use of words that may astonish the teacher. Pupils often know specific labels of objects or can name events and processes. If a child cannot think of a term, it can be supplied. Scope and accuracy of word knowledge can be checked as well as enriched.

Toys serve as excellent props for oral-language usage—either toys brought from home or toys available in school. A pupil can say all kinds of things about a toy: why he likes it; where he got it; how long he has had it; why it is his favorite; why others can play with it; how Daddy repaired it; and so on. Again, the possibilities are tremendous. Toys may be more effective than pictures because they are "originals" and not "reproductions." They require less projection of imagination and make fewer demands on memory.

Pets are useful in a similar way. Of course, pets pose problems that toys and pictures do not, but provisions can be made. Parents may bring pets to school and stay with the pet while it is being seen and talked about. One young fellow's mother brought his pet duck to school, and this provoked a tremendous amount of interest and oral-language usage. The children listened and imitated the "quack" sound. They called the duck "the talking duck."

The schoolroom provides numerous opportunities for oral-language usage. The front of the room, the back of the room, the rocker corner, the books, the clothing closets, the lavatory, the windows can all be talked about and compared with similar things at home.

Similarly, the school building can provide many stimuli. Visits can be made to the principal's office, the school nurse, the cafeteria, the auditorium, the playground, the parking lot. A good feature about such trips is that they can easily be made more than once. Recontact may help fix some of the language used and the ideas learnd. The richness and variety of television programs can also be stimulating.

Visits to other classes and by other classes at the same grade level and at higher grade levels is useful. Show-and-tell sessions had their origin in the desire to promote, among other things, oral-language usage.

Readiness books may also be used. Of course, the stimuli for oral-language usage and development in the readiness book that accompanies a basic-reader series are pictures, the chief asset of which is that all in a group have access to the same pictures. So, at this early stage in a simple—yet direct— way, all the assets that accrue to the dynamics of a group seeing and reacting together to the same clues can be set in motion and can be used to advantage. In a sense this adds up to a pint-sized version of a group Directed Reading-Thinking Activity.

Children learn to listen to each other, to note how different pupils see and react to different picture elements, to hear their language usage, and so on. Imitation helps many along the road to seeing and talking and sharing.

Some reading series readiness books are accompanied by *Big Pictures.* In many instances the *Big Pictures* are large reproductions of readiness-book pictures. This means that a teacher can mount the *Big Picture* on an easel and direct the group by having all focus from time to time on her *Big Picture* copy. Also some children see likenesses and differences better in the big-picture reproduction, or they can spot things better, or see motion lines better.

Pupils giving their version of a readiness-book picture scene can stand by the *Big Picture* reproduction and speak from it. This helps the group keep their attention focused on the pupil speaking and on the picture, rather than shifting back and forth from speaker to readiness book. Furthermore, the reluctant or anxious child can use the easel and the *Big Picture* as a psychological prop. He can stand by it as he talks, or partially behind it. He can use a pointer, if he wishes, and thus have something to occupy his hands.

An Illustration for Language Development. The following illustration is typical of the type of readiness-book pictures that are planned to promote oral-language development. This is the second such picture in the *Teachers' Edition for Ready to Go* (34).

The picture is similar to the first picture. It gives the children an opportunity to revisit a familiar picture environment, to reidentify previously recognized items, and to meet again the same characters. This dealing in the "known" is desirable, since it promotes recall by providing many

original stimuli and encourages children to feel at ease. Both of these factors stimulate greater oral-language response.

There is enough newness present in this picture to excite interest. The same house appears in the background, but attention is focused on activities on the lawn. The same characters—Bill, Susan, and Spotty—are presented in a new episode that still involves elements of the first. The action is one familiar to most children. The fact that the action is not complete as depicted allows for freedom of interpretation; imagination is stimulated, and recall of similar personal experiences will lead children to predict a possible outcome. As a result much oral-language usage may follow. The unfinished story plot excites the children, and they are eager to tell how they think it will end and why it will end that way.

Each child can look at the page and be given time to study and react to this picture. Oral-language reaction to the picture may then be started by the question, "What do you think is happening in this picture?" It is well to use this type of question before directing attention to details. Have different pupils tell what they think. As they talk, be alert to the extent to which they recognize and use details in the picture.

If necessary, ask questions that will cause them to re-examine and react to certain relevant details of action and feeling. "What is Spotty doing? Why is she going toward the ball? Do you think Spotty will get to the ball before Bill?" "Is Bill running or walking? Why? What do you think he will do with the ball?" "What is Susan doing? Why is she sitting down? Is she laughing or crying? Who threw the ball? Do you think Susan will try to get the ball?"

After the children's stories have been told, they can be led to appreciate certain number concepts as shown in the picture. For example, ask, "How many pets do you see? How many balls do you see? How many children do you see?"

An activity of this type can be used not only to promote oral-language usage but also to see relationships of picture characters, setting, and action, to predict outcomes, and to support conclusions.

Another Illustration. Two pictures may be used showing two episodes of the same event. The events are separated by time of occurrence (sequence) and plot development (story continuity). Both of these two pictures (pp. 220–221) depict a major and a minor action.

In the first picture the major action centers around Bill and Nancy; in the second picture it shifts to Susan and the puppy. Two sets of characters are in the total action, but they can be linked separately with the major and the minor action. The actions and feelings of the characters are depicted by picture and plot. This should evoke much oral-language usage that reflects the human-interest factors suggested: Susan's plan, her anticipation, her delight; Nancy's and Bill's preoccupation with Red and the stick; and the surprise of all three.

After pupils have reacted either individually or as a group to the "story" in the two pictures, the episodes can be dramatized. Children love to do this, and five of them can be involved. A screen can be used as a tree. This kind of role-playing is a good way to involve "feelings" and stir thoughts through the emotions.

All this may be climaxed by having a "story writing" session. Select two pupils. One will tell or dictate the story in the first picture. The other will continue the story by telling about the second picture. The first pupil may sit or stand next to the teacher and dictate his story. The teacher writes the story in manuscript style on a large piece of newsprint or, if a typewriter with primer type is available, she may type the story. Typing a story has many advantages and controls. The letters are of uniform size and shape, upper-case letters are easy to distinguish from lower-case letters, words are evenly spaced, lines are equal distances apart, more content can be put on a page, and, above all, it looks like a page from a book. Furthermore, more than one copy can be prepared at a time.

Effort should not be made to put what the children say into short sentences so that a sentence can be put on a line. Quite to the contrary, runover sentences should be used.

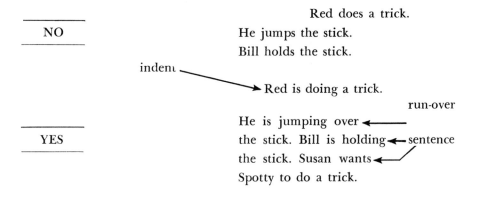

Avoid breaking words at the end of a line. Long "and then" sentences should be adjusted by means of punctuation. Effort should be made to record the story pretty much as it is dictated. Total verbatim reproduction is not necessary and, at times, not wise.

Writing or typing the story in the presence of the group permits them to see that writing is no more than talk written down. They note, too, that the next day or week or month the teacher can read back this story just as she read it the first time.

Appointing two people to tell the story means that the teacher can more readily follow the dictating. It is a far cry from the situation where five or six are trying to talk at the same time. Recording after the group has talked about the story readies pupils to talk. The speaker can use ideas

given by others during the discussion of the picture. Listeners in the group may supply a word or give a line if the speaker seems at a loss.

After the story has been written or typed, the teacher and the pupil dictator read the story back, together. The teacher reads the story orally at a slow, even pace, pointing to each word as she proceeds. The pupil repeats after the teacher, word-by-word. Pupils are not asked to read the story or to locate words on their own.

This procedure can be followed with a two-picture story, a four-picture story, or even stories with more than four pictures. A different pupil may be designated to tell a story for each picture, or one pupil may tell the whole story. Regardless of the procedure for telling, pupils are not to be asked to even try to read the story orally on their own. The purpose of the chart is being accomplished as the pupils see their talk being written down and see that it can be read back.

Some stories will be longer than others. Some may be so short as hardly to qualify for the label *story*. For instance: "The dog jumps over the stick." Length of story should not be used to prod a child. Repeated opportunities will do this as confidence and security and satisfaction influence production.

A teacher once asked her supervisor: "How many experience charts should I get?" To which the supervisor replied: "One million."

At times so-called group charts may be obtained. This is the situation in which each member of the group may contribute. Sometimes this is the best approach when dealing with a group of reluctant talkers. The preferred method is to obtain individual charts. (See Chapter 8.)

When using readiness materials of the kind illustrated, the teacher may give the group the names of the children represented in the picture. The children illustrated appear throughout the first-grade-level program. This way the pupils get to "know" the characters and their names (Bill, Nancy, Susan, Red, Spotty).

One other source helpful in promoting oral-language usage and development is the "field trip." Field trips can serve to great advantage or be efficient time killers. Trips should be planned in such a way that the things the teacher wants her class to observe will be within their reaction range.

One teacher who took her class to see a post office planned carefully with the postmaster in advance of the trip. She wanted the children to see a dramatization of how to buy a money order. When the children returned to school and were asked to "tell" about their trip, they all wanted to talk about the boy who fell off the bus at the post office. None spoke about the money-order window.

Obviously "bus riding" and "falling" were within their reaction range. The human factor caught and held their attention. By contrast, the money-order episode most likely escaped most of them. This is not to imply that the dramatization idea was not good, but rather to point out the need for realistic expectancies.

In this instance the teacher got what she wanted—oral-language usage. Fortunately she took full advantage of the situation by prompting and encouraging the pupils to talk. After exhausting the bus episode, some went on to talk about the post office.

In this instance, as in other field-trip incidents, the teacher recorded the pupils' stories in experience charts. Pupils could then illustrate their charts. Seeing correct words in print such as *post office, stamp, postmaster* helped some pupils remember the words for oral-language usage and helped a few actually recognize the words in print.

Pupil illustrations of their own dictated experience charts promote many worthwhile educational ideas. First, the picture is another symbol system. As such it helps pupils "see" better how symbols are associated with experiences to form a concept. The picture represents the experience as well as a word or words. Second, the picture is produced by the pupil. This active participation on the part of the pupil promotes retention and recall of ideas and language. Third, the scene chosen by a pupil for illustration does not, of course, show all that happened. Moving pictures might show "all," but stills cannot. Grasping this helps pupils see other pictures in a more functional way and better prepares them to deal with the pictures in a basic-reader story. Fourth, each item in the illlustration shows what elements of a concept the child reacted to, remembered, and reproduced. Each item or facet of an item represents an attribute of a concept. A table may have either two legs or four. A horse may have only two legs. A tree may have many branches and leaves, and pupils can be asked to distinguish between them. This is a good practice since it helps reinforce word-experience relationships. Fifth, the quality of pupils' drawings may be a good gauge of their intellectual potential expressed through a medium other than words. The Goodenough Man-Drawing Test (13) can provide a substantial measure of intelligence. Scores correlate well with Binet Test results. Teachers, given a brief period of supervised scoring, get fairly reliable results on the Goodenough Test. Sixth, the child's choice of and use of colors can be observed. Did he remember the post office as black or red? Is everything colored red? Are colors used selectively? Seventh, motor coordination and dexterity may be noted. Budding artists may be observed. Eighth, diligence, originality, and independence may be noted. Ninth, the picture can be used in almost the same way as a title is used by pupils who can read. When selecting a story posted in the room or locating one in a pupil's collection of stories, the picture may be the means of identification.

Pupil illustrations are not busy work when linked with pupil stories in the way described. Many things can be learned by the teacher as well as the pupil. Pictures can be used as a basis for classroom observation and/or clinical observation. A projective technique (35) to study anxiety is both useful and suggestive. In this test a pupil is presented with a picture showing a familiar scene. One of the figures in the picture has a blank head and the pupil is to insert either a "happy" face or a "sad" face. He decides the kind

of face according to his response to the situation. The "anxiety score" is the percentage of the total number of pictures to which the child affixes a "sad" face.

A pictorial guess-who test shows how children respond socially to each other (18). A child is shown a drawing of a child sucking his thumb, for example, and is asked who at school is like that. Results show pupil and

teacher ratings that are pretty much in agreement and quite informative.

A pupil self-portrait may be very revealing and promote a considerable amount of oral-language usage. Similarly, pupil portraits of a classmate, a parent, or a sibling may be informative.

Pictures can be useful in many ways. Those made by the children themselves serve a practical purpose, and those they are asked to react to may be quite informative. All in all, pictures can do a good deal more than promote oral-language usage.

Seeing Relationships

In the process of reacting to a picture, many children note relationships of action and predict events to come; others do not. Some recall accurate mental images of important details when trying to visualize the picture; others do not. Seeing relationships, making accurate predictions in terms of information available, and accurate recall of experiences are essential to dealing with language-experience relationships. These skills need not be refined in dealing with oral language, since they serve identical purposes in dealing with printed language or reading.

Remembering things seen by linking them meaningfully with a picture story and with the oral language used to tell the story is a reliable method of learning. It is also a good way to build and retain concepts. Using spatial relationships along with story associations help some to visualize elements of a scene.

In the activity on pp. 224–225 the children are given an opportunity to play a memory game. A gradual step-up in demands upon memory can be made by reducing the number of clues needed for recall of an original situation. Doing so alerts pupils to techniques for accomplishing voluntary recall by means of studying and remembering techniques.

Other activities that may be used are (34, p. 6):

1. Play games in which the items are identified by color descriptions. For example, a child could say, "I see something that is red, white, and blue. What is it?"

2. Have children sort and classify various items according to color likeness, to common color combinations, and to shades of one color. Following are some examples.

a. Ask all the children who are wearing something red (or some other color) to raise their hands. Then check and discuss their responses.

b. Discuss colors that are seen together frequently such as those peculiar to various holidays: green and red of Christmas; black and orange of Haloween; purple and yellow of Easter; red and white of valentines; and red, white, and blue of patriotic holidays.

c. Ask all the children wearing something blue to rise and stand at their seats. Then discuss the various shades of blue represented: dark blue, very dark blue, light blue, very light blue.

In their world of sight, children are constantly looking upon a wide view. It is obvious that it would be almost impossible for them to react to all or even to a great proportion of the stimuli within sight. As a result they become intuitively conditioned to viewing much and seeing little. This passive conditioning causes many to observe far less than they could. A common experiment with adults is to have a group observe the same scene and then compare what each sees. The experiment repeatedly indicates that people "see" only that to which they react, that they react according to their previous experience, and that different people see different things when looking at the same scene.

It is also known that people can be trained to be more alert to what they see by having them use the tried and successful methods of remembering: purposeful seeing, meaningful association, seeing again and again, and using the information gained.

Activities may be planned to develop pupils' abilities to "see" more. For example, the visual-discrimination activities on pp. 226–227 deal with gross discrimination of color and size. Pictures presenting very common experience areas may also be used. Such pictures will permit many to react according to their previous experiences.

In the process of training children to "see" more, they must be equipped with "seeing" techniques. The most common and effective method is to

note likenesses and differences. This is done by *sorting* according to size or condition, purpose or destination: *arranging* according to sequence, relationships, or adjustment; and *organizing* into units according to type, kind, or species. Such noting of likenesses and differences will not only help the child deal more adequately with the physical world but also with the intellectual world of words and ideas.

In the activity on p. 229 children are being encouraged to note attributes and observe criterial properties exhibited by each animal and to go beyond this to identify classes of animals. This method of categorizing develops further insight into the network of inferences that are or may be set into play as concepts are developed.

Elliot W. Eisner (8) raises a most interesting question in his paper on "Knowledge, Knowing, and the Visual Arts." What place can the visual arts justly claim in the curriculum?, he asks. In the course of his discussion he refers to a study made by Lawrence Downey (6) in which educators and laymen ranked aesthetic development twelfth and fourteenth respectively out of sixteen items, including patriotism, citizenship, and physical development. Eisner goes on to say that (8, pp. 211–212):

Symbols mediate experience and the language systems in which they exist often act as a buffer, a mediator, a screen for the child's percepts. All too often the child learns to substitute the symbol of the thing experienced for the qualities of it. Instead of seeing it, he learns to symbolize it. Recognition replaces vision.[1] He moves from precept to concept, from the sense of the thing to the idea of it, a process so firmly reinforced that by the time he is nine the child who was once able to generate the poetic image of an oil slick as a dying rainbow is no longer able to do this.[2] The language of the intellect is substituted for poetic vision. And as the use of language becomes more theoretical its power to alienate man from the subtleties of feeling strengthens.

----

[1] Both John Dewey in *Art as Experience* and Ernest Schachtel in *Metamorphosis* discuss the distinction between seeing and recognizing. For Dewey "Bare recognition is satisfied when a proper tag or label is attached, 'proper' signifying one that serves a purpose outside the act of recognition. . . . It involves no stir of the organism, no inner commotion. But an act of perception proceeds by waves that extend serially throughout the entire organism. There is, therefore, no such thing in perception as seeing or hearing *plus* emotion. The perceived object in a scene is emotionally pervaded throughout. When an aroused emotion does not permeate the material that is perceived or thought of, it is either preliminary or pathological." And Schachtel, speaking of how language may function in perception says: "The word, of course, never can take the place of the object or the quality or the activity which it designates or indicates. But most of the time, when we listen to the spoken or read the written word, we neither perceive nor imagine the referent of the word but are in contact only with the words (concepts). We behave as if the word were really all there is to the object which it designates. The label (sign) becomes a substitute for its reference, and thus, in listening or reading we are divorced from any experience of that which the words point to."

[2] Lawrence Kubie, speaking of the iconic character of the preconscious in its role in creative behavior suggests that where the child is tied too firmly to the demands of external reality either through pressures from adults or from a formal system such as logic he is apt to have his preconscious processes impeded and thus his ability to function creatively hampered. See L. Kubie, *Neurotic Distortions of the Creative Process* (Lawrence, Kansas: The University of Kansas Press, 1958).

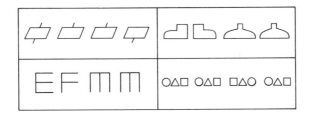

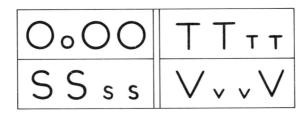

It is not to be thought that the visual-discrimination skills and abilities referred to thus far are in any way the answer to the questions raised by Eisner and others, but at this stage of school learning, they do represent a start. Seeing can go beyond just looking; symbolization can be an aid to an increasingly firmer grasp of concepts and more refined categorizations.

First children develop skill in noting likenesses and differences on a tridimensional level as described. Then they are ready to take a next step in sharpening visual discrimination and deal with both geometric and letter-like forms. An example of such an activity is seen above.

Jean Turner Goins' recent good study pointed up again the need for visual-perception training. She says (12, pp. 101–102):

> The results of the study as a whole also indicate the fruitfulness of the search for interrelationships among aspects of visual perceptual abilities and show that there is some relation between them and the reading process. The evidence points to the need for a broader concept than has formerly prevailed concerning the assessment of the visual abilities of beginning readers. The assessment should include not only visual screening tests but also an inventory of perceptual capacities and skills.

Auditory Discrimination

Both parents and teachers often wonder when to begin phonic training. When to start depends on the interpretation given to *phonics.* Language has a phonological sound system as well as a grammar. Usually it is assumed that a passive control of phonological features antedates an active control. In other words, a child hears a phonetic contrast such as that between "s" and "sh" before he can produce the sounds. When the infant begins to use meaningful words, he starts to use an active phonological system. Susan M. Ervin and Wick R. Miller say (9, p. 116): "By the fourth year, the child's

phonological system closely approximates the model, and the remaining deviations are usually corrected by the time the child enters school."

It is this active use of sounds that provides the foundation for phonetic-analysis training. The answer to the question of *when* to start is, as soon as the child enters school begin to sharpen his ear for sounds and make him articulate about them so that he can deliberately apply his knowledge to

printed words. A way to start this training is by means of auditory-discrimination activities.

Oral-language facility provides the foundation needed to make the transition from oral to printed language. Articulateness about the sounds represented by printed language prepares the reader to use one of the most important word-recognition skills—phonetic analysis. Since oral language and its various sounds are so crucial in learning to read printed language, it is imperative that auditory skills be carefully appraised and developed. To do this, it is most appropriate to start with the child's world of nonvocal sounds, because, to differentiate these sounds, he does not usually have to have the precision needed to deal with vocal sounds. Yet, in dealing with nonvocal sounds, various qualities that differentiate sound can be distinguished: intensity, pitch, duration, and timbre.

Long before the child enters school he has learned to discriminate between vocal sounds sufficiently to differentiate one word from another and to obtain understanding. Seldom, however, is the preschool child able to identify syllable sound units that are alike and are heard in different words. It is extremely unwise to assume that a child who hears and understands words is by the same token able to tell how words are alike or different by sound elements alone. This is a skill that forms the foundation for phonetic analysis and should be carefully developed.

Before the child enters school, he has had experience with nursery rhymes and jingles, particularly television commercial jingles, and has developed some sensitivity to rhyming words. Usually he has also acquired some sensitivity to rhythm and time. The general awareness of the uniform recurrence of a beat, an accent, or rhyming words readies a child to deliberately identify words that have similar sound units and can be used in a rhyme.

In the first two auditory-discrimination activities (pp. 232 and 233), the children were directed to perceive likenesses and differences in nonvocal sounds and to perceive the sound of recurring rhyming words. This should prepare them to hear words that rhyme and contrast them with words that do not rhyme. The ability to perceive differences as well as likenesses is essential to auditory discrimination. Ability to recognize sound units that agree or do not agree with a rhyme pattern is necessary if children are to use the more advanced skills in phonetic analysis.

At all times be careful not to distort a word by exaggerating a sound. The quality of a sound unit is determined by an almost imperceptible blending of sounds. For all purposes of phonetic (phonic) analysis, the sounds should always assume their conventional qualities as an interacting part of the sound unit of which they are a member. There is no "tee" sound in *cat*. It is sufficient to know that the sound as represented by the letter *t* is a part of the total sound unit *cat*, which is similar to *bat, hat, fat,* and so on.

Proceed by having the children name each item first to be sure they know the correct spoken word. Some may be alert enough so that you may start by asking, "Which two of these three names rhyme?" or it may be necessary to say, "Let's make a rhyme using two of these names." It may be necessary to be still more obvious by asking, "Which of these two rhyme: cat and bat or cat and stick? Let's make a rhyme using these names. The cat saw the bat."

Some of the children may need to try five or six different times before they understand. When they do understand, have them proceed individually by making up nonsense rhymes: The cat sat on the bat. The fan stood on the pan. The rose was on the hose. The nail was in the mail. The lock was on the clock. The star was in the jar. The bell fell on the shell. The spoon jumped over the moon. Encourage as much originality as possible and permit as much recognition of the humor of some patterns as the situation will allow. Pupils may then draw lines connecting the two pictures in each block whose names sound alike.

Sometimes, after a series of trials and errors, children begin to succeed. They are not certain about how or why they are succeeding, but the dynamics of the situation seem to produce the needed response. However, after a lapse of time and the resultant interruption of other activities, when they return to an operation demanding the accurate use of the skill, they have forgotten the principle. This tends to be especially so in activities that demand greater acuity for sounds.

The enthusiasm with which such activities are presented should be keen. Neither should the "game" aspect be overexploited. Children love realism and honesty and will cooperate where these are practiced.

Just as rhyme helps the children hear words that sound alike, alliteration will help them become sensitive to words that begin with the same consonant sound. Alliterative effect is evident, for example, in tip, tap, toe.

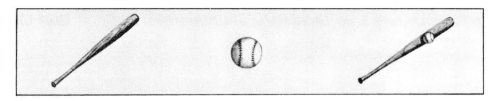

The above activity encourages the use of visual clues and functional clues to help make the association of words that begin with the same sound.

All the pupils should react to each auditory activity. Even though the more advanced children may quickly identify the words that fit together by sound, they should be able to explain that this is because the words have the same beginning sound.

Have the children name each item. (A bat, a ball, a bat and a ball, or a ball on a bat.) Then ask, "Who can make a song with these two?" You might get a reply like: "A bat, a ball, a bat on a ball." Ask the pupils, "Which words seem to go together? (Bat, ball.) "Why do they go together so well in a song? Yes, because the words begin with the same sound." You might use the tune and rhythm of "A Tisket, a Tasket."

The ability to recognize that spoken words can begin with the same consonant sound is essential to the sound analysis (phonetic analysis) of

BILL

NANCY

printed words. Therefore, in developing skill for recognizing initial consonant sounds, one needs to provide activities that permit frequent and varied repetition and that capture as much rhythmic movement as alliteration and voice modulation can give. Some children will have difficulty in perceiving the rhythmic pattern of alliteration and will need frequent "hearing" opportunities. Once the pattern is acquired, they are ready to deal with the reason words agree with one another: i.e., because they begin with the same sound.

The activities on pp. 236 and 237 deal with auditory discrimination of two initial consonants. It differs from previous activities in that the printed words <u>Bill</u> and <u>Nancy</u> are also used. This is a first step toward visual-auditory discrimination and prepares the children to attack words phonetically.

As in previous activities, the approach is almost entirely auditory. This is fitting, since *sound* is the foundation for phonetics. The spoken words to be compared are the names of pictured items. All of the pictured items are common, and most children will name them readily.

If the children know the names of the letters in the words <u>Bill</u> and <u>Nancy</u>, they may name the two beginning letters. Since the name of each pictured item begins like either <u>Bill</u> or <u>Nancy</u>, the decision is relatively simple; it is one of two.

Many other similar activities can be used. The following suggestions are illustrative (34, pp. 4, 5, 12, 21, 35, 43):

1. Play a sound discrimination game. Let one child cover his eyes. Choose another child to make different sounds (tap on glass, rap on a desk, beat a drum; start a fan; clap erasers, clap hands; strike a high note on the piano). Allow the child with eyes hidden ten seconds to identify the sound made.
Let the rest of the class see the noisemaker in action.
2. Place a screen in front of the piano. Have one pupil behind the screen use the loud or the soft pedal; strike a high or a low note; then strike a key and hold it for a long sound or release it immediately for a short sound. The other pupils will decide whether they heard a high or low note, a loud or soft note, a long or short note.
3. a. Have the children make rhymes with names of people rhyming with names of food, or with other items, such as:

I saw Sam	I see Mabel
Eat a ham.	Clean the table.
I see Anna	I saw Paul
Eat a banana.	Paint the wall.

b. Play a picture-name matching game. Place different pictures along the board in the chalk tray. One pupil names one of the pictures (cat), and another finds a picture whose name rhymes (hat). This might be timed to add interest.
4. Present orally some simple phrases using two words whose initial sounds are to be compared, such as, "I saw a boy. He had a. . . ." Then present two pictures; one of a baseball bat, one of a glove. The pupils will decide that *bat* and *boy* begin

with the same sound. Sometimes children need much practice with activities like this in which they select one of two words. Be certain that the two words represented by the pictures have strikingly different beginning sounds.

5. Some of the verses written by Laura Richards are both interesting and have alliterative patterns. In her book, *Tirra Lirra,* which you may find on your shelf of old books or in the library, turn to "Master Jack's Song" on page 111, and particularly use the chorus:

> Where the jam-pots grow!
> Where the jam-pots grow!
> Where the jelly jolly, jelly jolly jam-pots grow.
> The fairest spot to me
> On the land or on the sea
> Is the charming little cupboard where the jam-pots grow.[3]

Also use: "The Baby Goes to Boston," pp. 123–124; "Was She A Witch?" p. 145; and "Eletelephony," p. 31 in the same book.

6. The teacher might proceed as follows: "I am going to say two words. Listen carefully so that you can tell whether or not the two words begin with the same sound.

soda—some	far—fat
sand—sing	feet—fence
say—boy	pet—down
fan—see	do—door

Sometimes children grasp the sound differences well during a training period, only to have great difficulty a day later. Such pupils need frequent experience at spaced intervals. It may be good procedure to conduct a brief auditory-discrimination activity in the morning and again in the afternoon; then extend the time span between practice periods to every day; then to every other day, and so on.

Speech Appraisal

In paying close attention to each child's ability to recognize rhyming words, the teacher may have noted many variations in quality of speech. Some of the variations may have been marked enough to be labeled substandard. Others may seem very minor. Nevertheless, all who seem to deviate from the conventional pattern, even if only slightly, should be considered for further study. These children may exhibit various signs of concern because of speech problems: withdrawing from a group, being very quiet in a group, refusing to stand in front of a group to talk. Each sign may be a clue to the alert teacher. Then, too, careless speech habits may reflect inadequate auditory discrimination. Therefore, some of the pupils who had difficulty in the previous auditory-discrimination activities may also have speech problems. Where this is true, the teacher could work on the causative factor—auditory discrimination, rather than on its symptom, speech.

---

[3] From *Tirra Lirra* by Laura E. Richards (Boston, Little, Brown, 1932).

The activities on pp. 240 and 241 deal with the production of consonants as influenced by the interaction of other letters in a word or speech unit. The consonant sound may be at the beginning of a speech unit, at the middle, or at the end. In each position the consonant is blended into the speech unit and is influenced by the other sounds.

Six letter sounds are checked, each in an initial, medial, and final posi-

tion in a speech unit. The letter sounds are p, b, f, v, t, d.

The letters p and b represent lip sounds formed with essentially the same adjustment of lips and velum, but the p is voiceless because the vocal bands do not vibrate, whereas the b is voiced. The letter p ordinarily causes little difficulty other than to be weakly articulated. Children with a Germanic background often substitute p for final b.

The letters f̱ and v̱ also represent lip sounds formed essentially alike, except that the v̱ is v̄oiced. Children with Spanish and Germanic backgrounds often confuse v̱ and f̱ and v̱ and w̄.

The letters ṯ and ḏ represent tongue-tip sounds formed essentially alike, except that the ḏ is v̄oiced. The ṯ and ḏ sounds are frequently confused. It might be well̄ not to declare to̱ the children the purpose of the activity to avoid any possible embarrassment and a resulting restriction on speech.

Naming each picture and talking about each item will permit the teacher to hear speech sounds in a single word and when used in a larger language context. Guide this naming and general discussion in small group situations, working with three or four children at a time. All the children should be checked. Select them at random so that the arrangement will be different from the previous groupings. This puts flexible grouping into practice. As you identify variations of pronunciation in the group situation, make notes. If possible recheck the questionable responses by working with each child individually.

If it is apparent that psychological and physiological factors are causing much substandard speech, refer the children in question to a speech specialist at once. If only minor variations occur, the teacher might, after this activity is completed, initiate a corrective program. Alert the child by having him hear the difference between his speech and more acceptable speech, and by developing a program of auditory training. Then provide opportunities that stimulate the use of words involving the particular speech difficulty. It may be necessary to work on the sounds in isolation as well as in word and sentence contexts.

Similar activities can be structured for the consonants g̱, ḵ, ḻ, m̱, ṟ, s̱, ṉ, j̱, sẖ, cẖ, sṯ, and tẖ (voiced). The sounds represented by j̄, sh̄, st̄, and th̄ require complicated tongue and lip movements. Some are frequently spoken incorrectly. Illustrative words for each letter and each combination are as follows: g̱irl, wag̱on, dog̱; ḵite, basḵet, checḵ; ḻadder, baḻḻoon, baḻḻ; m̱irror, ham̱mer, com̱b; ṟing, caṟrot, chaiṟ; S̱anta Claus̱, bicycḻe, g̱lass̱; nos̱e, peṉny, paṉ; j̱ar, soḻdier, cag̱e; sh̄eep, dish̄es, fish̄; ch̄imney, pitch̄er, match̄; st̄ick, toast̄er, nest̄; th̄imble, tooth̄brush, teeth̄.

Listening

One of the chief avenues of learning for the preschool child is listening. He learned to talk by listening, learned new words by being very attentive to their sounds, and acquired many ideas and expressions by hearing others use them. Frequently during the years he has surprised and amazed grown-ups by the things he has heard and then remembered and repeated. While he may not be articulate about how he has learned by listening, experience has taught him *when* and *how* to listen (when interest or necessity prompt him), so that he seems to do it intuitively. He has experienced real listening for years and can be a fascinated, interested audience; or with utter disregard for amenities, he can turn his attention to something else very quickly and return just as quickly when again interested.

What one hears is remembered better if it is interesting and/or familiar, has plot unity, is illustrated, and is well told. The more meaningful the associations are that can be made while listening, the better the retention will be.

The activity below presents three folk tales about animated beasts in never-never land. The tales are simple, repetitive, cumulative, and brief. The plots are developed in such a way that the children can easily identify themselves with these marvelous creatures from the world of imagination. Human-interest factors so evident in the actions and feelings of the animals help make this possible.

The purpose of the activity is to have the children listen to and retell the stories. The complete story about "The Three Billy Goats Gruff" may be found in the *Anthology of Children's Literature* (23, pp. 180–181). Here is a brief synopsis. This, however, should not be considered a substitute for reading the complete story.

THE THREE BILLY GOATS GRUFF

Three Billy Goats with the family name of Gruff were to go to the hillside to eat grass. On the way they had to cross a bridge under which lived a Troll. The smallest goat was stopped by the Troll but was freed when he persuaded the Troll to wait for the next goat, which was bigger. This also happened to the second goat. But when Big Billy Goat Gruff came, he was too big for the Troll and killed him. The Billy Goats Gruff became big and fat.

Have the pupils retell the story with or without picture clues. Have them dramatize the story. Proceed in the same way with "Henny-Penny" in the *Anthology of Children's Literature* (23, pp. 111, 112).

HENNY-PENNY

Henny-Penny was eating in the yard when something hit her on the head. She thought the sky was falling and ran to tell the king. On the way she met Cocky-Locky. She told him her story and he went with her. They met Ducky-Daddles, Goosey-Poosey, Turkey-Lurkey, and Foxy-Woxy. The latter tricked them into coming to his cave where one by one he ate them. But Henny-Penny escaped and ran home and never told the king that the sky was falling.

Encourage the children to make up a story about the pictures at the bottom of the page. (See p. 244.) Perhaps it will be about two little dogs who want a third dog to live in the empty house. Welcome ideas with enthusiasm, and worthwhile results will be forthcoming. Some children may want to act out their stories.

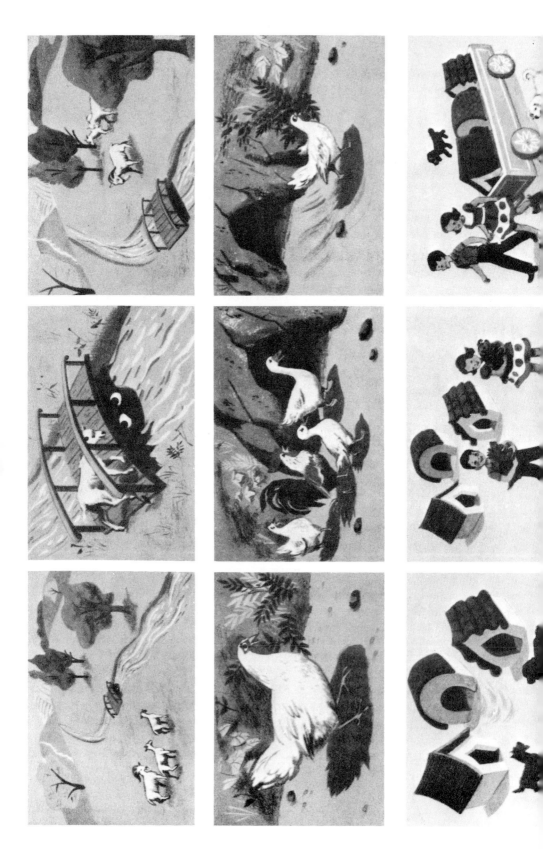

Have pupils tell other similar stories they may know. Tell them other folk tales such as "The Three Little Pigs," "The Old Woman and Her Pig," "The Gingerbread Man," and modern fanciful tales like "Millions of Cats," by Wanda Gag. The following activities may also be helpful.

1. Discuss: How did the story start? How did it end? What part did you like best?

2. Invite a skilled storyteller to visit the room and tell stories.

3. Divide the class into small groups and promote storytelling in the groups.

4. Ask the children to bring pictures of personal experiences and have them tell the story illustrated.

Social and Emotional Adjustment

Good mental hygiene within a peer group is essential to learning. Security, self-confidence, acceptance, tolerance, and a sense of belonging are the foundation for attitudes that encourage fair play, free expression, emotional poise, and participation in effective learning experiences. The implications of social and emotional approaches to learning emphasize the necessity for planning with and for the children in terms of everyday all-around growth in their present-day world.

Early school experiences are important ones. Maintaining happy, relaxed, stimulating relationships among the entire group and between each child and the teacher promotes growth of personality that in turn advances achievement. The stimulating situations that are provided should foster individual creativity and exploration and at the same time help to fix learning where needed. In such situations some competition is recognized, and mistakes are considered as attempts and accepted as ways of learning. "Try, try again—you were almost right," says the more experienced person (the teacher) in the classroom to the less experienced one (the pupil).

The purpose of an activity like the following one is to give children an opportunity to react to and talk about actions demanding appreciation for the dynamics of common social experiences. (See pp. 246 and 247.)

This is an activity in which the entire class can participate. The attitudes that are fostered cut across levels of achievement and potentials for achievement. All children need to develop appreciation for the basic principle involved: taking turns. Encourage individual pupil interpretation, being sure to elicit the basic concept of sharing opportunities and privileges.

Let the children dramatize the scenes. Let them take turns at pretending to wash their hands, eat their lunches, and get on and off the bus. In each scene leadership may be varied.

Encourage the correct use of labels common to each scene, the social amenities common to each, and the use of the "magic" social phrases *Please, Thank you, Excuse me,* and *I beg your pardon.* Allow the children a free hand in elaborating on the rather stereotyped situations. In this way

they may incorporate new challenges, new lines and actions, new feelings and emotions.

What child starting to school does not experience mixed feelings about school and about home! What happens in the home before the child starts to school and during the critical in-between period of the first few weeks at school often determines his adjustment and attitudes. Often it is some chance remark or misunderstood observation that leads children to doubt and be anxious. Sometimes particular family situations or family secrets have made them anxious and insecure. An opportunity to explore their feelings through structured reproductions (pictures) of different family situations often provides such children, as well as their teacher, a means of acquiring insight. The purpose of the picture situations in the activities on pp. 250–251 and the possible resultant "stories" is to help both the teacher and the child acquire more insight into some of the reasons for the different social and emotional adjustments revealed.

From her first meeting with her class, the teacher presumably studies and directs each child and gives each of them frequent opportunities to succeed. As was stated earlier, success is the highest form of motivation and the most important form of therapy any child can experience. But success alone may not be sufficient to unravel the varied adjustment knots that are unique to different children. Therefore, it may be helpful to try to understand what takes place psychologically as the children's stories unfold.

One or more of the four pictures shown may in some way be related to a child's needs. Each picture may cause the child to show a different side of his personality, and each may give rise to different attitudes, defenses, and motivations. What items in the picture does the child use or ignore in telling his story? What motives does he assign to the characters? Remember that the children have only their own experiences, direct or indirect, to draw upon; thus everything they say or imply has relevance.

Adjustments need to be made and are constantly being made by all children. The basic attitudes involved in relationships within a family are of the utmost importance for each child's adjustment and achievement. The pictures in this activity should be discussed one at a time in groups as small as time will permit. This is an excellent opportunity to cut across group lines established by the levels of competencies in oral language. Doing so avoids false notions about permanent membership in any groups.

Permit and encourage as much individual spontaneous response to a picture as possible. Note how different children respond to different elements in the picture: some respond to a member of the congregation at the church door, some to the colored window, to the rope on the tree, to Father pushing Susan, to Father reading to Susan, to Mother knitting, to Father saying good night, to children going to bed, and so on.

Note also how the children respond to character actions and interactions. Some children may consistently react to the total picture, whereas others react only to parts. Some children may use a theme such as "Father doesn't" or "the bad boy" to describe the action in each picture, even though the action does not indicate such implications. Others may give a stereotyped response to each picture, such as reacting only to "little" Susan. Some may concentrate on the "formal" aspects of the picture, or consistently ignore certain people. Others may not react to color or may overreact to it.

Do not diagnose the child's personality or that of his family on the basis of his responses, as some children deliberately make up stories or give unusual comments to get attention. If you obtain a number of unusual responses that are made with sincerity, however, consult the school psychologist, social-service worker, or home visitor.

Principles concerned with social learning in a democracy need to be grasped because to a considerable degree individualizing of instruction, or teaching at the child's level, is accomplished only to the extent that teachers have a proper perspective on learning and living and sharing. It is only as knowledge of reading instruction and of human growth and development and self-control and concern for others lives in the hearts of teachers that maximum learning can occur.

If reading is to be taught as a thinking process there must be a belief in, a development for, and a protection of the individual's right to be himself within the confines of the group or class in which he works. Three aspects of the individual's freedom need to be appreciated: freedom of consent, freedom to follow one's own purposes as dictated by personal needs, wishes, and values, and freedom of association. Similarly, groups have their responsibilities as well as their freedom. If pupils are to use freedom responsibly, they must learn the following essentials, as discussed by Edna Ambrose and Alice Miel (1, p. 10):

respecting one's own and others' opinions, ideas and forms of expression; being creative and responsible in one's use of symbols; looking for excellence in everyone; making value judgments and knowing their bases; disciplining oneself; working out the appropriate balance of freedom-restraint; keeping in balance other interrelated behaviors such as cooperation-competition, leadership-followership, majority-minority, dependence-independence; being selective in the authority with which one cooperates and knowing the bases upon which one chooses leaders and delegates responsibilities.

The simple framework that the authors suggest adults follow to develop in children the basic faiths that encourage self-acceptance and openness toward others is (1, p. 47):

1. Recognizing the individuality of each child
2. Listening to, respecting and using children's opinions
3. Accepting their feelings
4. Accepting the aggressive, rough and tumble play of exuberant youngsters
5. Planning work and play so they can use their abilities
6. Giving time and thought to them and their needs; endeavoring to meet their needs
7. Allowing opportunities for them to be with their friends

8. Using power with them. Exercising the type of control they need to learn to exercise with others
9. Participating with them in pleasurable activities
10. Having a sense of humor, laughing and joking with them.

In addition, Muriel Crosby (3) and John J. DeBoer (4) point out how the community influences language growth and affects a pupil's adjustment. The church, the civic organizations, the community playgrounds and parks, the town library, the newspapers, and the local industries all contribute to making the child the kind of student he will become.

Reading Inventories

An informal reading inventory of a pupil's readiness or maturity level can be an effective means of initiating differentiated instruction. Studies (21, 24) do show that the subjective judgments of teachers, particularly experienced teachers, are quite reliable in estimating pupil readiness for reading instruction. Even so, the use of reading-readiness tests or intelligence tests is urged.

Standardized Reading-Readiness Tests

Standardized tests of reading readiness, combined with the judgment of able teachers, provide a good measure of pupil achievement. The general purpose of such tests is to predict a child's ability to learn to read.

Tests available usually have subsections designed to check on different aspects of reading readiness, such as the ability to make visual discriminations of objects, symbols, letters, and word forms, to make auditory discriminations, to name letters, and to understand vocabulary. They also provide information on the student's learning rate, ability to perceive relationships, ability to interpret feelings and make inferences, and so on. None of the standardized tests measure all of these areas. The range and completeness of subtests varies considerably. For example, one of the widely used tests—the Lee-Clark Reading Readiness Test—has four subtests measuring recognition of likenesses, discrimination of differences, experiential background, including understanding of vocabulary, and ability to discriminate among similar but different letter and word forms. The test requires only fifteen to twenty minutes. The Harrison-Stroud Reading Readiness Profile has seven parts: using symbols, making visual discriminations (two parts), using the context, making auditory discriminations, using context and auditory clues, and giving the names of letters. It is recommended that the tests be administered in three sessions, and it is estimated that the testing time is eighty to ninety minutes.

As Helen M. Robinson (31) points out in her review of the American School Reading Readiness Test, usually only six to ten items are used in subtests, and this number is too small to provide reliable information. When the sample size is so small there is considerable doubt about the predictive value of the scores obtained. In this regard, this particular test is no different from others on the market. In addition, manual directions accompanying such tests usually indicate that each subtest contains both easy and difficult items, which increases the predictive-value burden placed on subtests.

James R. Hobson reviewed the Lee-Clark Tests and voiced the kind of caution that might be exercised in using any standardized reading-readiness test (22, p. 777):

After using it for more than 20 years in the last month of kindergarten, this reviewer can report that in practice it is very effective in screening out those children with gross and usually rather obvious hindrances to success in beginning reading, such as mental immaturity, deprivation in experiential background, nervous instability resulting in short interest and attention span, and gross sensory handicaps. It sometimes serves to give evidence of excellent ability and probable success in reading on the part of children who, lacking somewhat in physical size, social forwardness, manual dexterity, or oral verbosity, have not previously been rated high by their teachers.

Neither the test itself nor any of the technical data presented in the manual would appear to support the rather elaborate normative and interpretative tables. These are attractive and logical enough; but in the absence of any experimental support or statistical verification, it must be assumed that they have been more or less subjectively derived and that their validity for such exact and detailed analysis is in question.

Nila Banton Smith, in her thorough article on "Readiness for Reading," indicates that the relationship between intelligence-test results and reading-readiness tests has led to a number of conclusions (32, p. 15):

1. When intelligence tests are used in conjunction with other tests, intelligence is one of the most significant indices in predicting readiness for beginning reading. . . .
2. Intelligence is a major factor in reading success at any level. . . .
3. Too many bright children are failing at all levels. . . .
4. A mental age of from 6 to 6½ years is considered by many investigators to be essential for success in beginning reading. . . .
5. No one mental age is a guarantee of beginning reading success.

Probably the most widely quoted conclusion is the one concerned with the mental age needed for beginning reading. M. V. Morphett and Carleton Washburne reported the following conclusions in 1931 (26, pp. 502–503):

4. When the Detroit test was used as a basis for determining mental age groups, the children who had a mental age of six years and six months made far better progress than did the less mature children and practically as satisfactory progress as did the children of a higher mental age.
5. When mental age was measured by the Stanford Revision of the Binet-Simon Scale, the children with a mental age of six years and six months again made much better progress in reading than did those of less maturity, but they made less satisfactory progress than did those whose mental age was six months greater. The gain in ability up to six years and six months of mental age, however, was much greater than the subsequent gain. . . .

7. Consequently, it seems safe to state that, by postponing the teaching of reading until children reach a mental age of six years and a half, teachers can greatly decrease the chances of failure and discouragement and can correspondingly increase their efficiency.

Subsequent studies (10, 11, 36) indicated that no one mental age is a guarantee of success in learning to read and gave support to the idea that a constellation of factors determines readiness for reading and that these factors differ from individual to individual. Now, as a matter of fact, some manuals (16) accompanying standardized readiness tests recommend that the test be used in conjunction with an intelligence test. So the caution to teachers of beginning reading voiced by Nila Banton Smith is very timely (32, pp. 16–17):

> She will not place her sole and undivided confidence in the six-to-six-and-a-half-mental-age criterion as determining when all of her pupils are ready to begin reading. While this is the norm which has been found in several different places, there are individual differences in children, in material used for beginning reading, and in the type of procedures used. Furthermore, the other elements contributing to total maturation must be considered.

Again, reference to Dolores Durkin's recent study seems timely (7), especially to the fact that the intelligence quotients of the pupils she observed ranged from 91 to 161. In addition, other factors usually considered relevant to readiness for reading seemed to contribute to success in different ways.

Standardized reading-readiness tests do provide information that is useful in determining the range and level of achievement children have attained by the time they are required to enter school. If the results are used in conjunction with other sources of information, such as intelligence tests and informal reading-readiness tests, a substantial picture of each child may be obtained. The end result of all this study should be a program of instruction in reading that is paced by each pupil's potential.

Kindergartens and Reading Readiness

If it is acknowledged that individual differences exist even at the preschool level, there can be no question about the role of a kindergarten program in the total reading-instruction program. If we accept the fact that children show a range of differences at the first-grade level of at least five years, it must be recognized that similar differences exist at the preschool level. As a matter of fact, M. Lucile Harrison wrote in 1936 that "Many studies have been made of the importance of kindergarten training for children as it affects their later school progress. With few exceptions these point to the fact that the instruction given in pre-primary years in school definitely promotes success to a measurable extent through the early grades in the elementary school." (19, pp. 15–16.)

The 1924 report of the National Committee on Reading had a section entitled "Experience and Training Which Prepare Pupils for Reading—Kindergarten and Early Part of First Grade." The major part of the instruction they described was to "be given in a kindergarten which provides a rich and varied course of study" (27, p. 26). They went on to say that (27, pp. 27–28):

Kindergarten and primary teachers should provide a wealth of interesting, vivid experiences about the home, the community, animals, flowers, trees, and the common relations of group and community life. Various group activities should be organized, such as gardening, caring for pets, building bird houses and constructing playhouses. . . . The pupils should be encouraged to discuss such experiences freely and to add rapidly to their stock of ideas. . . .

Simple stories, poems, and songs form a second source of valuable experience. If pupils talk about the experiences described in stories, they become familiar, not only with their content, but also with their forms of expression. Drawing or illustrating facts or events which are described also results in a clearer understanding of them.

They do caution, though, that "formal instruction in reading should not be given to most pupils before they enter the first grade" (27, p. 30).

It is apparent then that recommendations about reading instruction at the kindergarten level have been supplied to educators for at least half a century. It is also apparent that individual differences have been recognized for many years and that teachers have been urged to teach accordingly. It is both strange and disturbing that, as Dolores Durkin reported (7), parents are getting the notions from teachers that they should not help their children—eager and ready to learn to read—to do any reading before they enter first grade. Arthur I. Gates (10) pointed out that "method of teaching" was a more important determiner of reading success than a pupil's intelligence. Apparently, method of instruction is a vital and fundamental factor.

If "formal" instruction is interpreted to mean the memorization of a reading vocabulary through endless drill and through word repetition of the kind exemplified by preprimers, the caution voiced by the authors of the *Twenty-Fourth Yearbook on Reading,* by the teachers in Durkin's study, and by Gates are timely. As long as such practices of indoctrination are employed, caution—the utmost caution—must be exercised. Actually, what is needed is a more appropriate approach to initial reading instruction —an approach that is premised on the psychology of learning, on human growth and development, and on knowledge of thinking and cognition.

The Association for Childhood Education International publishes a *Portfolio for Kindergarten Teachers* in which Elizabeth Neterer indicates that the kindergarten year can be the best time for preparation for learning to read (28).

Kindergarten teachers in the Madison, Wisconsin, public schools prepared a portfolio called *Guides for Kindergarten Teachers.* In "Looking Forward to Reading Readiness," they say (25):

Reading readiness, as viewed in Madison Public Schools, is not something merely to wait for. Nor is it a condition or state of being to be trained by means of pencil-and-paper activities. Rather, it is looked upon as a stage of development in which the kindergarten makes a contribution through its many wholesome and varied activities. The aim is not to make all children equally ready for first-grade reading, but to help each child to develop to his fullest possibilities.

This aim is typical of what can be found in other similar bulletins or guides. Reading readiness seems to be viewed in much the same manner as was suggested by earlier advocates of such programs.

Some teachers have added individualized teacher-pupil conferences to their kindergarten programs. Esther K. Harris (18) reports using a conference approach much like that used by teachers who take an individualized approach to reading instruction in the grades. Among the values of a conference approach, she cites such things as the pupil's warm response to the teacher contact, learning specific skills of book selection, knowing many more books by title, and so on.

Recently Fred M. Hechinger (20) devoted his column in *The New York Times* to the issue of reading instruction in kindergarten. He opened his article by refering to a comment made by John Fischer when he was inauguarated president of Teachers College, Columbia University. Fischer indicated that many children can learn more and do so earlier than many teachers ever thought possible. But he added that what a child *can* do and what he *should* do are not necessarily the same thing. This is a sound idea if it is interpreted not to mean No, but rather to mean adjusting to individual differences.

Much interest in earlier reading instruction is being evidenced on the national scene, and rightly so. For too long a time, education has been unrealistic in its attempt to slow down those who might move faster than programs geared to average pupils allow. In the Denver Public Schools a study on reading-readiness instruction and parents is under way, aided by the Carnegie Corporation. The Denver schools have already found promise in their reading instruction in kindergarten programs and, since home influence seems to play so important a role in pupil readiness for reading, the study is to help determine how this "home" help can be improved. Parents—as well as some teachers—must be cautioned not to push those who are not ready to be pushed, while at the same time pushing those who are ready.

SUMMARY

Certain words take on meanings in the course of time that were not originally associated with them. Some words move us strongly, others do not. How these changes came about, how the nuances developed, is shrouded in mystery, though we know that they came about in the marketplaces of our communities.

As pointed out earlier, the terms reading readiness and readiness for reading seem to have taken on controversial and puzzling meanings. Reading readiness originally meant a level to be attained before "formal" instruction in reading was started. Then it came to mean not something to wait for until a child grew older, but something that was promoted. Third, the phrase took on another dimension and seemed to point an accusing finger directly at parents, citing their reading habits, their race, and their socioeconomic level as reasons for their children's difficulties with reading. Fourth, with this censure came a note of hope; rescue might be possible. Fifth, the somewhat apologetic explanation was advanced that *readiness* did not really refer to any one level but to all levels.

It has been suggested in this chapter that the positive connotations associated with the word *maturity* be linked with the preschool period and be referred to as *maturity in reading (beginning reading stage)*. Maturity refers more to a process than a level; granted, of course, that, as Willard C. Olson points out (29, p. 4), it is used on occasion to refer to that period when "structures and functions have attained their adult status." In reading, though, as William S. Gray and Bernice Rogers (15) indicate, a person works toward maturity all his life. Olson also suggests that maturity, when compared with immaturity, sets up expectancies for stages of development but does so on the fluid basis of growth and change. Maturity does all this without disparaging the intrinsic merits of those early preschool years.

Individual differences, even at the preschool age, can be an asset rather than a liability. Ample evidence is available to show that differences do exist. It is reported that tests show a range of at least five years insofar as maturity at the beginning reading stage is concerned. The likelihood is that more precise measuring instruments would show an even greater range. This being the case, it is all the more important that beginning reading instruction not be of the procrustean variety. It is no more possible to fit all five- to six-year-olds with a single shoe size than it is to fit them all into the same instructional group. The interaction of a constellation of physical, mental, social, and emotional factors and the continuity of experiences can provide the legend with which to caption a picture of preschool-age children.

The miracle, of course, is that some children do learn to read before they start to school. How does it happen, *especially* since they have not had any "formal" reading instruction? At one time it was thought that this could be accounted for by intelligence, but this is not the answer. Then it was thought that socioeconomic level or race accounted for the phenomenon, but this was not the answer either.

It must be that initial reading instruction is not as complex as it is thought to be; otherwise children with I.Q.'s as low as 91 and coming from "low" socioeconomic levels could not learn to read almost completely on their own. At least they were on their own in that they were not taught to read by teachers trained to teach reading. Must the learning be attributed to the fact that they are described as persistent, perfectionistic, and competitive children? Since these are largely acquired personality characteristics, they, too, do not answer the question. Or, could it be that the constant repetition of being read to on a two-lap-book approach did the trick? Regardless, each child who succeeds casts further doubt on what goes on in the name of formal beginning reading instruction. Apparently rote memorization, whether of words or phonetic generalizations, is not the answer. Apparently, too, the fear voiced by first-grade-level teachers concerning what to do with the child who can read when he starts to school further indicates that something is drastically wrong.

The maturity of children of preschool age can be used to full advantage if the teacher recognizes the individuality of each child and sees to it that reading is done to communicate and to understand—not to memorize words and parrot them.

REFERENCES

1. Ambrose, Edna, and Alice Miel, *Children's Social Learning*, Washington, D.C., Association for Supervision and Curriculum Development, 1958.
2. Betts, Emmett A., *The Prevention and Correction of Reading Difficulties*, New York: Harper & Row, 1936.
3. Crosby, Muriel, "Community Influences," *Factors that Influence Language Growth*, Chicago, National Council of Teachers of English, 1952 and 1953.
4. DeBoer, John J., "Some Sociological Factors in Language Development," *Child Development and the Language Arts*, Chicago, National Council of Teachers of English, 1952 and 1953.
5. Dewey, John, *Experience and Education*, New York, Macmillan, 1938.
6. Downey, Lawrence, *The Task of Public Education: The Perceptions of People*, Chicago, Midwest Administration Center, University of Chicago, Press, 1960.
7. Durkin, Dolores, "Some Unanswered Questions About Five-Year-Olds and Reading," *Changing Concepts of Reading Instruction*, J. Allen Figurel, ed., New York, Scholastic Magazines, 1961.
8. Eisner, Elliot W., "Knowledge, Knowing, and the Visual Arts," *Harvard Educational Review, 33* (Spring, 1963), 208–218.
9. Ervin, Susan M., and Wick R. Miller, "Language Development," *Child Psychology*, Sixty-second Yearbook of the National Society for the Study of Education, Part I, Chicago, University of Chicago Press, 1963.
10. Gates, Arthur I., "The Necessary Mental Age for Beginning Reading," *Elementary School Journal, 37* (March, 1937), 497–508.
11. Gates, Arthur I., and Guy L. Bond, "Reading Readiness: A Study of Factors Determining Success and Failure in Beginning Reading," *Teachers College Record, 37* (May, 1936), 679–685.
12. Goins, Jean Turner, *Visual Perceptual Abilities and Early Reading Progress*, Supplementary Educational Monographs, No. 87, Chicago, University of Chicago Press, 1958.
13. Goodenough, Florence L., *Mental Testing: Its History, Principles, and Applications*, New York, Rinehart, 1949.
14. Gray, William S., "The Nature and Organization of Basic Instruction in Reading," *The Teaching of Reading: A Second Report*, Thirty-sixth Yearbook of the National Society for the Study of Education, Part I, Bloomington, Ill., Public School Publishing Co., 1937.
15. Gray, William S., and Bernice Rogers, *Maturity in Reading*, Chicago, University of Chicago Press, 1956.
16. *Group Tests of Reading Readiness: The Dominion Tests*, Department of Educational Research, Ontario College of Education, Toronto, University of Toronto, 1955.

17. Harris, Cornelia, "Individual Reading Conferences in the Kindergarten," *Elementary English, 35* (February, 1958), 96–101.
18. Harris, Esther K., *The Responsiveness of Kindergarten Children to the Behavior of Their Fellows,* Monographs of the Society for Research in Child Development, Vol. 11, No. 2, Serial No. 43, 1946, Washington, D.C., Society for Research in Child Development, National Research Council, 1948.
19. Harrison, M. Lucile, *Reading Readiness,* Boston, Houghton Mifflin, 1936.
20. Hechinger, Fred M., "Early Start?—Trend of Reading in Kindergarten Opens New School Controversy," *The New York Times,* November 18, 1962, Section E, p. 9.
21. Henig, Max S., "Predictive Value of a Reading-Readiness Test and of Teachers' Forecasts," *Elementary School Journal, 50* (September, 1949), 41–46.
22. Hobson, James R., "Tests and Reviews: Reading-Readiness," *The Fifth Mental Measurements Yearbook,* Oscar Krisen Buros, ed., Highland Park, N.J., Gryphon, 1959.
23. Johnson, Edna, Carrie E. Scott, and Evelyn R. Sickels, *Anthology of Children's Literature,* 2d ed., Cambridge, Mass., Riverside, 1948.
24. Kottmeyer, William, "Readiness for Reading," *Elementary English, 24* (October, 1947), 355–366.
25. Madison Public Schools, "Looking Forward to Reading Readiness," *Guides for Kindergarten Teachers, No. 8.,* Madison, Wis. Curriculum Department, Madison Public Schools, 1953.
26. Morphett, M. V., and Carleton Washburne, "When Should Children Begin to Read?," *Elementary School Journal, 31* (March, 1931), 496–503.
27. National Society for the Study of Education, *Report of the National Committee on Reading,* Twenty-fourth Yearbook of the National Society for the Study of Education, Part I, Bloomington, Ill., Public School Publishing Co., 1925.
28. Neterer, Elizabeth, "Kindergarten's Responsibility Toward Reading," Leaflet No. 8, *Portfolio for Kindergarten Teachers,* ACEI Bulletin No. 2, Washington, D.C., Association for Childhood Education International, 1951.
29. Olson, Willard C., *Child Development,* Boston, Heath, 1949.
30. Olson, Willard C., "Reading as A Function of the Total Growth of the Child," *Reading and Pupil Development,* W. S. Gray, ed., Chicago, University of Chicago Press, 1940.
31. Robinson, Helen M., "Tests and Reviews: Reading-Readiness," *The Fifth Mental Measurements Yearbook,* Oscar Krisen Buros, ed., Highland Park, N.J., Gryphon, 1959.
32. Smith, Nila Banton, "Readiness for Reading," *Readiness for Reading and Related Language Arts,* NCRE Research Bulletin, Chicago, National Council of Teachers of English, 1950.
33. Stanger, M. A., and E. K. Donohue, *Prediction and Prevention of Reading Difficulties,* New York, Oxford, 1937.
34. Stauffer, Russell G., and Alvina Treut Burrows, *Teachers' Edition for Ready To Go.* New York: Holt, Rinehart and Winston, 1960.
35. Temple, Rita, and Elizabeth W. Amen, "A Study of Anxiety in Young Children by Means of a Projective Technique," *Genetic Psychology Monographs, 30* (November, 1944), 59–113.
36. Thomas, George I., "A Study of Reading Achievement in Terms of Mental Ability," *Elementary School Journal, 27* (September, 1946), 23–33.

Chapter 8 ⚡ The Language Experience Approch

Thus far in this text a number of conditions have been discussed that need to be taken into account if reading instruction is to be provided for six-year-olds. Most of the conditions are commonplace and hardly original. Even so, they warrant repeating and re-establishing.

First and undoubtedly foremost is the fact that the range of differences among typical six-year-olds is at least five years. This means that, if reading instruction is to be based on ability, the range and frequency of pupil distribution has to be determined and dealt with. Second, reading is to be thought of and taught as a communication process. Meaning is the important thing, not saying words. Reading is a thinking process, not a parroting process. Third, individualized reading procedures as well as group reading procedures are to be used. Fourth, written materials used must convey meaning in much the same way as does the oral communication of six-year-olds. Stilted artificiality must be avoided and no excuse trumped up for its use. Fifth, the vocabulary, concepts, and cognitive processes that children have developed for oral communication must be used to the full advantage in a similar way by having written words trigger the same concepts. Sixth, word-attack skills need to be taught as a "first aid" to meaning. Words must be introduced in a communication context so that, as the reader moves along, meaning clues to recognition may always be a first-order functional source of help. Phonic elements must be taught in a pronunciation unit or context and not in isolation. Seventh, pupil interests, experiences, and knowledge must be used as a basic source of funds and must be extended and refined. Eighth, reading skills must be taught and paced in such a way that individuals are able to assimilate them and use them. Ninth, the rules of the psychology of learning must be observed. Tenth, the freedoms and responsibilities of self-selection must be initiated from the beginning. Eleventh, a love of and an appreciation for what reading can do for people must be fostered.

GETTING STARTED

Most children come to first grade eager to read or learn to read. The few that can read will want to show that they can do so. Others will be eager to show that they want to try. An immediate or early start should be made. The object of the start is to show pupils that reading is no more than talk written down.

A good way to accomplish all this is by means of a pupil-dictated experience story. Arrange to have available in the room some item that will catch and hold the interest of the pupils. One teacher got under way by using a white mouse. Obviously this was unusual, but this contributed to its value as an attention-getting device and a means of stimulating oral language. Teachers could use a puppy, a chick, a baby rabbit, a parrot, a novel toy, a well-illustrated book for children or a story well told.

The teacher who used the white mouse placed the cage in the center of a pupil-viewing-level table. The pupils gathered around and watched the mouse move around in his cage. They saw him stand up on his back legs with his front paws up on the side of the cage. They saw him eat from his food tin. Then the teacher took the mouse out of the cage and allowed him to walk along the top of the desk. She showed no concern about handling the mouse, and her confidence and poise very much influenced the class.

As the pupils watched they talked and exclaimed: "Look, he's standing up!" "He has pink eyes!" "See, how long his tail is!" When this comment was made, the teacher asked the class to say how long they thought the tail was. Estimates were given that ranged from six inches to four feet. Regardless, the teacher's question had caused all to look again and to look with a purpose. "What should we name him?" asked the teacher. This evoked a number of responses such as "Whitey," "Snow White," and "Pink Eyes." The class preferred "Snow White."

The teacher put the mouse back into the cage, covered the cage, and set it aside. Then she gathered the class around an easel on which she had tacked a large piece of newsprint. (Newsprint is lined paper approximately two feet by three feet in size.) After writing the name *Snow White* on the top line, she invited them to talk about the mouse, indicating that she would write down what they said, just as she had recorded the mouse's name.

Dick said: "Snow White scratched around in his cage." Jane added: "Snow White has pink eyes." Alice said: "He stood up on his hind legs and looked at us." As each child offered an idea, the teacher wrote it on the newsprint, using appropriate manuscript writing and a heavy black crayola crayon. Pupils noted immediately that she could not write as fast as they talked. Even so, she wrote at a good pace, and the waiting time was not long. After each idea had been recorded, she read it back to the group in general and to the pupil dictating in particular. Altogether she recorded the ideas of six different pupils, completely filling the news-print sheet. All this took but a few minutes, and the pupils were fascinated by the performance and were eagerly attentive. The account read as follows:

Snow White

Dick said, "Snow White scratched around in his cage." Jane said: "Snow White has pink eyes." Alice said: "She stood up on her hind legs and looked at us." Jerry said: "Her tail is two feet long." Bill said: "Snow White ran around on the table." Nancy said: "Snow White is soft and furry."

Now the teacher read the entire story to the class. As she read, she pointed quickly and briefly to each word, the pupils saying the words with her. Even though this made for some arhythm, a surprisingly even-paced performance resulted.

Next she gave each pupil an eight-by-eleven-inch sheet of white paper and asked them to make a drawing of Snow White. While the children were drawing she went around the room, writing the words Snow White at the top of each pupil's paper. This gave some a chance to show that they had already learned to copy writing as they proceeded to label their own paper.

The following things had occurred as a result of this experience.

1. Pupils saw that reading was no more than talk written down.

2. They saw that the teacher could read back or play back all of the story or parts of it.

3. They followed the reading process on a left-to-right basis.

4. They made return sweeps from the end of one line on the right to the beginning of the next line on the left.

5. They saw that letters were made differently. Some few were capitals. Snow White always started with capital letters.

6. They saw the use of punctuation in a meaningful language context.

7. They experienced the thrill of "reading" as they read with the teacher.

8. Some of the pupils saw their names and ideas in writing.

9. They had displayed *curiosity* as they watched and examined the mouse and *creativity* as they told about their reactions.

10. Oral-language usage was stimulated as they reacted to the mouse.

11. Ideas were shared in the dynamics of a class situation and in response to an immediate experience.

12. Teacher questions had caused them to observe more carefully.

13. Each had opportunities to listen to others speak, to hear their ideas, and to discover how others reacted to the same circumstances.

14. Each had an opportunity to vote and express preference for a name for the mouse and to learn how to accept the decision of the majority.

15. Each had an opportunity to make his own drawing and thus show the attributes about Snow White that he was reacting to and reproducing.

16. The name <u>Snow White</u> written on each illustration gave pupils an opportunity to link two symbols for the same referent: a printed name and a picture.

In addition, the teacher had an excellent opportunity to discover the following things about her class.

1. their curiosity about the mouse

2. their concern or lack of concern about seeing the mouse out of the cage and on the table and their reluctance or readiness to touch the mouse

3. their willingness to move around the table and among each other

4. oral-language usage, particularly their choice of words

5. their attention span, persistence, and cooperativeness

6. whether some could read; as the story was being read back by the class, some few ran ahead and did so correctly

7. ability to use crayons and to illustrate ideas; the illustrations were some index to maturity and revealing in ways similar to the Goodenough Draw-A-Man Test (12)

For all concerned, this was a profitable experience. To be sure, the parents heard about the event. They also heard that reading had been done. "I read a story about Snow White," said one girl to her mother. "Oh," was the pleased reply. "You read about Snow White and the seven dwarfs?" "No, Mother. We read about a white mouse. We named him Snow White. See, here is his name on my picture. He is standing up looking at us."

All this is in sharp contrast to the "Oh! Oh! Oh!, Look! Look! Look." approach. The differences are so striking that it is hardly necessary to enumerate them.

The next day this teacher divided the class into three groups on a random basis. In each group were two of the children who had dictated lines that were recorded in the "Snow White" chart. Then she had each group gather with her in the back of the room around the chart of the previous day.

She started each group session by rereading the chart to them. Then they all reread it together as she pointed to the words. Next she invited Jerry to stand by her and read the chart with her. She started by merely pointing to the name of the chart and Jerry immediately supplied <u>Snow White</u>. Each time the name <u>Snow White</u> appeared in the story, Jerry hurried ahead and read the words. He also recognized his name. "Reading" for Jerry had been a booming success.

Jane stood by the teacher next. Jane read the title, too, as did Jerry. However, each time the words <u>Snow White</u> appeared thereafter, Jane hesitated. All the teacher needed to do, though, in each instance was point to the same words in the title and Jane responded immediately. She, too, read her own name.

Others in the group were given opportunity to "read," too. The teacher stayed alert to the interest of the group and the activities of the rest of the class. Some were looking at books that had been placed on the library-corner table. Others were in the house corner, playing. Still others were drawing. Some sat together; some preferred to work alone. The teacher was careful not to overplay the attention span and interest of the group sitting with her or of others in the class.

In the next group Nancy did a fine reading job. She read Snow White each time it appeared. She read the name of each pupil and the word said: "Dick said," "Jane said," and so on. When they got to the sentence she had dictated, she read all of it: "Nancy said, 'Snow White is soft and furry.'"

Dick needed a little help with the story name. All the teacher did, though, was to make an s-s-s sound, and Dick caught on. This help was needed each time. A pause on his name was sufficient to prompt him to remember that this was his contribution and therefore his name.

In the third group Alice performed as Jerry had. Bill, however, astonished the group. He read almost the entire chart, needing help only with scratched and furry. Now the teacher went a step further. She asked Bill to locate certain words. First she said: "Point to your name." This he did quickly. Then she had him point to Dick, Jane, Nancy, Jerry, and Alice in that order. He found each name almost as quickly as he had located his own. Next she asked Bill to count the number of times Snow White appeared on the chart. He proceeded to count as he pointed, starting with the title, and gave the number five.

By this time the teacher had gathered the entire class around. Next she had Bill locate the words table and around. Both appeared in his contribution, so she had felt reasonably confident that he would succeed. Then she said: "One of those two words appears at some other place in the chart. Which one?" This was a challenging question. Bill needed to compare words and to make a decision. In a few seconds, though, he had located the word around in the second line.

Now the teacher tried one more thing. She saw that all this was holding the attention of the class. Also she realized that she was being given an ideal opportunity to make points about reading and how interesting it can be. She printed the word table on the chalkboard and asked Bill to read it. This he did instantly, even though it was in isolation. Then she wrote the number two on the board and he named it. Next she wrote the word pink. On his own, Bill walked to the chart and found the word there, and then announced that the word was pink.

Many things occurred during this second go-round with the "Snow White" story that were very desirable from both a pupil and a teacher point of view. From a pupil point of view the following observations are particularly relevant.

1. Pupils had an opportunity to work in a group, as well as to work on their own or with some other classmate.

2. When they were not in the reading group they had an opportunity to decide what they would do from a list of opportunities prescribed by the teacher.

3. They could do some "book selecting" at the library table.

4. They could read. As is evident by the detailed reports on the six dictators, the reading performance varied according to their ability to do so.

5. They could listen to others read.

6. Each pupil that had a chance to read had a chance to "succeed." Some read only the title but some, like Nancy, read six or more words.

7. The range of words read varied from Dick—who knew two words with a bit of hissing help from the teacher—to Bill who knew thirty-five of the thirty-seven different words and who read fifty-four of the fifty-six running words.

8. Visual discrimination of words was accomplished this early in the school year; and it was done without drawing shadow boxes, an extremely artificial crutch at best.

Neither did the teacher have to frame any of the words with her hand. This, too, is a weak sort of aid.

9. Visual-auditory discrimination occurred each time the pupils located in the story a word the teacher spoke and each time they read with her.

10. The sounds that letters represent were being linked on a phonetic word-attack basis, especially when the teacher helped Dick recall Snow White by making the *s-s-s* sound.

In many respects the teacher was able to make an informal inventory of readiness for reading, for each pupil's performance allowed her to note his skills. For example, she knew that Bill could read many words. He had already indicated that he knew thirty-five words. This total is higher than that found in the first two preprimers of any series of readers. He knew words in isolation as well as in context. But, above all, he knew how to use context clues to word meaning. When Bill returned to the chart to locate and identify the word pink, he showed awareness of one of the most important skills in a reader's word-attack repertore—meaning clues.

On the other hand, Jerry indicated that he recognized three words: Snow, White, and Jerry. He knew Snow White each time it occurred in the chart, indicating clearly that he had a visual image of the word and that he linked the right auditory image with the right visual image.

This stands in sharp contrast not only to the content of preprimers, but also to the *memoriter* approach to word learning. This teacher did not give the class a list of words to take home, so that distaste for reading could be reinforced at home as well as in school. Rather, she got their attention through an old "psychology of learning" trick. She used a novel experience, different, vivid, and within their grasp. Then she allowed the pupils to react by talking rather than by imposing her ideas. She arranged to have recontact or reinforcement of learning within twenty-four hours. It is during the first twenty-four hours that forgetting occurs at a rapid rate. This is true of logical as well as rote learning. Each time a pupil read the chart, others in the group had recontact with the words.

By the third day this teacher had reproduced the "Snow White" story on hectograph and had a copy available for each pupil. This gave each pupil an opportunity to pore over the story as much as he wished. She moved about from individual to individual and, in the private person-to-person session, read through the story with each pupil, underlining each word a pupil could read on his own. In some she underlined only the title, but on Bill's copy she underlined every word. In addition, the teacher wrote the name of each pupil at the end of the story. In a few instances pupils were able to write their own names.

On the library table was the story of "Snow White and the Seven Dwarfs." Pupils gained a great deal of pleasure from the fact that they could read the words Snow White in a book. In addition, the teacher had a booklet about a snow man, and some pupils discovered they could read the word snow there, too. Some could read the word snowman. One little girl brought with her from home a copy of *Jack and Jill* in which appeared a story with a winter setting. In the story the word snow was used a number of times.

So these children were encouraged to make a transfer of their reading knowledge immediately to different contexts. And, interestingly enough, they made the transfer without raising any questions about the differences in form and shape of the letters in type and the letters in handwriting.

In the meantime, the teacher started the informal reading-readiness inventory, proceeding as described in Chapter 7. She already knew a great deal about each pupil. About some she knew more than about others. For this teacher, every contact with her pupils was "diagnostic" in nature. She got to know each pupil better and better under the various circumstances and demands of the beginning school program. She learned their names, assigned seats and desks, pointed out closets and the lavatory, the room and the teacher next door, the school nurse, the principal's office, and so on. She read to the children, told stories, had them listen to music, and soon had them settled into the business of school life.

Not all of the school day was being devoted to the inventory, nor was all the reading time. She continued with other experience stories of the

"Snow White" type in which the pupils dictated in response to a shared and immediate first-hand experience. The school librarian stopped in one day and told a story to the class. This was used as a prop for pupil-dictated stories. A group of third-grade-level children visited and did a puppet show. This was an excellent source of stimulation.

When the inventories were completed, this teacher had a good idea of the language facility, interests and tastes, intelligence, and social-personal poise of each pupil. Now, in order to differentiate reading instruction and pace the learning of each on as nearly an individual basis as possible, she organized the class into four groups, her purpose being to give her an opportunity to obtain individually dictated stories and to obtain enough of them to be useful. Moving around the room from pupil to pupil was not as efficient for systematic help as working out of smaller subgroups. The groups were roughly divided according to the four levels as described. Bill and five others were in a Level IV group. Nancy and seven others were in a Level III group. Jerry and eleven others were in a Level II group. And Dick and five others were in a Level I group.

In the Level IV group Bill was way ahead of the others. He already had a sizable reading vocabulary and was having a grand time reading his way through the books in the library corner. This teacher, with her modified individualized reading approach, had made provisions for Bill and the other budding Bills. Bill was keeping his own record of books read and was sharing his enthusiasm and book knowledge with others in the room. This sharing he did informally on a friend-to-friend basis, a classmate-to-classmate basis, and already he had discovered that he could share on an interest-to-interest basis. Two others in his "dictating" group were catching on fast and doing a good deal of reading.

Dick and the pupils in his group were miles apart from Bill. Even so they were doing just what Bill was doing. They were dictating stories just as he was. Often, they dictated stories about the same experience areas as he did. This was especially true when the interest source was one in which the whole class participated. They "read" their stories on the two-voice level. They read, and that was the important thing! They got books on the library shelf and "read" them. Then, too, at times Bill would sit next to Dick in the library corner and in a low whisper read a story to him. Furthermore, at times Bill would help Dick with words when he was "rereading" his old experience stories or reading a library book.

All in the class knew that Bill was just about the best reader, but all also knew that Dick was coming along. Dick knew this too. So did Dick's parents and so did Bill's parents. The climate that prevailed in the classroom was indicated by the rising enthusiasm, good will, and self-reliance.

Once the class was organized into dictating groups, a teacher-group-contact cycle was developed. The plan permitted her to sit with each group to obtain pupil dictation on an average of twice a week. This cycle will be enlarged upon later. First, it seems timely to study carefully how the teacher worked with the Group IV people and the Group I people.

Group IV was Bill's group and had five members. At the appointed time the five pupils came to the dictating corner. The arrangement was such that pupils sat in a semicircle facing the teacher. The topic of the day was a turtle that one of the boys had brought to school. Earlier in the day all the children had gathered around to watch the turtle and to hear Bob tell how he found it.

The turtle was in a box containing grass, twigs, a small rock, and a pie tin filled with water. Stones were in the pie tin to help anchor it. The group was gathered about this exhibit, watching and talking.

The teacher then moved to the dictating table. This was a small table at pupil height. On it she had sheets of lined paper approximately eleven by fifteen inches and a black crayola. A small screen was used to provide some privacy by screening the pupil dictating from the group and the class. Then, one at a time, the pupils in the group took turns sitting with the teacher and dictating. Bill dictated the following story.

THE WALKING FORT

I called the turtle "The Walking Fort" because that is what he is. He carries his fort on his back. When he walks along, if he sees some trouble, he pulls in his neck and his feet. Then he is safe in his fort. I told my Dad about the walking fort and he said the turtle was like an army tank. But I like "The Walking Fort" better.

After Bill had dictated the story, the teacher read it back to him to see if everything was in order. Bill said the story was right. Then the teacher gave the story to Bill, and he returned to his regular seat with it. There he could do a number of things with it. First, he reread it. Bill was already so facile at learning new words that he was asked to underline only words he did not recognize or was not sure about. In this instance he could read the entire story. He paused at only the word carries, but he was able to recognize this word when he read on. Even so, he drew a light wavy line under the word carries.

This done, he turned to his vocabulary book or new-word book as he called it. This was an alphabetized notebook that his mother had given him. However, Bill could have alphabetized it himself. He already knew the alphabet and could write many of the letters. The few he was not sure about he copied from the alphabet chart along the room wall. In this book he entered only words that were "new and interesting" to him. From this story he chose turtle, fort, carries, trouble, neck, army, tank, and better.

While Bill was doing this, the other four members of the group were taking turns dictating. Edna, one of the four, dictated the following story.

RACE

I could run a race with the turtle. He has four feet but he can't go fast. I have only two feet but I could win the race.

The story was read back to Edna and then she went to her seat. None in the group was as advanced as Bill. Even so, they were well enough along to underline only words they did not know or were not sure about. In this story Edna underlined could, can't, and only. Then she started to draw a picture to go with her story.

She had barely started with her picture when all in the group had finished dictating their stories. Then they all reassembled with the teacher and took turns reading their stories to each other. One at a time they came and stood by the teacher and reread the story orally. This procedure allowed the teacher to follow the oral reading and to note which words were underlined. So, she could be ready to supply the unrecognized words and thus help the oral reading and help the listener to get the story. In Edna's instance, she needed teacher help with could and only. As is often the case, the oral rereading of the story led to her recognition of the word can't. Somehow the demands of the oral reading, the language rhythm, and the flow of ideas seem to do the trick.

When the group meeting ended, all returned to their seats. Bill continued with his vocabulary book. Edna and three others continued drawing the illustrations to accompany their stories.

At another time that day the teacher sat down with Dick and his group of six. They, too, assembled around the turtle box and talked again about the turtle. Bob told again how the turtle came out of the water when his Dad was fishing. With this group the teacher did more perception prodding as the pupils watched the turtle move about in the box. She kept saying: "See how he pulls his head in"; "See how he goes around the rock"; and so on. Then she drew up the easel with a piece of newsprint thumb-tacked on it to record what the members of the group had to say. She used the "group" story approach with these pupils because they seemed in need of the intradependence thus obtained. They needed the stimulation of each other and got more of a story or an account than when they dictated alone. The account recorded in this instance was as follows:

BOB'S TURTLE

My Dad saw the turtle when he fished. The turtle is little. The turtle can pull his head in. He has spots on his back.

Bob

Mae

Gale

Jimmy

The names at the end were those of the four pupils who dictated sentences. The fact that not all contributed was of no concern. Some days all added an idea; some days only a few contributed. Some days the group picked one member to tell the story for the group.

After the story was dictated, the teacher read it to the group, pointing to each word as she proceeded. Then different pupils took turns standing by the easel and reading the story together with the teacher. Bob was up first. He knew his own name and said the word *turtle* when he read the title. When they got to the word *turtle* in the first sentence he did not recognize it again. Instead of telling him the word immediately, she pointed to the word in the title. Before he could answer, Jimmy popped up with the word. Bob knew the word *fished* when they got to it, and he knew the word *turtle* the next two times it occurred.

Two more pupils read through the story with the teacher. Then they all returned to their seats to draw pictures to go with their story. They knew that by the next day the teacher would have reproduced a copy of the story for each. Bob drew a picture of his father fishing. Jimmy drew one to show the spots on the turtle's back. Dick drew a turtle on a rock, and so on.

By the time the teacher was through reading the story with the group, Bill had already read it from his seat, as had Edna. Interest in reading and curiosity about what the others said prompted this. And, of course, Bill was interested in how Dick was doing.

The next day the group of twelve—Jerry's group—met around the turtle box. On occasion, this group at this early stage dictated a group story as did Dick's group. However, whenever a story or account was dictated as a result of a first-hand experience, particularly one that could be examined and re-examined as this one could, individual stories were obtained.

Teachers are often concerned with time when a situation develops in which twelve individual stories must be dictated in one period. Time should not be a factor and was not in this case. This does not mean that the concern voiced by such teachers is unfounded, but the feat is not impossible, as the following account proves.

A demonstration with a comparable group was timed. The demonstration was performed in the Seaford, Delaware, Central Elementary School and was observed by five teachers. The presence of these teachers added some extraneous factors that might have interfered with the progress of the demonstration, but it did not.

The group was assembled and the interest area briefly discussed with the pupils. Ideas were shared, and thinking was stimulated. Then one at a time the pupils sat down with the teacher and dictated their accounts.

The stories were recorded as previously described for the Group IV people. The stories were short and averaged about three sentences per story. This occurred in September of the school year and the pupils already had experience dictating stories and expressing their own ideas. Some were more verbose than others and some more creative. Each had his own ideas and voiced them in his own, individual way.

After each child had dictated his version, he returned to his seat and reread the story. As he reread he underlined with a single black line each word he felt he knew. Guesses were not to be underlined—only words they felt sure about.

When all had dictated their stories and the last one had had a few minutes to reread and mark his story, all reassembled in the dictating area. There, one by one, they read their story version to the group. The teacher clipped each child's story on the easel at pupil eye level. Then the teacher and the pupil read the story together. The teacher pointed to each word as she proceeded, pausing long enough every time to encourage the child to say the word if he knew it or thought he did. Again, as with the Group I pupils, the language pattern and the on-goingness of the idea often helped the pupil recall and speak words that he would not have known on his own.

The time for this whole procedure was thirty-three minutes. Twenty-three minutes were used in the dictating and recording phase and ten minutes in the oral rereading and sharing phase. The whole procedure was unhurried, nevertheless.

Some typical stories are as follows.

Mr. Turtle

Mr. Turtle walks on four feet. He is very slow.

*

The Funny House

The turtle walks around in his house. His house has a hard roof. It's a funny house.

*

Spotty

The turtle has spots like my cat. I called him Spotty. That's my cat's name.

*

The Turtle

When the turtle eats he sticks his head out. His eyes are open.

*

Slow and Easy

I like a turtle. I like to watch him crawl around. He is slow and easy.

The words underlined are those the pupils felt they knew when they reread their stories at their seats. Underlining known words is a positive approach to word learning, for it emphasizes what is known. It also calls for a facing up to the facts; either one knows or does not know or guesses. So the act requires a certain amount of intellectual honesty. The need to "prove knowledge" occurs when the oral reading is done. The teacher will pause a bit longer on each underlined word. If the word is unrecognized the teacher supplies the word and the underlining is marked: |＿|＿|＿|＿|＿|＿|.

The pupils are now ready to prepare a picture of a turtle or a turtle scene. Pictures of turtles may be available in old magazines. If expendable, the pictures may be cut out and used instead of a pupil drawing.

Next the Level III group, or Nancy's group, was assembled. All eight gathered around the turtle to watch and talk and share ideas. Then one by one they sat down with the teacher and dictated their accounts of their turtle observations and their ideas creatively. Some of the accounts were much like those dictated by members of Bill's group in length and originality; other were more like the Level II group accounts. Nancy dictated the following.

THE LONESOME TURTLE

I believe the turtle is lonesome. He walks around so slow and looks so sad. Sometimes he looks out at us and then he pulls his head in again. I believe he is lonesome.

Nancy returned to her seat and underlined words she did not know or was not sure about. Nancy was a cautious person—more inclined to underestimate her knowledge than to overestimate it, and the underlined words reflect this. Nancy's reaction to the turtle also reflects her personal disposition and motives (1). Her response to the turtle suggests a strong and compelling regard for the welfare of others. The sensory cue of the one little turtle in the big box apparently was sufficient to arouse this flow of ideas. Nancy's general disposition finds many stimuli that are functionally equivalent and guide her to a form of behavior that already is being labeled as, "That's Nancy for you." This is not only Nancy's way of reacting to her environment, but her way of meeting it.

At the risk of being repetitious, this seems like an opportune time to repeat Ben Jonson's counsel implied in the statement, "Speak that I may judge thee." Every dictated story gives pupils an opportunity to speak and to "show" themselves. Similarly, every dictated story or account gives teachers an opportunity to "see" pupils' essential characteristics, because dispositions are in continuous flow. As Gordon W. Allport says (1, p. 373): "Interests, ambitions, compulsions, phobias, general attitudes, inclinations, hobbies, values, tastes, predilections—all are personal dispositions (some only secondary) and are at the same time motives."

Rick dicated the following story and revealed his personal dispositions.

THE EXPLORER

This turtle is an explorer. He goes around exploring. He came out of the water to explore. He explores our box.

A fascinating and stimulating feature of the dictated-story approach is the opportunity it provides pupils to be creative. Once pupils are encouraged to "open up" and "give," so to speak, each dictation session can become a revelation. These wondrous acts of revelation can be awesomely impressive and almost oracular. The oportunity to know pupils, to understand them, to bring out the best in them is unique.

Rick, like Nancy and others in this group, underlined only words he did not know. Already his stock of known words or sight words was so large and so reassuring that he could face up to unknowns and deliberately take the first step toward wisdom: "to know that you do not know is the beginning of wisdom."

Contrast this with the many children who cower in the web of a sinister drudge who day after day parboils them in the cauldron of rote memorization. This is why the words "Oh! Oh! Oh! Look! Look! Look!" echo so imploringly across the land. These tortured and retortured children are pleading and repleading. Add to this the wails of the "buh, aah, tt" children thrust from the "Oh! Look!" cauldron into the "buh! buh! hum! buh!" cauldron, and it is easy to understand why all the concern about initial reading instruction chills the nation's brick-and-mortar school palladians.

On this second day the teacher also met again with the Level IV and Level I groups. The Level IV people used the group assembly for a dual purpose. First it served as a waiting pool as each took turns sitting with the teacher and reading again their dictated turtle accounts. Bill recognized the only word he had been uncertain about—carries. He had brought with him to this private conference his New Word book and indicated that he had entered in it the word carries. Edna also recognized the three words she had underlined: could, only, can't. Now the teacher performed another interesting job. She carefully printed these three words on small rectangular pieces of substantial white paper approximately three-eighths of an inch wide and one and one-half inches long. These small cards give each pupil a private file of words.

The private file serves any number of purposes. First of all, it provides the children an opportunity to manipulate the words on their desk tops to produce stories or accounts of their own choosing. This is an especially effective way to get children to use and reuse these words and to do so with a purpose—a purpose they want to accomplish. They could also use the cards to produce stories with the help of a Pupil Word Card Holder.[1] By pressing his cards on the surface of the Holder, the pupil can make the words adhere until he wishes to remove them. The Holder may be held either horizontally or vertically, and cards may be lined up in straight lines by placing them on the impressed rules.

Peggy, a member of the Level III dictating group, set up the following story on her World Card Holder:

		Pets		
I	like	pets.		
The	Turtle	is	a	
pet	in	our	room	.
Do	you	like	pets	?
		Peggy		

Even though each word had been placed on a card three-eighths of an inch by one and one-half inches, Peggy—as did all the other children—cut the cards down to the size of the words: | I | | I | ; | the | | the |

Placing the words on a Holder has many advantges. First, the cards stay in place. Second, the Holder can be moved about with ease without upsetting the word arrangement. Third, pupils can swap Holders and thus exchange stories. Fourth, the words can be removed with ease and refiled for future use.

Pupils could write notes to each other. Edna wrote a note to Patsy:

| May | I | read | your | turtle | story | ? |

Patsy put the answer on her Holder: | Yes |

While the teacher was working with the Level III group, Dick, with the help of Bill, put this question on his Holder:

| May | I | use | the | easel | to | paint | my | picture | ? |

At this stage Dick could read only three words in that question:

| May | I | picture |

but he knew what the question was. Even though the teacher was busy in a private pupil conference, Dick walked up to her and waited quietly until she could turn to him. Then he handed his Holder to her. She read the message, added the word | yes | , and returned the Holder to him. This com-

---

[1] Russell G. Stauffer (New York: Holt, Rinehart and Winston).

municating act took but a few seconds, and did not disturb the room. Dick had waited quietly until the teacher acknowledged his presence. This was communicating with a purpose.

Pupils could play word-matching games. Joanna and Frances played a visual-discrimination word-matching game. Joanna put the word ⌞turtle⌟ on her board, and Frances put the same word on her board. Then Frances put up the word ⌞the⌟ , and Joanna matched it.

Carl and Ray did an initial-consonant visual-discrimination matching. Carl put the word ⌞ball⌟ on his board, and Ray put up a word that also began with the letter "b": ⌞boy⌟ . Then he put up ⌞stop⌟ , and Ray put up ⌞stone⌟

Jean and Ed were working together doing a very timely auditory-visual-discrimination word matching based on initial single consonants and consonant blends. Jean in a low whisper pronounced a word, and Ed had to find a word in his file that had the same beginning sound. Jean said the word "table." Ed found the word ⌞turtle⌟ in his file and put it on his Holder for Jean to see.

If in the process of writing a Holder story a pupil needed to use a word not yet in his file box, he turned to the teacher and had her put the word on a card. For example, Jerry wanted to use the word *running* so the teacher put it on a card for him: ⌞running⌟ This word was not added to Jerry's vocabulary notebook until he could recognize it at any time, anywhere.

All in all the Pupil Word Card Holders render a considerable service. Teachers are always looking for activities that pupils can do on their own. The activities described here kept many children occupied, fruitfully occupied. These pupils were busy creating, assembling ideas, manipulating words, increasing their reading vocabularies, fixing more permanently retention of words previously learned, refining word-attack skills (both phonetic-analysis and structural-analysis skills), teaming up and working together, sharing, and so on. One other factor was also true: the room was astonishingly quiet. These six-year-olds were busily engaged in reading activities in which they were interested and which were within the range of their capabilities.

The second purpose of the second-day gathering of Level IV pupils was the swapping of stories. Pupils loved this part of the get-together even more than the pupil-teacher visit. Not only was it a pleasure and a privilege to read someone else's story, but also it was gratifying and inspiring to have someone else read your story. Pride of authorship is stimulating and ego building. These children were not only budding readers but also budding authors. Language arts were truly communication arts.

When the Level I dictating group reassembled on the second day, the group chart was made available. Then, one by one, each member of the group took a turn "reading" the story orally. Again, each child stood by the teacher and followed her voice as they read the story together. Today, though, there was one *big* difference. The pupil had the pointer and pointed from word to word as the story was read. Another big difference was that the teacher toned down her voice and her rate of reading so that much initiative rested with the pupil. In some instances a pupil literally took over and read ahead. This teacher was acting much as a swimming instructor does on occasion. As the novice is paddling along, the instructor withdraws his support, and almost without realizing it the learner swims along on his own.

After each had read the story orally the teacher moved a step further. She pointed to words (she *did not* cup the words in her hand) and asked pupils to name them. Dick knew twelve of the words: turtle (appearing four times), Bob, Dad, fished, in, back, spots, little, and in. Next the teacher covered the chart and wrote certain words on the board in isolation. Everyone recognized turtle in isolation. Four knew Bob's name. One knew fished. Three knew spots. Five knew little, and so on. Each word a pupil knew in isolation was placed on one of the small cards. Again the pupils in the Level I group were "doing" all the things being done in the Level IV group.

Now the teacher and the Level I people went to the library table. There they found the word turtle in the title of a book. They also found the word in different pages in the book. Then they turned to an encyclopedia and found the word turtle in the index. The teacher then turned to that page number. Why did she do this? She was building the "encyclopedia habit" from the very beginning of the educational career of these budding scholars. Even the Level I pupils could, when on their own, pick up an encyclopedia and turn to the section on turtles and enjoy the pictures.

During this "turtle" week, pupils brought in magazine items and newspaper clippings about turtles. The interest in turtles and words spilled over into the after-school hours. This happened not because the teacher sent home a list of turtle words to be memorized, but because these children were interested. Again this circumstance is a far cry from what happens all too often. The thirty-one pupils in this room had no need to pull in their reading necks behind a protective shutting-out shell. There was no anxiety and fear—only eagerness and pleasure.

At the end of the "turtle" go-round when the Level II and III pupils had had their second day and the Level I pupils had had a third day, all the stories were clasped together and placed in the pupil-story file. This teacher used wire clothes hangers with skirt-holding clips attached. The stories were all clipped as a stapled package to the clothes hanger and hung on a story birch rod. Now pupils could go to the story rod any time they were free and take down the "turtle" stories. As the year progressed, the story birch rod filled up, providing pupils with a catalogue of their own creations all packaged together. It was fun, even in November, to go back and select the "turtle" file and reread the stories and reminisce about the long-ago week with the turtle. In addition, pupils could readily see what progress they had made in learning to read. By November many of the pupils could read all of the stories suspended from the "turtle" hangers on the rod. Here was a teacher who did not believe in "sparing the rod and spoiling the child."

The "turtle" stories were told in response to a first-hand experience situation. All had seen the turtle, examined him, and talked about him. Dictating an account or a story about him prompted the use of vocabulary known to each pupil.

A dictating cycle was set up by this teacher and flexibly followed. Roughly, it was a plan to meet with two groups on one day to record a story and with the other two groups on the next day. On the second day she met again with the two groups started on the first day to give them an opportunity to reread their stories and check on word retention after twenty-four hours.

This phase of the working cycle might be charted as follows:

DICTATING GROUPS SCHEDULE

	Mon.	Tues.	Wed.	Thurs.	Fri.
Level I	dictate	reread and word study	reread and word study	dictate	reread and word study
Level II	other activities	dictate	reread and word study	reread and word study	dictate
Level III	other activities	dictate	reread and word study	other activities	dictate
Level IV	dictate	reread and word study	other activities	dictate	reread and word study

This plan could be adapted as circumstances warranted. On occasion the Levels I and II groups did not have a second rereading day. On occasion activities related to a single experience area and a single chart or set of charts require the five days of the school week. Sometimes, too, the Levels III and IV groups needed a second rereading day. Of course, it must be kept in mind that the levels as charted here represent children grouped because of the results obtained on the informal reading-readiness tests and the standardized-reading-readiness test. Thus the Level IV group was most mature and the Level I group the least mature.

How to keep the cycle going should not prove a problem. The world abounds like a well-stocked stream with many, many areas of interest. Children are by nature wide-eyed and curious, so that the two of the world and the two of the children can result in a rich and colorful four. Children, like adults, like to talk about themselves, their possessions, their home, their family, their pets, their friends, their neighbors, their relatives, their trips. The question is not so much *what* to talk about as it is a matter of selecting. In addition, the special events in the school year as well as the holidays provide innumerable diamonds: school plays, festivals, assemblies, visitors, playground, Halloween, Thanksgiving, Christmas, Lincoln's birthday, Valentine's Day, Washington's birthday, Easter. Combined with a readiness book or two, these provide a larder full and overflowing.

This teacher prepared a guide-plan of interest areas that could be used for a month or more. She listed four areas per week, even though she knew that most likely only two would be used. In addition she allowed for rich incidental and unexpected events such as Bobby's lost tooth, Dolores's cat's baby kittens, the welcome home extended a local boy who was a World Series hero, the crash into a local lumber yard of an abandoned aircraft. Her guide gave the comfort that she sought in regard to interest areas. She knew that she would never exhaust the opportunities. She also knew that field trips could be quite useful if wisely planned, though there was always the possibility that they would be time consuming and yield few returns.

Individual charts permit and encourage each pupil to use his own words to express his ideas. They are, in fact, a veritable gold mine, for they reflect a pupil's language facility as well as his own curiosity, interests, and creativity. They are as valuable in this respect as they are for word usage. Reexamine the charts already presented in this text and note how each of these factors is in evidence.

Even though the same interest area, "turtles," was used to motivate chart dictation, the words used reflect individual preferences and differences. When Bill's account (p. 268) is compared with Edna's account (p. 269), the differences are well illustrated. Bill used forty different words, and Edna used twenty; only six words are common to both (*I, the, turtle, he, feet, but*). The differences are equally as striking when the five accounts (p. 271) dictated by five members of the Level II group are examined. Now one might conclude that, because the accounts are short and were dictated by less fluent pupils, the number of common words would be considerable. Quite to the contrary, only *one word* is common to all five stories, the word turtle—the interest area around which all stories are built. The number of different words in each is as follows: ten words, thirteen words, fourteen words, thirteen words, and fourteen words. A comparison of the titles gives a ready indication of interest differences: "Mr. Turtle," "The Funny House," "Spotty," "The Turtle," and "Slow and Easy." Creativity is apparent in the titles, but it is even more so in the contents account.

Examining just this one set of stories has already supplied abundant evidence supporting the value of dictated stories. The stories that follow confirm and reconfirm this. If the vocabulary of these stories is compared with that of any preprimer, it becomes apparent that the meager, stereotyped, repeated vocabulary is entirely too meager, too stereotyped, and too repetitious.

Individual charts encourage the same kind of creative freedom in choice of pupil illustrations. What to illustrate and how is determined by each pupil. Individual charts permit and encourage the exchange of charts. As chart after chart is accumulated, a rich chart library is built. Children love to go to the chart library and choose a chart or a set of charts to read. In this case it is doubly exciting to select and read because all authors are known. Each is a celebrity in his own right.

One of the most thrilling experiences encountered took place during a consultation visit to schools in Kent County, Maryland. In a particular first grade, one of the boys was making very slow progress. In October, he was dictating accounts using only a very few words. In December, on a return visit, he read orally a dictated story and did a fine job. But then his face really lit up with bursting-at-the-seam news. He had read his neighbor's story and would now, if the observers wished, read his own story! This he did, reading rhythmically and with great delight.

Individual charts about the same interest area, such as the turtles, can be packaged together and posted that way. A pupil who wants to reread the Turtle charts weeks later can get the package, take it to his seat, or sit on a rocking chair in the library corner, and read and remember the pleasant memories of those early school days. Even then learning to read was a pleasant, gratifying experience! Now he finds that he can read practically all of the charts. As a matter of fact, he can read Bill's chart with its forty-one different words almost entirely.

Individual charts can be reproduced and swapped. "I'll give you a copy of my turtle chart for a copy of your Post Office chart," said one pupil to another. Individual charts fit well into a personal chart notebook or folder. Each pupil can be provided with a chart notebook in which he staples or pastes all of his charts. This gives him a running inventory of his own progress. Each chart is dated as it is entered, and at the end of the year each has a fine chart chronology. These notebooks should be substantial enough to survive an occasional taking home.

Every individually dictated story represents a personalized word-usage record. In the eyes of the pupil the words in his chart are: "My words in writing." Possession may be recognized as nine-tenths of the law; in word learning, it is nine-tenths of retention. Every time a pupil marks a word in his chart as a known word, he is underlining the "my spoken word—my printed word" idea. In a way he is awarding himself a gold star. Each underlined word in the stories on pp. 271 and 272 represents a pupil-recognized achievement. He knew the word and he drew the line. Should he forget the word, as he may do, being human and not infallible, his total story plus his picture or illustration will provide many meaningful clues to recognition. As stated earlier, the teacher writes the words he encounters on small cards three-eights inch by one and one-half inches and puts them into one of the child's word banks. The cards may be kept in a word box for ready use on a Pupil Word Card Holder. When eight or ten words have been accumulated, the pupil begins to see the need for putting the words in some order. This is the time to set up an alphabetized word-bank box. For this purpose one pupil brought to school an egg box with twenty-four compartments. Each compartment was indexed with a letter of the alphabet, except that the last one was marked X, Y, Z. Now the words he had accumulated could be filed alphabetically and thus made more readily available for use. Another child brought a box that had been used to house Christmas balls. Some children used small envelopes labeled aphabetically and assembled in a box. Various types of "boxes" can be used. The important thing is the experience of filing words alphabetically—requiring the giving of attention to the initial letter of a word and requiring the pupil to deal with and learn the use of the alphabet in a very practical and meaningful way.

Some children put each word on the top line of a three-by-five-inch card and then filed the cards in a box alphabetically. On the card they put the name of the story in which the word was first underlined and the sentence from the story in which the word was first used. Whenever possible, they illustrated the word or found a small picture that could be cut out and pasted on the card, thus assembling in a sense their own picture dictionary. In addition, when circumstances permitted, the pupil found the word in other places such as newspapers, old magazines, and very old books, cut the word out, and pasted it on the card. They could also copy a sentence from someone else's chart or from a book on the library table. All this provided highly profitable busy work.

Other children put their words into a word-bank notebook. One girl brought a notebook to which she and an older sister had attached alphabet indexing stickers. Most of the notebook users labeled pages alphabetically by hand. Notebooks were easier to handle in many ways and could be taken home. In addition, they looked like private dictionaries. These people also copied a "first use" sentence and found other uses in other sources. Pupils soon discovered, though, that card users had an advantage in that they could alphabetize words that began with the same letter, e.g., about, along, an, army. Words recorded in a notebook did not allow for this without a great deal of erasing and rearranging.

These word banks provided the security of a sound investment. The account could be drawn on at any time without depleting the principle when using the Pupil Word Card Holder, when doing word-recognition activities either under teacher direction or in collaboration with another pupil, and especially when doing creative writing and faced with a spelling need. The interest on each investment in the word bank far exceeded anything available on the world economic scene.

Furthermore, the pupils were acquiring the "dictionary" habit. It would not be difficult to progress from their own dictionaries with their alphabetized arrangement and illustrative sentences to picture dictionaries, and then to standard dictionaries.

MODIFIED BASIC-READER APPROACH

The methodology described thus far has represented a modification of an individualized approach to initial reading instruction. As pupil's reading vocabularies grow, the teacher begins to plan on initiating group-type Directed Reading-Thinking Activities, so that all the habits and skills that accrue to this kind of reflective thinking and reading instruction can be started.

Quite adequate group-directed reading-thinking activities can be conducted using materials at a primer level. Some primer-level stories have enough content and plot to justify their use for such purposes. This being the case, a teacher can select wisely and then compare the vocabulary demands made by the selected primer with the vocabulary accumulated by each individual in a group.

Preprimers usually introduce about sixty words. So, to get started with a primer and fit into its vocabulary demands and also take advantage of the vocabulary new-word introduction controls, each pupil in the group should know practically all of the words introduced in the preprimer. Usually by the time pupils have accumulated a vocabulary of 100 to 120 words, they will have enough overlap with a preprimer vocabulary so that they can read each word.

The comparison is readily made. Each pupil has been maintaining a vocabulary bank against which he can now check the primer words. A good procedure is to give the preprimer list to the pupils, especially the better readers, and let them make the check. If this is not done, pupil and teacher can sit down together and check through the preprimer list to see how many words the pupil knows.

On occasion, a word appearing in a preprimer list but not in the pupil's vocabulary bank may be used as a stimulus source for dictated-experience stories. The word *umbrella* was used in this way, and it resulted not only in excellent dictated stories but also in an increase in the children's vocabularies.

Another procedure to follow that may accomplish the same purpose is to let the pupils in the group read the three preprimers independently. The size of each child's reading vocabulary, plus the fact that each has been reading books in the library corner, provides the confidence needed to read the preprimers. When this is done, the children prove to themselves that they can read these three books and, in turn, gain the security that results from this knowledge. Now the pupils will not be as concerned about the senseless repetition. They will read it once and forget about it. They will not have to Oh! Oh! Oh! for days over Look! Look! Look! Once the three books have been read, they can be taken home for show and reading purposes. Other books will have been taken home in the interim, so this procedure will not seem at all unusual.

Children like those in Bill's Level IV dictating group learn as many as six to eight new words per experience story. By the time they have dictated and dealt with twenty experience-story accounts, they usually recognize more than enough words to read a primer. This is especially so if the teacher has been keeping an eye on the preprimer vocabulary and introducing on occasion experience-story material that would invoke the use of certain words. At the rate of two to three stories a week, Level IV pupils can be ready for group Directed Reading-Thinking Activities within seven weeks, or by mid-October.

Once group D-R-T-A's are introduced, the reading-instruction time can be divided between group D-R-T-A's and a modified individualized approach. Doing this, pupils soon discover that, insofar as word learning is concerned, they are adding more words to their reading vocabulary via the experience stories than they are through basic-reader material. This should not be disconcerting, because emphasis is on reading for meaning, and not just learning words.

As the reading vocabularies of the other pupils at Levels, III, II, and I approach the right size, they, too, are introduced to group Directed Reading-Thinking Activities. Sometimes it is necessary in order to keep peace in the family to start Level I on group D-R-T-A's at a third preprimer level. This should be avoided, though, whenever possible. Content of even third-level preprimers is not up to minimum prerequisite for such purposes. On the other hand, sometimes a Level IV group makes such rapid progress in word learning that it is wise to wait to introduce group D-R-T-A's until a first reader can be used. Even though group D-R-T-A's have been started with the I, II, and III Level groups, they also continue with the dictated-story plan.

INDIVIDUALIZED READING

Thus far at the first-grade level reference has been made only to the modified individualized plan. This has represented an adaptation essential to the kinds of demands made by beginning reading instruction. Obviously it is impossible for a child to select a book and *read* it when he cannot read. True, he might seek teacher help with each word he does not know. However, the books available other than preprimers do not have even a controlled vocabulary. Hence, a pupil may meet four or five words that he does not know in a single sentence or as many as ten to twelve on a single page. No person will or could persist for very long in the learning-to-read effort when the odds against success are so great. More than teacher help and enthusiasm would be needed.

However, as pupils acquire a reading vocabulary and go about the business of locating words they know in as many other places as possible, they begin to discover that they can read some of the books in the library. Currently books of the *I Can Read*[2] type make this transition much more likely. Now book reading can be deliberately planned and approached on an individualized basis much as described in Chapters 6 and 7.

Planning get-togethers can be started. A good way is to have a group or a class gather in the library corner or in the school library. Then the teacher or the librarian can present book after book, discussing each briefly and advising the group where to find it. Pupils who have been successful in learning to read and who have a favorable attitude toward reading will respond to such sessions eagerly.

Of course, this is not to imply that pupils should not be introduced to a library corner or a school library until they have acquired some reading skill. Quite to the contrary, as has been shown on many occasions throughout this chapter and the previous one, pupils will have been introduced to and will have turned to the library on many, many occasions. Now, though, they are doing so with a different objective in mind. Now sharing sessions will be planned and various methods of sharing, such as oral reports, dramatizations, pictures, and group reports, will be used. Now, too, pupils will have a better idea of how to attack unknown words on their own. The extensive training in word recognition during the experience-story time, along with the refinement and extension of skill learning during the group D-R-T-A's, will have prepared them to move ahead on the on-their-own word-recognition road.

WORD-RECOGNITION TRAINING

The experience story or modified individualized reading approach provides innumerable top-priority opportunities to teach word-attack skills. Every story recorded and witnessed by the pupils has provided opportunities for both visual discrimination and auditory discrimination. Children can see each spoken word become a printed word. They see each letter being formed. They note differences in letter configuration and word configuration. Some letters, b, d, f, h, k, l, and t, extend above the line; some, g, j, p,

---

2 New York: Harper & Row.

q, y, and z, extend below it. Some are on the line: a, c, e, i, m, n, o, r, s, u, v, w, x. Some words are long; some are short. Some look very much alike: *in, on, an, no.* All this they learn to "see" as they watch chart after chart being prepared, and as they "read" through chart after chart with the teacher. And all this is learned without pressure to memorize and is done in a very functional setting—the recording and rereading of stories. There is nothing artificial or stilted or forced about it. On the contrary, it is meaningful, continuous, and paced. It is as C. DeWitt Boney so aptly put it (2), "learning to read as they learned to talk." It is learning to deal with printed words in a real, live communication circumstance.

Gradually and often quite quickly, pupils begin to discriminate words. When they find how often a word appears on a chart as described on pages 262–273 of this chapter, selective and purposeful word discrimination is being done of both a visual and an auditory nature, and both acts are done in conjunction with a reading act and are not divorced from it, as they are when they are taught in isolation.

Once words are recognized, they can be used to teach specific word-attack skills selectively. In fact, the child can be introduced to word-attack skills the moment he can read *one* word. For example, a child who can read only his name can be asked to decide whether another name begins or ends in the same way as his does. This can be done either by sight or by sound.

When Dick can read his name, the teacher can ask him to decide whether or not the names she says begin the same way. She can also print the name, David, Bill, Darlene, and Nancy, say, on the board or on paper and ask him to underline each name that begins with the same letter as his name: David, Darlene.

When Dick can read two or more words, the complexity of the demands can be increased. Now the teacher confronts Dick with the two words he knows, Dick and, say, turtle. She says: "I am going to say a word that begins like one of these two words. Point to the right word." Then she pronounces desk, table, door, down, toy, tent. Note that the spoken word always fits one or the other circumstance. The same can be done visually. Also, similar practices can be initiated with inflectional changes and derivatives: walk, walking; run, runs; fly, flying; carry, carries. The opportunities for such activities are legion.

Filing the words or preparing a word dictionary requires further attentiveness to word structure. Not only are single-letter beginnings dealt with but also letter combinations when filing such *blends* and *dipthongs* as black, she, the, and tree. Now the letters in the alphabet take on functional significance as they are used to put words in order. The filing allows the students to deal with these situations in circumstances that are rich with meaning and bristling with purpose. *Letter names* serve a real purpose and are different from *letter sounds.* Chapter 9 deals with the total word-recognition problem in detail.

RECORDING METHODS

In previous chapters, reference has been made to different ways of recording experience stories. For emphasis and clarification they will be dealt with again briefly.

Thus far, the teacher method of recording pupil stories has been to write them with either crayola, chalk, or similar writing instruments. This is effective and graphic and has certain intrinsic advantages. Pupils see how the teacher writes, how she holds the crayon, how she dots *i*'s and crosses *t*'s, how she slants letters, how she makes capitals, and so on. Seeing her do this time and again is equivalent to repeated demonstrations in writing. Children are quick to ape, and this provides an opportunity for pleasurable aping. They see too how she places paper and slants it, how she follows across a line, how she moves from right to left, how she indents, how she uses punctuation. Seeing all this is obviously helpful.

A primer typewriter provides another top-flight means of recording pupils' stories. As already indicated, pupils can see the typing being done, see the words being printed, note the carriage shifting from right to left, see the carriage move to the left as a line is being typed. The magic of printing occurs in front of their eyes. Also, the teacher can type enough copies at a time to supply everyone in a group. For Bill's group, for example, six copies of a story could be typed at one typing. Then all in the group receive a copy immediately.

Because typed copies can be neat and tightly packaged, the resulting copies can be filed much more readily than the longer hand-written copies. Story booklets can be kept with greater ease, and stories can be exchanged with greater ease. All this is very helpful.

When the typewriter is not being used by the teacher, pupils can be given access to it. Pupils love this and show considerable facility at it. This is an excellent stimulus for writing stories. Of course, this kind of activity needs to be kept under control. Typewriters are costly and must be taken care of. They are not so costly, though, as some of the booklets that are being bought to shore up *memoriter* approaches to beginning reading instruction.

THEY ALL WANT TO WRITE

They All Want To Write (3) is the title of an inspiring, sound, and far-reaching book published in the late 1930s by a group of teachers who were practicing what they were preaching. The book has been revised since 1939, but its philosophy and methodology remain the same. It is the kind of book all elementary-school teachers should own and all first-grade-level teachers should have on their desks ready for constant use. As the title suggests, the subject is creative writing and, as Paul Witty says in his foreword to it, "this volume brings out . . . the fact that creative writing offers an excellent vehicle for recognizing, respecting, and cultivating individuality" (3, p. vii).

One of the hardest-worked words in educational circles is the word *functional*—everything has to serve a function, and rightly so. To be functional something has to serve a purpose and have utility value for the user. Thus, functional spelling represents the skill needed to spell while one is writing a letter or a report or a paper or a book. A principal value of creative writing is that it invariably is functional writing: stories, accounts, notes, letters, posters, advertisements, book records, word files, and so on. These kinds of writing activities can serve pupil purposes without being drummed up by a teacher. If children's writing is done to the accompaniment of the steady tum-tum beat of contrived teacher copying, pupils quickly develop that veiled look of whipped attention and the overexaggerated cackle of enthusiasm that can ring so hauntingly in one's ears. Yes, the children are laughing, but . . . ?

Early writing experiences (4) involve writing a name, notes to a teacher, or to someone at home, get-well letters, birthday letters, permission for trips, thank-you notes, invitations, telling and writing about the seasons or about the weather, and so on. At first copying is hard work and requires much elbow room—big pencils and big paper. Control and improvement is brought on quickest by the need to communicate. If someone has to read your writing and a hoped-for answer is dependent upon their reading, motivation soars rapidly. This is true even if the "hoped-for answer" is *only* a word of praise. Children need to be encouraged and helped. Expectancies must be adjusted to individual differences in writing, just as they must in all skills. Handwriting experts and fortune tellers can distinguish one handwriting from another, and the concept of individual differences in handwriting has finally made its way into handwriting classes. Legibility, yes, but not goose-quilled uniformity!

Gradually children acquire writing skills that enable them to write their own stories as well as dictate them. Written stories or notes or accounts take more time and usually are shorter than dictated accounts. This is not a liability of written stories, but rather an asset of dictated accounts. In fact, during the early writing days a teacher may step in and rescue a piece by writing an ending for the pupil (3).

Without a doubt pupils cannot spell all the words they want to use, but the remarkable thing about their spelling attempts is the degree of accuracy they achieve—phonetic accuracy. The astonishing phonetic accuracy of children who want to write and are encouraged to do so is evidence again —if more is needed—that children who have learned to talk do have an ear for sound, and that phonetics cannot be the monster of rules and regulations it is made out to be or children would not fare so well on their own. The examples below illustrate this.

clinb	for climb	cilled	for killed
dag	dog	stared	started
geting	getting	astonot	astronaut
Monaday	Monday	likeed	liked
Autumu	Autumn	fends	friends
skaed	scared	astronoutnot	astronaut
woching	watching	hose	house
dansing	dancing	floteing	floating

MY MARKET

This is my maknet [magnet] fishing. My mother is woching me⁚ [watching]. And so is my sister.

THE BIG STORM

Five of the children dice. That was very, very bad. No one like it.

THE STORM[4]

Pets do not like the wind. It was floded. Housed were floteing. And Pets and People were sat.

The following stories written by first-graders are reported in Ivah Green (6).

MY DANSING DRES

I have a dansing dres. You shod see it wen I twrl. It twrls way owt. I can dans in it. I can stan on my toes too.

MY TOSSLS

Do you know that I am going to have my toslls takeing out. I will have them takeing out this spring. I went to the hsptll the other night to get my errs tested.

MY DOLLY

My dolly is buerock. Her lag came off. My brother buerockn it. I am not happy now.

Ivah Green added this comment following these stories in her article (6, p. 383):

---

[4] These three stories were made available to the author by three teachers in the West Seaford Elementary Schools, Seaford, Delaware.

An adult's first reaction may be: "What a lot of misspelled words!" And there are a good many. But the spelling is so nearly right in places as to be almost phenomenal, when one considers how unphonetic English spelling is, for the most part. And these are the writings of children who were six years old in September. But a good many are spelled correctly, and surprisingly so. And in some words the correct letters are all there, but simply disarranged.

Once children start writing, they soon discover that their reading word bank has additional dividends to pay. Words they want to write and that they cannot remember how to spell may be in the bank. Interestingly enough, pupils can make this discovery on their own. From the private word banks to a picture dictionary is an easy step. On occasion, too, a pupil finds himself using a word in a creative-writing job that he wants to add to his word bank. Then he goes to the teacher with a scrap of paper and asks for the correct spelling. This is motivation of the highest order.

SUMMARY

It has been said that while one may trust a man's probity one may not trust his predilections. Predilection implies a strong liking that results from one's treatment, one's principles, or one's previous experience that predisposes one to prefer certain kinds of friends, or books, or methods, or to accept something without subjecting it to any other test (7).

The temper of the statements in this chapter should clearly reflect the strong feelings that inspired them, and the principles should clearly reflect a belief that learning to read can be accomplished with the same communication effectiveness and motivation as learning to talk, that memorization is no substitute for understanding, that repeating facts is no substitute for reflective thought, and that permanent reading habits are not acquired in the quicksand of gold stars and scarlet letters. Experience as a teacher, a clinician, a consultant has fostered the conclusion that all our children bring with them to the Inn in Trochate excellent bread, meat, and wine, which can be converted into an unprecedented literacy. It is a pity that in the midst of such abundance one finds famine. Resources are not the problem. The difficulty is man. The contraceptive methods of lockstep teaching and rote-memorization learning need to be replaced with the art of personalized discovery and reflective thought. Initial reading instruction is one area in which we can get "off the beach."

REFERENCES

1. Allport, Gordon W., *Pattern and Growth in Personality*, New York, Holt, Rinehart and Winston, 1961.
2. Boney, C. DeWitt, "Teaching Children To Read as They Learned To Talk," *Elementary English Review*, 16 (April, 1939), 139–141, 156.
3. Burrows, Alvina Treut, June D. Ferebee, Doris C. Jackson, and Dorothy O. Saunders, *They All Want To Write*, New York, Prentice-Hall, 1952.

4. Burrows, Alvina Treut, Russell G. Stauffer, and Elizabeth H. Vazquez, *American English Book I*, New York, Holt, Rinehart and Winston, 1960.
5. Goodenough, Florence L., *Mental Testing: Its History, Principles, and Applications*, New York, Rinehart, 1949.
6. Green, Ivah, "All Words Belong to First Graders," *Elementary English, 36* (October, 1959), 380–384.
7. *Webster's Dictionary of Synonyms*, Springfield, Mass., Merriam, 1942.

PART V
DEVELOPMENTAL
SKILLS

Chapter 9 ❧❧❧❧❧❧ Developing Skill in Word Recognition ❧❧

Do you remember when you learned to read? The average literate man on the street is apt to answer, "No, I don't remember." Such an answer is strange, is it not? Reading is a complex process, as earlier chapters bear witness and as authorities through the years have testified, and learning to read is a most difficult phase of this complex process. Why, then, does almost no one remember it?

Could it be that learning to read was so challenging and so demanding that the majority of people have subconsciously blocked out the memories of it? This hardly seems likely. While this might be true in some instances, it would not be true generally. Could it be that learning to read was so easy that most people had very little difficulty and as a result do not remember? This hardly seems to be the answer either. It is likely, though, that the true answer lies somewhere between these two extremes, and perhaps it is nearer the "easy" side of the issue than the "difficult" side.

Many people know someone who could read before he started to school, someone who may have had some "teaching" help at home during those sacrosanct preschool years or may just have learned to read much as he learned to talk. Experience has taught first-grade-level teachers in particular that some children come to school possessing some techniques by which they recognize words. Some teachers greet these early readers with warmth, but many others are anxious and concerned because these children do not fit into the scheme of things. Studies have shown that such children from varied social-cultural backgrounds and with varied degrees of intelligence enter school in a steady stream. However, it is not only these few who do not remember how they learned to read, but also the many more who needed "formal" instruction in order to get started.

When pressed to recall their first years of reading instruction, many people have a recollection of teaching and learning experiences related to learning to read. Recalled are occasions in which pupils made sounds in response to teacher-written letters and letter combinations, yet they knew no phonic rules. Some have labeled this the grunt-and-groan phase of their learning-to-read program. Is this the only imprint that the complex process of learning to read has left in minds of literate man? If so, why?

Teachers and prospective teachers reveal a considerable lack of knowledge about phonic generalizations (1, 40). On whom does this reflect—the teachers, the teachers of teachers, or the functionality of phonic generalizations? Our teachers are able people. Most of them have completed four years of college. As a group, their I.Q.'s may not be as high as those of scientists and engineers, but certainly they rank among the most intelligent people in the general population. There seems little likelihood that it is teachers' inability to grasp phonic generalizations that accounts for their lack of knowledge. Mary Austin and Coleman Morrison in *The Torch Lighters* (4) suggest that more teaching of reading at the prospective-teacher level is needed. Why, though, have teachers who are teaching phonic generalizations year after year not learned the generalizations? This is a real paradox. Could it be that phonic generalizations are not particularly functional, especially to the person who can read? The myriad rules most likely are not very serviceable to the reader who either readily recognizes many words or who has learned to trust a dictionary.

On many occasions parents at P.T.A. meetings and the like have been asked to name the syllable rule that applies in the word *pinnate,* and in most instances they cannot do this. When asked what phonic generalization applies to the first syllable, again most cannot do it. Most do know the rule applying to the second syllable, but when asked to state the accent rule that applies, again they are lost. These same requests have been made of teachers on many occasions, and in most instances the results are the same as with parents.

Subjective and objective evidence indicates that neither parents nor teachers, even though they can read, know or use phonic rules.

Phonic generalizations are taught in grades one, two, and three. Is this the level at which phonic generalizations are most useful? If so, why?

WHAT WORD-RECOGNITION SKILLS?

What does a child, or any individual for that matter, do when he stops at a word he does not recognize? Obviously, he *sees* the word, or, in other words, he uses *visual perception.* But seeing the word is not enough, for it does not help him to recognize it. Next he tries to *sound* the word by means of visual clues first and sound clues second. He analyzes the word to discover letter clues to the sounds that they may be representing in this particular word context. Then he blends these sounds together so that, along with the appropriate accent, he can say the word. All this may not be sufficient because *meaning* clues also determine phoneme sounds and accents; he may need to read on to determine the appropriate meaning.

In other words, word-recognition skill involves the ability to use context clues or meaning clues, phonetic clues or sound clues, and structure clues or sight clues. This all sounds very complex and makes the learning-to-read circumstance seem most difficult. This being the case, how does one account for the fact that year after year many bright children learn to read on their own?

The success of these children implies three things. First, the skills of word recognition cannot be too complex or else these preschoolers would not be able to work out their own quite reliable system. Second, there must be some pattern to the development of these skills or else the children would develop as many different systems as the well-meaning adult phoneticists have done. Third, there must be a tremendous latent power residing in meaning and communication, or else the words would remain unknown.

Compare the situation when the word is not recognized immediately with a reading performance when no difficulty is encountered. Now the recognition process becomes the simultaneous and instantaneous act of seeing the word and identifying the appropriate meaning. Meaning directs the entire process. Apparently, then, since meaning plays a dominant role in both situations (dealing with words that are not immediately recognized at sight, and words that are), it provides the most functional key to word recognition. This is the position taken throughout this text, because it keeps *communication* in the fore. All other aids are subordinate and auxiliary to it. One deals with the phonetic elements not merely to say a word, but to help one in grasping its meaning. The same condition is true about structural aids.

MEANING CLUES TO WORD RECOGNITION

Meaning clues or context clues are then the most functional aid to word recognition, and the skills associated with meaning clues should be given first-order attention. The context in which words are presented for learning purposes should in turn be as rich with meaning as circumstances permit. For initial reading instruction, words taught should be words that children have learned to use for oral communication. Studies of children's vocabularies (oral and written) indicate that the number of words children use at age six is quite large. Minimum estimates are as high as 1,500, so the number of words available for use in preparing initial reading materials is large.

Accordingly, attention should be focused on the communication being done and not on the words being used. As already seen, instruction focused on communication yields much better results than when focused on word recognition and vocabulary control.

In Experience Stories. Compare the context and content of Bill's story and Dick's group's story on turtles with a first story in a typical preprimer.

THE WALKING FORT

I called the turtle "The Walking Fort" because that is what he is. He carries his fort on his back. When he walks along, if he sees some trouble, he pulls in his neck and his feet. Then he is safe in his fort. I told my Dad about the walking fort and he said the turtle was like an army tank. But I like "The Walking Fort" better.

Bill

BOB'S TURTLE

My Dad saw the turtle when he fished. The turtle is little. The turtle can pull his head in. He has spots on his back.

Bob
Mae
Gale
Jimmy

RED

Nancy, come here.
Come here, Bill. (55, p. 5)

HERE, RED

Come here.
Come, Red. (55, p. 6)

Bill, Bill.
Come here.
Come here, Bill. (55, p. 7)

Come here, Bill.
Here, Nancy.
Come here.
Here, Red.
Come here. (55, p. 8)

The contrast is so sharp that it seems unnecessary to say more. Even so, it must be pointed out that the first story in *Come Here* (55, p. 4) is not really typical of similar first stories in basic-reader series. The five words used in the story quoted were introduced in a readiness book. This does not make this first story any more palatable; neither does it make it more of a communication act. If this "story" were to be adjusted to be like a first story in a first preprimer of most basic-reading series it would look like this.

Come (p. 1.)
Come, come. (p. 2.)
Here, here, here. (p. 3.)
Here, Here.
Come here. (p. 4.)

Disgusting, is it not? And to think that 90 to 95 percent of the children in this jet-aged, rocket-mellowed, interplanetary-minded country of ours are being fed this kind of pablum. Even more disconcerting is the thought that this has been the diet for the past forty years, and that it is apt to be the diet for the next decade at least. These circumstances should be dreadfully embarrassing to any author whose name appears on such material and much more embarrassing to publishers who insist on producing it, despite the fact that in some instances they are being strongly advised not to.

At this point, some timid soul is sure to say that the preprimer story as presented here is divorced from its context. This is true; the pictures are not there. Note though that the context from which this language has been lifted is a picture context. Is the purpose of this material to teach pictures or words? The answer is: words. So Peter has not been robbed to pay Paul.

No defense can be marshaled in behalf of such material. It is devoid of all the principles that make for sound learning and for communication.

Of course, much the same thing could be said of other books for children that are like this. Books like *The Cat in the Hat*[1] robbed of its pictures would be very uninteresting. Only one big difference exists, and this alters the circumstance entirely. *The Cat in the Hat* is not being sold as a preprimer or accompanied by a 110-page manual of directions.

Recall again that Bill could read every word in his story—a total of *forty* different words—and had doubts about only one word, *carries*. Recall too that this story was dictated by Bill early in September. Even if Bill had been permitted to read the first story in a preprimer such as the one described, he would have dealt with only *five* different words. He dealt with eight times as many in one experience story. Or, if he had been allowed to read the more common first preprimer-type story, he would have dealt with only *two* words.

Now examine again the performance by Bob in the Group I situation (page 270). He recognized and remembered three words: *Bob, turtle,* and *fished.* This is equal to the number of words he would have learned in the preprimer first story. Here, however, he was learning the words in Sep-

---

[1] Dr. Seuss (Theodore Seuss Geisel), *The Cat in the Hat* (New York: Random House, 1957).

tember, whereas by the preprimer method he would not have learned them until February.

What are the word-recognition factors that weigh so overwhelmingly in favor of the dictated-experience-story approach? Why should Bill and other Bills around the country recognize so many words? Why should Bob at the other end of the scale recognize even a few words? The answer is readily apparent.

1. The children think of the ideas. They are the *thinkers*.

2. The ideas reflect each child's experience and knowledge—his *creative* effort.

3. The words used are the pupils' words. Not only are these words in their speaking-listening-meaning vocabularies, but also they can produce them in response to a stimulus. Children are the *producers*.

4. The order of the ideas is *theirs*. Each child arranges the events he observes in his own pattern. Each sees *sequences* and *consequences*.

5. The children see their own spoken words being recorded. They can *recognize*, if they have not before, that each printed word represents a spoken word. They know this or are cognizant of it.

6. They experience the pride of authorship. They can sense all the rights and privileges appertaining to being *authors*.

7. They hear their own stories being reread orally. They can feel *emotion* as they listen to their own words being spoken by others.

8. Paced by the simultaneous oral reading by the teacher, they can identify the words they know and not words that some cold and logical word count had told the teacher they should learn first. Because they use their own mental constructs, the *reconstructing* process—with printed words as the stimulus source—is facilitated.

9. They make visual *discriminations* of words without such artificial props as shadow boxes or basal brackets or some other kind of word sty.

10. They make visual-auditory discriminations and associations between each word they speak and the teacher writes, and between each word the teacher rereads orally.

The factors in the dictated-experience story procedure that facilitate retention or aid memory are equally significant:

1. A first in any learning situation is to so arrange the situation that the major initiative rests with the learner.

2. The more vivid the impression created through color, novelty, participation, and so on, the better is the recall.

3. The use of sensory modalities facilitates learning. The pupils saw the turtle, talked about it, and dictated their own impressions about it.

4. The opportunity for some incidental learning along with the directed learning makes for more effective retention.

5. The teacher direction helps pupils discover cues to word recognition by making vivid oral-printed language associations, by giving hints and

suggestions, by encouraging pupils to name all words they think they know, and by allowing them to identify their own *memoriter* clues.

6. The material dealt with is adapted to the perceptual level of the learner.

7. The circumstance encourages the pupil to be intellectually honest without penalizing him.

8. The innumerable opportunities for meaningful reuse of words learned provides a form of wholesome repetition.

Furthermore, the language context can always be enhanced by supporting it with a pupil-prepared picture. Such a picture can facilitate word recognition and retention. It can also serve as a title aid, especially for pupils like Dick and Bob.

The fact that other pupils dictate stories about the same experience area offers to each pupil many interpretations of the same experience. It also exposes each pupil to many uses of the same words that he used.

Another major advantage of this rich language-context approach to initial reading is the constant opportunity available to the child to "go back" to the original context and rediscover the word.

Thus children acquire an attitude toward reading in general and word recognition in particular that is thoroughly charged with meaning. It is the communication of the child's own ideas that provided the crux of the communicating act and the word-learning situation. Context—a rich personalized context—makes the difference. If a word is not remembered the practice of turning to context for meaning clues is initiated and becomes thoroughly instilled.

In Basic-Reader Stories. When instruction in basic readers supplements the experience stories, a deliberate effort is being made to increase a pupil's reading vocabulary on a "paced" basis. As described in Chapters 2, 3, and 4, basic-reader materials, if appropriately structured, are especially useful in a group-directed reading-thinking situation.

Two values result from the use of basic-reader materials. First, all in a group are reading the same material at the same time. They are examining the same evidence, making conjectures based on the evidence, doing so according to their individual experience and knowledge, and reading to prove whether or not their hypotheses were correct. Second, because the rate of word introduction and concept introduction is controlled, skills of word recognition, concept development, and comprehension can be put to work without frustrating the reader, as may happen in material that is not similarly controlled or paced.

Group instruction using basic readers can accomplish certain skills of reading and thinking. Individualized instruction using all kinds of materials can accomplish other essential skills of reading and thinking. Among the skill learnings common to both approaches are those leading to independence in word recognition. Both approaches are needed if independence is the objective, as it should be. Of course, materials other than basic readers may be used for group-instruction purposes, but they do not allow for the accomplishing of the skills with the same efficiency.

One of the reasons for the preparation of basic readers is for the control or pacing of vocabulary. Words new to a series are introduced on a paced basis. (See Chapter 2.) The pacing varies from no more than two new words on a page at the primer level to as many as six or eight at the sixth-grade level. Paralleling this range is a similar one in the number of running words per page. Even though the number is not controlled by prearranged plan, type size, line spacing, picture size, and frequency of occurrence influence this greatly. Whereas a primer may average 65 running words per page, a sixth reader may average 360 words per page. The words are usually selected according to available evidence of frequency of usage as tabulated in various vocabulary studies. In fact, both frequency of usage and commonness of meaning are considered. At the primary level, particularly, great care is taken to select words that are *known* to children, or words that are in their functional speaking-listening vocabularies. This kind of meaning guarantee on an oral level is sought as an aid to written word recognition. In other words, both meaning and oral usage are controlled, so that attention can be focused sharply on recognizing the written symbol and associating it with its meaning(s).

In addition, each word is embedded in as rich a meaning context as author and artist ingenuity can create. First, new words are always introduced in a sentence context. Doing this not only surrounds the "new" word with known words, but it also takes advantage of the completed thought contribution to recognition that a sentence can make. Second, new-word introductions are paced on a page, or separated by a minimum number of running words. This number has been set at twenty running words. Setting the number so high often means that one or two sentences may separate new-word introductions at the primary level, and at the intermediate level it usually means no more than one new word in a sentence.

Pictures are carefully planned so that new words introduced on a page are supported by picture clues. (See Chapter 3.) When *dog* is introduced the accompanying picture shows a dog. When *conveyor belt* is introduced it is illustrated. When *sweeping* is introduced, as used in the game of curling, it is illustrated. All this is done to help the novice reader along the reading-for-meaning road.

The total context for a word is the language context *plus* the picture context. A well-trained reader will take full advantage of the total context at all times, especially as he learns to appreciate the fact that a good picture may be worth a thousand words and as he learns that all graphic aids serve to enhance meaning.

What does the teacher do about the new words introduced in a basic-

reader story when she is directing the reading of a story? This is an extremely important question, and its answer is equally important. It is one of the key points at which basic-reader word-recognition training has bogged down.

A "new" word in a basic reader means only that it is the first time that the word appears in a particular set of readers. At the primary level in particular, "new" words are "known" words. At the intermediate level, glossaries are provided to help make "new" words known words. "New" words are paced in introduction. "New" words are supported by graphic aids. "New" words are selected so as to give a reader an opportunity to try out the word-attack skills he has learned. For this reason the number of new words is controlled so that the reader will not be frustrated by too big a demand on his skill-analysis abilities. "New" words are reused in the story in which they are introduced and in subsequent stories because the psychology of learning has always stressed meaningful repetition. At the primary level word reusage is very carefully controlled in basic readers.

For these reasons "new" words introduced in basic readers are never presented to pupils in advance of the reading of a story. To do so is to deny pupils the only well-controlled opportunity they will have to try out the word-attack skills they have learned and to try them out under teacher supervision. In addition, to teach new words in advance of the reading of a story rejects one of the basic reasons why so much arduous preparation goes into basic readers and why they are called *basic.* This understanding about new words is as essential at the intermediate level as at the primary level. At the intermediate level, pupils are learning when and why and how to use a glossary. If glossary words are pretaught, pupils cannot learn the when and why of glossary usage.

It would be naïve—very naïve—to think that this condition applies to all instructional situations, that in science class or arithmetic class new words would not be dealt with in advance. However, a basic reader designed to teach reading skills and built with a carefully controlled vocabulary is not a science book or an arithmetic book. The purpose of a basic reader is different. However, even science books and arithmetic books and the like use both context clues to meaning and glossaries. Authors of these texts make every effort to develop accurate concepts, and this is as it should be.

Therefore, context clues to word recognition are equally as important to the budding reader when he reads experience stories and when he reads basic-reader stories. Meaning—reading to understand—is always the guiding star, the one by which he charts his course.

What does a pupil do if when reading in a basic reader he meets a word he does not recognize? Obviously he first looks at the word; otherwise he would not know that he does not know it. Quickly he calls to mind all the skills he has of a structural-analysis nature. Then he notes the sounds that he thinks the letters represent in this instance and blends them together, giving attention at the same time to the place where he thinks the accent will fall; then he may read on to find language clues, or he may study the picture to see if that context provides any hints to meaning. Depending on his reading level he may turn to a glossary or dictionary. Finally he may turn to the teacher. The first steps should be accomplished readily if the child is reading at his word-recognition ability level. Turning to a glossary may take a little time, and turning to a teacher may take more time.

A preferred plan is to train pupils to use context clues first if they do not recognize the word on sight. With meaning clues in mind, the word may then be analyzed for structure and sound clues. This order is proper, because meaning plays a dominant role in word recognition. It influences how a word may be syllabified, how the phonemes may be sounded, and where the accent falls (*record*: rĕ kôrd or rĕk′ rd?) (*rebel*: rĕb′ l or rĕ bĕl′?). While it is true that these examples represent the exceptional word, it is also true that seeking for meaning always facilitates the getting of meaning; and this certainly applies to word recognition. Words are but symbols—cogs in the meaning wheel.

In Individualized Reading. Context clues to word recognition abound in *experience stories,* as already described. This is one big reason why experience stories are an ideal way to get the incipient reader started on the reading road. From the very beginning the rich source material of experience stories fosters the attitude that meaning in reading always comes first and that the habit of searching for meaning should be constantly practiced.

Context clues to word recognition abound in basic readers from the primer level up. The controlled pacing of new words, of word-recognition skills, and of context (language and picture) clues makes basic readers ideal for the extending and refining of skills initiated through experience stories. Basic readers provide the only controlled materials available that permit the reader to try out his word-attack skills without being frustrated. This is why "new" words are *never* taught in advance of the reading of a basic-reader selection.

The object of the training in word-recognition attack skills started via experience stories and extended and refined via basic readers is to develop readers who can deal with words *on their own.* The proof, therefore, of the effectiveness of the experience story and the basic-reader training program is what children do when reading materials other than experience stories and basic readers; in other words, how effectively children can deal with words when reading trade books, periodicals, newspapers, and the like. Or, put in question form, do the word-attack skills learned in *controlled* reading materials function in uncontrolled reading materials? Will pupils use skills they have learned under the watchful eye of a teacher when they are reading on their own?

The history of the transfer of knowledge is not at all encouraging and can be summed up in the words "one learns that which he practices." For teachers of reading this means that if pupils are not given an opportunity to try their word-attack skills while reading in an almost completely "on-their-own" situation, they will not become proficient in word recognition. The objectives set as the outcome of word-recognition training will not be reached.

The conclusion that follows logically from the facts advanced is that, to complete the cycle of word-recognition training, children must be given the opportunity to participate in an individualized reading program with its self-selection privileges.

What does a pupil do if, while reading on his own, he meets a word he does not recognize at sight? He can skip the word, but he will never do this if the attitude and habit of reading for meaning have been fostered and developed in him from the very beginning of his in-school reading life. Habits of seeking and demanding meaning are not easily acquired. Habits of self-discipline, self-reliance, and self-assurance are acquired only in an atmosphere that encourages their formation.

The sheltered atmosphere of a group may or may not promote some of these character attributes. Much will depend on the leadership. The sheltered atmosphere of an individualized reading situation may or may not result in pupil acquisition of these characteristics. Again much depends on the leadership. However, some of the characteristics are apt to be acquired in an individualized reading situation even of the weakest kind. And in a situation in which the teacher practices described in Chapters 5 and 6 are carefullly followed, there is considerable likelihood that the characteristics listed will be acquired. Prerequisite, of course, is that the teacher understand that individualized instruction is an essential in a sound, well-founded program of reading instruction.

If these preferred conditions exist, the child who meets a word he does not recognize on sight will put to work all the skills at his command and will seek teacher help only as a last resource. He will proceed as already described. The teacher needs to be sure only that the pupil seeking her help has fully utilized all the skills he has learned.

When a child asks for teacher help with a word, the first question the teacher asks is, "What do you think it is?" This question implies quite clearly that the pupil has done all he can and invites him to say: "Well, I read on. Then I tried to blend the sounds together and I think this is it." His answer will be particularly helpful to the teacher. He will show her where and how he is wrong if he is wrong. The child who says *trick* for *truck* must realize that *truck* does not make sense. In turn, the teacher will know that the difficulty is with the medial vowel. If she had not asked him, however, she could never be this specific about his need.

Or, on the other hand, the child who asks for help with the word *cache* and can pronounce it correctly must be seeking meaning help. In this instance the teacher should be curious as to how the pupil learned to pronounce the word. This is an account of an actual situation, and the pupil in question had turned to a dictionary and obtained the correct pronunciation but had failed to check on the meaning. The word sounded like *cash* and the pupil assumed this was the meaning, but this meaning did not make sense; so without double-checking in the dictionary he double-checked with the teacher. He was learning a valuable lesson though, and the teacher was provided with a priceless teaching opportunity. Words that sound alike (homonyms) do not usually have the same meaning; and to obtain the pronunciation of a word is not of much help if it is divorced from meaning. Meaning always take precedence. However, this child was well on the way toward acquiring on-his-own habits and had the presence of mind to stop reading when *cash* (*cache*) did not make sense.

Pupils reading in different sources and doing so on their own should know as much about context clues to meaning as it is possible to teach.

Language-Context Clues

What does a teacher mean when she tells a pupil to read to the end of a sentence or paragraph to see if he can identify an unrecognized word? She is asking the pupil to use meaning clues as an aid to recognition. What is the writer trying to say?, she is asking him. What words would you, the pupil, use to say the same thing? She is inviting the pupil to reconstruct the author's ideas and to think.

Pupils have had many experiences doing the same thing when communicating orally. Often when two people are having a conversation a speaker hesitates on a word and, before he can supply it and finish his idea, the listener has supplied it for him. How does the listener know what word to supply? He does so because he is listening intently and has grasped the speaker's ideas. So, with his attention focused on meaning, he is ready to step into the oral-communication breach and supply the word. It is this same kind of intentness on meaning that should characterize the circumstance in which a pupil reads on and uses printed language-context clues to word recognition. The author and the reader are talking with each other almost as if they were in a face-to-face situation.

Using language-context clues to recognize a word is much like tests involving the missing-word device. As reported by Marion D. Jenkinson (34), this approach was used by Cyril Burt (13) as a supplementary test in his English revision of the Binet scale. He used two passages and in scoring made no allowance for synonyms. Burt felt that this completion-test method was largely a test of reading comprehension. As such it was a means of measuring knowledge acquired and using information gathered from previous experience.

Examples of a cloze test are: I heard a _____ bark. George _____

_____ was the _____ president of the United States. The cat turned quickly and ran _____ the street.

Starting with M. R. Trabue (63), the completion method was used to test reading comprehension. Then in 1953 Wilson L. Taylor (59) used the completion method to measure readability of reading material and called it the "cloze procedure." Marion Jenkinson reports that, "The term 'cloze' is derived from the Gestalt notion of closure, the tendency to fill in a missing gap to make a well structured whole" (34). This is not a "guessing" technique but a use of the intellectual processes of logical analysis—imagery, reasoning, evaluating, judging, and problem-solving.

When a child is asked, therefore, to use language-context clues to recognize a word, he is not being asked to guess. Quite the contrary, he is being asked to use his intellectual powers to their fullest, to comprehend so thoroughly that he can make logical cognitive deductions. Convergent-type thinking is being required as the pupil focuses all the information at hand on the missing word or concept.

Certainly the process of reading comprehension is arrested when an unrecognized word retards comprehension. The pupil facing up to the fact that he does not know is taking the first big step toward wisdom. The cost to the learner in terms of time to stop, think, reflect, and act is infinitesimally small as compared to the cost of ignorance.

Marion Jenkinson (34) classified student-verbalized responses on the cloze test into three categories: structure of language, semantic aspect, and subject's approach. Of particular interest here is the subject's use of semantics or his methods of obtaining meaning from a passage, methods the author identified as literal, contextual, and ideational. When the subjects used contextual aids they did so through the anticipation of ideas and meanings, the retrospection of the passage, and the reconstruction and extension of meaning. The high scores on the Jenkinson cloze test revealed a greater number of discrete ideas that were more precise, had greater relevancy, indicated more effective use of context, and gave evidence of being more actively engaged in the process of interpretation. They also revealed a greater knowledge and use of word meanings and language structure, showed more verbal fluency, and made more use of certain intellectual processes.

Every reader—the highly skilled as well as the semiskilled—uses context clues to meaning, because, as Constance M. McCullough put it (39, p. 225), "The verbal woods are full of context aids to reading." Not every reader, however, is articulate about what he does. This is a function of a good instructional program.

What are the context aids to reading that are available to the reader as he makes his way through the verbal woods? Constance McCullough lists and defines context aids to reading as follows (39, pp. 226–227): experience clue, the comparison or contrast clue, the synonym clue, the summary clue, mood or situation clue, the definition clue, and the familiar-expression clue.

a. Experience Clues. Experience clues draw heavily upon the reader's life experience. They rest quite solidly upon the degree to which he has examined and reflected over happenings in his sensory world.

> "This is a good book," she said.
> "Is it for Mother?"
> "No, it is for Dad's brother," said Bill.
> "He is my <u>Uncle</u> Jack." (56, p. 14.)[2]

*

> Then, as quickly as it came, the rain stopped. At the same time two girls ran out of the house. They were both watching the sky. "Look!" cried one girl. "There it is. It is the most beautiful <u>rainbow</u> I have ever seen."

*

> Now the sun was high overhead. Already the day was hot and dry. There was not a <u>cloud</u> in the sky.

In each of the illustrations the underlined word is one of the new words being introduced. The word *Uncle* is the only new word presented on the page and is surrounded by seventy-five running words, all of which had been introduced earlier in the series. In addition, the word occurs more than once on that page. It is readily evident that a pupil reading for meaning would supply the word *Uncle* almost automatically because it is the word that fits. Even if a blank space had been employed, most children could fill it with the right word. This is one more reason why new words should not be pretaught. To do so denies pupils the opportunity to think and predict and to use phonetic clues. Practice exercises could be provided in which the pupil is given some letter clues to recognition. For example:

> "No, it is for Dad's brother," said Bill.
> "He is my Un_____ Jack."
> or
> "There was not a cl_____ in the sky."

Exercises like this help pupils understand how phonic clues plus context clues provide the reader with a very useful skill.

It is readily evident, too, that life experience plays a significant role. This is true with the word *Uncle* as well as with *cloud* and *rainbow*. Note, too, how the context provides a tone that enriches the meaning and facilitates comprehension.

b. The Comparison or Contrast Clue. In such a context the reader grasps the new word when he compares or contrasts it with a known word. Likeness and difference clues provide one of the best ways to obtain understanding and insight.

---

[2] These and subsequent selections are from Russell G. Stauffer *et al.*, Winston Basic Readers (New York: Holt, Rinehart and Winston), 1960.

All day her new hat went on and then off.
When night came, she put the box down by her bed.

*

One of the men was watching Willie. He called over. "Take it easy, my boy.
Take it easy. You try too hard."

*

I'm so hungry. I never get enough to eat.

*

I guess if you had only ten cents spending money every Monday and you had
to make it last through Saturday. . . .
"Why I never heard of such a thing!" said the dragon. "Ten cents a week—
why, that's just plain stingy."

In some circumstances the opposite word appears in the immediate context as in day and night, and easy and hard in the examples above. Also,
in some instances the opposite word appears ahead of the word being
introduced. In other instances it follows. Thus the reader needs experience
in using the context surrounding a new word.

There are many occasions when the opposite word is not given, but when
other words provide the contrasting setting or circumstance. This is true in
the "always hungry—never get enough" situation. Here the qualifying
words always and never play an important role. In the paragraphs where
stingy is presented, a larger context is used to create the impression of not
plenty (only ten cents—make it last—I never heard of such a thing). In each
instance the reader intent on meaning will get the tone and intent of the
situation and grasp the meaning of the idea being conveyed and in turn
may recognize the word. Again when the context clues are coupled with the
phonetic clues, the likelihood that pupils will recognize the word is greatly
increased.

c. The Synonym Clue.   This clue occurs when in the same sentence or a
following sentence appears a word that is a repetition of the same idea or
word.

Nancy laughed as she ran. She looked like a happy girl.

*

"I cannot believe it," King Charles thought. "No one can live without care.
Everyone has trouble. Everyone has something to worry about."

*

His other hand was squeezed tight around the stone from Edinburgh Castle.

At first consideration the idea of synonyms seems to be particularly fertile.
One is apt to think that words that mean the same thing abound. This is
not the case. According to *Webster's Dictionary of Synonyms* (67, p. xxvii),
a synonym "will always mean one of two or more words in the English

language which have the same or very nearly the same essential meaning." Then it points out that this is not a matter of mere likeness in meaning but is, rather, a likeness in denotation. So, synonyms are "only such words as may be defined wholly, or almost wholly, in the same terms." Synonyms are interchangeable only within limits.

It may be wise, therefore, rather than to look only for a synonym, to look for other words as well and to search for the mood, tone, and intent of words. Approaching synonyms this way will result in a better understanding of words, as is evident in the illustrations cited. Happy and laughed are better appreciated as the reader grasps the larger picture of how the girl looks and why she is running. This is true, too, of worries and cares, and squeezed and tight. Even though this is the case, synonym usage is one of the best ways to get understanding. To be gay, is to be blithe, glad, joyful, cheerful, happy, and so on, and to understand gay is to understand these other terms, too, in part.

d. The Summary Clue. This is the circumstance in which one word appears to describe a whole set of conditions as if in summary. Or, it might be said that a whole set of circumstances appears to add up to one big circumstance that is labeled by one word.

> Very soon Railroad Street was full of people, all hurrying to the station. It was lined with cars from the railroad crossing to the stores. Once again Topton was a very busy place.
>
> *
>
> It was a hot summer evening. The window in Charles' room was open, so he sat down near it.
> Suddenly a strong breeze came through the window. It blew some papers across the room. Then, just like that, the breeze stopped blowing.
>
> *
>
> Even though Omar hated his brother's teasing, he had great respect for him.
> Now he admired the way Gomez grabbed the heavy spear and shot downward through the water. He seemed to glide along easily. It took a few seconds before he bobbed up again with his first catch.

The details provided in each description lead the reader to a generalization. In the first illustration the street was full of people; all were hurrying; the street was lined with cars. The reader gets the idea that this was a busy place and time. The same is true in the illustration of breeze and admired. The summary word does not always appear at the end of a description, as can be seen, but regardless of the word's position, the reader is supplied with enough facts to grasp the idea.

e. Mood or Situation Clue. As already pointed out in a number of illustrations, the word may be suggested to the reader because of tone and mood in a particular setting.

The day did not look good, but the children wanted to go.

By and by Nancy called to Jack. "Now we cannot have a picnic. Look at the <u>rain</u>."

*

At last a tall man came into the room. He was carrying a big prize in his arm. Then all was quiet.

"Friends," he said. "We are here today to find the <u>most</u> beautiful cat."

*

The farmer loved his wife, but he was worried about one thing. She could never get enough of anything. She always wanted more than her share of the comforts of life. It was this <u>greediness</u> that worried him.

In the first illustration the reader catches the spirit of the circumstance by means of the different specifics. The day does not look good. (How doesn't it look good? Why? What is wrong?) The children wanted to go even though the day did not look good. What did they want to do? Where were they going? What is it that they might do even if the day is not good? Apparently the picnic must be called off. What was happening on this not-so-good day that a picnic could not be held? Most likely it is rain. By the time the reader gets to the word <u>rain</u> he is ready to bark it out.

In the third illustration the mood elements are also strikingly apparent. The farmer loves his wife but he is worried about something. She always wants more than her share.

In both instances, the <u>rain</u> example and the <u>greediness</u> example, the moods are created near the beginning of the story. As a result they influence the reader's "set" or expectancy for the rest of the story. What will the children do on this rainy day now that picnic plans have been called off? Or, what will happen because the wife is greedy? The reader gets a feel for the story and for the new word introduced.

f. The Definition Clue. This is the clue in which the word is defined in the immediate context either preceding or following the word.

"I've been invited to a Christmas party, and I want to go dressed as a fairy. But the <u>costume</u> takes much money.

*

For two days and two nights the wind blew, and the rain beat down. This was one of the <u>wildest</u> storms of the year.

*

"I got it in school," Ray said. "I gave my new glove to Donald, and he gave me his whistle. We like to <u>swap</u> things."

The definition or explanation clue is perhaps the easiest to recognize and to use immediately. The author eases the reader along the road to fuller meaning by providing a full explanation. The whole procedure is like a built-in dictionary.

g. *The Familiar-Expression Clues.* These are clues that are derived from certain language patterns that have become common and familiar.

The cat turned quickly and ran <u>across</u> the street.

*

That night Mr. Que sat long with his books. "Who rules <u>least,</u> rules best," he read.

*

"The price seems very high, dear. We'd better talk to your mother about it."
Oh, dear! Oh, my! Grown-ups were always saying that. Without a <u>doubt</u> there would be NO HAT.

A reader who gets caught up in the web of a familiar expression finds himself reading on through the passage with ease, even though it may contain words that appear strange in print. Oral-language usage and meaning familiarity will do the trick. The association is readily made because the response has been thoroughly established through frequent oral repetition. Children recognize readily the swing of "quick as a wink" or "hungry as a bear."

A. Sterl Artley (3) lists other context aids that a reader can use as clues to word meanings. Even though some of the aids he classified are similar to those listed by Constance McCullough (39), they merit repeating: typographical aids, structural aids, substitute words, word elements, figures of speech, pictorial representations, inference, direct explanation, background experience, subjective clues. Some of these that are different from those on the McCullough list are illustrated in the following lines.

a. **typographical aids**
   quotation marks:

"Look, Bill," said Susan. "Red is pretty and clean. He wants to go to school with you."

italics:

Princess: Ned, did you see the ball game on television last Sunday?
Ned: Oh, yes, Princess. But I wasn't very happy about it.

bold face:

The Free Fall (b.f.)
The fact that a man falls faster when he first jumps from a plane led to the idea of the delayed jump.

parentheses:

He told Harvey that the schooner could not return to Gloucester until all the salt in the bins (100 hogsheads) was "wet."

footnote:

* Author's note: The words may not be printed lest someone use them to work magic.

glossary:

a-cad-e-my (ā Kăd′ e-mĭ), 200. 1. A place of training, a school. 2. A group of learned men united to advance art or science.

b. **structural aids**
   nonrestrictive clause:

The engineer—for that's who the man was—carried Tom into the station.

apposite phrases:

It was a valentine—an old-time valentine.

*

This had been a hard winter for Broken Dream's people, the Atsina Indians.

parenthetical expressions:

"First, never try to hurry a hog."

*

As for Cousin Bill, he never had much to say.

*

"Upon my word, lad, how come you to ask such a question?"

c. **word elements**
   roots, prefixes, suffixes:

"As the boat disappeared across the sea . . ."

*

He is unpredictable.

*

Both thermoplastic and thermosetting plastics have many uses.

d. **figures of speech**

It is as black as night.

*

I see the Moon Lady. She is round like the moon and has a dress of silver.

*

His quickened ears heard wings.

Language, used to communicate, is a storehouse of meaning. This is true whether the language is oral or written. The printed page is a reading detective's paradise of clues. Every word, every word order; each idea, each idea order; every line, sentence, paragraph, and page; all punctuation; all mechanics—all aid the knowing reader in his search for understanding.

The innumerable demands on oral language made by day-to-day living forces every child to face up to the consequence of what he hears. He catches tone, mood, intent, word order, because they influence what he wishes or does. Children will learn to be equally as attentive to the meaning of printed words if their experiences with them demand meaning. Learning to use printed words to communicate requires direct and continuous teaching. Learning to use all the many context aids to written communication also requires direct and continuous teaching in a situation that demands understanding.

Reading or the recognition of words may not be thought of as a parroting situation. Printed words must be dealt with by each reader as they occur in a communication context. They must not be predigested for him. He must learn to take full advantage of every clue available in the search for meaning.

Over and over again pupils must be given an opportunity to search for meaning as they read—to unlock every word. The context clues described thus far must be taught again and again so that each pupil will in the course of his reading training become as accomplished in his use of these clues as he is in the use of oral-communication clues.

If to the context clues as enumerated by McCullough (39) and Artley (3) are added the clues defined by modern structured linguistics, a quite complete picture is obtained. The linguists' approach to language meanings is by way of language signals. And, even though linguists are on occasion charged with neglect of meaning, Charles C. Fries points out that he and others have constantly insisted that meaning cannot be ignored. He says (25, p. 97):

> All language, as we view it here, concerns itself with meanings. Or, perhaps, we should say rather that human beings are basically concerned with meanings and use language as their tool to grasp, to comprehend, and to share meanings. It is the linguist's business to turn the spotlight on the tool—language—itself in order to examine the physical material of which it is composed and to determine the ways this material has been selected and shaped to accomplish its function of mediating meaning.

Language as the storehouse of man's experience and of the meanings that grow out of that experience provides man with a means whereby he can share his experience. Just as semanticists point out that "the word is not the thing," so linguists point out that "the language itself is not the meanings." Language is a code of signals. The person wishing to communicate effectively learns the language signals by which meanings are sent and received. The signals can be dealt with discretely for analysis purposes, but in operation they function as a continuous system. In fact, the systems or patterns are, through frequent and intensive usage, learned so thoroughly that they become a part of an undifferentiated background. The identification and recognition of the patterns in speech are almost instantaneous and automatic. People are not conscious of the code through which messages come and go, of learning to talk or having to learn to talk; they are conscious only of the messages conveyed, unless something interferes.

According to Fries (25, pp. 65, 105, 106), there are several important layers of signaling patterns; lexical, grammatical, and social-cultural.

Lexical signals are the morphemes or words that function in our language code. They consist of two contrasting patterns. First, the difference in lexical meaning represented by different words, e.g.,

Every *step* seemed harder to take.
Every *stop* seemed harder to take.

In speech the difference between *step* and *stop* is signaled solely by the difference in their vowel sounds. *In print it is signaled by the vowel shape.* These two words (*step* and *stop*) are similarly separated from *stoop, steep, strap, strip.* In writing as in speaking, or in reading as in listening, it is the particular message or meaning to be transmitted that determines the sequences to be used and how they are to function as signals. When the lexical signals *step-stop* and the meanings connected with the pattern "Every (stop, step) seemed harder to take" are known so completely that identification and recognition of the language signals is instantaneous, then attention to the carrying physical patterns (speech or print) sinks below the threshold of attention. When they are not known so completely, conscious effort must be given not only to the lexical signal or signals that are not instantaneously recognized, but also to the meanings connected with the total pattern. Meaning is essential to accurate identification and recognition, even at the structural unit level of lexical signals or at the word level.

The second pattern is the co-occurrence of other lexical sets that identify a particular meaning out of a variety of meanings that a lexical signal or word may represent. The lexical item *spread,* for instance, represents different meanings. In each of the following sentences the co-occurrence of other lexical items helps determine the particular meaning applicable in each sentence.

"With canvas spread, she was following the Adventure."
"Soon they were out where the full wind caught the spread sail."
"He would not put on a full spread of canvas in a strong wind."
"Tiger was her cat. Spread out on Patty's knees Tiger was dreaming of . . ."

Listeners and readers familiar with our language usually are not conscious that they use lexical sets in recognizing a particular meaning out of many that a word may have. Such responses are acquired, though, in the learning of a language. The reader is apt to grasp instantaneously the meaning of "spread canvas," "full spread," and "spread cat" without giving deliberate attention to the co-occurring lexical sets.

While it may be true that pupils will, when reading, deal successfully and effortlessly with lexical sets that have been learned in their speaking-listening communication world, it is also true that teachers may not assume that all meaning shifts are grasped. Pupils need to articulate such changes.

This can be done by requiring them to single out for discussion such varied meanings as are illustrated, for example, by *spread*. Other uses can then be dealt with such as *spread butter,* a *table spread,* a *bedspread,* and *spread eagled,* and attention can be given to co-occurring lexical sets.

Grammatical signals are the signals of meaning carried by grammatical structures, of which there are three patterns. First are the contrastive arrangements on the form-class level, or words as "parts of speech." In these patterns of grammatical signals it is not individual words that function as the structural units but classes of words. In the context of actual usage, the words become marked as belonging to one of four major form classes (25). It is the markers that signal the form-class or part of speech. In fact, even a nonsense word will take on a particular form-class meaning when so marked. By way of illustration see how the nonsense word *diggle* becomes a noun, an action verb, an adjective, and an adverb, as it takes on the different form-class meanings (25, pp. 104–109):

Noun. Diggle: A diggle was sick.
Two diggles were sick.
Action verb. Diggled: A woggle diggled another woggle.
Adjective. Digglier: This woggle is digglier than that woggle.
Adverb. Diggly: This woggle uggled another woggle diggly.

Also, by way of illustration, see how the words *plain, toll, alarm,* and *produce* become nouns, verbs, adjectives and/or adverbs as they take on different form-class meanings.

Noun: The cattle and the oxen had run off to join the buffaloes on the plains.
Adjective: And it was plain to him that she was a laughing girl and not at all a serious one.
Adverb: Its lights showed the men plainly to the Indians who were . . .
Noun: To help pay for the roads the people had to pay a toll each time they used the roads.
Noun and Adjective: Because of the toll the roads were often called toll roads.
Noun: The alarm spread.
Adverb: Lambs tripped over one another in alarm and fear.
Noun: A producer and several assistants conduct rehearsals and the final show.
Verb: There are writers and editors who produce the script.

Form-class changes of the kind illustrated should be dealt with at whatever levels they occur. Pupils can be asked to note the changes in meaning as a first step. When noun, verb, adjective, and adverb usage has been dealt with in English class, this nomenclature and meaning for parts of speech can be added to the discussion of context clues to meaning. At the same time it can be noted that some of the form-class changes are accompanied by structure changes: plain-plainly; produce-producer.

Second are "function" words —words that one must know as items and for which it is impossible to substitute nonsense words such as *diggle, uggle,* or *woggle*. The number of function words is small as compared with the four major form-class markers.

In the arrangement: "Who is coming tomorrow?," who is a function word; and in this arrangement it signals the grammatical meaning "question." A rearrangement of signals is required in "He is coming" to get the grammatical meaning "question" as in, "Is he coming?"

Third are the signals of meaning carried by patterns of "intonation" and the use and significance of sequence of pitch changes. Some example are:

He ran to the ╱ green ╲ house.

He ran to the ‾green‾╲‾house.‾

Social-cultural signals provide not only linguistic meanings of utterances, but "total meanings." A perfectly clear linguistic meaning must be cast into a social frame of organized information if the full meaning is to be grasped. For example, "They won the series through four successive victories" may be clear linguistically but not socially-culturally. But when the reader fits this statement into a social-cultural framework of organized information, the meaning becomes full. If, for example, the reader learns that it is the Dodgers who won four successive games and that it is the Yankees who were beaten not in spring training but in the World Series, that meaning approaches much closer to total meaning.

"We have to go to town this morning.
Sheriff Williams said something about wanting to see you."

The social-cultural meaning of these two sentences does not become clear until they appear as a part of organized information. Out of context many meanings can be attributed to the two sentences. In the context of "Whitey Steers Ahead," the reader knows why the Sheriff wants to see Whitey. In fact, if the reader were stopped at the point in the story where the quotation occurs, he would most likely predict that an award of some kind is in order for Whitey. Pauses to predict help readers grasp such influences as social-cultural-economic forces exert. As is apparent, full grasp of meaning is essential to reading, regardless of whether the passage is to be read orally or not. It is apparent, too, that to have effective intonation and pitch changes, all the signals of communication must be utilized.

Skill and efficiency in the use of language-context clues for word-recognition purposes is of number-one priority because of the premium it places on understanding. Reading without understanding is not reading, and the mature reader makes a determined effort to get as close to perfect comprehension as circumstances permit. Therefore, he uses every available technique to unlock meaning, and for him, "unlocking words" means to unlock the meaning of words.

Skill and efficiency in the use of language-context clues for word-recognition purposes is accomplished only through constant, diligent effort. To be able to "read to the end of a sentence" is only a crude beginning, but it is a beginning, and it initiates the attitude and habit of seeking meaning.

Daily practice should be provided to develop skill and efficiency in one or more of the different techniques described above. By so doing, children will grasp the idea that "getting the meaning out" is of first-order importance and that "sounding out" is only an aid to achieving that purpose. The many illustrations that have been provided can serve as pattern guides for the identification of similar opportunities so that the teaching of the use of language-context clues becomes a daily practice.

It should be apparent, too, that the need for and the use of language-context clues occurs from the very beginning of the learning-to-read program. As the syntactical, grammatical, and semantical demands of language become more complex, the need for training in the use of language-context clues becomes more urgent.

If initial reading instruction is begun with the meager diet provided by preprimers, the wherewithal for the use of language-context clues is not available. Turn again to the section in this chapter concerned with experience stories and see how the opposite is true when this approach is used. When a first-grade girl dashes to her experience chart to get help in recognizing a word in isolation that she did not recognize on sight, she is indicating that she is learning how to take advantage of context. She is acquiring the right attitude and the right habits. She is learning to put first things first. This is impossible when material as devoid of meaning as that in preprimers is used. Not only is it impossible, but pupils try to memorize word forms and look for *memoriter* signals to help them distinguish one word from another. The end result is that words become confused, signals fail, and either the word-learning process grinds to a stop or it creeps along at a snail's pace. Even the endless repetition of flash cards and the soliciting of help at home seldom do the trick. This is why parents frequently are told by teachers not to worry about their child's slow progress but to give him more time. Such teachers have noted that on occasion, when given sufficient repetition, most pupils do learn some words.

Picture-Context Clues

It is impossible to write a book about the teaching of reading and put the entire discussion of word-recognition into one chapter. A look at the index will show how discussion of word recognition occurs at many points, throughout this text, especially in Chapters 2, 3, 4, 7, and 8. This is to be expected, since ability to recognize words and the use of word-recognition skills is a constant, on-going part of the reading act.

The use of picture clues for word-recognition purposes was first discussed in Chapter 2. In that discussion the point was made that when basic readers are carefully structured, they will reflect the deliberate effort taken to provide picture clues to word recognition as well as language clues. This kind of structuring should be done throughout a basic series, especially at the beginning-to-read level. Reread pages 47–48 in Chapter 2 concerning the discussion of the build-up for the word family. Ample language clues were provided, and in addition a family was shown in the picture. In this respect the setting or context for the word family was like that of a picture dictionary. Given was the new word family, a language definition, and an illustration. These conditions are met so often in a well-structured basic-reader series that the pupil is being supplied literally with a built-in picture dictionary.

Words and illustrations are the hallmarks of any well-structured dictionary—even an unabridged dictionary. As a matter of fact, unabridged dictionaries would be more useful if they provided more illustrations. Picture dictionaries like the *Winston Pixie Dictionary* or the *Golden Book Picture Dictionary* provide very little more help, if any, for a word like *family* than is provided in a basic reader.

To a good degree simliar principles operated in pictograph language. Pictures were used because they provided symbolically some of the elements or attributes of those of the original. Thus the pictograph symbol for *house* had a roof, walls, rooms, floors; it was not nearly so abstract as the word *House.*

At the intermediate level and beyond, pictures play equally as important a role in the total word-attack skill repertory. In fact, the role of pictures, maps, graphs, and charts may be even more important in the search for meaning. The Courtis-Watters *Illustrated Golden Dictionary for Young Readers* (16) is designed for those children who have outgrown the picture-dictionary stage. Even the word change in the title from *Picture* to *Illustrated* indicates the greater scope of the more advanced dictionary. The illustrations consist of pictures, maps, graphs, charts, and so on. For example, the illustrations for the word *dam* fill half a page and show an earth dam, a mill dam, a beaver dam, a rock-fill dam, a timber-crib dam, a multiple-buttress diversion dam, a horizontal-arch dam, and a multiple-arch dam with reinforcing buttresses. On the other half of the page appear six word entries and definitions, including the word *dam,* and two more illustrations.

Glossaries in basic readers usually contain both picture and word definitions. For example, the word *harpoon* is introduced in the following sentence of a fifth-level reader: "Bob and Hank had their harpoons with them." The story is about fishing at Cape Cod. The word *harpoon* appears in the glossary, along with an illustration of a harpoon and a harpoon gun. If a pupil also turned to a dictionary such as the *Basic Dictionary of American English* (5), he would find there two illustrations of a harpoon.

In the same fifth-level reader the word *kilt* is introduced in a story about Scotland in the sentence: "One or two soldiers in the dark green kilt of the famous Black Watch leaned carelessly against a cannon." On the following page are shown two soldiers in kilts, and thus picture aid to meaning is provided. On the other hand, even though the word appears in the glossary it is not illustrated there. If, however, a pupil turned to a dictionary such as the *Basic Dictionary of American English* he would find an illustration of a kilt.

Picture-context clues can be most helpful to the beginning reader as well as the maturing reader, and even to the most advanced reader. Illustrations so specifically pointed as to provide ideas to support or elaborate on the meaning of a single word are worthy of careful study. Basic-reader pictures and glossary illustrations provide built-in picture-dictionary-type help. These sources can contribute greatly to word-recognition processes and to comprehension. They not only are the equal of a thousand words but also can supply the wherewithal to clarify one word.

The desirable path to pursue, then, to acquire word-recognition skill is to give first-order priority to the value of context clues—both language and picture clues. The plan described here is more than a blueprint for glory. It is realistic and far-seeing. Its important facets are immediately apparent from the early phases of the learning-to-read program. The superiority of starting with an over-all design concerned with meaning and long-range efficiency within the framework of ordered excellence goes far beyond the piecemeal prescription of a program that seeks only phoneme or grapheme constancy.

SOUND CLUES TO WORD RECOGNITION

Skill in word recognition needs to be taught. It involves ability to use context clues or *meaning* clues, phonetic clues or *sound* clues, and structure clues or *sight* clues when decoding a word that is not recognized at sight.

Phonic Analysis Defined

The terms *phonics* and *phonetic analysis* are often used interchangeably, and this has on occasion confused some and puzzled others. A definition of phonetics that appears universally acceptable is the one offerd by Charles K. Thomas. Phonetics, he says, is "the study of oral sounds used in communication" (60, p. 3). He goes on to give us the purposes of phonetic study: "The broadest answer is that phonetic study sharpens our understanding of the tool of speech which we use in the varied social situations of daily life" (60, p. 32). He adds that "On a more pedestrian level, the objective of phonetic study is the improvement of substandard speech" (60, p. 33). If in this last sentence one were to substitute the word *analysis* for the word *study,* the resulting statement would be, "the objective of phonetic analysis is the improvement of substandard speech." Obviously this is not what reading specialists mean when they write about phonetic analysis.

In 1929, Anna P. Cordts said that *"Phonics* is the term usually applied to the study of sounds as they are related to reading. The aim of this study is to give the child power to identify words independently. For this reason it is considered a part of the problem of learning to read" (15, p. vii). Emmet A. Betts put it this way in 1946:

II. **Phonetics and Phonics.** These terms are often used interchangeably by teachers. The term *phonetics* has been used . . . to designate the science of speech sounds. . . . *Phonics* is a term used to designate the application of phonetics to the teaching of reading. (6, pp. 623–624.)

Dolores Durkin, after making a critical assessment of the claims and counterclaims prevalent today, had this to say about phonetics and phonics:

Phonics is an adaptation of the highly specialized field known as phonetics. The phonetician, unlike the teacher of reading, concentrates on a study of speech sounds as an end in itself. He is therefore interested in the most subtle variations in sounds, and even in their physiological and acoustical characteristics. . . . Phonics . . . is the end-product of an attempt to select from the findings of the phonetician whatever is useful for reading and spelling. As such, phonics concentrates on the most common sounds in our language, and on the letters or combinations of letters most often used to record them. (17, pp. 1–2.)

At a point further along in her discussion, she says: "That symbols representing speech sounds are used to record our language makes phonetic analysis both possible and productive in identifying words" (17, p. 5). This she does without defining *phonetic analysis* or telling why she uses this term rather than *phonic analysis*. It would seem that *phonic analysis,* because it concentrates on the common sounds in our language and on the letter or letters used to represent them, would be the more precise term. However, because *phonetic analysis* has become so well established as the label for these circumstances, both terms are used interchangeably.

Dolores Durkin points out that the use of highly specialized knowledge like phonetics to identify unfamiliar words could result in irregularities from exact pronunciation (plastic, complex) to close approximation (chair, formal) to misleading combinations (walk, tongue) (7). Accordingly, she makes a plea for realistic teaching of phonics. The plea for a realistic approach is sound, but only a phonetician would know that the combination of sounds in the six words she gives could range from exact to approximate to misleading information. It seems wise, therefore, to add that realistic expectations should be declared with regard to the teaching and use of phonics. Children are not phoneticians. Phonic techniques for word analysis can be taught and be quite functional when used as one of a combination of skills for dealing with unfamiliar words. As a matter of fact, as pointed out earlier, some children develop on their own quite an effective system for "sounding out" words.

Phonics must be used on a "combination of skills" basis because of the influence of grammatical functioning of certain words on their pronunciations. By way of illustration, there are adjective-to-verb shifts as in *ab' sent* and *ab sent'*; noun-to-verb shifts as in *des'ert* and *de sert'*; and noun-to-adjective shifts as in *min'ute* and *mi nute'*.

How Phonics Can Be Used

Many people do not know the word represented by the following letters: p i n n a t e. Naming each letter does not help them to recognize it. (Recognition means not only to say a word but to know its meaning in the context in which it is being used; or, if it has only one meaning, to know that one.) This evidence eliminates what one author described as reading (24): "Reading means getting meaning from certain combinations of letters. Teach the child what each letter stands for and he can read."

For those who still do not know the word, let us examine it further. As literate adults you probably could speak the word almost instantly, even though you did not recall having seen it before. Ask yourself, then, whether in speaking it you used some of the common phonic rules represented by the letter combinations of the word, or the common syllable rule.

Did you know that the word had two syllables? Did you know that the syllable break occurred between the two *n*'s? Did you know the rule applying?

If there are two consonant letters between two vowels in a word, the first syllable usually ends with the first of the two consonants. (29, p. 86.)

Now examine the first syllable. Do you know the common phonic rule that applies?

If there is only one vowel letter in a word or accented syllable, that letter usually represents the short vowel sound unless it comes at the end of the word. (29, p. 226.)

Do you know the rule that applies to the second syllable?

If there are only two vowel letters in a word or accented syllable, one of which is final *e,* usually the first represents the long sound and the second is silent. (29, p. 227.)

Do you know the rule or rules that apply to two-syllable words? (Neither of the two generalizations recommended for use with two-syllable words applies here.)

Two like consonant letters following the first vowel letter (cannon, furrow) are a clue to an accented first syllable and to a short vowel sound in that syllable except when the vowel sound is controlled by *r*. . . .
Final *e* or two vowel letters together in the last syllable (parade, complain) are a clue to an accented final syllable and to a long vowel sound in that syllable. (29, pp. 240–241.)

This illustration reveals two things. First, while you most likely could pronounce the word *pinnate,* you did not know precisely the rules involved.

This being the case, your knowledge of phonics was not very complete, and you would be considerably handicapped if you had tried to say a word that was not composed of such common elements. Second, even though you could pronounce the word correctly, you had no idea concerning the meaning of the word. Therefore, you did not know how the word could be used.

Of what use is phonics to a child learning to read? As some parents and most teachers of first grade can substantiate, some bright children learn to read almost completely on their own, or so it seems. They apparently, somehow, learn to read in much the same way that they learned to talk. In addition, these alert, enterprising children usually make up their own system of word attack, including phonetic analysis. Often they need only teacher reassurance that what they are doing is correct or nearly so.

This implies three things. Effective skills of word attack cannot be too complex, or children, generation after generation, would not be able to deduce their own rather reliable system. Second, the skills they develop are fairly uniform and almost standard. This suggests that there must be present a rather readily identifiable system; otherwise different children would deduce quite different systems. Third, the skills developed by a resourceful child in a first-hand situation—a situation in which the child is reading to get meaning, where the need is clearly recognized and the skill used does a job—are apt to be very functional.

From this we can conclude that there are skills of word analysis that are useful and, therefore, functional. Second, if alert readers do so well when using their own system, they will become even more skillful and efficient when using techniques teachers have found to be useful. If this is true for these children, certainly it is equally as true for the less resourceful.

It is established, then, that certain children work out their own system of phonetic analysis when reading for meaning, and that from this we may conclude that phonetic skills are helpful when reading for meaning.

Second, as one bright five-year-old said, "If I can say the word, then I know what it is." The secret of the process resides in already "knowing" the word.

All this leads to a major conclusion: when basic reading materials are structured using words common to children's speaking vocabularies, the children using meaning clues, sound clues, and sight clues may recognize words and read. This in turn means that a packaged primary-reading program, to be effective, should provide a carefully planned word-recognition program, presented frequently and systematically, and based on words known to be common to children's speaking vocabularies. As has already been pointed out a number of times, pupil-dictated experience stories provide a ready source of words that are in children's speaking-meaning vocabularies.

When to Start Phonic Instruction

A question teachers are asked frequently is, "When do you begin instruction in phonics?" The most acceptable answer is, "From the very beginning of a child's school career." A child meeting an unfamiliar word tries to blend sounds together so he can speak the word. It may be that he will recognize the spoken word and this way help fix in his mind the printed symbol as a sign for the word. It is the blending together of sounds as represented by the printed letters that does the trick. Knowledge of sound, then, is the key element in phonics.

In Chapter 7, "Readiness for Reading," there is a lengthy discussion on auditory discrimination. In that discussion it is pointed out that by the time children come to school the size of their speaking vocabularies is ample evidence that they have an ear for sounds. It is an astounding feat of blending auditory-speech-meaning capabilities when a child hears a new word once or twice and then uses it correctly without formal instruction. Yet this astounding feat occurs again and again in the preschool years of a child. On occasion, it is true, some words are taught deliberately; but the majority of the words learned are not so taught. Otto Jesperson says:

> A Danish philosopher has said: "In his whole life man achieves nothing so great and so wonderful as what he achieved when he learnt to talk." When Darwin was asked in which three years of his life a man learnt most, he said: "The first three."
>
> A child's linguistic development covers three periods—the screaming time, the crowing or babbling time, and the talking time. But the last is a long one, and must again be divided into two periods—that of the "little language," the child's own language, and that of the common language or language of the community. In the former the child is linguistically an individualist, in the latter he is more and more socialized. (35, p. 103.)

Once a child comes to realize that cries of a certain kind bring responses of a certain kind, he is taking the first big step on the road to voluntary use of language; and, as Jesperson puts it, this is when many parents discover that the child has learned to exercise a "tyrannical power." When children have progressed to the language of the community level, it is almost incomprehensible to realize that they can remember what sounds have to be put together to bring about exactly this or that word.

Even more astounding is that the child eventually comes to correct his own speech mistakes. It seems that there may be two possibilities to account for the mistakes. One is that the child may hear the correct sound before he is able to produce it correctly. The other is that the child learns how to pronounce a new sound at a time when its own acoustic impression is not yet quite settled. This is the time when, if parents are in too great a hurry to correct a child's false pronunciation, they may only produce speech troubles. As Jesperson says (35, p. 110): "The path to perfection is not always a straight one."

It is truly remarkable, is it not, how well children observe sounds, how they learn to correct their own speech errors and those of others about them? The "sound" wealth children bring with them to school is fabulous. Even the poorest among them is wealthy.

Children can be taught to be articulate about the sounds they bring with them to school if the instruction is paced so that for some it is not too hurried and for others not too exacting.

The road to sound articulateness or to deliberate use of sound knowledge to unlock a word is through the recognition of likenesses and differences of sounds. As described in Chapter 7, the approach is easiest through the use of language patterns of rhyme and alliteration. For this oral-language facility furnishes a rich storehouse.

The Alphabet

For centuries prior to the rise of comparative linguistics, Latin was the chief language taught. It was taught chiefly as a written language, and (35, p. 23) "this led to the almost exclusive occupation with letters instead of sounds . . . and very often where the spoken form of a language was accessible scholars contented themselves with a reading knowledge." All too often what was considered "logical" in language was determined by whether or not it conformed with Latin usage. "This disposition, joined with the unavoidable conservatism of mankind, and more particularly of teachers, would in many ways prove a hinderance to natural developments in a living speech" (35, p. 26). This account of linguistic progress and attitudes may reflect the continued emphasis on the value of knowing the names of the letters in the alphabet as a learning-to-read aid at the early stages.

The *names* of the letters and the sounds the letters represent are not the same in most instances. More than forty sound symbols are needed to represent the English language and, since the alphabet contains only twenty-six letters, it is apparent that there are not enough letters to produce a one-letter-for-one-sound circumstance. Ernest Horn found forty-eight different situations of the letter *a* alone (32). Similarly, the short *i* sound is represented in fifteen different ways. So it is readily apparent that the same *letter* may represent different *sounds* and that the same *sound* may be represented by different *letters*. It is equally as apparent that letters do not "make" sounds. The letters in the word *cat* do not say a thing, no matter how intently one listens. The letters, however, do represent sounds.

On the other hand, rather extensive study of initial reading instruction done under the direction of Donald D. Durrell (18) indicates that knowledge of letter names is the most important part of the phonics program. This includes knowledge of letter names as well as perception of letter forms. Alice Nicholson's study of 2,000 first-grade children led her to conclude that (42, p. 24) "A knowledge of the names of letters provides the greatest assurance of learning to read. Tests which measure association with name and form of letter show the highest correlations with learning rates for words." Nicholson's findings concerned with knowledge of letter names are supported by Arthur V. Olson's findings (44). He followed the growth in reading and word perception of the same 2,000 children, and concluded that knowledge of letter names provided the best predictions of success in reading when September test results were compared with February findings. In these studies early instruction in letter names and sounds followed by applied phonics and practice in meaningful sight vocabulary produced higher results than incidental teaching. Even so, it could not be said that a knowledge of letter names and sounds assured success, but a lack of such knowledge could produce failure. Knowledge of letter names and sounds could then be both symptomatic and causative of a certain maturation in the cognitive processes. While high mental age did not assure success, children with high mental ages did have better letter knowledge.

Again an aspect of the total pupil-teaching situation that appears highly significant is that of human variability. Just as some pupils come to school able to read, so some come knowing all of the alphabet. On the other hand, some come unable to read a word, and others are unable to name but a few, if any, of the letters. Of first-order importance is the need for differentiated instruction.

The constellation of skills thus far referred to might be thought of as readiness for phonics: functional speaking and listening vocabularies, auditory and visual discrimination, and knowledge of letter names. To think of it thus, though, suggests a discreteness in the hierarchical structure of phonic skills that seems unwarranted. This is especially so if it is agreed that phonics is the study of sounds as they are related to reading, or the application of phonetics to the teaching of reading. In this setting, phonics encompasses all facets of "sound" knowledge, and the components listed here are a part of the constellation. Furthermore, all of the components most likely do not make equal contributions, and this makes it difficult to place one above another.

Yet on the other hand, it is true that the cluster of elements of the constellation thus far described all have occurred before any, or at most only a few, printed words have been learned. This means that the knowledge of sounds has not yet been applied to the analysis of a printed word. In this sense the skills referred to might be labeled *phonic readiness.*

Carter V. Good has defined phonics as "the act or process of breaking up words into visual or phonetic elements for the purpose of blending these into word wholes" (28, p. 29). If this definition is accepted, the skills referred to represent phonetic skills and could be considered readiness for phonics. But again, this is divorcing the idea of sound knowledge from the total act of phonics: "the application of sound knowledge to printed symbols."

This point is belabored because it is believed that if teachers think of phonic-readiness skills as discrete items they will offer their students insufficient training in auditory discrimination. Twenty years of experience in a reading-study center have shown the author that most of the children who are tested to determine the extent of their reading disability lack word-attack skills, especially auditory discrimination. What seems to be happening is that teachers have children attempting to recognize printed words before they have a sufficient knowledge of sounds and the letters used to represent them on an auditory level.

Developing a Sight Vocabulary

"Following a readiness program in which the names and sounds of letters have been learned, a child in the first grade acquires a sight vocabulary," according to Donald D. Durrell and Helen A. Murphy (19, p. 11). This suggests quite clearly that a child should not be taught to recognize any words until he has learned the names and sounds of twenty-six letters. By "sounds of letters" they mean here only the single sound that is represented by the name of a letter. They say further (19, p. 11): "Growth in this vocabulary is dependent upon many factors including the rate at which new words are introduced, the difficulty of the words, the methods of presentation and the provision for adequate practice."

At this point the reader is urged to reread pp. 261–284 in Chapter 8. Note that, in the language-arts-experience approach to initial reading instruction, no artificial learning walls are declared. A sight vocabulary is not learned after a readiness program, for to do so would be to separate highly interrelated language skills into artificial teaching units.

In the language-arts-experience approach pupils are led to associate word sounds (word names) with word sights (printed word) in a circumstance that is highly similar to the learning-to-talk process. Every story recorded and witnessed by the pupils provides untold opportunities for them to make visual and auditory discriminations and word-sound and word-sight associations. The discrimination and association process occurs in highly functional situations. The rate of the discrimination and association process of any one child is determined by that child's ability to hear, to see, and to remember.

No artificial word-learning rates are declared or imposed. No artificial word-learning gimmicks need to be used, such as "colorful words," "words with pictures," "word-enrichment techniques," "obvious," "partial," or "no-clue" context clues, "flash cards," "words in phrases," "classifying and finding the main idea," "telling words," use of "manuscript and cursive writing," "tabulating word-perception errors," or "pacing the number of new words at five a day, three a day, or one a day." (19) All these gimmicks have been found to be of varied degrees of effectiveness in those teaching-learning situations in which a basic sight vocabulary is taught via the stilted, artificial, asinine approach set up in preprimers. And, interestingly enough, even the gimmicks are no guarantee to learning, nor do they stimulate the naturalness of a "learning to read as one learned to talk" circumstance. The studies (19) provide abundant proof that the preprimer approach to word learning bolstered by gimmicks continues to be highly ineffective and is a breeding ground for reading disability and for dislike of reading, although some learn to read in spite of the technique. Reread now the arguments developed on pages 295–299 with the perspective of the present discussion.

Developing and acquiring a sight vocabulary can be done in a way that stimulates the learning-to-talk process. Sound and sight are not divorced. The rate of "new" words is not determined by some artificial, illogical plan of one or two words per page or one or two words per basic-reader "story." Children can acquire sight words at their own pace based on their own experience with and knowledge of the spoken counterpart and not on a forced Oh! oh! oh!, run! run! run!, fail! fail! fail! basis.

Developing Visual-Auditory Discrimination for Consonants

This might be considered the most essential skill in the entire phonetic-analysis program. This skill requires the pupil to associate known "sound" and "sight" knowledge in new situations. The training can be started as soon as a pupil has a sight vocabulary of *one* word. Instruction does not need to be delayed until a pupil recognizes fifty or a hundred words on sight. To do so is to lose invaluable teaching opportunities and, what is more damaging, to develop habits of word guessing and wrong attitudes toward reading.

If a child knows his name on sight, the training program can be started. Let us assume that a child recognizes his name, Bill. The training steps to follow are:

1. Place the printed word Bill in front of the child. Either type it on a small word card, or print it on a word card, or write it on a chalkboard.

2. Place an unknown word under the word Bill, perhaps the name of another pupil, Nancy.

3. Ask the pupil to point to his name. (To do this he must read his name and choose one of the two printed words.) Reading his name provides the *visual* element of the visual-auditory circumstance.

4. Tell the pupil to *listen* to a word you will say (speak the word without distortion) and decide if the word rhymes with his name or has the same ending sound. The rhyming element is the vowel element and needs early teaching.

5. Say one-syllable words, some that rhyme with Bill and some that do not. Each time the pupil must indicate whether the spoken word rhymes with his name or whether it does not. Use such words as hill, pill, still, fill, ball, run, car, will, chill, right.

6. It is best to start with words that rhyme (hill) and then to use a word

that is distinctly different (ball). This facilitates the recogniion of like and unlike sounds. It also places emphasis on the vowel sound and thus alerts the pupil at this beginning stage to recognizing the value of and use of vowels.

7. Then shift to beginning consonant sounds and follow the same procedure. Some children experience more difficulty distinguishing between beginning sounds. What is needed is sets of words in which alliteration is readily heard: as Bill, bats, ball; the use of beginning word sounds that are sharply different, such as Bill and cat, Bill and run, or Bill and man; and frequent opportunity to listen and decide. Once visual-auditory training using initial single consonants is started, two or three short training sessions per day should be held.

When a pupil recognizes at sight two, three, or more words, the complexity of the visual-auditory training task can be increased. This requires that the pupil listen carefully, link the right sounds with the letters that represent them, and make the right choices. At first, two printed words can be placed together:

Visual clues	{ Bill	neck	better
	{ turtle	tank	fort
Auditory key words	{ (baker)	(Tom)	(face)

All the pupil needs to do is point to the printed word that has the same beginning sound as the spoken word. Then increase his task by using three or four printed words, such as:

Bill	better	he	Dad
turtle	tank	back	his
neck	fort	pull	like
		safe	but

Not much is to be gained by using more than four key words. The complexity of the decision-making task is demanding enough with a three- or four-word list.

This kind of training can be done on a teacher-pupil basis or a pupil-pupil basis. Required, of course, when pupils team up is that both can read the printed words being used and that both can think of spoken words that have appropriate beginning sounds.

There is considerable likelihood that such training can be started early in the school life of every first-grade pupil. In the first week of school some may be able to start with two or three printed words; some may start the second week and use only one printed word, their name. Training is readily paced according to each pupil's ability.

A next step is to have pupils underline a right word. This helps the pupil coordinate hand-and-eye effort, and it helps him focus more carefully on the word being underlined. Be certain that the line does not touch the word or in any way mutilate it.

(Sight words)	<u>B</u>ill <u>t</u>urtle	<u>n</u>eck <u>t</u>ank ←(pupil underlining)
(Auditory key words)	baker	Tom

A subsequent step of considerable importance is to have the pupils underline only the beginning letter, which represents the beginning sound. This helps the pupils focus on specific letter-sound associations.

(Sight words)	B̲ill turtle	neck tank̲
(Auditory key words)	baker	Tom

As soon as the sight vocabulary permits, blends and digraphs may be similarly dealt with, as may ending sounds. Now the pupil is asked to underline the two letters that represent the beginning sounds, or the ending sounds.

(Sight words)	Glen storm f̲lood	bring flew̲ start
(Auditory key words)	step	fly

As the number of sight words increases, the pupil faces the need to organize them so that they are readily available for use. The best procedure is to set up an alphabetized word bank. Bill, the boy referred to in Chapter 8, had a list of forty words and needed to use fourteen of the twenty-six letters for filing purposes. This was true for him after dictating only one experience story. He not only faced an immediate need for an alphabetized list, but had a continuous demand for it as his list of known words grew.

Two to three dictated stories per week soon result in a considerable supply of words available for study. As pointed out in Chapter 8, at first pupils underline in their experience stories only the words they know. As they progress and their sight vocabulary increases, they soon reach the point where they underline only the words they do not know. This shift is to be encouraged when a pupil appears to know as many as three-fourths of the words dictated. For some, this changeover may occur when they know only slightly more than half the words. Others may need the security of knowing as many as 90 percent of the words. Whenever the change does occur from underlining known words to underlining unknown words, focus is being placed on the unknown and on the likelihood of doing something to help recognize the unknown words.

Consonant and Vowel Substitution. This is the time when pupils are to be aided and abetted in the phonetic analysis of the words in their experience stories that they do not know. The circumstances for doing this are most opportune both as to moment and condition. The words in the story are "known" to the pupils on an oral-language level. They dictated the stories and chose the words. They were the producers. Many of the words in the story are "known" to the pupils on a printed-language level. They underlined only those words they did not know. So they must be making accurate and selective visual discriminations and must be making use of visual-auditory discrimination skills. They associated the right sounds with the right printed words. They are using cues to word recognition, particularly context or meaning clues, and visual clues. Next, give them training in the use of phonetic or sound clues. If the pupils can "say" a printed word, we know they will instantly recognize it again as a known oral-language symbol.

The following sentence occurred in a dictated-experience story of a first-grader named Wayne.

The <u>man</u> <u>broke</u> into <u>the</u> store <u>and</u> got some <u>money</u>.

The words underlined by Wayne were known words. Four words were unknown: <u>into</u>, <u>store</u>, <u>got</u>, <u>some</u>. On rereading the story the pupil substituted <u>office</u> for <u>store</u>; even though this was a wrong substitution, he had made a <u>good</u> association. The man had actually broken into the office in the store.

This teacher started by writing the word <u>store</u> on a piece of paper.

<u>store</u>	<u>got</u>
<u>stop</u>	<u>not</u>
<u>into</u>	<u>go</u>
in	got
to	<u>some</u>
into	<u>come</u>
	<u>see</u>
	<u>some</u>

Under the word <u>store</u> she wrote the word <u>stop</u>, which was in Wayne's word bank. Wayne recognized <u>stop</u> at once. Then the teacher underlined the <u>st</u> in both words. Wayne re-examined the story and then said <u>store</u>. The help with the <u>st</u> in a known phonic context enabled him to try the sound in a new context.

For the word <u>into</u>, just breaking the word into syllables was enough to enable Wayne to recognize it. The teacher listed the words on the paper as shown in the left-hand column above.

For the word <u>got</u> she used the known word <u>not</u>. Then she used the known word <u>go</u>, but Wayne was unable to blend the sound elements together and say <u>got</u>. The best he could do was gōt (goat).

The teacher dealt with the word <u>some</u> as follows. First she placed the word come from the pupil's word bank under some. Then she placed the word see under some. Wayne was still unable to blend the two sounds together and recognize some, so the teacher told him what both words were.

All this took but a few minutes. It was done on a person-to-person, teacher-to-pupil basis, using a language context supercharged with meaning, and it helped the pupil go from knowns to unknowns.

At another time that day Wayne and the teacher reviewed the word-attack activity. This time the teacher proceeded as follows. First she wrote the word store in isolation to see if Wayne recognized it. Then she added the other words.

store	stay
stop	day
stand	

Wayne failed to recognize stay but did so when the word day with its vowel clue was added. Thus Wayne had four opportunities to blend sounds together by obtaining sound clues st (consonant blend) and ay (vowel digraph) from known sound contexts.

At this point the teacher called together five other children to watch and listen and learn. She proceeded by writing the following words on the chalkboard.

got	some
not	come
dot	see
lot	some
pot	
hot	

Next she used words that had been underlined by Wayne as known and had him blend sounds together by lifting known sound elements from other sound contexts. She proceeded as follows:

man	broke
can—cat	bring—sing
pan—pet	brown—town
fan—for	brake—take
tan—to	brook—book

The aid words like cat, pet, sing, and town were in Wayne's word bank and again provided vowel clues. The only words he had some trouble with were brake and brook. He was able to say brook by using the vowel clue oo in book but did not know what brook meant.

Note that in one situation the beginning consonant was changed from word to word while the vowel-consonant-ending was held constant. This was then an exercise in beginning consonant substitution—a key skill to acquire. In the second situation the beginning blend *br* was held constant while the vowel-consonant endings were changed. This way the vowel is kept in a sound context and is not dealt with in isolation.

Note also that this activity was built by using phonic elements in known phonic contexts. This is an extremely important aspect of the learning situation.

Once visual-auditory training in consonant substitution is initiated, training exercises should occur daily. This can be done either individually, in small groups, or on a class basis. This is one way to keep a class fruitfully occupied while it is waiting its turn to go to lunch or to the school bus.

The total amount of time devoted to such training should equal twenty minutes or more per day. The psychology of learning states that frequent, meaningful repetition in situations where new decisions must be made is the best way to acquire and retain a skill. When this psychology of learning is practiced, artificial gimmicks need not be resorted to.

Another story by Wayne was used similarly.

Pepper

Pepper came out of the dog house. He went over to the roses and got stung on the tip of his nose by a bee.

The word *over* was dealt with as follows. The teacher covered the second syllable and asked Wayne to say the first syllable. The moment he pronounced the vowel o he turned to his story and said o ver in a questioning, am-I-right sort of way.

Got was dealt with as before.

got	game—came
not	
hot	

The teacher realized now that apparently Wayne's difficulty was in recognizing and blending the sound as represented by the letter g in words like got. The only other word in Wayne's word bank that could be useful was the word came in which g could be substituted for c to make the common word game.

All of this was done for Wayne in late September and early October. If, on the other hand, Wayne had been required to follow the lock-step pattern of a basic-reader readiness and preprimer program, he might not have made this much progress until mid-February. By that time his interest in reading and in school could have been so stifled that he might have been well on the way to becoming just one more bright boy with a "reading" problem.

The basic principles essential to consonant and vowel-consonant substitution can be restated as follows:

1. Provide adequate auditory-discrimination training.
2. Be sure pupils know the names of the letters used to represent sounds.
3. Have as a base a list of sight words.
4. The unknown word or the word to be dealt with through phonetic analysis should be a part of a meaningful language context such as an experience story.
5. Clue words used to identify the sounds represented by the letters in the unknown word must all be well-established known words.
6. Place clue words and unknown words together, one above the other, so that pupils can see readily the visual similarity that exists.
7. Allow time for the pupil to try to blend the sounds together and "discover" the word.
8. Encourage the pupil to try saying the word.

These principles operate from the beginning of phonic instruction and are useful in all circumstances involving consonant and vowel-consonant substitution possibilities. On occasion, words occur that do not lend themselves to such phonetic analysis by a neophyte reader. Such words must be taught as sight words. It would be impossible at this point to try to illustrate all the possibilities for consonant-substitution training.

Avoiding Phonics in Isolation

The idea expressed in this topic heading could have been stated positively, as "Always teach phonics in context," but this would have resulted in less attention and perhaps less understanding. "Thou shalt not sin" could be stated as "Always be good," but the latter is not so attention-getting.

What is a phonic context? The concept can best be understood through analogy with the concept "word context." The meaning of a word is determined to a large degree by the language context in which it is used.

> a hard<u>wood</u> floor
> <u>wood</u>ed land
> aged in <u>wood</u>
> the <u>wood</u> box
> cut fire<u>wood</u>
> a <u>wood</u> block print
> Mr. <u>Wood</u>
> the <u>wood</u>chuck
> the <u>wood</u> thrush
> painting the <u>wood</u>work
> the <u>wood</u> worker

Similarly, the sound value of a letter is determined to a large degree by the sound context in which it is used.

paper	had
ate	at
fail	parent
praise	care
play	air
great	prayer
	wear
able	call
bible	fault
robber	daughter
bee	saw
blue	aye
tub	

Anna D. Cordts says in *The Word Method of Teaching Phonics* (15, p. 4) that "The pupil learns each letter sound not as a detached element, but in the very position and environment in which it occurs. This is an important factor in the learning process." A phonic context, or sound context, or pronunciation unit can be a syllable as well as a word. So a child asked to generalize about a sound is asked to deal with the sound in a sound context, as illustrated for the sounds represented by *a* and *b* above.

A child cannot answer the question "What does the letter *a* say?" In the first place, the letter *a* is not a talking letter and therefore does not say anything. In the second place, the letter *a* can only represent a sound. And, in the third place, since the letter *a* represents many different sounds, the question "What sound does the *a* represent?" is unanswerable. The setting or context in which the letter *a* occurs and represents a sound must be identified. A legitimate question is, "What sound does the letter *a* represent in the word *play*?"

For a child to know all of the variations in sounds that the twenty-six letters of the alphabet can represent is well-nigh impossible. Even teachers' knowledge of the variations is astonishingly limited (49, 1). On many occasions when speaking to parent groups, I have asked them to recall some of the most commonly used phonic and syllable rules only to find that they did not know them. Only the most learned phonetician is likely to know the rules and to know how to apply them.

It has been said that the age of wisdom is from six to sixteen. At age six children ask all the questions, and at age sixteen they can answer all the questions. Similarly, it has been said that the age of phonics is from grade one to grade four. In grade one a start is made in teaching phonic rules, and by grade four the rules have been forgotten. Although those sayings are repeated with tongue in check, they make an effective point about the truth of the circumstances.

A reliable and useful approach to phonetic analysis is by means of known key-sound units such as syllables and words. Pupils are more apt to recognize similarity in sounds and letters used to represent them when they go from known words to unknown. As Donald Durrell *et al.*, say (20):

The irregularities in English phonics make an *inductive* approach (learning phonics through extensive practice) more effective than a "rules and exceptions" method. Words in the child's speaking vocabulary are best for the application of phonics. At best, phonetic analysis yields only an approximate pronunciation of a word but this is usually adequate if the word is known to the child. When the word is not known there is no sure way of knowing vowel sounds and accented syllables except by using the dictionary.

Ernest Horn, in his 1929 report on a child's early experience with the letter *a,* said (32), "The actual difficulty confronting the child in interpreting a new word is not quite so great as the tables indicate since approximate sounds, together with the reading context, may be a sufficient clue to the word. . . ."

At best, then, it appears that for a child to get the approximate sound(s) of a word by dealing with its sound elements as a part of the total sound context (or word) and by recognizing the meaning of the word in the reading context is the ultimate skill to attain. Both elements require a context. The letter or letters require a phonic context and the word requires a language-meaning or semantic context.

Phonic contexts useful for attacking certain words may be illustrated as follows:

stimulus word	phonic context aids
sleep	*sl*ow, *see*, ca*p*
cone	*c*at, st*one*
rose	*r*un, n*ose*, *cl*ose
get	*g*o, *p*et
star	*st*op, *car*, *ar*e

At this point the reader is urged to reread those sections that deal with phonetic analysis, especially pages 48–50 and 118–122.

Vowel Keys

In dealing with the consonants, a basic principle is consonant substitution. This is so because in the phonic respelling of words in a dictionary, consonants are frequently substituted so as to represent the appropriate sound. For instance,

> bottle (bŏt′ əl)
> calm (käm)
> circus (sûr′ kəs)
> dislodge (dĭs lŏj′)
> foxy (fŏk′ si)
> hawk (hôk)
> impartial (ĭm pär′ shəl)
> link (lĭngk)

In addition, at the bottom of each right-hand page in a dictionary there usually is an abbreviated pronunciation key. There the reader is given help only with vowels. Further help with some of the words above would be:

bŏt tle (bŏt′ əl)   hŏt ə=a in alone
calm (käm)   ärt
circus (sûr′ kəs)   ûrge ə=a in alone

A full pronunciation key usually lists consonants also, but lists them only in single beginning and single ending positions. By way of illustration, some of the consonants appear so: b back rub; d do bed; f fit puff. Consonants are either retained in the phonetic respelling as they appear in the entry word (bottle bŏt′ əl), are substituted (calm käm), or are dropped (hawk hôk). Vowels, on the other hand, may appear as they do in the entry word or substitute(s) and are coded as to sound by means of diacritical marks.

circus (sûr′ kəs)

The vowel *i* is replaced with the vowel *u,* and this vowel is coded by a circumflex. The vowel *u* in the second syllable is replaced by a schwa: ə. In the instances where the schwa is substituted, this is done because such vowels due to lack of stress tend to lose their value and merge into a reduced sound. In other words, the schwa occurs only in unaccented syllables and indicates the sound of a in alone, e in system, i in easily, o in gallop, and u in circus.

Students should be taught early to use a vowel pronunciation key. A good procedure is to use the key provided in the dictionary they are using. For example, if the class is using the *Basic Dictionary of American English* (5), the key provided there may be used: ā as in fāte, ă as in făt, â as in fâre, ä as in fär; ē as in bē, ĕ as in bĕt, and so on.

Each child should have his own vowel key on a three-by-five-inch card. The card should be constantly available for use in attacking unfamiliar words and for use in skill-training activities. A child's card may be started by illustrating either the long or the short sound of a, or both.

Vowel Key
fāte
făt

It is recommended that auditory-discrimination training be started with the long a sound because it is the sound commonly heard and associated with the letter a. Once again, training is accomplished by using simple, one-decision circumstances. For example, a pupil records the word fate or ate on his vowel card. Such words as the following may be used:

gate	day	same	lake
go	cane	it	Jane
ice	cut	some	me

When quick and accurate decisions are made on the visual-auditory level using only long a situations or sharply different vowel situations involving other vowels, other situations of a may be used as auditory cues.

car	saw	late	rain
cat	sat	mail	far
call	date	man	cap

Follow a similar procedure with the short vowel a as in făt.

hat	can	lap	lad
net	tin	step	rid
it	sun	lip	rot

and

car	saw	late	rain
cat	sat	mail	far
call	date	man	cap

Then the two vowels are dealt with simultaneously. Now the pupil must decide whether or not in the spoken word the sound represented by the letter a is the same as that in āte or in făt.

When this has been accomplished, follow a similar procedure with sounds as represented by the letter o. First nō is added to the card, and visual-auditory skill training is done. Then nŏt is added, and more training is done. Next the two vowel situations represented by o, the long and the short, are dealt with simultaneously. Finally the four situations are dealt with simultaneously.

Vowel Key	
āte	nō
ăt	nŏt

This is the procedure followed until a pupil's card looks as follows:

Vowel Key				
āte	nō	bīte	ūse	bē
făt	nŏt	bĭt	fŭn	bĕt
fâre	nôr		fûr	
fär				

By the time a pupil's vowel-key card lists all these vowel sounds, he will be so far along that the dictionary and its pronunciation key will rapidly replace it.

A principal purpose for developing skill in consonant substitution and in the use of a vowel key is to be able to use a dictionary effectively. At times this objective is lost sight of when skill training in phonetic analysis supersedes reading for meaning and/or when phonetic analysis is treated lightly.

Consonant Blends and Consonant Digraphs

A consonant blend represents a combination of consonants in such a way that, even though the sound of each consonant does not lose its identity, the sounds the letters represent are in essence blended together. There are two- and three-letter consonant blends, as the following list illustrates.

bl	dr	gl	sc	sn	tr
br	dw	gr	sk	sp	tw
cl	fl	pl	sl	st	scr
cr	fr	pr	sm	sw	str

Consonant digraphs may be defined as two consonant letters representing one speech sound. Illustrative combinations are ng, kn, ld, ch, gh, ph, ah, uh, th, wh.

A thorough study of consonant situations in a primary-reading vocabulary was done by Elsie Black (7) to determine the incidence of certain consonant situations according to their initial and final syllabic situations. The situations analyzed were single consonant letters, consonant digraphs, consonant trigraphs, consonant blends, and syllabic consonants and blends.

She found that 68 percent of all the consonant situations identified were single consonants—38 percent in the initial part of the syllable, and 30 percent in the final parts—and they appeared at all reader levels checked.

Two-letter blends represented 15 percent of the total; and three-letter blends 1 percent. Of the two-letter blends, 8 percent were in the initial part of the syllable, as were over half of the three-letter blends. Of the consonant digraph situations, 3 percent were in the initial part of the syllable and 7 percent in the final part.

She identified 4,063 consonant situations in 2,503 syllables, embracing 1,996 words. Of this total, 26 were consonant trigraph situations, and all appeared in the final part of syllables. In addition, there were 130 syllabic consonants and 16 syllabic blends appearing only in final syllables.

It may be safely assumed that the results obtained by Elsie Black are typical. This being the case, a number of conclusions about teaching children how to deal with such situations discriminately are in order. First, they should be taught control over blends and digraphs and trigraphs in the same inductive way as described earlier for single consonants. Second, because these letter combinations occur at all levels, they should be taught whenever they occur and not postponed on an arbitrary basis until a second- or third-grade level.

Special Consonant Circumstances

The consonant w represents a consonant sound in such words as we, war, and win and a vowel sound in cow and how. Similarly, the letter y represents a consonant sound in yes and yellow and a vowel sound in sly and cry.

Eight consonants represent only one sound: b, h, j, l, m, p, t, v, and nine consonants represent two or more sounds: c, d, f, g, n, r, s, x, z. The letter s represents the sound of zh in words like measure, as does the letter z in azure, and si in confusion. The letters gh after a vowel are silent as in nigh and night. The letters ph represent the sound of f as in Philco, Philadelphia, and phosphate.

Vowel Situations

In another thorough study, Ruth E. Oaks (43) examined the same 1,996 words studied by Elsie Black (7) to determine the types of vowel situations and the principles basic to their pronunciation. She defined a vowel situation as "one which embraces a given vowel letter or combination of vowel letters used to represent a vowel sound in a given syllabic setting." In the 2,503 syllables, she identified eight phonic principles that appeared to operate in the pronunciation of the vowels embraced.

1. When a stressed syllable ends in e, the first vowel in the syllable has its own "long" sound and the final e is silent.

2. When a stressed syllable containing only one vowel ends with that vowel, the vowel has its own "long" sound.

3. When there is only one vowel in a stressed syllable and that vowel is followed by a consonant, the vowel has its "short" sound.

4. When a word of more than one syllable ends with the letter y, the final y has the sound of "short" i. When a word of more than one syllable ends with the leters ey, the e is silent and the y again has the sound of "short" i.

5. When a syllable contains only the one vowel, a, followed by the letters l or w, the sound of the a rhymes with the word saw.

6. When there are two adjacent vowels in a syllable, the first vowel has its own "long" sound and the second vowel is silent.

7. When, in a word of more than one syllable, the final syllable ends in the letters le, the l becomes syllabic (i.e., it functions as a vowel) and is pronounced, but the e is silent.

8. When, in a word of more than one syllable, the final syllable ends in the letters en, the n becomes syllabic and is pronounced, but the e is silent.

Oaks found 103 different single vowel situations, 53 different vowel digraph situations, 5 different diphthong situations, and one trigraph situation. The percentages of applicability of phonic principles was as follows:

Principles 4, 7, 8: 100%
Principle 5 ranged from 85% to 100%
Principle 2 ranged from 71% to 89%
Principle 3 ranged from 66% to 74%
Principle 1 ranged from 53% to 71%
Principle 6 ranged from 47% to 51%

The last five principles listed by Ruth Oaks accounted for approximately 70 percent of the different vowel situations and 80 percent of the total vowel situations. In addition, she found that 67 percent of the vowel situations occurred in stressed syllables, 14 percent in unstressed syllables, and 19 percent were "silent" vowel letters. She also noted that 35 percent of the different situations appeared at the primer level, 21 percent at the first-reader level, 28 percent at the second-reader level, and 16 percent at the third-reader level.

It might be safely assumed that the results she obtained are typical of what would be found if other similar studies were undertaken. Thus it might be concluded that control over the basic principles and the exceptions to them should be taught in an inductive way. Second, because a need to use the principles may occur at all levels, the skills should be dealt with when the need occurs rather than by arbitrarily assigning the teaching of the skills to a certain level.

Oaks used the following definitions:

long vowel sound	the sound which is the same as the name of the letter and indicated by a macron
short vowel sound	the sound represented by the vowel when a breve is placed above the vowel
vowel digraph	two adjacent vowels representing a single speech sound
vowel diphthong	a union of two vowel sounds pronounced in the same syllable
open syllable	one which ends with a vowel
closed syllable	one which ends with a consonant
unstressed	one which does not receive an accent

Special Vowel-Situation Illustrations

In a short word ending with a final e, the e is *usually* silent and the preceding vowel is long: gate, complete, bite, nose, cute; and live, come, done.

When there is only one vowel in a pronunciation unit or syllable and it is followed by a consonant, the vowel is usually short, as in at, set, it, of, and up.

When two vowels are adjacent in a pronunciation unit or syllable, it is impossible to generalize about what either of the vowels say. A recent thorough study of adjacent vowels reported by Alvina Treut Burrows and Zyra Lourie (12) makes this point quite clear. Earlier studies by Theodore Clymer (14) and Ruth Oaks (43) reported similar findings. Burrows and Lourie take the widely known rule, "When the two vowels of a word are together, the first vowel is *usually* 'long' and the second vowel is silent" and point out that all one may rightly ask is, "When two vowels go out walking, what does either of them say?" (12, p. 81.) Then they go on to say that "A considerably larger number of words refute the 'rule' than obey it."

Burrows and Lourie studied the 5,000 words of highest frequency on the Rinsland (47) list and found a total of 1,728 words with *two* adjacent vowels, including a, e, i, o, u, y, and w. Of this total, 389 words were of the diphthong variety (oy, ow, oi, ou, ew). Of the remaining total, there were 668 in which the long sound of the first vowel dominated. They also examined the vocabulary of the beginning readers of five publishers and found similar results.

Burrows and Lourie concluded that the only safe generalization is that one must be versatile in the use of vowel sounds. This versatility should be accomplished by helping the beginning reader note what vowel sound is used in the words he meets. Doing this will help him realize that vowel sounds vary. It will also help him avoid being the victim of an unsound generalization.

When Burrows and Lourie examined subgroupings of words, they found that the ea combination appeared most frequently. However, of the total 268 such words, 111 did not follow the "first-vowel-long" rule. The ie combination appeared in 122 words, and 81 of these did not fit the "first-vowel-long" rule. One might expect that the ee combination would yield a set of words with high consistency, but the effect of a following r (a murmur diphthong) made an important difference: cheer, deer, steer. Extreme exceptions were most interesting in such words as: been, trial, diary, aviation, museum, geography, rodeo.

Durkin presented the following list to show variability and to point out that phonetic generalizations should be used only as starting points in word analysis (17, p. 69).

Vowel-Vowel Combinations

I

ay (say)
ee (meet)
eu (feud)
oa (coat)
oi (oil)
oy (toy)
uy (buy)

II

au (auto, laugh)
ey (they, honey)
oe (toe, shoe)

III

ai (paid, aisle, said)
ea (each, steak, dead)
ei (either, height, eight)
ie (pie, chief, friend)
oo (book, pool, flood)
ui (built, guise, suit)

IV

ou (out, ought, dough
soup, cautious, could)

SIGHT CLUES TO WORD RECOGNITION

As stated before, when a pupil encounters a word he does not recognize on sight, it is obvious that he must have "looked" at the word. Visual perception was involved, seeing was involved, but recognition—meaning "to know again"—was not involved. Sight clues must have been used; otherwise the pupil could not have known that he did know the word in question.

The extent of the pupil's use of sight clues is uncertain. Undoubtedly the total configuration of a word provides clues. If the configuration was unique, as in the word *apple,* then there was little likelihood that the word was confused with another similar word. On the other hand, when configurations have practically no unique distinguishing features, clear visual differentiation may be a challenge, as in *house, horse.* Degrees of differences may be illustrated, as follows:

apple	other	run	come
three	mother	running	some
house	one	over	purpose
horse	ten	oven	suppose

Studies (27, 19) show the need for training in visual discrimination. And, as Jean Turner Goins points out, what is needed is a broader concept than has previously prevailed.

Children can sort words and note that two words are alike or different. They can do this with words they cannot read and should be taught to do more than sort or arrange words on a configuration basis or a word-physiognomy basis—a basis largely divorced of meaning. Pupils must learn to deal with printed words in situations in which communication takes precedence. If the words to be recognized are in a context in which the primary purpose is to communicate ideas, the approach to the recognition of printed words will simulate the approach to the recognition of oral language and will do so on a high level. Such conditions exist in pupil-dictated stories, as described in detail in Chapter 8.

In dictated stories "recognizing again" means the recognition in print of the words the pupil chose to use to communicate ideas orally. Now the sorting and organizing of words is done because ideas are to be communicated and not just to compare the shape of words.

Sight clues go beyond the discrimination level when words are dealt with in a language context. The structure clues that become useful to the reader are those that modify or change meaning. Such changes can be classified as inflectional word changes and derivative word changes.

Children use these changes in their oral communication, even at the preschool level. What is more, they do so quite effectively (37, 58). They use the same changes in the stories they dictate. It is only in a basic reader—preprimers and primers and in some first readers—that these changes are so limited that children who learn to read with so meager a diet are not faced with a need to analyze printed words. If a child is taught to read with the curtailed vocabulary of a basic reader as the principle source of word usage, such statements as the following are in order (6, p. 652): "After he has achieved "primer" level of reading ability, his attention is directed to word variants—such as *ed* and *ing* words—in his reading vocabulary. By the time he has achieved "first-reader" level of reading ability he notes plurals formed by changing *y* to *i* and adding *es*, and the *er* and *est* of comparison."

Inflectional Changes

Inflectional changes and derivative changes are changes in the form of a word that indicate a change in meaning. Five parts of speech are modified by inflectional changes:

Nouns: gender, number, and case. Most of the changes are affixed to the ends of nouns to form plurals and possessives: *boy, boys, boy's.*

Verbs: voice, number, tense, person, mood. Most of these changes are past tense, the third person singular, and the present participle: *laugh, laughed, laughs, laughing.*

Adjectives: comparison and number. Most of these changes are those of comparison: *small, smaller.*

Adverbs: comparison; *slower, slowest.*

Pronouns: gender, number, case, person.

A derivative or derived form is a root word to which a prefix or suffix or both have been added: *scribe, subscribe, describable*; *marine, submarine, mariner*.

Children will use derivatives in the stories they dictate or in their creative writing, and with them a start can be made in teaching the use of structural changes to unlock words not recognized at sight. Generally speaking, such skill training is most useful when it is coupled with the use of a glossary or dictionary. Then precision and accuracy can replace educated guesses such as might be made about words like *ascribe* or *mariner*.

Millard Black (8) studied the same vocabulary that was studied by Ruth Oaks (43) and Elsie Black (7). One of the purposes of his study was to determine the incidence of five-word variants at each reader level in the primary grades. The five variants he chose were plural or possessive, *s, ing, ed,* and the comparatives or agents *er* and *est*. His choice of these five was based on Margaret M. Bryant's report on the "five living inflections in modern English" (10).

Millard Black found that:

the inflectional ending *s*, accounting for at least one-half the total word variants used at any reader level studied, decreased in proportion to the total vocabulary as the reader level increased. Its incidence ranged from 76.4% of the total variants used at the pre-primer level to 52.3% at the third-reader level.

The incidence of other inflectional changes tabulated (*ing, ed, er,* and *est*) increased at each successive reader level. The inflectional ending *est* was not used at the pre-primer level; all other endings were used at all levels encompassd in this study. The incidence of these endings tended to increase in proportion to the total vocabulary (8, p. 58).

Again, one most likely may safely assume that Millard Black's findings are typical of what might be found if similar vocabulary studies were made. This being the case, it is apparent that almost from the very beginning of a learning-to-read instructional program, even one as narrowly conceived as a basic reader, pupils should be taught how to deal with these inflectional changes. The safe and sound approach is always to teach the change inductively and in a meaningful context—one in which the learner needs to make a decision.

```
                      doll.
The girl has two
                      dolls.
              walk
The boy is            to school.
              walking
              bigger
John is the           boy.
              biggest
          paint
John              the box.
          painted
```

Conditions such as the following should be noted.

1. The root word is not changed or altered by adding or dropping a letter when an inflectional change is made.

run	paint	slow
runs	painted	slower
	painting	slowest

2. The root word is altered by the addition of a letter.

sun	big	stop
sunny	bigger	stopping
sunning	biggest	stopped
sunnier		
sunniest		

3. The root word is altered by the dropping of a letter.

smile	rose	tame
smiled	nose	tamer
smiling	rosy	tamest
	nosy	

4. The root word is altered by changing letters.

dry	penny	funny
dried	pennies	funnier
		funniest

It is readily observable that the changes illustrated represent spelling changes. As a matter of fact, when reading is taught with communication of meaning as a chief purpose, the children learn to deal with the changes described here without being articulate about each specific change. James A. Fitzgerald (22) has pointed out that many of the most persistently misspelled words are among the words of highest frequency in reading. In other words, even though pupils learn to spell many words through reading (the correlation between reading and spelling, while high, is far from perfect), there are many who need to be taught. Stated differently, one of the four spelling rules that applies to a large number of words and should be taught is the following (33, p. 1,345): "(a) the rules for adding suffixes (changing y to i, dropping final silent e, doubling the final consonant)." The four conditions listed here to be taught in reading are also listed to be taught in spelling; they appear to be of greater use when such words are to be spelled than when they are to be read. That this is so is common knowledge among experienced teachers. In brief, then, it is the meaning or meanings of a word along with some attention to structure that leads to effective recognition of inflected forms.

Derivatives

Grammatical changes in word endings to show changes in case, number, gender, tense, voice, mood, and comparison are called inflectional changes or word variants. A derivative word is derived by adding affixes to a root word and thereby modifying its meaning. An affix is either a prefix or a suffix. A prefix is a syllable or word placed before and joined with a word and modifying its meaning. A suffix is a syllable(s) placed after and joined with a word and modifying its meaning. A root word or base word is that element of language that cannot be further broken down and, accordingly, forms the base of a vocabulary.

root word: *play*
prefix, plus root word: *replay*
root word, plus suffix: *playable*

Most classroom teachers and experts favor the teaching of vocabulary, especially by direct instruction. To make such instruction effective, lists of root words, prefixes, and suffixes have been identified as being important for language-usage purposes. Philip Sauer (52) recommended that students be taught 100 root words. George C. Kyte (36) proposed a general vocabulary of 663 words as a core vocabulary in the language arts. James Fitzgerald (23) proposed a similar list of 644 words as a "Basic Communication Vocabulary." James E. Bullock (11) also compiled a communications core vocabulary for fourth-grade-level children. J. I. Brown (9) provided a list containing frequently used root words as well as prefixes and suffixes. Research on the effectiveness of methods of word study is very meager and limited primarily to the secondary level and beyond (50). Even so, all seem agreed that vocabulary should be taught.

A reading program in which basic readers represent only one source of instruction material and in which they are considered a very limited kind of abridgement of a library will have pupils turning to a library and dealing with many words. This being the case, instruction in the recognition and use of common roots should prove timely and useful.

David H. Russell's comprehensive study concerned with the dimensions of children's meaning vocabularies in the fourth through the twelfth grades investigated the breadth of their vocabularies in science, social studies, mathematics, and hobbies and recreations (48). He found that both boys and girls improve their vocabularies rather consistently from fourth through the twelfth grades, but that the vocabulary abilities become increasingly specialized as the children mature. Walter Loban discovered that children tend to speak more words in each succeeding year during the first seven years in school. He also noted that "Both the low and high groups of subjects use the same number of words among the 12,000 most commonly used words in the English language" (37, p. 83). At the same time, studies (64, 51) show that wide reading is apt not to be sufficient to develop a wide vocabulary.

Roots. It seems, then, that specific vocabulary instruction should be accomplished. This being the case, instruction in the recognition and use of common root words should be helpful. And, since sharp inroads are being made into reading programs that are exclusively basic reader and since practices of individualized reading instruction with the library as the source of materials are being used, the need to teach about root words at an earlier level than high school and on a *depth*-of-understanding basis is of considerable importance.

How to approach the teaching of root words is in many ways more important than the decision that they should be taught. Walter J. Moore voiced his concern about the importance of placing stress on meaning thus: "stress on meaning . . . *cannot* be permitted to interfere unduly with the child's budding interests. The perceptive teacher, then, learns ways of achieving this rather neat balance between overemphasis upon words and their meanings, and the deepening, broadening interests of their pupils" (41, p. 394).

"Words are interesting" is the first sentence in Margaret Ernst's Foreword to her book *Words* (21, p. v). Then she goes on to say: "When you begin to know which ones belong to the same families and who their forefathers were, they become fascinating." By expressing her attitude about words this way, she seems to be making a fine and appropriate distinction between *interesting* and *fascinating*.

As Walter Moore has wisely cautioned, stress on words may not interfere with a child's budding interest. What Margaret Ernst is implying is that, if instruction starts with a child's interest in words (because words are interesting) and goes on to word families and forefathers, the child can be led to be fascinated by words (because words become fascinating). If children first select words from their dictated-experience stories for further study, then words from their creative writing, then words from basic readers, and then words from their self-selection reading, their *interest in* words can be converted to a *fascination by* words.

In her book, which can be used in elementary as well as secondary schools, she asks, "Do you know that words are like trees, with a firmly gripped root, and branches and leaves flowering from the root?" (21, p. 3). As an example, she illustrates with the Greek root *graph,* meaning "to write," and *gram,* meaning "letters" (21, p. 52):

graph	gram
graphophone	monogram
addressograph	grammar
photograph	gramophone
biography	diagram
paragraph	telegram

She further suggests that words be dealt with as follows (21, pp. 53–55):

$$\text{phonograph}$$
$$\text{sound} \; + \; \text{write}$$

To make roots grow she recommends the following:

I. Tell what each root means.

II. List three words built on each root.

III. Give the meaning of each word you list as you did with the <u>graph</u> family.

IV. Use each word in a sentence.

<u>fer</u> as in transfer

<u>port</u>. You will find that there are two <u>port</u> roots, one meaning "carry," one meaning "doorway." Work with the one meaning "carry." <u>Port</u> has an enormous number of descendants or derivatives.

<u>form</u>	<u>manu</u> or <u>man</u>
<u>meter</u>	<u>duc</u> as in educate or conductor
<u>scope</u>	<u>tract</u>
<u>phone</u>	<u>vis</u> or <u>vid</u>
<u>auto</u>	<u>cede</u> as in precede
<u>bio</u>	<u>ped</u> as in pedal
<u>aqua</u>	<u>cent</u>
<u>logy</u> as in zoology, geology	<u>lit</u> as in literature
<u>dic</u> as in dictation	<u>viv</u> as in revive
<u>geo</u>	<u>aud</u> as in audience
<u>litho</u>	<u>cap</u> as in capital
<u>mono</u>	<u>micro</u>
<u>multi</u>	<u>labor</u> as in laboratory
<u>photo</u>	<u>anni</u>
<u>phys</u>	<u>mit</u> or <u>miss</u> as in transmit or dismiss
<u>tele</u>	<u>terra</u>
<u>spec</u>	<u>cred</u>
<u>fort</u>	<u>bene</u>
<u>scrib</u> or <u>scrip</u>	<u>sect</u>

Picturesque Word Origins will help convert one's interest in words to fascination. The following excerpt considers two words from Latin.

Sacrifice: a thing made sacred

Latin *sacer*, "sacred," with a combining form of *facere*, "to make," gave *sacrificare*, "to make sacred," "to devote, or offer, to the god." Since this offering generally entailed death to the thing offered, and its destruction on the altar, the word came to mean "to kill or destroy." The corresponding Latin noun, *sacrificium*, was borrowed in Old French and Middle English as *sacrifice*.

From the live sacrifice to one's god, it is a far cry to the modern world's "sacrifice sales" and baseball's "sacrifice hits."

Salary: originally, salt money

Roman soldiers, as a part of their pay, drew a special allowance originally for the purchase of salt, in ancient times not always so easily obtained as now. The allowance "for salt" was called *salarium*, from *sal*, "salt." The word was later used to mean "pension." Latin *salarium* was borrowed in English as *salary*, "fixed regular wages," but used in connection with civilian workers only, not soldiers. A soldier draws his "pay," not a *salary!* (46, pp. 103–105.)

Wilfred Funk, in his book on word origins and their romantic stories, writes, "Every word was once a poem. Each began as a picture. Our language is made up of terms that were all originally figures of speech" (26, p. 1). He further inspires us with, "In the end this book has one main intent. I can only wish that the reader might be encouraged to walk among words as I do, like Alice in Wonderland, amazed at the marvels they hold" (26, p. 4). He groups words as "business terms," "words of your house," and "words of your garden," to cite just a few; the romantic stories he provides are just that—"romantic."

Prefixes. A syllable or syllables or even a word, put at the beginning of another word to modify its meaning, is a prefix. Curious about what prefixes to teach, I spent six weeks one summer analyzing the vocabulary of the 1932 edition of Edward L. Thorndike's *The Teacher's Word Book of 20,000 Words* (61) with the following results.

1. Of the 20,000 words, 4,922, or twenty-four percent had prefixes.

2. Fifteen prefixes appearing most frequently accounted for 82 percent of the 61 different basic forms of prefixes studied.

3. Each of these fifteen prefixes had its number well-scattered over the 20,000 words, with no sizable clustering at any one level. In other words a pupil reading a book with a vocabulary range equivalent to the fifteenth thousand rating in the Thorndike list would need practically the same knowledge of prefixes as if the book's range in vocabulary were limited to the first few thousand in the Thorndike rating.

4. Twenty-six of the different basic forms used had various assimilated forms. These are forms that have the same meaning as the basic form but have different spellings. Ten of the fifteen prefixes appearing most frequently had assimilated forms. For example, *ab* as in *abstract* had the assimilated forms of *a* as in *apart* and *abs* as in *abscess.*

The list of fifteen prefixes appearing most frequently, together with the number of times each appeared in the Thorndike rating, is as follows:

Prefix		Frequency
ab	(from)	98
ad	(to)	433
be	(by)	111
com	(with)	500
de	(from)	282
dis	(apart)	299
en	(in)	182
ex	(out)	286
in	(into)	336
in	(not)	317
pre	(before)	127
pro	(in front of)	146
re	(back)	457
sub	(under)	112
un	(not)	378

Suffixes. A syllable placed at the end of a basic word and modifying its meaning is known as a suffix. The most comprehensive study of suffixes was done by Thorndike in a desire to prepare a teacher's reference book on suffixes. The book should help teachers (62, p. 2) "in whatever systematic or incidental treatment they give to suffixes and word formation." He points out that "The meaning or force a suffix actually has in real words may not be the meaning it might be expected to have from its origin. It is therefore useful to examine the words themselves. . . . Such a list of words will do much the same service for suffixes that the illustrative sentences of the Oxford Dictionary do for words" (62, p. 3). This makes the availability and use of a book like Thorndike's on *The Teaching of English Suffixes* as essential to the study of suffixes as a dictionary is to the study of words.

Thorndike distinguished between incidental teaching and systematic teaching, and indicated that both approaches had great merit. He felt that incidental teaching was more apt to be a teaching of genuine meanings in genuine contexts. He felt that in such situations, because the seeking of meaning was being so ardently pursued, the reader would acquire a living habit or tendency of thought. Even so, he believed that a reasonable amount of deliberate and systematic teaching should be planned and carried out wisely.

For each of 93 suffixes among the 50,000 words used, Thorndike sought answers to the following questions (62, pp. 4–6):

1. How many words of each degree of frequency are made by the suffix? . . .
2. What meanings does the suffix have, and what is the frequency for each? . . .
3. How easy is it to see that the words are composed of the suffix plus some word or part of a word, modified somewhat? . . .
4. How easy is it to infer what the word means from knowledge that it equal x + the suffix and that x means so and so? . . .

Thorndike lists the following twenty-four suffixes and indicates that pupils should become acquainted with them by Grade 10.

-able	-ary	-ic	-less
-age	-ate	-ical	-ment
-al	-ence	-ion, -tion, -ation	-ness
-an, -n, -ian	-ent	-ish	-or
-ance	-er	-ity, -ty	-ous
-ant	-ful	-ive	-y

In discussing incidental and systematic instruction, Thorndike suggests that from "two to five lessons on suffixes in each grade from 6 to 10" would be useful (62, p. 72). He emphasizes strongly that words are living things and are constantly shifting and changing in meaning, and that people must keep in mind that most of the suffixes represent a range of meanings and that they must think in terms of variables as well as constants.

Thorndike gives a total of 4,300 words as being formed with the 93 suffixes. The number of words for the five most frequently used suffixes is as follows (62, pp. 66–69):

-ion	1095
-er	978
-ness	719
-ity	580
-y	576

The number of words of each degree of frequency in which the suffix *-ion, -tion,* or *-ation* appears is (62, p. 19, pp. 66–69):

331 words outside the 20,000 most used words
165 words outside the 16th to 20th thousand
201 words outside the 12th to 15th thousand
180 words outside the 10th to 11th thousand
 31 words outside the 9th thousand
 80 words outside the 6th to 8th thousand
107 words outside the 1st to 5th thousand

Estimates of the distribution of meanings of the 800 *-ion* words are as follows (62, p. 14):

Meanings	Number of words
1. act of Xing,[3] as in *abdication, mediation*	327
2. process of Xing, as in *fusion, germination*	38½
3. fact of Xing, as in *contradistinction, levitation*	51
4. practice of Xing, as in *litigation, prostitution*	6½
5. state or condition of being Xed, as in *addiction*	93½
6. fact of being Xed, as in *propagation*	14½
7. thing made by Xing, result of Xing, as in *abbreviation, conflagration*	83
8. thing that Xs, as in *affliction, illustration*	31½
9. thing that is Xed, as in *contribution, narration*	16½
rare and special meanings	138

Generally speaking, the analysis scores for the *-ion* suffix groups are low, indicating that they are difficult to recognize. As a matter of fact, Thorndike says (62, p. 14), "In speaking and writing he [a student] should avoid *-ion* and *-ation* words unless he knows that they mean what he wishes his hearers or readers to think." Then he adds that in his opinion it would be better to use the active meaning residing in such words as *abdicating, abolishing, abrogating,* rather than *abdication, abolition,* and *obrogation.*

This is in sharp contrast to the circumstances surrounding the 137 words that contain the suffix *-ful.* Analysis is usually easy, as an *armful, beautiful,* and *cheerful.* Even so, in words like *fitful, lawful, manful,* the meanings are more variable and capricious than appears to be the case at first sight or first thought (62, p. 15).

---

[3] X = the word minus the suffix.

Thorndike's thoughts about the suffix -ly (forming adjectives) are illustrative (62, p. 51):

Meanings	Number of words (estimated from 50)
1. X, as in *cleanly, kindly*	6
2. of X; pertaining to X; with respect to X as in *earthly, fleshly*	14
3. like X; like that of X, as in *beastly, loverly*	17
4. characteristic of X; suitable to X; befitting X, as in *gentlemanly*	15
5. causing X; causing to be X; making X, as in *deathly, deadly*	6
6. characterized by X, as in *leisurely*	3
7. every X; once every X, as in *daily, hourly;*	6
rare and special meanings	22

"By grade 6," Thorndike says, (62, p. 51) "pupils should have learned that -ly forms adjectives as well as adverbs. If not, their attention should be called to *brotherly, costly, daily, deadly, earthly, friendly, heavenly, kindly, lonely, lovely, manly, weekly,* and *yearly.* They may learn then or later that -ly means like or characteristic of in about one case out of three."

In summary, while the study of roots, prefixes, and suffixes can be interesting and fascinating, it can also be very challenging. Instruction must be geared to the idea of variability and the need to examine the circumstance in which the word is being used. It also appears wise to deal with words as whole words and then, as conditions permit, deal with prefixes, roots, and suffixes as parts of a word. Constancy of meaning can then be recognized on an inductive basis, and cautious generalizations can be made.

USE OF THE DICTIONARY

Of all the aids to word recognition, the dictionary ranks second in importance only to that of context. Of all the skills of word recognition, those essential to effective use of the dictionary rank second in importance only to those of context. Adults use a dictionary. It is one of the aids they learned to use in school that they also use out of school. Dictionary usage has life-time value, and skills of dictionary usage have life-time utility.

Adults do not know phonics and phonic generalizations. This does not mean that they cannot read or that they do not know how to deal with a word they do not know. The chief reason adults do not know the generalizations and rules referred to is because there are so many of them. When uncertain about a word, they know that the best way to deal with it is to turn to a dictionary. To deal with words independent of a dictionary would require persons to be trained as competent phoneticians, semanticists, linguists, and lexicographers.

The dictionary is a number-one aid. It provides the user with information about the English language. It records the usage of speakers and writers of our language. It does not prescribe usage but informs about usage, and unabridged dictionaries may actually record dialect usages. The dictionary provides information about the meaning of a word, its pronunciation, its spelling, its history, its part of speech, its synonyms and antonyms.

Elizabeth Vazquez puts it this way (65, p. 9):

We can get six main ideas about what we find in dictionaries, as follows:
1. How to Find Words: a dictionary lists words in alphabetical order.
2. Word Meanings: a dictionary tells what words mean (in the various ways they can be used).
3. Pronunciation: a dictionary tells how to pronounce words.
4. Spelling: a dictionary tells how to spell words.
5. How to Use Words: a dictionary may show how to use words (in the right combinations and order to say what we want them to say).
6. Word Histories: a dictionary may tell us where words come from.

Dr. Samuel Johnson, in the Preface to the first edition of *A Dictionary of the English Language* in 1755, wrote as follows about his work:

Thus have I laboured to settle the orthography, display the analogy, regulate the structures, and ascertain the signification of English words, to perform all the parts of a faithful lexicographer: but I have not always executed my own scheme, or satisfied my own expectations. The work, whatever proofs of diligence and attention it may exhibit, is yet capable of many improvements: the orthography which I recommend is still controvertible, the etymology which I adopt is uncertain, and perhaps frequently erroneous; the explanations are sometimes too much contracted, and sometimes too much diffused, the significations are distinguished rather with subtilty than skill, and the attention is harrassed with unnecessary minuteness.

Stuart A. Courtis and Garnette Watters wrote as follows about the purpose of their *Illustrated Golden Dictionary for Young Readers* (16, p. 5):

A dictionary is a book all about words. This dictionary will help you pronounce words correctly. It will help you spell them correctly. It will make clearer the meanings of words you already know. It will teach you new words and their meanings.

In this book you will discover interesting facts to add to your knowledge. You will also find many brightly-colored pictures and maps which will tell you many things you wish to know.

Your dictionary will be both useful and fun to use. It will help you at home and at school.

Ellen Wales Walpole, in her note to parents and teachers about *The Golden Dictionary*, explains (66, p. 94):

The Golden Dictionary is a book for parents and teachers to share and enjoy with children. It will be of great value to children in building an easy familiarity with words and their uses. It will also help them to form good dictionary habits early in life—to understand alphabetical order, to develop speed in finding words, appreciation for the meanings of words and sensitivity for their correct usage.

Regardless of the nature and scope of dictionaries, the purpose is always the same. This makes it immediately apparent that dictionary usage can no longer be confined by the lock-step of a basic-reader program. On the contrary, at whatever level words are used, these dictionaries are to be used also. William S. Gray says, "Even though the dictionary is not usually introduced until fourth grade, the understanding pupils in the primary grades acquire about the variant meanings of words, the use of context clues, and the use of structural and phonetic analysis prepare them for learning how to use the dictionary" (30, pp. 29–30), and later, "During the middle grades most children learn to use a dictionary," but such remarks cover only those circumstances in which reading instruction is confined within the limits of a basic reader. Reading instruction as defined in this text has pupils building their own dictionary in first grade as they learn to read via the language-arts–experience approach, using picture dictionaries for creative writing purposes as well as for reading purposes, and, at an early stage, because of the reading done during the individualized instruction time, facing the need to look up words not immediately recognized.

A second grader used a dictionary to check on the different meanings of *wind*. He discovered that the same four letters represented *wind* as in "the wind did blow," *wind* as in "to wind a watch," and *wind* as "to wind along a country road." He had read it as used in the third illustration. Similarly, a first grader, who during the individualized reading session came upon the word *hive*, turned to a dictionary and found that it meant "a box or house for honey bees." In the same way, a third grader, reading about Indians in a book he had selected, encountered the phrase, "They had a brush with the Indians." Turning to the dictionary he found that the fourth meaning listed for *brush* was "a short, quick fight."

As early in school life as possible, children should be led to regard dictionaries as the writer Erskine Caldwell did. Helen F. Olson quotes Caldwell as saying that, of all the books he owns, "I value the dictionary by far the highest and would certainly have endeavored to hold on to it the longest. I not only consulted it frequently, but in my free time I read the dictionary instead of reading novels and magazines; in my estimation, nothing had been written that was as fascinating, provocative, instructive, and fully satisfying as a book of words and their alluring meanings" (45, p. 365).

The attitude that a dictionary is truly a golden book of treasures should be developed from the beginning of school life. Similarly, the habit of turning to a dictionary should be initiated from the beginning. First-grade classrooms should not only have picture dictionaries, illustrated dictionaries, and pupil-built dictionaries, but also an unabridged dictionary. Nothing could be more appropriate than to have first-grade children see and use and watch the teacher use an unabridged dictionary placed on a dictionary stand and looking for all the world like a family Bible—and commanding some of the regard of a family Bible.

How to Find Words

A student who meets a word while reading that he does not know or is not sure about and turns to a glossary or dictionary for help wants to find what he is looking for in the shortest time possible. With the thinking reader, "on with the story" or "on with the article" is always the motto. Also with the thinking reader "read-with-understanding" is always the motto. Obviously, to deal with words and not grasp the ideas they are intended to communicate is not reading. Efficient use of the dictionary is therefore essential. Training needs to be started early in the school life of every pupil and to be continued until mastery is accomplished.

In the first grade, pupil construction of their own picture dictionary or word file or vocabulary bank is a first practical approach to learning dictionary skills. First, a child learns that the order of word entry is by beginning letters arranged according to the alphabet. For example, the first thirty words that Robin put in her picture dictionary required her to use eighteen of the twenty-six letter sections. By the time she had entered forty-six words she had used all the letter sections except X and Z. This prompted her to dictate two stories: one about an X-ray and another about a zoo. Now she had a word filed under each letter section. Now she had learned, too, that the letters X and Z occurred at the end of the alphabet and were in the back of her dictionary box. She also learned that there were not very many words that started with either of these two letters.

As Robin added words to her file, she learned not only that X and Z were at the end of the alphabet, but also that A and B were at the beginning and that M and N were in the middle. Each time she filed a new word or refiled an old word she moved back and forth in her dictionary box and thus dealt in a very practical way with the order of letters to each other, both a forward order and a reverse order. All this was done for a practical reason —the need to file words. Furthermore, the filing occurred many times during the school day as Robin worked with her dictionary box, and the practice did not have to wait for some trumped-up teacher situation. Robin did not have to wait until Norman had filed a word for every letter in his box, nor did she delay anyone who progressed more rapidly than she did.

One day, though, the teacher gathered together a group of nine first graders, all of whom had at least one word under each letter in their picture dictionaries or dictionary boxes. Then they played a dictionary game. First, each pupil placed four markers in his book or box. The number 1 marker was placed in front of the letter a words; the number 2 marker, between d and e; the number 3 marker, between l and m; the number 4 marker, between r and s. Then the teacher uncovered, one at a time, words she had placed on a piece of newsprint. These were words she knew were common to all boxes. The pupils located the words as quickly as they could, using the division markers as an aid.

From their own dictionaries to picture dictionaries was an easy step. This teacher had two picture dictionaries available. She had the children take turns using the picture dictionaries rather than their own. When she uncovered a word, for example, *dog,* seven of the pupils looked for the word in their personal dictionary books or boxes, and two looked in the professional picture dictionaries.

At another time the teacher showed the *Basic Dictionary of American English* (5) to the group and had them note how this dictionary was like a Pixie Dictionary and in turn like their personally constructed dictionaries. All this kept attention focused on use and serviceability. Children learned in a first-hand way how to use a dictionary, how to use an alphabet, and how to do so quickly and efficiently.

This was the procedure followed by this teacher with other children in the room as their filing needs increased and as their reading vocabularies grew. Later, these children learned to file words not only by the first letter but by the second and third letters also.

In a subsequent session, pupils were taught how to use guide words. They were led to *discover* that the word at the left-hand top of the page is also the first word on the page and that the word on the right-hand top is the last word on the page. Then exercises were used to develop speed and efficiency.

Quick and efficient location of words can become almost a rote skill, one that requires a low minimum of reflective thought. This being the case, another skill involved is that of skimming a column of words. Training can be accomplished this way. Pupils can be asked to set up on their desk tops or on their Pupil Word Card Holders[4] a list of words in alphabetical order, one word for each letter. Then the teacher stops at each desk and names one of the words, which the pupil then locates as quickly as possible by skimming the list from top to bottom. Or the teacher can name a word and all in the group skim their lists to see if they have the word on their lists. Later, or at a higher grade level, pupils can be asked to open their dictionaries to a certain page; for example, page 398 in the *Basic Dictionary of American English* (5). The teacher names one of the words on that page, and the pupils skim to locate it. For instance, she may name *kite* in the first column or *kitten* in the second column, and so on. Practice will produce quick and efficient performance.

Word Meanings. The most exciting aspect of words is the varied meanings they represent. Truly, words are poems! Words are rich according to the degree to which we ascribe meanings to them. The multiple uses of a word are a tribute to man's ability to see relationships between things and ideas and to make associations. The fact that *run* has been given 104 different usages (see the *American College Dictionary*) (2, p. 1,062) does not mean that it is a more useful word than the word *rumple*; it means only that the concept for *run* has caused men to identify the myriad attributes now associated with it. Words are fun, and some words or expressions cause men to smile when they perceive what might otherwise be most incongruous

---

4 Russell G. Stauffer, New York: Holt, Rinehart and Winston.

associations. *Sleeping pills, cigar box,* and *running board* are examples. Words have a rhythm and a roll as in *Tippecanoe* or *paraphernalia* or *humming bird.* Words are one of the great imponderables conceived by the mind of man. A word is a symbol. A symbol is a token, a sign. Words have a long history of serving as something spiritual. As a combination of letters forming a unit of language, a word may designate a person, place, or thing, assert being and mode of being, assert a specific action, or express a relationship or connection.

A dictionary meaning may help a reader obtain a clearer understanding of a known word used in an unknown way or of an unknown word met for a first time. In the sentence, "Pat had exhausted the subject of dolls," students may not at first grasp the meaning of *exhausted.* From the sentence the reader might conclude that Pat had done something with or about dolls. The reader may know the meaning of *car exhaust* or of *exhausted* signifying *tired* and thus be able to bring some meaning to this sentence. The dictionary provides the following:

exhaust (ĕg zôst′) 1. to empty; drain; use up: He had *exhausted* our supply of water long before we reached the spring. 2. to tire (oneself) out completely; He *exhausted* himself playing tennis. 3. to discuss or treat thoroughly: They *exhausted* the subject of politics. 4. discharge of used steam or gas fumes from an engine after each stroke of a piston: The air was black from the *exhaust* of the car. 5. the pipe through which discharged steam or gas fumes escape. 6. discharged steam or gas fumes. (5, p. 266.)

Now the pupil understands that Pat had discussed dolls thoroughly. In the process the pupil may either on his own or by wise guidance be led to rummage about among the other meanings of *exhaust* and see how they are alike and how they are different. It may be noted that the first three meanings appear to have certain attributes of *exhaust* in common and that they differ from certain other attributes that appear to link the last three meanings together. This word has a richness that is not readily exhausted.

In the sentence, "Dark ominous clouds foretold a storm," the word *ominous* may be completely unrecognized. Apparently it contributes meaning to a dark cloud—one that seems to be predicting a storm—but what could *ominous* be adding? The dictionary gives the following information:

ominous (ŏm′ ə nəs) like an omen of bad luck; threatening evil: Dark *ominous* clouds foretold a storm. *om-i-nous-ly.* (5, p. 494.)

So the word *ominous* tells the reader that the sky contains not only dark storm clouds but also dark storm clouds that suggest evil or danger or bad luck. Maybe dangerous lightning will result; or a heavy downpour will cause a flood; or a strong wind will blow things down; or large hail stones may cause much damage. Whatever the result, it is evident, according to the sentence, that the dark cloud is *ominous.*

Exercises of this kind and of a similar kind may be used to show pupils how the dictionary helps with word meanings.

Pronunciation. The dictionary provides help with pronunciation and is far more reliable than almost any pupil's best attempt at independent word analysis for pronunciation purposes. Knowledge of rules of accent and syllabification are so extremely complex that even the most skilled phonetician can be puzzled.

It is best to face up to the matter of accent and syllabification realistically. Memorizing a few rules that tend to have some constancy will enable children to parrot the rules when asked to do so. When he is faced with a need to unlock an unknown word by sound, however, there is little likelihood that the rules will result in anything at all reliable or accurate, for, as Donald Durrell has said on many occasions, these rules are usually applied backwards. In other words, if a child knows the word *colonial* he may be able to provide adequate explanation about accent. Even so, it is difficult to imagine him doing this, as the following illustrates (30, p. 189): "The suffix *-ial* is a visual clue to primary accent in words—the primary accent usually falls on the syllable preceding *-ial.*

official   of-fi-cial   (ə fish′ əl)

To apply this suffix visual clue successfully, the pupil would also need to know that "1) an accent (primary or secondary) always occurs on the first or second syllable of English words; 2) a common pattern of accent in longer words is a secondary accent on the first or second syllable, an unaccented syllable, and then the primary accent" (30, p. 187).

The reader of this text will discover difficulty in repeating this rule accurately immediately after reading it. To memorize the rule, he will need a fair amount of time. Furthermore, he must know it so well that he will not misuse it when dealing with a word that ends in *-ate.* In such words the accent falls on the second syllable preceding the suffix *-ate.*

Knowledge about the visual-clue value of certain suffixes represents only one aspect of the total accent situation. This is apparent when one examines the index listings on *accent* in William S. Gray's thorough *On Their Own in Reading* (30, pp. 243, 246).

Teachers do not know these rules; pupils do not know them; parents do not know them; and, most likely, only the most skilled phoneticians do. It is for these reasons that it is urged that practical good sense serve as the teaching guide. The dictionary supplies all the aid that is needed. Pupils should from the earliest encounter with unknown words be taught how to turn to a dictionary and use it efficiently.

No pupil has learned to be on his own in reading by memorizing the hundreds of rules supplied in *On Their Own in Reading* (30). A pupil, to be on his own in reading, must acquire the skills as defined in *Maturity in Reading* (31). Then efficient use of the dictionary will serve as a first-rate aid to comprehension. It is unfortunate that *Maturity in Reading* was not titled *On Their Own in Reading*. If it had been, comprehension skills and word-recognition skills would have been kept in proper focus. As it is now, many teachers own *On Their Own in Reading*, whereas few even know about *Maturity in Reading*.

To teach children to deal with *accent* start with words they already know and speak distinctly. Training may be started with a list of two-syllable words such as:

copper	hilly
dial	jacket
empty	lilac
fable	matter
giant	primer

A good procedure is to have pupils compare words which differ in meaning depending on where the accent falls. At times it helps to have pupils tap out the rhythm of these words with a finger.

pres′ ent	pre sent′
rec′ ord	re cord′
ob′ject	ob ject′
des′ert	de sert′
sus′pect	sus pect′

Then proceed to three-, four-, and five-syllable words. Emphasize the stress and duration of syllables. Such words as the following may be analyzed:

wea′ ri some	sus pi′ cious
un war′ y	se′ ri ous ness
un ut′ ter a ble	sep′ a ra′ tion
ter′ ri fy	sen′ si bil′ i ty
sur vi′ val	res′ to ra′ tion

A next step is to use words that are new to the pupils and that will require them to try their sound and blending ability in "sound blind" circumstances. Adults soon discover when dealing with a word they have never heard spoken that, even though they may speak it as recommended by a dictionary, they are uncertain about the correctness of their pronunciation. As a result even at their advanced level they are eager to hear someone speak the word correctly.

Syllable rules are of some value in spelling, and it is in spelling class that they are frequently taught. They are of some value in the early learning-to-read stages when on occasion, if a child syllabalizes a word and then speaks it, he may identify it as a spoken word he knows. However, once a child goes beyond this speaking-meaning vocabulary, the lack of consistency of spelling rules makes them of limited value.

Three common rules that may be of some utility value in the learning-to-read life of a pupil are as follows:

1. When a word has two consonants next to each other, many times the first consonant ends one syllable and then the second consonant begins the next syllable.
2. In many words when one consonant stands in the middle of two vowels, that consonant begins the second syllable.
3. Many times when a word ends in *le,* the consonant before *le* is added to the *le* and begins a new syllable. (57, p. 17.)

These rules should be taught inductively and frequently reviewed. As soon as the dictionary proves to be the most reliable source, pupils should be taught how to use the syllable arrangement of words both in the entry word and the phonetic respelling. Again pupils must learn to hear syllables and to identify them. A good procedure is to give pupils a list of new words that are syllabified, as follows:

dec′ i bel	(dec i′ bel, dec′ i bel)
dex ter′ i ty	(dex′ ter i ty, dex ter′ i ty)
grat′ i fi ca tion	(grat i′ fi′ ca tion, and correct)
lex′ i cog ra pher	(correct, and lex′ i cog ra′ pher)

Then the teacher gives two pronunciations for each word and the pupil must decide which one is correct according to the syllabification and accented form he is seeing.

Word Histories. Appropriate examination of definitions in dictionaries will yield word histories like the following ones:

batter (băt′ ər) 1. to beat or strike with repeated blows; pound: The rescue squad *battered* down the door. 2. to damage by use or misuse: The boys soon *battered* all the new furniture. (1*batter* is at least in part from a French word [battre] meaning "to beat.")

2 **batter** (băt′ ər) thin mixture of flour, liquid, and other ingredients: *pancake* batter. (2*batter* is 1*batter* in a later and special use.)

3 **batter** (bat′ ər) the player who is batting or whose turn it is to bat. (3*batter* is a word growing out of 1*bat.*)

*

1 **gall** (gôl) 1. bitter substance made by the liver and stored in a sac in the body called the *gall bladder.* 2. rudeness; impudence: The salesman had the *gall*

to walk in without knocking. (¹*gall* is from an Old English word [*galla*] meaning "bitter substance"; "bile.")

² **gall** (gôl) 1. sore on the skin caused by chafing, especially on a horse. 2. to make sore by chafing. 3. to annoy; vex; irritate: He *galled* me by his constant criticism. (²*gall* is probably a form of ¹*gall*.)

³ **gall** (gôl) a swelling or growth on a leaf or stem, caused by the attack of certain insects, bacteria, or fungi. (³*gall* comes through the French [galle] from a Latin word [galla] meaning a "gall of the oak tree, shaped like a nut.")

*

¹**lime** (līm) 1. chemical compound of calcium and oxygen made by burning limestone, bones, or shells. It is used for making cement, for making soil less acid, etc. (¹*lime* is a form of an Old English word [lim].)

² **lime** (līm) 1. small yellowish-green citrus fruit, somewhat like a lemon. 2. the tree that bears it. (²*lime* is from an Arabic word [limah]. It is related to the word *lemon*.)

³ **lime** (līm) the linden tree. (³*lime* is the changed form of an Old Enlish word [lind] meaning "linden.")

lined, lining. (¹*line* is a form of an Old English word [line] meaning "a cord." It goes back to a Latin word [linea] meaning "linen thread".)

sack (săk) 1. bag, especially a large one of rough cloth: a *potato* sack. 2. any cloth or paper bag. 3. the amount a bag can hold. 4. to put into a bag: to *sack* wheat. 5. loose jacket, especially for women or children: *a baby's sack* (¹*sack* is a form of an Old English word [sacc] that comes through Latin [saccus] from a Greek word [sakkos] of the same meaning.) (homonyn; sac). (5, pp. 95, 306, 418, 419, 625.)

A discussion of the origin of words does alert pupils to the long history that many words have. It also should alert them to changes that have occurred through the centuries as well as to how words have crossed from one language to another. Pupils might be led to see how a tracing of words might result in a history of man—his searchings and conquests and ideas.

Similarly pupils should be alerted to new words entering our language and to words that have gained new meanings or lost meanings or become obsolete.

atomic-powered	geiger counters	lend-lease
baby-sitters	freeways	H-bomb
litterbug	king-sized	hot rod
	malarky	evacuees
		de-icer

Old words that have taken on new meanings are:

absentee	circle	grain
ache	defy	hick
boot	fleet	life
		murk

Some words that have lost meaning since 1930 are:

acre	inner
chip	list
disdain	mash
fame	mold

The utility value of a dictionary as a source of help to obtain meaning, pronunciation, spelling, word history, and derivation, and so on is unquestionable. The answer to the question, "Of what use is a dictionary?" is an irrefutable, positive answer, as shown here. Substitute methods for word interpretation are worthless.

Language security, an insurance plan relating to lifetime habits of effective communication and allowing for fixed periodical consideration of words and their meanings, can be offered to pupils on a contributory basis. Dictionary usage can be taught.

PHONIC RULES

Throughout this chapter many references to rules have been made—rules for using phonetic (sound) analysis and structure (sight) analysis to deal with an unfamiliar word. Ways of utilizing context clues for both pronunciation and meaning were also discussed at length. The "ways" listed are seldom referred to as rules, because "rule" is a regulation that exercises authority of a sovereign nature. It is always right. In context no simple regulation can do the job. Much depends on the way in which a word or words are being used. The meaning provided by each word in a sentence, the semantic relationship of words to each other, and the relationship of sentences to each other are so varied that rules governing them can hardly be formulated. Rules also suggest a scientific orderliness of the kind that context clues do not provide. Context can provide help if the reader is intent on obtaining meaning and refuses to go on without meaning.

On the other hand, the regulations governing phonetic analysis and structural analysis are to help the reader recognize words; that is, to know the *meaning of the words.* The reader is reminded again that, even if he deals with a word like *pinnate* phonetically and structurally and still does not know its meaning, it gaineth him nothing. The reader is asked to select one of the following words—a word that he has not seen before if there is such a word in the list:

fillister	rowel
palatine	tellurian

First deal with pronunciation. Most readers after using their knowledge of pronunciation rules, will probably be uncertain which of the following phonetic respellings represents the one listed in a dictionary:

fĭl′ ĭs ter	fĭl ĭs′ ter	fĭl′ ĭs ter
pā lā′ tĭn	păl′ ə tĭn′	păl′ ə tĭn′
rōw′ əl	row′ əl	rou əl′
tĕl′ yər ĭ ən	tĕl ye′ rĭ ən	tĕ lōōr′ ĭ ən

Even if the reader selected the right respelling in each instance, he still did not have the meaning and needed to refer to a dictionary. For the word *fillister* the first listing is correct; for *palatine,* the second one; for *rowel,* the second one; and for *tellurian,* the third one. Correct use of a dictionary would have been the quickest and most accurate step to take.

The four studies (7, 8, 12, 43) previously referred to on pages 337–341 of this chapter spelled out at some length the complex circumstances of the factors involved in the pronunciation of words when the words were limited to frequently occurring ones. A study was also made by Theodore Clymer (14) to test the utility of forty-five phonic generalizations, which were selected somewhat arbitrarily from among 121 different generalizations. Clymer's main criterion was: "Is the generalization stated specifically enough so that it can be said to aid or hinder in the pronunciation of a particular word?" The word list developed on which to check the generalizations was a composite list of all the words introduced in four basic readers, plus the Gates Reading Vocabulary for the Primary Grades, for a total of 2,600 words. Clymer took the following steps:

1. The phonetic respelling and the syllabic division of all words were recorded. Webster's *New Collegiate Dictionary* was used as the authority for this information.
2. Each phonic generalization was checked against the words in the composite list to determine (a) the words which were pronounced as the generalization claimed and (b) the words which were exceptions to the generalization.
3. A "percent of utility" was computed for each generalization by dividing the number of words pronounced as the generalization claimed by the total number of words to which the generalization could be expected to apply. For example, if the generalization claimed that "When the letters *oa* are together in a word, *o* always gives its long sound and *a* is silent," all words containing *oa* were located in the list. The number of these words was the total number of words to which the generalization should apply. Then the phonetic spellings of these words were examined to see how many words containing *oa* did have the long *o* followed by the silent *a*. In this case thirty words were located which contained *oa*. Twenty-nine of these were pronounced as the generalization claimed; one was not. The percent of utility became 29/30 or 97. This procedure was followed for all generalizations. (14, p. 254.)

Clymer then set two criteria as his opinion of what constituted a "reasonable" degree of application. First, he felt that his list should contain at least *twenty* words as the minimum total number of words to which the generalization could be expected to apply. He selected twenty because he felt that if a generalization applied to fewer words it had low utility value and did not warrant instructional time. Second, he set at 75 percent the criterion of utility value. In other words, if the word list contained twenty words to which a generalization could be applied, the generalization should work in fifteen of the twenty words.

In his report Clymer uses the word *generalization* rather than *rule* because all of the forty-five statements being checked had exceptions. He felt that a rule could not have an exception. The following table gives the results of the analysis of the forty-five phonic generalizations.

Generalization*	No. of Words Conforming	No. of Exceptions	Per Cent of Utility
1. When there are two vowels side by side, the long sound of the first one is heard and the second is usually silent.	309 (bead)†	377 (chief)†	45
2. When a vowel is in the middle of a one-syllable word, the vowel is short	408	249	62
middle letter	191 (dress)	84 (scold)	69
one of the middle two letters in a word of four letters	191 (rest)	135 (told)	59
one vowel *within* a word of more than four letters	26 (splash)	30 (fight)	46
3. If the only vowel letter is at the end of a word, the letter usually stands for a long sound.	23 (he)	8 (to)	74
4. When there are two vowels, one of which is final *e*, the first vowel is long and the *e* is silent.	180 (bone)	108 (done)	63
*5. The *r* gives the preceding vowel a sound that is neither long nor short.	484 (horn)	134 (wire)	78
6. The first vowel is usually long and the second silent in the digraphs *ai, ea, oa,* and *ui.*	179	92	66
ai	43 (nail)	24 (said)	64
ea	101 (bead)	51 (head)	66
oa	34 (boat)	1 (cupboard)	97
ui	1 (suit)	16 (build)	6
7. In the phonogram *ie,* the *i* is silent and the *e* has a long sound.	8 (field)	39 (friend)	17
*8. Words having double *e* usually have the long *e* sound.	85 (seem)	2 (been)	98
9. When words end with silent *e,* the preceding *a* or *i* is long.	164 (cake)	108 (have)	60
*10. In *ay* the *y* is silent and gives *a* its long sound.	36 (play)	10 (always)	78
11. When the letter *i* is followed by the letters *gh,* the *i* usually stands for its long sound and the *gh* is silent.	22 (high)	9 (neighbor)	71
12. When *a* follows *w* in a word, it usually has the sound *a* as in *was.*	15 (watch)	32 (swam)	32
13. When *e* is followed by *w,* the vowel sound is the same as represented by *oo.*	9 (blew)	17 (sew)	35
14. The two letters *ou* make the long sound.	50 (own)	35 (down)	59
15. *W* is sometimes a vowel and follows the vowel digraph rule.	50 (crow)	75 (threw)	40
*16. When *y* is the final letter in a word, it usually has a vowel sound.	169 (dry)	32 (tray)	84
17. When *y* is used as a vowel in words, it sometimes has the sound of long *i.*	29 (fly)	170 (funny)	45
18. The letter *a* has the same sound (ô) when followed by *l, w,* and *u.*	61 (all)	65 (canal)	48

Generalization*	No. of Words Conforming	No. of Exceptions	Per Cent of Utility
*19. When *a* is followed by *r* and *final e*, we expect to hear the sound heard in *care*.	9 (dare)	1 (are)	90
*20. When *c* and *h* are next to each other, they make only one sound.	103 (peach)	0	100
*21. *Ch* is usually pronounced as it is in *kitchen, catch,* and *chair,* not like *sh*.	99 (catch)	5 (machine)	95
*22. When *c* is followed by *e* or *i*, the sound of *s* is likely to be heard.	66 (cent)	3 (ocean)	96
*23. When the letter *c* is followed by *o* or *a* the sound of *k* is likely to be heard.	143 (camp)	0	100
24. The letter *g* often has a sound similar to that of *j* in *jump* when it precedes the letter *i* or *e*.	49 (engine)	28 (give)	64
*25. When *ght* is seen in a word, *gh* is silent.	30 (fight)	0	100
*26. When a word begins *kn*, the *k* is silent.	10 (knife)	0	100
*27. When a word begins with *wr*, the *w* is silent.	8 (write)	0	100
*28. When two of the same consonants are side by side only one is heard.	334 (carry)	3 (suggest)	99
*29. When a word ends in *ck*, it has the same last sound as in *look*.	46 (brick)	0	100
*30. In most two-syllable words, the first syllable is accented.	828 (famous)	143 (polite)	85
*31. If *a, in, re, ex, de,* or *be* is the first syllable in a word, it is usually unaccented.	86 (belong)	13 (insect)	87
*32. In most two-syllable words that end in a consonant followed by *y*, the first syllable is accented and the last is unaccented.	101 (baby)	4 (supply)	96
33. One vowel letter in an accented syllable has its short sound.	547 (city)	356 (lady)	61
34. When *y* or *ey* is seen in the last syllable that is not accented, the long sound of *e* is heard.	0	157 (baby)	0
*35. When *ture* is the final syllable in a word, it is unaccented.	4 (picture)	0	100
*36. When *tion* is the final syllable in a word, it is unaccented.	5 (station)	0	100
37. In many two- and three-syllable words, the final *e* lengthens the vowel in the last syllable.	52 (invite)	62 (gasoline)	46
38. If the first vowel sound in a word is followed by two consonants, the first syllable usually ends with the first of the two consonants.	404 (bullet)	159 (singer)	72
39. If the first vowel sound in a word is followed by a single consonant, that consonant usually begins the second syllable.	190 (over)	237 (oven)	44

THE UTILITY OF FORTY-FIVE PHONIC GENERALIZATIONS (continued)

Generalization*	No. of Words Conforming	No. of Exceptions	Per Cent of Utility
*40. If the last syllabe of a word ends in *le*, the consonant preceding the *le* usually begins the last syllable.	62 (tumble)	2 (buckle)	97
*41. When the first vowel element in a word is followed by *th, ch,* or *sh,* these symbols are not broken when the word is divided into syllables and may go with either the first or second syllable.	30 (dishes)	0	100
42. In a word of more than one syllable, the letter *v* usually goes with the preceding vowel to form a syllable.	53 (cover)	20 (clover)	73
43. When a word has only one vowel letter, the vowel sound is likely to be short.	433 (hid)	322 (kind)	57
*44. When there is one *e* in a word that ends in a consonant, the *e* usually has a short sound.	85 (leg)	27 (blew)	76
*45. When the last syllable is the sound *r*, it is unaccented.	188 (butter)	9 (appear)	95

* Generalizations marked with an asterisk were found "useful" according to the criteria.

† Words in parentheses are examples—either of words which conform or of exceptions depending on the column.

Source: Theodore Clymer, "The Utility of Phonic Generalizations in the Primary Grades," *The Reading Teacher, 16* (January, 1963), pp. 256–258. Reprinted with permission of Theodore Clymer and the International Reading Association.

Examination of this table shows that:

1. If 100 percent accuracy were required and if the generalizations were declared *rules,* only nine of the forty-five could be taught as rules.

2. If to this list of nine rules the first criterion is applied, a frequency of application of twenty or more words, then four of the rules would not merit teaching. This leaves the following five rules as meriting teaching time:

20. When *c* and *h* are next to each other, they make only one sound.
23. When the letter *c* is followed by *o* or *a* the sound of *k* is likely to be heard.
25. When *ght* is seen in a word, *gh* is silent.
29. When a word ends in *ck*, it has the same last sound as in *look*.
41. When the first vowel element in a word is followed by *th, ch,* or *sh,* these symbols are not broken when the word is divided into syllables and may go with either the first or second syllable.

Note also that in two instances, rules 25 and 41, the number of words conforming totals only thirty. This suggests that the list might be further reduced to *three* rules.

3. If one adheres to the two criteria set up (a frequency of application of twenty words, and a 75 percent utility value), then only eighteen of the forty-

five generalizations merit teaching. They are numbers 5, 8, 10, 16, 20, 21, 22, 23, 25, 28, 29, 30, 31, 32, 40, 41, 44 and 45.

The range of the number of words conforming varied from a high of 828 with generalization number 30, to a low of 30 with generalizations numbers 25 and 41. Note also that only six of the generalizations had a total of 100 words or more to which the regulations could be applied.

4. Clymer states:

"A group of generalizations seem to be useful only after the pupil can pronounce the word. Generalizations which specify vowel pronunciation in stressed syllables require that the pupil know the pronunciation of the word before he can apply the generalization. (See, for example, generalization 33.) This criticism assumes, of course, that the purpose of a generalization is to help the child unlock the pronunciation of *unknown* words."

5. Regional pronunciations would also influence the usefulness of some of the generalizations.

6. If the eighteen generalizations are re-examined to determine what percentage of the 2,600 words the number of words conforming represent, the following picture results:

Generalization	Percentage of 2,600
5	18
8	3
10	1
16	6
20	4
21	3
22	2
23	5
25	1
28	13
29	1
30	31
31	3
32	4
40	2
41	1
44	3
45	7

If one arbitrarily said that the generalization should apply to at least 5 percent of the total vocabulary, we could conclude that only six of the generalizations merit instructional time: numbers 5, 16, 23, 28, 30, and 45. Only one of these six—generalization 23—applies in all instances. One might conclude, therefore, that the only generalization meriting teaching time is the one which states that "when the letter *c* is followed by *o* or *a*, the sound of *k* is heard."

It must be kept in mind, of course, that the reading vocabulary of children, even those in the primary grades, will not be limited to 2,600 words.

Thus the number of words conforming to the generalizations listed here may be larger, as may the exceptions. Also, as the number of polysyllabic words increases, the number of generalizations will also increase.

This examination of the *rule* circumstance points up quite clearly the futility of either *rules* or *generalizations*. It can account for the fact that children, teachers, and parents do not know the rules and therefore do not use them. It accounts for the reason why only phonetic specialists and not even reading specialists know the rules. It suggests loudly and firmly that from the beginning of reading instruction attention should be focused 100 percent on comprehension rather than on word-recognition rules, because 100 percent comprehension will always have 100 percent utility.

SUMMARY

Of all the facts and ideas presented in this chapter, the one most difficult to understand and most shocking to one's beliefs is the teachers' lack of knowledge of phonic generalizations. Surveys clearly show that teachers say they believe in phonics and that they teach phonics, and yet tests of their knowledge of phonic generalizations show that they do not know them. This lack of knowledge of phonics is not limited to first-year teachers, but it true of experienced teachers as well. How can such a perplexing circumstance exist?

The answer cannot be attributed to low intelligence level of teachers, for teachers test among the top 10 percent of the population. Neither can this lack of knowledge be attributed to lack of opportunity to learn. They have "taught" the rules year after year and so have had frequent contact with them—a basic tenet of the psychology of learning. The rules cannot be too difficult for teachers to learn and remember, or else they would not be taught to first, second, and third-grade-level children. What is the answer? Two answers appear to be plausible. First is the moot point of *utility*, and second is that of *practicability*.

Phonic generalizations are useful only if the person can be sure that the word he is pronouncing is reasonably accurate (allowing for local differences) and if he already knows the meaning of the word. In other words, as long as the printed word being spoken is in the person's speaking-meaning vocabulary, the "analysis" can be of value. Why this may happen with greater frequency at grades one, two, and three, or during the "learning to read" process is readily apparent. And why this may not happen beyond this level or stage of progress has been clearly illustrated with the word *pinnate*. At this later stage even the most skilled phonetician and linguist may not know what to do and may need to consult a record of the English language prepared by scholars, specialists, and editors to help readers, speakers, and writers who want to know the meaning of a word, its pronunciation, its spelling, and so on—in one word, a dictionary.

Phonic generalizations are practical only when they are consistent. Each inconsistency or set of inconsistencies or each exception results in a new rule or generalization. The studies referred to in this chapter point out clearly the large number of generalizations that exist. In fact, the number is so great that the word "rule" is dropped by some educators in preference to the less definite word "generalization."

Is the following syllogism accurate?:

Step One.   Knowledge of phonic generalizations is essential to reading.
Step Two.   Teachers do not know phonic generalizations.
Step Three. Teachers cannot read.

Obviously, no one will accept this conclusion. Teachers can read and do read even though they do not know phonic generalizations. The same condition is true of adults other than teachers and of most schoolchildren. They, too, can read, even though they do not know the phonic generalizations.

Apparently, then, what is needed is to keep phonics in perspective and to recognize its contribution to reading and to the learning-to-read process. The following generalizations about word-attack skills in general and phonics in particular are timely and relevant.

1. Children should *always* be reading for meaning.

2. Words to be dealt with should *always* appear in a meaningful context, preferably that of a story or an article.

3. Context clues to word recognition should *always* be tried first, even at the primary level, and in controlled vocabulary material.

4. Phonic generalizations are particularly useful during the learning-to-read process. This is true at this stage because the printed words being dealt with usually are already a functional part of the subject's speaking-meaning or oral-language vocabulary.

5. Structure generalizations are useful during the learning-to-read process. This is true at this stage because knowledge of common inflectional changes and common affixes may help the reader deal with a word already a part of his speaking-meaning vocabulary.

6. Ability to substitute consonant sounds, to recognize variations of vowel sounds as marked by a diacritical key, and to blend sounds together are essential to dictionary usage.

7. A dictionary provides word-recognition help for both pronunciation and meaning. For pronunciation purposes a dictionary provides phonetic respellings. Respellings use consonant substitution, diacritical vowel markings, syllabification, and accents. The dictionary also provides a diacritical pronunciation key for the convenience and accuracy of the user. Meaning clues are provided through definitions, illustrative usages, word histories, and illustrations.

8. Rules are so great in number and so complex in detail that only the most skilled phonetician is apt to know them and use them correctly. All

readers other than the few phoneticians referred to depend on a dictionary for help. Therefore, students from the first grade on should be taught how to use a dictionary.

The American Heritage

Two hundred years ago, Thomas Jefferson advocated free elementary schooling for all future citizens, the selection and encouragment of promising secondary-school students, and free university education for those qualified. This Jeffersonion tradition is finally becoming the American tradition in the latter half of the twentieth century. Thomas Jefferson, the author of the Declaration of Independence, put the higest value on education so as to protect individuals in the free exercise of their natural rights, emancipate them from prejudice, divest them of all bias, fix reason firmly in her seat, call to their tribunals every fact and opinion so that both sides of a question might be clearly presented, question with boldness, make inquiry without fear of its consequences, be answerable for the uprightness of their decisions, make observations founded on examined experience—all this so that they will be precious to their country, dear to their friends, and happy within themselves.

In 1955, Dora V. Smith wrote:

It is the fashion these days to urge the schools to go "back to the 3 R's" though it would be difficult for most of us to find one that has actually departed from them. What many of these critics want, as has already been illustrated, is that we should teach children accuracy in getting the thought from the printed page and leave until they are older any consideration of what has been said. Certainly accuracy in getting the thought is a fundamental end of the teaching of reading. Stopping there would furnish all the training necessary for a follower of Hitler, or Stalin, or Mussolini, who has but to grasp instructions in order to obey; but it is only the first step in the teaching of reading in a land where freedom of speech, we hope, prevails. Devotion to truth, learned through careful examination of ideas, is the aim of the teaching of communication in a democracy. Use of slanted or emotional language, fallacies in reasoning, stereotyped or prejudiced thinking, and substitution of the devices of propaganda for clear presentation of evidence must be recognized for what they are. . . .

Clearly, future citizens of the United States must be protected by their own training against the deliberate slanting of news and the cheap devices of propaganda.

The temper of our times demands clear thinking in the face of malicious innuendo, hysterical pleading, false analogies, and, on occasion, deliberate misrepresentation of facts and principles of our country's heritage. . . .

In the face of this situation, it is clear that the schools must keep before the youth of the nation Kipling's challenge of fifty years ago:

> If you can keep your head
> when all about you
> Are losing theirs . . . you'll be
> a man, my son.

(53, pp. 19–23.)

This is the yardstick by which every American teacher of reading should judge the children she teaches, her methods of teaching, and her objectives. Such is the resource of spirit and mind upon which sound reading instruction is premised. The struggle to make these principles prevail is the common challenge to us all and should be dignified by the name American Reading Instruction.

REFERENCES

1. Aaron, I. E., "What Teachers and Prospecitve Teachers Know About Phonics Generalizations." *Journal of Educational Research, 53* (May, 1960), 323–330.
2. *The American College Dictionary,* New York, Random House, 1961.
3. Artley, A. Sterl, "Teaching Word Meaning Through Context," *Elementary English Review, 20* (February, 1943), 68–74.
4. Austin, Mary, and Coleman Morrison, *The Torch Lighters, Tomorrow's Teachers of Reading,* Cambridge, Mass., Harvard University Press, 1961.
5. *Basic Dictionary of American English,* New York, Holt, Rinehart and Winston, 1962. By special permission.
6. Betts, Emmett A., *Foundations of Reading Instruction,* New York, American Book, 1946.
7. Black, Elsie B., *A Study of the Consonant Situations in a Primary Reading Vocabulary,* unpublished Master's thesis, Philadelphia, Temple University, 1950.
8. Black, Millard H., *A Study of Certain Structural Elements of Words in a Primary Reading Vocabulary,* unpublished Master's thesis, Philadelphia, Temple University, 1950.
9. Brown, J. I., *Efficient Reading,* Boston, Heath, 1952.
10. Bryant, Margaret M., "The English Inflections and Form Words," *Word Study* (Springfield, Mass.), vol. 21 (October, 1945).
11. Bullock, James E., *The Compilation of a Core Communication Vocabulary List and Its Evaluation in Terms of the Word Recognition and Spelling Abilities of Fourth Grade Children,* unpublished Doctoral dissertation, Philadelphia, Temple University, 1956.
12. Burrows, Alvina Treut, and Zyra Lourie, "When 'Two Vowels Go Walking,'" *The Reading Teacher, 17* (Novmeber, 1963), 79–82.
13. Burt, Cyril, *Mental and Scholastic Tests,* London, King, 1927.
14. Clymer, Theodore, "The Utility of Phonic Generalizations in the Primary Grades," *The Reading Teacher, 16* (January, 1963), 252–258.
15. Cordts, Anna D., *The Word Method of Teaching Phonics,* Boston, Ginn, 1929.
16. Courtis, Stuart A., and Garnette Watters, *The Courtis-Watters Illustrated Golden Dictionary for Young Readers,* rev. ed., New York, Golden, 1961.
17. Durkin, Dolores, *Phonics and the Teaching of Reading,* Practical Suggestions for Teaching Series, No. 22, New York, Teachers College, Columbia University, 1962.
18. Durrell, Donald D., "First-Grade Success Study: A Summary," *Journal of Education, 140* (February, 1958), 2–6.
19. Durrell, Donald D., and Helen A. Murphy, "Boston University Research in Elementary School Reading: 1933–1963," *Journal of Education, 146* (December, 1963), 1–53.
20. Durrell, Donald D., Helen A. Murphy, Doris U. Spencer, and Jane H. Cattorson, *Word-Analysis Practice,* Tarrytown, N.Y., World, 1960.
21. Ernst, Margaret S., *Words,* 3d rev. ed., New York, Knopf, 1955.
22. Fitzgerald, James A., *A Basic Life Spelling Vocabulary* Milwaukee, Bruce, 1951.
23. Fitzgerald, James A., "An Integrating Basic Communication Vocabulary," *Elementary English, 40* (March, 1963), 283–289.
24. Flesch, Rudolph, *Why Johnny Can't Read and What You Can Do About it,* New York, Harper & Row, 1955.
25. Fries, Charles C., *Linguistics and Reading,* New York, Holt, Rinehart and Winston, 1963.

26. Funk, Wilfred, *Word Origins and Their Romantic Stories,* New York, Funk, 1950.
27. Goins, Jean Turner, *Visual Perceptual Abilities and Early Reading Progress,* Supplementary Educational Monographs, No. 87, Chicago, University of Chicago Press, 1958.
28. Good, Carter V., *Dictionary of Education,* New York, McGraw-Hill, 1959.
29. Gray, William S., *On Their Own in Reading.* Copyright 1960 by Scott, Foresman and Company.
30. Gray, William S., *ibid.,* rev. ed., 1960.
31. Gray, William S., and Bernice Rogers, *Maturity in Reading,* Chicago, University of Chicago Press, 1956.
32. Horn, Ernest, "The Child's Early Experience With the Letter *A,*" *Journal of Educational Psychology, 20* (March, 1929), 161–168.
33. Horn, Ernest, "Spelling," *Encyclopedia of Educational Research,* 3d ed., New York, Macmillan, 1960.
34. Jenkinson, Marion D., *Selected Processes and Difficulties of Reading Comprehension,* Doctoral dissertation, Chicago, University of Chicago Press, 1957.
35. Jesperson, Otto, *Language: Its Nature, Development, and Origin,* New York, Macmillan, 1949.
36. Kyte, George C., "A Core Vocabulary in the Language Arts," *Phi Delta Kappan, 34* (March, 1953), 231–234.
37. Loban, Walter, *The Language of Elementary School Children,* NCTE Research Report No. 1, Champaign, Ill., National Council of Teachers of English, 1963.
38. McAdam, E. L., Jr., and George Milne, *Johnson's Dictionary,* New York, Pantheon, 1963.
39. McCullough, Constance M., "Context Aids in Reading," *The Reading Teacher, 11* (April, 1958), 225–229.
40. McCullough, Constance M., "Phonic Knowledge Demonstrated by Prospective Elementary School Teachers," a paper presented at the American Educational Research Association meeting, Chicago, February, 1963, Mimeo.
41. Moore, Walter J., "The Contribution of Lexicography to the Teacher of Language Arts," *Elementary English, 41* (April, 1964), 388–394.
42. Nicholson, Alice, "Background Abilities Related to Reading Success in First Grade," *Journal of Education, 140* (February, 1958), 7–24.
43. Oaks, Ruth E., *A Study of the Vowel Situations in a Primary Reading Vocabulary,* unpublished Master's thesis, Philadelphia, Temple University, 1950.
44. Olson, Arthur V., "Growth in Word Perception Abilities as It Relates to Success in Beginning Reading," *Journal of Education, 140* (February, 1958), 25–36.
45. Olson, Helen F., "The Dictionary as a Basic Text," *Elementary English, 41* (April, 1964), 365–369.
46. *Picturesque Word Origins,* Springfield, Mass., Merriam, 1933.
47. Rinsland, Henry D., *A Basic Vocabulary of Elementary School Children,* New York, Macmillan, 1945.
48. Russell, David H., *The Dimensions of Children's Meaning Vocabularies in Grades Four Through Twelve,* University of California Publications in Education, vol. 11, Berkeley, University of Califonia Press, 1954.
49. Russell, David H., "Teachers' View on Phonics," *Elementary English, 32* (October, 1955), 371–375.
50. Russell, David H., and Henry R. Fea, "Research on Teaching Reading," *Handbook of Research on Teaching,* American Education Research Association, N. L. Gage, ed., Chicago, Rand McNally, 1963.
51. Sachs, H. J., "The Reading Method of Acquiring Vocabulary," *Journal of Educational Research, 36* (February, 1943), 457–464.
52. Sauer, Philip, "One Hundred Root Words for Vocabulary Building," *English Journal, 25* (November, 1936), 757–759.
53. Smith, Dora V., *Communication, The Miracle of Shared Living,* New York, Macmillan, 1955.
54. Stauffer, Russell G., "A Study of Prefixes in the Thorndike List To Establish a List of Prefiixes that Should Be Taught in the Elementary School," *Journal of Educational Research, 35* (February, 1942), 453–458.

55. Stauffer, Russell G., Alvina Treut Burrows, and Mary Elisabeth Coleman, *Come Here*, New York, Holt, Rinehart and Winston, 1960.
56. Stauffer, Russell G., Alvina Treut Burrows, Mary Elisabeth Coleman, and Evelyn Rezen Spencer, *Away We Go*, New York, Holt, Rinehart and Winston, 1960.
57. Stauffer, Russell G., Alvina H. Treut Burrows, and Edmund H. Henderson, *Studybook for Across the Valley*, New York, Holt, Rinehart and Winston, 1960.
58. Strickland, Ruth G., *The Language of Elementary School Children*, Bulletin of the School of Education, Bloomington, Ind., Indiana University, July, 1962.
59. Taylor, Wilson L., *Application of 'Cloze' and Entropy Measures to the Study of Contextual Constraint in Samples of Continuous Prose*, unpublished Doctoral dissertation, Urbana, Ill., University of Illinois, 1954.
60. Thomas, Charles Kenneth, *An Introduciton to the Phonetics of American English*, New York, Ronald, 1947.
61. Thorndike, Edward L., *A Teacher's Word Book of 20,000 Words*, rev. ed., New York, Teachers College, Columbia University, 1932.
62. Thorndike, Edward L., *The Teaching of English Suffixes*, New York, Teachers College, Columbia University, 1941.
63. Trabue, M. R., *Completion Test Language Scales*, New York, Teachers College, Columbia University, 1916.
64. Traxler, Arthur E., "Improvement of Vocabulary Through Drill," *English Journal*, 27 (June, 1938), 490–494.
65. Vazquez, Elizabeth, "You and Your Dictionary," *Basic Dictionary of American English*, New York, Holt, Rinehart and Winston, 1962.
66. Walpole, Ellen Wales, *The Golden Dictionary*, New York, Simon & Schuster, 1944.
67. *Webster's Dictionary of Synonyms*, Springfield, Mass., Merriam, 1942.

Chapter 10
Concept Development

The golden mean of concept development is not like the mathematical mean. It is not an exact average of points, scattered between calculable extremes. It fluctuates with the collateral circumstances of each situation. It fluctuates with the person, who brings with him his past relations to his world, his emotional dispositions, his capacity to think, and his expectancies for the future. It fluctuates with the nature of the concept to be acquired—its composition, structure, and operation. It fluctuates with the pressures that exist in the situation and with the consequences of the action to be taken. It is discovered only in the mature and flexible grasping of concepts formed on an abstract level and applied to new concrete situations.

Concepts are in good part the gift of innocent intent; but in the market-place of the scholar they are the achievement of experience, knowledge, and the higher intellectual functions. Required is a tough, not a tender, mind—a mind whose main features are reflective awareness and deliberate control, tempered by "warm-blooded" affective inference. These features are being formed and molded and used as the child passes from the stage of undifferentiated functions in infancy to the differentiation and development of perception, intention, and memory in childhood. School-age children possess these functions in some strength, and during the early school years they grow steadily in awareness and mastery, until they are capable of conscious and deliberate control and creative use. Concepts—scientific concepts—form the bases of a "mediated" attitude toward consciousness and deliberate use that characterizes that maturity of mind known simply as the art and method of correct thinking. This is a maturity that, even though it exacts order, does not exile that creative liberty which is the soul of art.

374

Concepts have in one form or another been of tremendous import in both theory and practice from the Greeks to the present day. Edith Hamilton (5) said that the great "either-or" contribution of the Greeks provided the thread of scientific development and helped them carry on their experiments and observations in a more varied and detailed manner. The direction for concept attainment was clearly pointed out by Aristotle, who indicated that meaning could be given to things only by classifying and generalizing them, and by Socrates, who investigated everything around him, uncovering assumptions and questioning certainties. *"Prudens quaestio dimidium scientiae*: to know what to ask is already to know half." (3) Across the centuries scholars have ridiculed rote memory and its alleged role in the learning-thinking process. Leo Tolstoy, for one, believed that children should not be taught by artificial explanations, compulsive memorizing, and repetition: "to give the pupil new concepts deliberately . . . is, I am convinced, as impossible and futile as teaching a child to walk by the laws of equilibrium" (11, p. 84). Needed, he said, is the chance for children to acquire new concepts and words from their general linguistic context.

Concepts are the cognitive structures that each child must develop in the course of intellectual functioning. It is only through functioning that concepts get formed. This is as true of the first simple habits established by the infant through the most elementary of sensory-motor acts as it is of the mature adult for whom representational thought has become hypothetico-deductive and is oriented toward possibilities, the lattice of all-possible combinations. As Jean Piaget and others argue, we do not inherit cognitive structures, but we do inherit a means for attaining them. And most important of all this mode of functioning remains essentially constant throughout life. It is always and everywhere the same. It is because of this constancy of functioning, despite the wide varieties of cognitive structures that can be created, that this way of functioning is referred to as a functional invariant (4) or as a functional constant.

Concepts are a unifying and an integrative force that, when acted upon by the child's cognitive skills, provide the intellectual wherewithal for dealing with a wide variety of overt and covert experiences. John H. Flavell provides a most useful generic image in this regard when he speaks of the child "for whom the world is beginning to stand still and stay put, a world which, like the child himself, knows something of law and order, and above all a world in which thought really counts for something, in which thought can be a more trustworthy guide to action than perception" (4, p. 415). In addition, it seems that in certain crucial respects a wide variety of cognitive areas (number, quantity, time) are mastered according to a common procedure, and this discovery, Flavell says, was "an act of creative inspiration" on the part of Piaget.

Concept development merits a first-order rating in the teaching of reading as a thinking process. This is so because concepts are cognitive structures acquired through a complex and genuine act of thought, and they cannot be absorbed ready-made through memory or drill. A concept is symbolically embodied in a sign, usually a word and, as such, a word represents an act of generalization. Printed words are the representational symbols used in reading and writing and are the written counterparts of speech. In mastering speech, the child starts out by expressing both the vocal and semantic aspects of a word dimly and amorphously. At first the word is a generalization. *Da-da* as applied to all men is gradually replaced by a generalization of a higher order and leads in the end to a truer concept of *father*. The child connects two or three or more words and gradually advances to simple sentences and then to complex ones. When this occurs, the structure of words no longer mirrors the structure of thought. That is why words in and of themselves cannot simply be added ready-made to thought. The relationship between thought and word is not a symbol-experience "thing" but a process—a process that is undergoing constant change. Syntactically, the child may start with one word, then two or three, and then simple and complex sentences. Semantically, however, he starts from a whole, a meaningful complex, and gradually learns to divide and master the separate cognitive structures. The structure of speech develops from the particular to the whole, from word to sentence; the structure of meaning develops from the whole to the particular (11, p. 126). For children to acquire concepts and words to represent them they must use, to varying degrees of efficiency, such intellectual functions as deliberate attention, logical memory, abstraction, the ability to note likenesses and differences, and so on. To successfully instruct a school child, methods must be employed that will require pupils to be articulate about and put to deliberate use such intellectual functions.

Comprehension as a functional invariant of all reading instruction requires that from the very beginning of instruction the reading-to-learn phase take precedence over the learning-to-read phase. The semantic and syntactical aspects of the developmental process of learning to read are essentially one, precisely because of their similar directions; whereas in speech this is so precisely because of their reverse directions. The child learning to read brings with him the rich supply of concepts, meanings, and words acquired in his world of oral communication and needs only to learn to recognize the printed symbols of speech. As this is accomplished, the instructional emphasis should rapidly shift from recognizing printed words to that of concept development. This is so because reading in all phases of the curriculum becomes a principal source of knowledge. The everyday concepts and words the child brings with him to school and builds on in his early school life are roughed and hewed from experience of the face-to-face concrete variety. The acquisition of concepts of an historical, geographical, sociological, numerical, and scientific nature evolve from a certain level of maturation of everyday concepts and a "mediated" approach that give them body and vitality (11, Chap. 6).

Concept development has been dealt with in earlier chapters of this book, and the reader is urged to reread these sections. Of special significance is the discussion on pages 137–147 in Chapter 4. The earlier references to this vital topic are a part and parcel of the topic and are essential to an understanding of concept development. A thorough understanding of this topic is far more essential to purposes of sound reading instruction than is a mastery of phonic and structural analysis. This is the chapter and this is the area of reading instruction that merits, as a subtitle, "On Their Own in Reading."

WHAT IS A CONCEPT?

Many diifferent authorities agree about the inferences, attributes, and categories of a concept, but their definitions differ as they reflect the author's point of view. Understanding seems best facilitated by illustration, and an account of concept formation and attainment may prove more useful than a definition. Interesting enough, in this regard, is that Bruner, Goodnow, and Austin do not define a concept until page 244 of their text, *A Study of Thinking* (1), where it appears as a summation of an extensive account of the process of concept attainment. L. S. Vygotsky (11) did likewise in his text, *Thought and Language.*

Basically, concept formation consists of the perception of relationships —relationships among stimuli, as B. J. Underwood (10) put it—or relationships between constituent-part processes, as others have put it (1). Bruner *et al.* go on to say that "The working definition of a concept is the network of inferences that are or may be set into play by an act of categorizing" (1, p. 244). They have found it more meaningful, however, to regard a concept as "a network of sign-significate inferences by which one goes beyond a set of observed criterial properties exhibited by an object or event to the class identity of the object or event in question, and thence to additional inferences about other unobserved properties of the object or event" (1, p. 244). To this definition they add clarity by means of an "apple" illustration. An object is seen. The object has criterial properties. A set of these criterial properties is observed as *red* (a shade of color), *shiny* (a degree of brightness or dullness of appearance), and *roundish* (shape). Undoubtedly other properties or attributes are observed, even though they are unlisted by Bruner, who assumes apparently that the three listed are sufficiently illustrative. Now the network of sign-significate inferences leads the observer to conclude that the object observed is an apple. As an apple, the object has class identity. To make this inference, the observer, as pointed out, undoubtedly noted other criterial properties of *apple*, since any number of other things also possess the properties *red, shiny,* and *round* (ball, nose, tomato, glass). Also observed must have been certain fruit qualities: texture of surface, shape, smell, and taste, perhaps. On the basis of the inferences made thus far, particularly the class identity, other assumptions may now be made. Assumptions or inferences may be defined as a weighted average of previous experience and knowledge. The inferences are based on unobserved properties and result from extrapolations—a going beyond the information immediately given. It could be assumed, for instance, that the apple is delicious and contains therefore a certain relation of sugar to acid, or that it is nonpoisonous and is uncontaminated by sprays. Or, it might be assumed that, if left unrefrigerated, it will rot after a certain period of time. It is apparent then that, when these complex concepts are wisely made and appropriately used, we can reach new generalizations or concepts for which we have no direct evidence at the moment.

It seems obvious, as Vygotsky says, that when a concept is a part of a system it can become subject to conscious and deliberate control. He defines consciousness as "awareness of the activity of the mind," and this self-reflective awareness of meaning always implies a degree of generalization. Generalization, he says, in turn means the "formation of a superordinate concept" that includes as a particular case the given concept. "A superordinate concept," he says, "implies the existence of a series of subordinate concepts, and it also presupposes a hierarchy of concepts of different levels of generality. Thus the given concept is placed within a system of relationships of generality" (11, p. 92). He illustrates this emergence of a system by analyzing the circumstance in which a child has learned the word *flower* and later learns the word *rose*. For a time, the child may now use the two words *rose* and *flower* interchangeably. When, however, *flower* becomes generalized and more widely applicable and includes and subordinates *rose*, the relationship of the two changes in the child's mind. Thus, he says, a system is taking shape, and the child's knowledge of flowers as a superordinate concept and rose as a subordinate concept is becoming systematized.

Herbert J. Klausmeier quotes Bruner's definition of a concept and indicates that it serves well as an operational definition in experimentation with strategies. Then he goes on to state how a concept is attained (8, p. 3):

> In general terms, an organism senses environmental phenomena, discriminates between and among them, perceives common elements among some of them, and categorizes or classifies various phenomena as belonging to the same class or kind. The resulting abstraction or concept, often represented in a word or other symbol, is comprised of the meanings—network of inferences—associated with the abstraction.

Reference is made here to Klausmeier's general account of concept attainment because he has maintained the experimentation-with-strategies focus, has described attainment in terms of an immediate perceptual act (the experimental use of cards with discriminably different information on each card), and has indicated that the abstractions obtained are usually represented by a word or other symbol. This interpretation is excellent for experimental situations of the perceptual variety studied in concept attainment experiments. It is necessary, though, for teachers of reading as a thinking process to keep in mind the fine distinction Bruner makes between "perceptual" and "conceptual" forms of categorizing or concept attainment.

In *perceptual* categorizing, the relevant attributes used are immediately present and can be examined at first hand. The fitness of an object to be judged a member of this or that category is determined by the attributes immediately at hand. In *conceptual* categorizing the relevant attributes are not available to sensory examination and therefore are neither as readily determined nor as readily weighed as to their relevancy. Two illustrations may help bring this aspect of categorizing into clearer focus. In the field of history, supposing one wished to show that in 1840 the Whigs chose William Henry Harrison as their candidate for the Presidency not because he was a well-educated gentleman-farmer and public servant who was fond of quoting the Latin classics, but because he was a popular military figure, hero of Tippecanoe, and a man the Whigs believed could defeat the incumbent, Martin Van Buren. This would require a difficult and careful search of attributes and, most likely, a validation by consensus. Similarly, to plan and prepare and accomplish a Manned Orbital Research Laboratory that can be used to study man's ability to live in space as a necessary step toward achieving interplanetary space travel is requiring a most exacting defining of attributes, as well as creating new categories on logical grounds, until appropriate means are available to prove that the conclusions reached are test-worthy and sound.

It is readily apparent that to judge an object as being an *apple* and testing to prove it so is far more readily accomplished than to judge an historical reason for nominating a Presidential candidate or scientifically putting into operation a Manned Orbital Research Laboratory. Readily as apparent should be the fact that operations of the perceptual type are quite concrete in nature as compared to the abstractness of "conceptual" operations. As a matter of fact, it might be less confusing to refer to them as concrete and abstract because of the likely confusion that may prevail if "concept" and "conceptual" are not carefully discriminated. Even though perceptual situations lend themselves to laboratory experimenting and conceptual situations tend not to, and even though perceptual cases deal with observable attributes and conceptual cases deal primarily with cognitive attributes, the basic process of categorization is the same.

In summary, a concept is a network of inferences that are discriminated and categorized as belonging to the same object or event (class or kind), provides the bases for inferences about other categories, and is usually represented by a word (s) or other symbol. Concepts may be defined on a subordinate and superordinate basis and classified as a part of a system. In addition, they may be classified as perceptual (concrete) or conceptual (abstract), depending on the source of the attributes being used. A next step, now, is to consider how concepts are formed and attained.

CONCEPT FORMATION AND ATTAINMENT

A first step en route to concept attainment is concept formation, according to Bruner *el al.* (1, p. 22). Concept formation reflects an intimate aspect of the formation of hypotheses. An attempt must be made to sort particulars into some meaningful set of classes in the interest of ordering their diversity and forming a concept. Bruner's mushroom illustration is apt in this regard. Suppose a subject were examining mushrooms (without any prior knowledge or experience with mushrooms) to determine whether or not they were edible. He would bring to this task, most likely, concepts about edibles and nonedibles, plants, food preparation, and so on. His experience would suggest that he study mushrooms before using them as food. To *attain* the concept that he had formed about mushrooms, he now would proceed to find predictive defining attributes that would distinguish edible mushrooms (examples or exemplars) from nonedible mushrooms (not examples or nonexemplars).

In many ways it might be said that concept formation is both a first step and a last step in a spiraling extension and refinement of concepts. As a last step, once a concept has been established, as in the mushroom example on a concrete-perceptual level, additional hypotheses on the abstract-conceptual level might be set into play about other unobserved properties. For example, from the nonedible mushrooms it might be inferred that an antitoxin could be developed. A network of predictive defining attributes would need to be distinguished so that an act of categorization could be accomplished.

Categorization

Categorization is a process—an "act of invention." As such, it is probably the most significant aspect of cognition and is that one great quality of the mind that permits man to adjust to his environment.

Under the concept of *cars* one can deal with a vast assortment of models, makes, and styles and can do so quite adequately. Under the concept *truck*, another and different grouping can be made without many fine discriminations, such as half-ton truck, two-ton truck, and so on. The uniqueness of such categories is their usefulness and their economy. The concept *car* or *truck* does not need to be relearned each time a car or truck is being recognized. The many particulars that distinguish one model and make of car from that of another need not enslave man intellectually. Additional particularization will not be necessary unless he wishes to or needs to further systematize his knowledge of cars and trucks. If this were not the case, and man were required in each instance to discriminate in minute detail before a concept could be attained and used, he would, as Bruner says, be a slave to the particular (1, p. 19). As it is, man's intellectual freedom and responsibility is achieved by his capacity to categorize.

Will Durant indicates that the need to deal with generalities as well as particulars was a distinguishing factor between the philosophy of the Socratic-Platonic school and the Aristotelian school (3, p. 59):

There was, in the Socratic-Platonic demand for definitions, a tendency away from things and facts to theories and ideas, from particulars to generalities, from science to scholasticism; at last Plato became so devoted to generalities that they began to determine his particulars, so devoted to ideas that they began to define or select his facts. Aristotle preaches a return to things, to the "unwithered fact of nature" and reality; he had a lusty preference for the concrete particular. . . ."

Yet, he goes on to say, Aristotle took on many of the qualities of Plato, and he too remained "a lover of abstractions and generalities, repeatedly betraying the simple fact for some speciously bedizened theory. . . ." (3, p. 60.) Excess devotion to generalities can be as enslaving and stifling as excess devotion to particulars. Professors are often accused of just such a love for ideas and lack of appreciation for the lusty particulars of reality.

Bruner's definition of categorization is significant here (1, p. 1): "To categorize is to render discriminably different things equivalent, to group the objects and events and people around us into classes, and to respond to them in terms of their class memberships rather than their uniqueness." To render things *equivalent* is to render a set of discriminably different things (Ford, Chevrolet, Plymouth) as the same kind of thing (cars). In each decisioned response certain particulars or properties of cars are considered relevant and others irrelevant. This is different from the category of identity in which a variety of particulars are identified as a part of the same object. So one can slip into a car in a parking lot and note almost as if by intuition that, even though this car is *like* one's car, it is not one's car. This is so even though the identity of one's car also "changes" from day to day.

In summary, learning to categorize is a matter of knowing how to use the discriminable attributes of objects and events as a means of determining their significant identity. If, for example, you wished to discriminate between cars passing by as either a Ford, a Chevrolet, or a Plymouth, you would start by noting the characteristics of each car. You would note its general appearance, the shape of the hood, the top lines, the trunk arrangement, the grillwork, the headlight arrangement, the tail-light arrangement, the fins, and so on. Then you would confirm your appraisal by checking the make of the car by the name on the front of the car. A next step would be to try your skill on passing cars and see if other investigators would distinguish cars as you did, whether they follow your directions for doing so. Thus, you were using the test of consistency to validate the identities you categorized.

Strategies of Concept Attainment

Studies of concept attainment indicate that the steps involved are successive decisions, with the early decisions clearly affecting the degrees of freedom possible for the later decisions. At the very beginning, even before a person has dealt with a single instance, he has to make a decision about the nature of the task. Then he must decide on the most efficient way to attain the concept. All this is influenced by the consequences of the decisions made.

A strategy, according to Bruner *et al.,* is "a pattern of decisions in the acquisition, retention, and utilization of information that serves to meet certain objectives, i.e., to insure certain forms of outcome and to insure against certain others" (1, p. 54). A pattern is inferred from the instances a problem-solver seeking to attain a concept decides to test, the inferences he makes, and how he changes these as he meets different contingencies. The ideal for any concept-attainment task is to attain a concept with a minimum number of encounters (rapid solution) and with the least amount of cognitive strain (cognitive economy). Among the objectives of a strategy are the following (1, p. 54):

    a. To insure that the concept will be attained after the minimum number of encounters with relevant instances.

    b. To assure that a concept will be attained with certainty, regardless of the number of instances one must test *en route* to attainment.

    c. To minimize the amount of strain on inference and memory capacity while at the same time insuring that a concept will be attained.

    d. To minimize the number of wrong categorizations prior to attaining a concept.

What is *most creative about strategies employed* is that the pattern of decisions used so clearly reflects the demands of the situation. There is no one ideal strategy applicable to all situations. They alter with the nature of the concept to be attained, the circumstances (social-personal-physical) that exist, the consequences that seem reasonable, and so on.

How do people achieve, retain, and transform information necessary for isolating, learning, and using a concept without exceeding their cognitive capacity? Verbal reports of direct experience provide insufficient data to determine how concepts are attained, and accordingly studies have aimed at externalizing observations of the processes of decision-making. This pattern of decision-making is influenced by a number of circumstances: a definition of the task, the nature of the instances encountered, the nature of the validation, the consequences of specific categorizations, and the nature of imposed restrictions.

It seems apparent that the act of concept or category formation—the inventive act by which classes are constructed—can be stripped down to the following (1, pp. 233–234):

    1. There is an array of *instances* to be tested, and from this testing is to come the attainment of the concept. The instances can be characterized in terms of their *attributes*, e.g. color, weight per volume, and in terms of attribute *values*, the particular color, the particular weight per volume, etc.

    2. With each instance, or at least most of them once the task is underway, a person makes a tentative prediction or decision. . . .

3. Any given decision will be found to be correct, incorrect, or varyingly indeterminate. . . . We refer to this as *validation* of a decision. . . .

4. Each decision-and-test may be regarded as providing potential *information* by limiting the number of attributes and attribute values that can be considered. . . .

5. The sequence of decisions made by the person en route to attaining the concept, i.e., en route to the discovery of more or less valid cues, may be regarded as a strategy embodying certain objectives. . . .

6. Any decision about the nature of an instance may be regarded as having consequences for the decision-maker. . . .

The scientist, the scholar, or any "learner" for that matter, is faced constantly with "the task of assimilating information, conserving cognitive strain, and regulating the risk of failure and folly." This is the behavior of problem-solving or thinking in everyday life. Taking the broad view, Bruner *et al.* believe that (1, p. 246) "virtually all cognitive activity involves and is dependent on the process of categorizing," and that the act of categorizing "derives from man's capacity to infer from sign to significance." Thus it seems that concept development and thinking are virtually synonymous. Bruner *et al.* also report that they have been struck by "the notable flexibility and intelligence of our subjects in adapting their strategies to the information, capacity and risk requirements we have imposed on them" (1, p. 238). Similarly, it may be added that in a parallel sense it is astounding to watch six-year-olds adapt to the rigors of a Directed-Reading-Thinking Activity. They show themselves to be very flexible and intelligent and resourceful in adapting their inferences to the information at hand. They display ability to reduce the number of cues available to fit a pattern, to deal with partially valid cues, and to resolve conflicting cues.

PIAGET AND COGNITIVE FUNCTIONING

The one person who has probably contributed most to our understanding of concept development and who has provided the impetus for others to do so is Jean Piaget. His method of studying child behavior is designed to get to the heart of a child's cognitive structure and describe it as it really is. His experiments are designed to permit a child to move on his own intellectually and to display the cognitive structure that is unique to him at that period in his development. Even though Piaget prefers the clinical method to the more standardized method, he is fully aware of the risks involved. As a matter of fact, he suggests a minimum of a year of daily clinical practice before an examiner is ready to move beyond the fumbling level. To operate clinically is no simple task and must be subject to the most strict criticism.

It is because of Piaget's distinctive contribution that a section of this chapter is devoted to him. And, it is because John H. Flavell (4) and J, McV. Hunt (6) have made such thorough studies of Piaget and have written so discerningly about him that their texts will be used as a principal source of reference.

Functional Invariants

A salient feature of Piaget's work is his interest in intelligence. He allies intelligence with biology in the sense that it conditions for us a mode of intellectual functioning. We do not inherit cognitive structures but a way of transacting cognitive business with our environment. This biological endowment of critically unstructured matter has two principal defining attributes that are said to be invariant over the whole developmental span—organization and adaptation. Flavell says (4, p. 43): "All living matter adapts to its environment and possesses organizational properties which make the adaptation possible." The invariant properties of intellectual functioning are the same as those in biological functioning.

The invariant processes of assimilation and accommodation also characterize the dynamic aspect of intellectual functioning. As a matter of fact, Piaget states that, when these two aspects of a cognitive act are in equilibrium or in balance, they constitute intellectual adaptation. Organization and adaptation are complementary processes in which cognitive organization presupposes some kind of interpretation of external reality, and adaptation is an assimilation of that something to some kind of meaning system.

Assimilation and accommodation is essentially a unitary event, and even the most elemental cognitive incorporation of reality means a coming to grips with the shapes reality presents. To assimilate an event is to accommodate to it. These are the two mechanisms of intellectual adaptation that make cognitive progress possible. When a newly accommodated-to feature is fitted into the existing meaning structure, it will assimilate to that structure and tend to change the structure and thus make possible further accommodatory extensions. This continuous process is a potent source of cognitive progress and makes possible deeper and deeper intellectual penetration into the nature of things. Furthermore the reason for the slow but steady cognitive progress rests in the fact that, as Flavell says, "the organism can assimilate only those things which past assimilations have prepared it to assimilate" (4, p. 50). By virtue of the fact that a primary function of assimilation is to make the "unfamiliar familiar," Piaget labels the process a conservative one.

The Concept of Schema

If new cognitive structures are going to be assimilated and accommodated so as to be functional, it presupposes some sort of enduring organization or structure system within the child. This Piaget refers to not as *structure* but as *schema*. Flavell defines a schema as "a cognitive structure which has reference to a class of similar action sequences, these sequences of necessity being strong, bounded totalities in which the constituent behavioral elements are tightly interrelated" (4, p. 53). As Flavell says, this is a rather forbidding definition. He goes on to say that schemas are named by their *referent action sequences* as schema of sucking, schema of sight, schema of intuitive qualitative correspondence, and so on. But even this is not a complete picture. When an infant performs an organized sequence of grasping behaviors, it implies also that a specific cognitive structure, an *organized disposition* to grasp, has been generated, and that a new behavioral totality has become a part of the child's intellectual repertory. "In brief, a schema is the organized behavior content which names it. . . ." The action sequence must have behavior components which when set into motion form a strong whole. Flavell says that "Schemas therefore refer to *classes* of total acts, acts which are distinct from one another and yet share common features" (4, p. 54). Being cognitive structures they are plastic organizations that adapt and change their structure to fit reality. Also, they are both created and modified by intellectual functioning.

Hunt says that Piaget takes the view that "the organism always acts in terms of the centrally organized, Gestalt-like structures which it has present. . . . Moreover, these structures . . . are observed as repeatable and generalizable pieces of behavior termed *schemata*. . . ." (6, p. 112.) He also points out that the ready-made reflexive schemata of the infant (such as the schema of sucking) become progressively transformed into the logical organizations of adult intelligence. Thus the picture of the development of intelligence is one of continuous transformations in the organizations or structures of intelligence.

A singular characteristic of schemas is their tendency toward repeated application. The organized behavior totalities such as sucking have an almost repetition-compulsion character of assimilation that Piaget speaks of as *reproductive* or *functional assimilation*. Once schemas are constituted, Flavell says, "they apply themselves again and again to assimilable aspects of the environment" (4, p. 55). Thus the newborn child soon attempts to adapt various objects into the global schema of sucking. Gradually, though, the infant begins to discriminate objects that are to be sucked only when one is hungry, and an element of recognition occurs within the initially undifferentiated schema of sucking. Thus we have seen the three basic functional and developmental characteristics of schema. According to Flavell, "Repetition consolidates and stabilizes it, as well as providing the necessary condition for change. Generalization enlarges it by extending its domain of application. And differentiation has the consequence of dividing the originally global schema into several new schemas, each with a sharper, more discriminating focus on reality" (4, p. 57).

A Conception of Intelligence

Piaget's observations concerning the interlocking systems of schema that develop through the continued operation of organization as well as assimilation and accommodation are crucial in determining the nature of cognition and represent fundamental properties of intelligence. Hunt says that Piaget's observations demonstrate empirically what the concepts of "a vertical hierarchy of information-processing operations and a continuous interaction between the organism and the environment mean. . . ." (6, p. 109.) He also points out that "a conception of intelligence as problem-solving capacity based on a hierarchial organization of symbolic representations and information-processing strategies deriving to a considerable degree from past experience" is emerging from several sources including, interestingly enough, Piaget's observations of children. Piaget conceives of the interaction between an organism and its environment as corresponding to inner organization and outer adaptation that results in continually reorganizing the structures of the mind. Because Piaget is primarily interested in investigating the qualitative development of intellectual structures, Flavell thought it timely to compare Piaget's position with four interpretations of intelligence: associationism, intellectualism, Gestalt theory, and the theory of groping.

It is no accident, according to Piaget, that as the child matures he develops a hierarchy of values and systems; rather it is dependent on the nature of the cognitive organization so far developed.

Action or actions apparently constitute the key aspect of all cognitive functioning. The overt slow-paced sensory-motor actions of the infant become progressively internalized and eventually are transformed into adult logical operations of abstract schema possessing reversibility, a group property called an inverse, and organized into systems of lightning-quick, covert operations. Thus overt actions (slow moving and concrete) and covert actions (internalized, mobile, and abstract) involve action as the common denominator of cognitive behavior.

PERIODS OF INTELLECTUAL DEVELOPMENT

It is Piaget's belief that, in educating a child, one should parallel the developmental process of the internalization of cognitive actions. Again in this regard he is placing emphasis on the action or active aspect of intelligence and is using this as a basis for theoretical emphasis on teaching and learning. This being the case, it is timely at this point to provide a description of the stages of intellectual development as he conceives of them.

The most difficult and demanding aspect of writing this chapter was to condense the abundant source material into a few pages. The discussion of Piaget, for example, barely scrapes the surface of his contributions, and the coverage that follows on the taxonomy of the developmental picture is at best only a very brief outline.

The Sensorimotor Period

The congenital sensorimotor schemata of reflexes or instincts apparently are the only "organizations" available at birth. This sensorimotor period extends from birth to about two years of age. It is the time when the infant moves from the reflex level to the forming of schemata that represent a relatively coherent organization of generalized, coordinated, and differentiated actions. The schemata apply almost entirely to the immediate environment and represent largely simple perceptual and motor adjustments. They do to a degree represent the elementary operations of cognitive functioning, even though the adjustments are primarily "to things" and do not represent internalized symbolic manipulations.

It is during this time and through a series of six major stages, as declared by Piaget, that the child begins to construct reality and begins to internalize schemata. The following account of the six stages is based on Flavell's description in Chapter 3 of his text (4): (1) the use of Reflexes (0–1 month); (2) the First Required Adaptations and the Primary Circular Reaction (1–4 months); (3) the Secondary Circular Reactions (4–8 months); (4) the Coordination of the Secondary Schemata (8–12 months); (5) the Tertiary Circular Reactions (12–18 months); and (6) the Invention of New Means Through Mental Combinations (18–24 months). Flavell makes two qualifications with regard to these levels. First, each stage is defined by the most advanced behaviors found within it. Second, the age intervals are at best only rough averages.

Preoperational Thought

This period might appropriately be divided into two subperiods: first, the period of preparation or preoperational representation; second, the period of concrete operations. The former extends roughly from ages two to seven; the latter from ages seven to eleven. The first is also the time in which the individual begins to come to grips with the world of symbols. The second is the period when his conceptual organization of his environment begins to take on stability and coherence and does so by means of a series of cognitive structures called *groupings*.

Again the reader is urged to keep in mind that this account represents a sharply curtailed digest of the original. At best it is not even a summary of a summary and requires the addition of another "summary" idea—one three times removed from the original. This forthright statement of circumstances is made not to alarm the reader but to impress him with the scope of the original and, perchance, to motivate him to read at least a comprehensive summary of the original, such as the one prepared by Flavell or the one by Hunt.

The preoperational subperiod is the time when the child moves from the level at which his best intellectual activity is a sensory-motor act to the point where he can do some manipulating of reality by means of inner, symbolic acts. A look at particular aspects of the general developmental evolution seems in order to introduce specific categories of experience or specialized types of intellectual achievements that are formed into "constructs." Reference is made in particular to the achievement of construction in imitation, play, objects, space, causality, and time. In all of this, keep in mind that the development proceeds from undifferentiation to differentiation, from unintentional to intentional, and from unintelligent to intelligent adaptations.

Advance in *imitation* is characterized by a child's ability to imitate "complex" new models, to imitate actions of objects, and to defer imitation by reproducing through memory an absent model or an act seen a day earlier. Advance in *play* is marked by true make-believe and circumstances in which models that are not at all like the original are used to re-enact play. Piaget describes the play action of a child who used a cloth as a pillow and played being asleep. A major breakthrough is made in dealing with *objects* when the child sees them as substantiated things that exist in space and exist independent of self. Piaget pretended to hide a coin in spot A, then in spot B, and finally did hide it in spot C; his daughter looked in each location in the A, B, C order until she found the coin.

THE ROUTE TO SYMBOLIC FUNCTION

Thus far the developmental aspects of cognitive functions have been defined primarily in terms of sensory-motor functions. Intelligence as such has been labeled as sensory-motor intelligence. This form of intelligence differs in profound ways from conceptual intelligence or representational intelligence. The chief intellectual requirement for representation is the ability to treat a sign as a means of signifying a perceptually absent event. The ability to do this, to make the act of reference, is called "symbolic function" by Piaget.

The route to symbolic functioning is characterized by a cognitive form that is far more encompassing than sensory-motor intelligence could ever be. First, representational thought, because of its symbolic nature, can recall the past, represent the present, and anticipate the future in one brief and mobile act, whereas sensory-motor functioning is a one-by-one succession of perceptual acts. Second, representational thought can reflect on, meditate on, or contempaltae a source of action. Sensory-motor functioning can pursue concrete goals but cannot search for truth reflectively. Third, representational thought can extend its scope to the past, to the future, and to the intangible, whereas sensory-motor functioning is limited to the manipulation of concrete acts and objects. Fourth, representational thought becomes socialized as a whole culture shares in a language—a system of codified symbols. Sensory-motor cognition by contrast is a private affair, limited to actions in reality as compared with the representation of reality.

As the child moves toward concrete operational concepts along the lines defined above, his progress is marked by a number of transitional phases. Two merit special note. First, he becomes increasingly more able to address himself to a specific task and to do so in an intelligent way, testing conditions as he proceeds. Second, in Flavell's words, "the rigid, static, and irreversible structures typical of preoperational thought organization begin, in Piaget's phrasing . . . to 'thaw out' and become more flexible, mobile, and above all decentered and reversible in their operation" (4, p. 163).

Concrete Operations

Thus far, intellectual development has been traced from birth through the sensory-motor period (about age twenty-four months), up through the preoperational or preschool period. The preoperational child differs from the sensory-motor infant chiefly in that he can operate on a representational level as opposed to direct action. The concrete-operational child operates on the representational level also and differs from the pre-schooler in that he has at his command a more coherent and integrated cognitive system that is flexible and plastic and yet consistent and enduring. This system of actions permits him to organize and manipulate the world around him more effectively. As the central neural processes become more and more autonomous, the development of symbolic behavior continues through the adaptive use of motoric and imagistic symbols to a representational activity that uses language as the predominant symbolic vehicle. Language becomes the mediator.

The *sine qua non* of representational thought appear to be reversibility (every logical or mathematical operation is reversible), mobile equilibrium (a system of balanced interchanges in which the transformations compatible with the relationships of a system compensate each other), and conservation (the cognition that certain properties remain invariant in the face of certain transformations). Most of the account of concrete operations is an elaboration of these points, with the meaning of operations taking on special significance. In Piaget's own words, to understand the development of knowledge the idea of an *operation* becomes central.

To know an object, to know an event, is not simply to look at it and make a mental copy, or image, of it. To know an object is to act on it. . . . An operation is an interiorized action . . . it is a reversible action; that is, it can take place in both directions, for instance, adding or subtracting, joining or separating . . . above all an operation is never isolated. It is always linked to other operations, and as a result it is always part of a total structure. For instance, a logical class does not exist in isolation; what exists is the total structure of classification . . . an operation is thus the essence of knowledge. . . . In other words it is a set of actions modifying the object, and enabling the knower to get at the structure of the transformation. (9, p. 8.)

Flavell says (4, p. 166): "A useful rule of thumb, one Piaget has used, . . . is to say that all the actions implied in common mathematical symbols like $+$, $-$, $\times$, $\div$, $=$, $<$, $>$, etc., belong to, but do not exhaust, the domain of what he terms *intellectual operation*."

Piaget believes that the languages of mathematics and logic provide the vehicle with which to formulate the properties of "concrete operations" and make models of the organization and process of cognition. Both these languages, he points out, reflect action. In an algebraic expression each term denotes specific action: $(+)$ refers to combining, $(=)$ expresses a possible substitution, $(-)$ a separation, $(\times^2)$ the action of reproducing 'X' X times, and so on. In the same way two classes can be added like numbers (deciduous and nondeciduous) (constitute all trees). The word *and* like the logical sign $+$ represents the action of combining. Classifying may be either an act of sorting or an implicit act. Or, two asymmetrical relations $(A > B; B > C)$ may be arranged in a series of increasing size by placing A, B, and C serially. Classifying may be done from several points of view and be said to correspond to overt actions and to operations of thought.

Formal Operations

Beginning at about age eleven or twelve a major transition occurs in that, instead of observation directing thought, the adolescent's thought directs his observations. As a result, two significant achievements are obtained. He now has the essential capacity for using the hypothetico-deductive scientific method, and he also acquires the capacity for social reform, because he can now compare imagined ideal conditions for society with the observed conditions.

In the concrete operational stage, the child must have objects to manipulate (dolls, walking sticks, leaves, etc.) in order to produce performances that show logico-arithmetical properties. But at the formal operations stage children acquire a capacity to deal with verbal expressions of logical relationships. This transformation shows in several ways. A child can operate by means of propositions; he can consider the hypothetical possibilities of a general law; his thought about what is hypothetically possible directs his perceptions and actions. Now he need no longer confine his attention to the real. Hunt says (pp. 230–231), "He can consider hypotheses which may or may not be true, and consider what would follow if they were true. He can follow the form of an argument while disregarding its concrete content. It is from this last characteristic that *formal operations* get their name." The abstract character of the formal operational structure shows in a number of ways. When combinations are involved, all possible combinations are taken into account. When comparison is involved it is made selectively by varying one factor while "all other things are equal" or "the rule of one variable."

The formal operations described in terms of their logico-mathematical properties include proportionality scheme, the sixteen binary operations of the Borlean logical calculus, and the INRC group structure. The account Hunt gives of the sixteen binary operations of two-valued propositional logic involves a combinational analysis of operations as distinct from a combining of classes. This corresponds with a structure which mathematicians call "lattices" and logicians call "the calculus of propositions." Suppose a proposition concerns classes of animals divided in two ways. (V) vertebrates and (I) invertebrates and into those that (T) live on land or are terrestrial and (A) those that live in the water or are aquatic. The concrete-operational child faced with the problem of describing the animals on a newly discovered planet would assign them to four possible classes based on the two-way classification (VT), (VA), (IT), and (IA). The formal-operations child would be capable of considering all the different classes of animals conceivable. He might set up a table similar to the following one before beginning his exploration (6, p. 232):

(1) No animals at all
(2) Only (VT)
(3) Only (VA)
(4) Only (IT)
(5) Only (IA)
(6) (VT) and (VA), but no (IT) or (IA)
(7) (VT) and (IT), but no (VA) or (IA)

(8) (VT) and (IA), but no (VA) or (IT)
(9) (VA) and (IT), but no (VT) or (IA)
(10) (VA) and (IA), but no (VT) or (IT)
(11) (IT) and (IA), but no (VA) or (VT)
(12) (VT), (VA), and (IT), but no (IA)
(13) (VT), (VA), and (IA), but no (IT)
(14) (VT), (IT), and (IA), but no (VA)
(15) (VA), (IT), and (IA), but no (VT)
(16) All four classes

Formal thinking, as it explains the adolescent's capacity to deal with the future and the hypothetical as well as his adaptation to the world of adults, is both thinking about thought and a reversal of relations between what is real and what is possible. "These are the two characteristics . . . which are the source of the living responses, always so full of emotion, which the adolescent uses to build his ideals in adapting to society" (7, p. 341). The adolescent reflects a new form of egocentricism. It must be kept in mind that, according to Piaget's theory, egocentrism is apt to increase whenever a subject copes with a new and untried field of cognitive functioning. For the adolescent it takes the form of a kind of naïve idealism in which he dreams of a glorious future and of transforming the world through ideas and tends to disregard the practical obstacles of the empirical world.

PIAGET AND EDUCATION

Piaget Rediscovered is the title of a report of conferences held at Cornell University and the University of California to re-examine some of Piaget's work on the cognitive development of children. The conferences were fruitful insofar as education is concerned; the papers appearing in the report testify well to this. The first paper is prepared by Eleanor Duckworth, a former student of Piaget's at the Institute of Genetic Epistemology in Geneva, Switzerland. She also served as Piaget's translator at both conferences referred to. Her paper is primarily concerned with the implications for educational practice of Piaget's approach.

She starts her paper by saying that everybody in education realizes that

Piaget is saying something that is relevant to the teaching of children. Of course, not everybody in education realizes this, but many do, and each year many more are learning about Piaget. The principal outcome of Piaget's theory of intellectual development is that "children be allowed to do their own learning." Teachers must present children with situations in which they themselves experiment by trying things out to see what happens, by manipulating things, by posing questions and seeking answers, by reconciling what they find at one time with what they find at another, and by comparing their findings with each other. She quotes Piaget as saying (2, p. 3), "The goal in education is not to increase the amount of knowledge, but to create the possibilities for a child to invent and discover. When we teach too fast, we keep the child from inventing and discovering for himself. . . . Teaching means creating situations where structures can be discovered; it does not mean transmitting structures which may be assimilated at nothing other than a verbal level."

Piaget also made two points about teacher education that are timely at this point. First, teachers can learn better by doing things than by being told about them. Second, prospective teachers should spend some time questioning children in a one-to-one situation. This way they would discover for themselves how difficult it is to understand what children mean, and perhaps even more important, how difficult it is to make oneself understood by children. This could have a sobering effect on the teacher who is thinking about teaching an entire class of children at one time.

Piaget believes the adage that experience is a good teacher but that it keeps a dear school. He says that experience is essential for intellectual development. But more than experience is required. The child must be active, must transform things, and must discover the structure of his own actions on the objects. By *active* he means two things: to act on material things; and to do things in social collaboration, in a group effort. This, he says, leads to a critical frame of mind because children must communicate with each other. Cooperation becomes co-operation, and this he considers an essential factor in intellectual development. Note how similar this is to the theoretical basis for a group-type Directed Reading-Thinking Activity and how the details of a D-R-T-A spell out the processes. (See Chapters 1–5.)

The one concept of Piaget's that a great many educators have heard about is *egocentrism*. It is also perhaps the most widely misunderstood, says Flavell, as he defines the concept (4, p. 60): "It denotes a cognitive state in which the cognizer sees the world from a single point of view only—his own— but without knowledge of the existence of viewpoints or perspectives and, *a fortiori*, without awareness that he is the prisoner of his own." It is when the individual is most self-centered that he knows himself the least. The process of "knowing thyself" is a continuous one and requires repeated reconstituting at different stages in life. The fabric of reality must be objectified and penetrated deeper and deeper if the self is to be conceptualized as a distinct and separate entity that sees reality from a particular viewpoint. In short, intelligent function, when equilibrium obtains, requires a fine balance between a person and his milieu so that both a realistic (accommodation) and meaningful (assimilation) rapport is secured. As Flavell says (4, p. 65), "cognition always begins on the margins of both self and milieu and works its way simultaneously into the inner regions of each." See again the discussion on play and imitation to note how these two kinds of cognition do not keep this balance. Play can be "riotously autistic" and allow dreams and dreamlike activity and various kinds of make-believe to be slavish and naïvely unrealistic. When a relative balance is maintained between assimilation and accommodation, some kind of adapted intelligence is operating. The needed logical structures are obtained only through internal equilibration and only by self-regulation and not by external imposition.

There are two basic premises upon which Piaget's prescriptions for education rest. One concerns the relation between a student and the content he is to learn. The other has to do with relations among students in the process of learning. It is the second major point—the role of social interaction—that fits into this discussion on egocentrism and leads to a highly relevant conclusion concerning teaching methods. Over and over again Piaget stresses the paramount importance of interaction with peers as the principal means of liberating a child from his egocentrism and as the principal means of gaining perspective. By pitting his thoughts against those of others and noting similarities and differences, the child can acquire the rationality and objectivity that only a multiperspective view can confer.

To the educator this means group activities, projects to be undertaken in common, planning sessions, discussions, sharing, and the like. The teacher must provide the wherewithal which the children can use to decide things by themselves. They must hypothesize and verify—experimentally in the sciences, deductively in mathematics, inductively in the social sciences.

Thus the first basic premise, or Piaget's major dictum to educators, rests on the word *action*. A student, in order to form stable and enduring cognitions, must be led to perform real actions on the materials that form the learning base, actions as concrete and direct as the materials allow. It is the teacher's task to analyze the content to be learned in terms of the operations implicit in it. This done, he must arrange the learning materials so that these operations can be carried out by the student himself. And above all, he must see to it that the student carries out the operations.

This leads to another key concept in Piaget's general theory that it is necessary for education to use. The role of concrete actions in situations that provide maximal perceptual support for such actions is of first-order importance. Gradually the transformation from the development and schematization of overt actions into mental operation occurs. The teacher must aid and abet this internalization and schematization process in the classroom. She must do this by getting the student to do the needed actions with less and less direct teacher support. She must have him proceed to cognitive anticipations and retrospections of operations until the originally external overt actions can take place internally and reflectively. This internalization-of-actions view of cognitive development is fundamental.

The child as a learning subject must be active because learning is possible only if there is active assimilation. In keeping with this is the concept that assimilation is the integration of any sort of reality into a structure. This applies not only in organizing and explaining certain known cognitive facts and relationships, but also in suggesting the existence of facts and relationships not yet discovered. Thus the approach can be both logical and empirical. The logical structures can be viewed as precise and parsimonious characterizations of ideal cognition in the realm of classes and relations and serve as a framework for investigating more specific intellectual attainments.

Finally, all development is faced with conflicts and incompatibilities. These must not be of such a nature as to overwhelm the subject but must permit him to discover relationships and thus reach a higher level of equilibrium. Also, of course, there must be present operative aspects that enable the subject to get at the structures of the transformation and thus from one state to another. Duckworth quotes Piaget as saying (2, p. 5):

> The principal goal of education is to create men who are capable of doing new things, not simply of repeating what other generations have done—men who are creative, inventive, and discoverers. The second goal of education is to form minds which can be critical, can verify, and not accept everything they are offered. The great danger today is of slogans, collective opinions, ready-made trends of thought. We have to be able to resist individually, to criticize, to distinguish between what is proven and what is not. So we need pupils who are active, who learn early to find out by themselves, partly by their own spontaneous activity and partly through material we set up for them; who learn early to tell what is verifiable and what is simply the first idea to come to them.

SUMMARY

The major purpose of most reading instruction is to improve comprehension. To comprehend means to understand as thoroughly as circumstances permit. The limiting factors are the maturity of the reader and the capabilities of the writer. Of course, it is the reader's purpose for reading that primarily determines how he will read, what he will read, and what he expects from what he reads. And it is the reader's purpose that is primarily determined by his level of conceptual development and his cognitive functioning. This is why concept development has been given so central a position in this text.

Reading is a mental process, as is concept development. To a large degree the processes are similar. The untrained child acquires concepts and functions cognitively much as does the trained child. The major difference is that the child being trained is taught to pursue excellence and to do so deliberately as he is brought into contact with the curriculum. Both processes are active processes—questioning, testing, inventing, and generally information-processing and -producing. It is not the processes themselves that produce excellence, but rather the active and voluntary use of the processes. Purposeful information-generating behavior yields cognitive-processing economy and reading-processing efficiency and makes it possible for the child to go beyond the information given.

It is not at all difficult to agree with Piaget's statement that the principal goal of education is to create students capable of doing new things—students who are creative, inventive, and discoverers. Cognitive functioning that pursues excellence requires just such performing. Reading performance in the pursuit of excellence makes similar demands. Each new word, each new phrase or clause, each new sentence, each paragraph, each page, each chapter requires the reader to create, to invent, to discover.

It is not at all difficult to agree with Piaget's second goal of education —to form minds that can be critical and can verify. If this is the grist of cognitive functioning, it certainly is of reading. The great danger today is of "slogans, collective opinions, ready-made trends of thought" transmitted either by voice or by print. The only way to resist is to do so individually. Each pupil must be taught to pursue excellence actively. Each pupil must learn to criticize, to tell what is verifiable, to distinguish between what is proved and what is not.

A problem solver seeking to attain a concept makes inferences, tests the inferences, and changes the inferences as he meets new contingencies. He has strategy that helps him make decisions. The ideal is to obtain a concept with a minimum number of encounters and with the greatest cognitive economy. What is creative about the strategies used is that the patterns clearly reflect the demands of the situation. No one ideal strategy is applicable to all situations. Strategies change with the nature of the concept to be attained, the circumstances (social-personal-physical) that exist, the consequences that seem reasonable, and so on.

As concepts are attained and reality is objectified, an increasingly undistorted knowledge of self is obtained. This self-realization goes on throughout life and represents a dual progression. It permits one to penetrate deeper and deeper into the concept of self, and it permits one to penetrate deeper and deeper into the fabric of reality. Egocentrisim can and does appear in various forms at different levels of development from childhood through adulthood. At all levels, clarity of a conceptual-symbolic nature comes about only as one learns to see things from points of view other than his own.

Intelligence is coming to be viewed as problem-solving capacity. This capacity is based on a hierarchical organization of symbolic representations on the one hand and information-processing strategies on the other —both deriving to a considerable degree from past experience. The interaction between an individual and his environment (accommodation and assimiliation) results in continually reorganizing the structures of the mind.

Action or actions constitute the key aspect of all cognitive functioning. Overt actions (slow moving and concrete) and covert actions (internalized, mobile, abstract) involve action as the common denominator of cognitive behavior. It is no accident that as the child matures he develops a hierarchy of values and systems, but rather it is the result of the cognitive organization so far developed.

The route to symbolic functioning is characterized by a cognitive form (representational thought) that is far more encompassing than perceptual or senory-motor representation and than iconic representation or imagery. Representational thought can recall the past, represent the present, and anticipate the future in one brief and mobile act; it can reflect on, mediate, or contemplate a source of action; it can extend its scope to the past, to the future, and to the intangible; it becomes socialized as a whole culture shares in a system of codified symbols. This suggests clearly that the symbolic function of representational thought is a general facility basic to both private symbols (dreams, symbolic play, imitation) and social signs (words and mathematical and scientific symbols). Obviously, though, language is the system *par excellence* without which thought could never become really socialized and logical. The *sine qua non* of representational thought appear to be reversibility (every logical or mathematical operation is reversible), mobile equilibrium (a system of balanced interchanges), and conservation (certain properties remain invariant in the face of certain transformations).

REFERENCES

1. Bruner, Jerome S., Jacqueline J. Goodnow, and George A. Austin, *A Study of Thinking,* New York, Wiley, 1956.
2. Duckworth, Eleanor, "Piaget Rediscovered," *Piaget Rediscovered,* a report of the Conference on Cognitive Studies and Curriculum Development, Ithaca, N.Y., School of Education, Cornell University, March, 1964, pp. 1–5.
3. Durant, Will, *The Story of Philosophy,* New York, Time Book Division, 1962.
4. Flavell, John H., *The Developmental Psychology of Jean Piaget,* Princeton, N.J., Van Nostrand, 1963.
5. Hamilton, Edith, *The Greek Way,* New York, Norton, 1942.
6. Hunt, J. McV., *Intelligence and Experience,* New York, Ronald, 1961.
7. Inhelder, B., and J. Piaget, *The Growth of Logical Thinking from Childhood to Adolescence,* New York, Basic Books, 1958.
8. Klausmeier, Herbert J., *Strategies in Concept Attainment,* a paper presented at the American Educational Research meeting, Chicago, February, 1963.
9. Piaget, Jean, "Development and Learning," *Piaget Rediscovered,* a report of the Conference on Cognitive Studies and Curriculum Development, Ithaca, N.Y., School of Education, Cornell University, March, 1964, pp. 7–20.
10. Underwood, B. J., "An Orientation for Research on Thinking," *Psychological Review, 59* (1952), 209–220.
11. Vygotsky, L. S., *Thought and Language,* New York, Wiley, 1962.

Chapter 11 ⋇⋇ Evaluation

"All teaching is diagnostic" is an axiom that should prepossess all teachers when they think about teaching and testing, particularly reading, because reading is a cognitive process—not a subject, like science and arithmetic. Every time a teacher directs a reading activity she should be gauging the effectiveness with which the pupils use the reading process. In other words, how effectively did the pupils achieve the purposes for reading by adjusting their rate and method of reading to the nature and complexity of the material?

If the teacher keeps this question in mind constantly, she will be able to focus her attention on the individual and his use of the process. Every time a pupil reads as a participant in a planned reading activity, he does so with his own particular aptitudes, abilities, and previous skill achievement. Every time the teacher has an opportunity to observe a pupil reading, she should be able to give a brief account of the reading-skill level at which he started and the advances he may have made to a new level of competency. Obviously, the better the teacher understands the reading process, the better she will be able to tell how effectively a pupil has used the process and describe his level of efficiency.

Teachers watching a demonstration of a group Directed Reading-Thinking Activity can make rather discerning observations about a group of children they are seeing in action for the first time. On many occasions the writer has used specially selected groups of children for demonstration purposes. On occasion a group is selected so as to have three good readers, four average readers, and three below-average readers. The classroom teacher of the children is asked to select a group representing this range of performance. The ten children are then directed as they read a selection from a basic reader chosen to be generally representative of the instructional level of the four average readers. After the demonstration, the observers are asked to identify the three good readers and the three below-average readers, and invariably they do so correctly. How can they do this?

There are symptoms of good and poor reading performances that are readily observable. Invariably, a first sign reported by the observing group is the number of requests the pupils made for help in word recognition. A second symptom is the oral rereading performance. A third is the time required when reading silently. Other evidences cited are lip movement, finger pointing, head movement, book position, pupil enthusiasm, and so on. These readily observable conditions represent some of the factors that characterize inefficient reading and are useful in telling where the learner is. Usually, the observers are astonished to note that they have discovered so many things about each reader in the course of one D-R-T-A, and they begin to realize that if they could see the same children perform again and again they would soon have a detailed and accurate account of each pupil's reading performance.

This is one good way to create among teachers the attitude that each D-R-T-A can be diagnostic. It is one good way, too, to have them realize that if so much can be learned about each pupil by an unsophisticated observer, there must be a lot more to observe.

If learning is thought of as "a change, due to experience, in the students' way of thinking, feeling, and acting" (3, p. 386), education may be regarded as "a system of learning experiences which bring about certain desirable changes in students." A system of learning experiences suggests that the experiences are selected and planned with a view to their effectiveness in helping the learner advance toward a given set of objectives. In this regard the experiences differ from a sequence of life experiences that occur at random. It is to be noted, too, that again the word *change* represents a key concept. It is the learner who must have the experience. It is the learner who must be affected by the experience. It is the learner who must change.

The teacher may be very active in creating and arranging the condition under which the learning is to take place. To do this she must be clear about the changes that the learning process is to bring about. It also requires that she determine whether the changes have been brought about and whether all the learners have been affected, and to what degree. In short, sound reading instruction must be based on a clear understanding of the reading process, full consideration of the characteristics of the reader, and a means for measuring the changes that may have occurred.

By virtue of the fact that reading is a process, determining what takes place in a reading situation is in sharp contrast to the use of pre- and post-tests to measure the products of reading. Certainly the teacher must find ways of penetrating beyond the symptoms of inefficiency (lip movement, finger pointing, slow rate, faltering oral rereading, and so on) to a more precise accounting of what takes place when one reads for meaning and is cognitively effective. To manage the reading process so as to develop a reader's command of knowledge requires, as Robert L. Ebel says (6, p. 41), "development of relationships between words and things, between instances and generalizations, between concepts and principles." Command of reading obviously involves thinking, which both requires and produces it. Proficiency in reading requires ready availability of relevant knowledge in science, mathematics, literature, and so on, and the understanding of the relations between things. The teaching of reading requires knowledge of the reading-thinking process and how this process is used most effectively to develop a command of knowledge.

INFORMAL TESTS

If every teaching situation is thought of as a testing situation, the meaning of *informal* takes on desirable dimensions. If teaching is thus conceived, the likelihood that reading instruction will be accomplished as described thus far in this text is considerably enhanced. Over and over again it has been pointed out that every time a student reads he does so with a purpose or purposes. He may have declared the purposes or may have adopted the purposes of others—classmates, a teacher, or a text. His reading act is not completed until he has found adequate answers to the purposes declared. Adequacy of answers may be determined by the usefulness of the information, by the acceptance by a group of peers, by checking against the authority of a teacher or a text, or by a test. So, the end result of almost any reading is to test the ideas garnered.

In group D-R-T-A's in which all members of the group are reading the same material, the testing of answers is aided and abetted by the fact that the group serves as the auditor. Answers must be proved to the group's satisfaction. The continuous interaction of pupils and teacher and authors can become more and more sophisticated as the clarification and refinement of purposes occurs and as students advance through the concrete operations on knowledge to the formal operations described in Chapter 10.

In individualized D-R-T-A's the over-all act has about the same dimensions (purposes, reading, proving) as for the group activities. The major difference is the pupil's need for self-responsibility. In addition, he may share answers with others and be faced with the need to be clear and articulate and with the need to answer audience questions that require a high order of verbal knowledge.

It should be apparent, then, that teaching without testing is unthinkable because it represents an essential feedback of learning (1). Testing is not an alternative; it is an essential for refining, extending, and summarizing knowledge.

D-R-T-A Inventories

Teacher observations and inventories provide an excellent basis for assessing pupil skills and performances. The broader and more specific the basis of observations on which evaluation rests, the better. This is so especially if in determining the final results they carry no more weight than their appropriateness and accuracy warrant.

An inventory can be made by using as a guide the D-R-T-A outline appearing in Chapter 2, pages 20–21. Inquiries that might be made are:

1. How readily does a pupil set purposes when reading fiction?_____ Non-fiction?_____
2. How varied are the purposes?
    seeking facts
    noting inferences
    checking vocabulary
    expanding concepts
    seeking relationships
3. Does the pupil adjust his reading purposes to
    the content?
    the social-personal conditions that exist?
    the consequences that seem reasonable?
4. Do the purposes declared permit him to penetrate deeper and deeper?
5. Do the purposes reflect ability to see things from points of view other than his own?
6. Do the purposes reflect a sound use of experience?
7. Do the purposes reflect a hierarchy of values and systems?
8. Do the purposes reflect goals and values that are becoming culturally mature and stabilized?
9. Can the pupil deal with hypotheses that may or may not be true?
10. Do his purposes reflect a certain amount of creative daring?
11. How attentive is he to the purposes of others in the group?
12. To what degree does he parrot or imitate the purposes of others?
13. Does the pupil adjust purposes in light of new evidence obtained while reading?
14. Do his attitudes and opinions cause him to limit either the nature or complexity of his purposes?
15. To what degree does the pupil adjust his rate of reading to the purposes declared and to the nature and difficulty of the material?
16. To what degree does he reread and reflect?
17. How effectively does he use phonetic and structural word-attack skills?
18. How effectively does he use a glossary or a dictionary?
19. Does the pupil seek teacher help in
    word recognition?
    concept development?
    comprehension?
20. How appropriate is his reading posture and performance?
21. How readily does he locate lines needed to support or refute a point?
22. What is the nature of his oral rereading?
23. How well does he listen to others prove points?
24. To what degree do either his purposes or proofs show a use of the language and concepts of the story or selection?

A similar inventory can be made of a pupil's performance during individualized D-R-T-A's. All the questions about purpose setting, adjustment of rate and method, attitudes, and seeking help apply again, except that in this context they take on new meaning. Added dimensions soon become apparent, and other inquiries need to be made.

1. To what degree does the pupil's choice of materials reflect examined interests and experiences?
2. How self-reliant and resourceful is the pupil in
    self-selection?
    reading independently?
    preparation for sharing?
    sharing?
3. To what degree does the choice of friends influence what he reads and shares?
4. How resourceful is he in using multimedia aids when sharing?
5. To what degree does the sharing reflect regard for the audience?
6. To what degree and how efficiently does the pupil use the varied communication skills?
7. How well does he use the library and show resourcefulness and persistence?
8. Is he an active listener, attentively interested?
9. How diligent is he in searching for facts and documentation?
10. How effectively does he use oral reports? Written reports?
11. What kind and quality of records does he keep?
12. How resourceful and thorough is he in developing new concepts?

A three- or a five-stage scoring on a quality scale may prove useful. Pupils may be rated as very poor, poor, average, good, and very good. If ratings are made periodically, comparisons can be made and progress noted. Of course, the competence of the rater is the key to the value of this process.

STANDARDIZED TESTS

Three questions about standardized tests need to be answered and understood if the issue of testing in reading is to be kept in perspective. What is a standardized test? What is the test supposed to assess? How is the information obtained best used?

What Is a Standardized Test?

A standardized test has been defined by Henry Chauncey and John E. Dobbin as (5, p. 9), "nothing more than a sample of performance related to the characteristic the examiner is trying to predict or estimate." To develop a test that would measure every aspect of a characteristic is virtually impossible. What can be done, though, is to sample a performance. It follows, then, that the longer the sample and the more carefully it is constructed, the more accurate will be the estimate or prediction. A reading test should consist of a set of test items or questions that are a representative sample. If a pupil scores well on one test of reading ability, it is usual to expect him to score high on another test, because the tests should represent samples of the same kinds of skills and experiences.

A standardized reading-achievement test is best described as one constructed by the use of scientific methods. Some of the distinguishing features of the scientific method are that it (1) is based on facts; (2) employs principles of analysis; (3) employs hypotheses; (4) is characterized by freedom from emotional bias; (5) uses accurate measurements; and (6) employs quantitative methods in the treatment of its data (7, p. 10). The procedure used for the preparation of the *Diagnostic Reading Tests* is illustrative.[1] This test was built by a group of skilled professionals working as a team and known as the Committee on Diagnostic Reading Tests. The Committee made a survey of opinions of teachers of reading and of others and then constructed tests in areas of instruction in reading. Test items were prepared and tried out experimentally. Final test forms were given to thousands of children in many schools, so that normative data could provide comparative samples of performance. As a result, the Committee made available a series of tests that possess a common design and a theoretical basis for measuring longitudinal growth and reading.

Even though the *Diagnostic Reading Tests* yield measures of vocabulary, comprehension (silent and auditory), rates of reading, and word attack—as well as a survey test of general reading proficiency—they are not perfect tests. The clarity, completeness, and accuracy of the test manuals have been questioned. Many of the test items are said to lack polish, and some are faulty. The norms have been considered inadequate (9). Apparently, even tests as carefully constructed as these are have limitations. On the other hand, it should be all the more apparent that subjective tests and the appeal to personal experience have greater limitations.

What Is the Test Supposed to Assess?

What a reading test is supposed to assess poses a big problem. If teaching a child to read will *change* that child in some way, the best way to find out if the change has been accomplished is to examine the child's reading performance. This means that it is necessary first to decide what the desirable changes are in terms of reading behavior. The first step is to decide how a pupil should be able to read after receiving reading instruction.

At this point the reader of this text might be asked to re-examine the preceding ten chapters to decide what tests would best measure the skills described. Doing this would help him realize better the scope and complexity of constructing tests.

To measure the recall or recognition of facts is not too difficult. To go beyond the recall of factual information is more difficult. In reading, this poses a thorny problem because reading is not a subject but takes all knowledge as its base. If facts are to be recalled, are they to be literary facts, scientific facts, social-science facts? If the process of gathering facts, drawing

---

[1] Published by the Committee on Diagnostic Reading Tests, Inc., Apartment 3G, 419 W. 119th Street, New York, New York 10027.

conclusions, testing hypotheses, suspending judgment, and gaining insights is to be tested, then again the process has to be applied to a content. In addition, if the essential characteristics of a good achievement test (5, p. 41) are to provide a set of tasks that require a student to recall, to generalize, to apply, and to discover, measuring reading skill becomes highly complex.

By and large, a teacher is interested in a variety of teaching approaches requiring several kinds of tasks (5, p. 40):

1. Several tasks that require the student to recall the most important pieces of the specific information he was expected to commit to memory.
2. Several tasks that require the student to generalize and draw conclusions—both from information he has remembered and from information provided.
3. Several tasks which require the student to apply newly learned generalizations to new unfamiliar information.
4. Some tasks which require the student to discover and reveal relationships between newly learned information and information previously learned.

These tasks provide the basis for an achievement test because they permit students to demonstrate the amount and quality of their learning. People who build tests for standardization should prepare items that call for demonstration of complex and insightful reading. This requires effort, professional know-how, and critical analysis. How well a test item or task does what it is supposed to do and how well a test as a whole does its task calls for "item analysis" and "test analysis." Professional test makers use refined statistical techniques to do these two jobs. In addition, they test large numbers of students, so that there will be reference groups with which to compare an individual's score and give it meaning.

Thus, a school system that uses standardized tests may make available to its teachers the following kinds of comparative data, adapted from Chauncey and Dobbin (5, p. 48):

1. Distribution of scores earned by all the students in the pupil's own class.
2. Distribution of scores earned by all the pupils in all the reading classes in the pupil's school.
3. Distribution of scores earned by all the students at the pupil's grade level in the local school system.
4. Distribution of scores earned by all the students at the pupil's grade level in the state.
5. Distribution of scores earned by all the students at the pupil's grade level in reading in a nationwide sample of schools. This information is usually provided by the test publisher.

This information will tell the teacher and the pupil how he compares with his classmates who have had the same teacher, textbooks, and curriculum. It also tells them how he compares with several kinds of competition.

One principle that must be kept in mind when test scores are interpreted is that fact that a score is only an *estimate,* and precise meaning should not be read into it. Because this is true, test publishers are now providing "band" scores. This means that an individual's score is a band or an interval and

not a precise score point. Thus, if a pupil takes a test and achieves a percentile score of 63, it might place him in a band of scores ranging from the
sixty-first percentile to the seventy-third percentile. If he takes the test
over again and again, his score would fall within this band at least two out
of three times. A grade-equivalent score of 6.8 may have a "band" score
ranging from 6.1 to 7.3. This forces one to recognize that a single test score
is only an estimate.

How Is the Test Information Obtained Best Used?

Any number of points have already been made about the use of information obtained from test scores determined by means of standardized tests.
Particularly relevant were the points just made about "band" scores and
estimates. Particular uses of tests may be grouped into six fairly distinguishable categories (5, p. 83): "to judge capacity to learn, to guide teaching, to
check learning progress, to discover learning difficulties, to improve teaching
techniques, and to assess teaching effectiveness."

Tests, whether formal or informal, are useful to teachers and schools for
planning instruction that will be at the level of the learner and geared to
his capacity to learn. Each of the subareas named in the discussion on
standardized tests may show a pupil's strength or weakness and help the
teacher plan more carefully. Pupils may need more help in the use of word-
attack skills, or critical reading, or concept development, and so on.

Tests on progress of learning should be made periodically and should
measure what has actually been taught. Pupils should be required to demonstrate those skills and abilities that are the goals of sound reading instruction. This means that not only should the teacher know what new skills
the student should learn or what old skills should be refined, but also the
student should know. Furthermore, the pupil should know what he must
do to prove that he has acquired a skill.

Learning difficulties can be identified, as has already been pointed out.
In reading, though, it is necessary that causes be identified and remedied,
and that symptoms be dealt with as symptoms. All too often time is devoted
largely to auxiliary skills of work attack and dictionary usage and not to
the fundamental skills required to read for meaning.

Testing to improve teaching and to assess teaching is, of course, a part of
every good teaching circumstance. Required is an appreciation of the goals
to be achieved. The better a teacher understands the instructional objectives to be achieved, the clearer she will be about assessing a student's
learning.

REPORTING PUPIL PROGRESS

The word *report* conjures a meaning of threat and anxiety in all too many
instances because of the grades-are-everything tyranny. Educators preach
on the one hand, about the importance of developing a child's mind, about

individual differences, and about human growth and development and on the other hand about using the home-work stick and saving the child by helping him earn only A's and B's. It would be a blessing if teachers would stop such double-talk and get on with the business of developing each child to his fullest and avoid breaking pupils' levels of aspiration over "norms" that have been falsely converted into "standards." These irresponsible practices have resulted in a deplorable waste of manpower that at times has been almost more than the spirit can bear. The gluttony for A's and B's has become the worst obsession of the post-Sputnik era. Maybe we would have been better off if we refused in 1958 to waste our time with such nonsense as individual differences, since nothing good could come from it anyway!

The report card requires teachers to face up to a strange paradox. They struggle vainly each marking period to fit each child into the A, B, or C bind. Teachers are educated to recognize individual differences, to see the wisdom of nongraded schools and their more flexible time schedules, to know their school's objectives, and to use teacher-made tests as well as standardized tests. What they need is more help on how to condense all the know-how about each pupil in each area of knowledge to fit a common yardstick.

No matter how reports are viewed, it must be agreed that, even though marking is a complex and difficult problem, marks are necessary. It is the uses made of marks that we quarrel with. Most commonly, reports are thought of as a means of communicating with parents. While this is a most useful purpose, this phase of reporting should stem from the accomplishment of a far more primary purpose—to report to pupils. If good teaching starts at the level of the learner, then good marking must also.

Reports to Pupils

Reporting to pupils is the focus that will best keep marks and reports in proper perspective. It is axiomatic that the pupil who knows *what* he is supposed to learn and *why* is far more apt to achieve than the one who does not. If the pupil knows what he is to do and why, marks can serve effectively as a means of stimulating, directing, and rewarding his achievement. Pupils know that teachers have expectancies and see many overt evidences of approval or disapproval. A teacher's comment, a smile, a nod, a pat on the back—these are evidences of "grading" that pupils recognize and do so with astonishing insight. A pupil who achieves a purpose that he understood will know to what degree he achieved and how rapidly he achieved. He knows what rating he merits, particularly if he has been led to face up honestly to a learning situation. He knows when he is working hard and achieving, and how his rate and method of working compare with those of his classmates. As a matter of fact, studies comparing students' rating of themselves with teachers' ratings show a great deal of similarity between the two ratings (11).

Programmed learning has as one of its major advantages that the goals to be attained and the skills to be achieved are spelled out in such detail and orderliness that the pupil can see quite clearly where he is and where he has to go and will have some idea about how long it may take him to get there. This is a constant form of "marking." Good teaching starts at the level of the learner and makes him an active participant in the purpose setting, in the purpose achieving, and in the use of new skills. It follows that a school could take a big step toward better education if it initiated periodic reports to pupils. Such practices would require an interesting type of honesty, could do much to promote pupil-teacher rapport and pupil self-understanding, and could do a great deal toward curriculum and course-of-study improvement.

Of the nine chapters in John I. Goodland and Robert H. Anderson's *The Nongraded Elementary School* (8), Chapter 6 on "Reporting Pupil Progress," could be the key chapter. If instruction is to be differentiated as described there, certainly the marking system should clearly reflect this. After a detailed account of reporting practices used in both graded and ungraded schools and identifying the preferred methods, the authors finally get around to the progress-information needs of the child:

> Up to this point the chapter has dealt primarily with the needs and the interests of parents and teachers insofar as the child's growth is concerned. In view of all this concern about reporting practices, and especially since so much is being said about "keeping the focus on the child," it is extremely curious that so little of the literature deals with the reactions and feelings of children in relation to the reports their parents receive. (85, p. 135.)

The authors make an earnest plea for doctoral studies and other research in this all-important area. Yet how timely it would have been if this chapter had more clearly reflected the "focus-on-the-child" philosophy and defined specific ways for doing so.

The reading teacher, in making a periodic semiformal report to each child, should place a grade value—A, B, C, or the like—on a pupil's effort. The report could be a two-part report: the first part telling the pupil how the teacher rates him in terms of himself, his potential for achievement, his previous school record, and his ambition, and the second part telling him how he compares with his classmates and the reading goals set for the year. So, a pupil might have an A rating in terms of himself and a C rating in terms of his class and the goals to be achieved. In some schools practices of this kind are being used. For example, a boy in third grade may be getting D-R-T-A instruction at a 2^2 basal-reader level. So the teacher may be noting that he is doing *A* quality work at the 2^2 level. In addition, at each conference the teacher could discuss the pupil's rate of progress, degree of progress, and use of reading. This would require her to account for the pupil's reading skills such as word attack, comprehension, concept development, versatility, variety of reading, depth of reading, and so on. It would also require that she account for her observations on the pupil's performance and cite the objective evidence that she used to determine her rating.

It is apparent that where such procedures are practiced the pupil can become an intimate part of the teaching-learning act. He will know what reading is and how to use reading to learn and for entertainment. He will see how he could keep an account of his own circumstances, and, just as when sound practices of individualized reading are accomplished, pupil records could become an integral part of the learning-to-read act. From this, teacher-pupil reporting to teacher-parent reporting will be readily accomplished.

Reports to Parents

Reports to parents represent the oldest and most widely used means of communication between the school and the home. As such they represent a tremendous public-relations influence. In this regard, Ruth Strang identifies guideposts to effective reports that warrant restating here (10, pp. 3–7):

1. Has your method of reporting to parents been developed cooperatively? . . .
2. Does your report to parents show trends in each pupil's development? , , ,
3. Does your report to parents show progress in the kinds of behavior that are most important for persons in a free society? . . .
4. Does your report to parents recognize individual differences in ability? . . .
5. Is your report to parents accurate? . . .
6. Is your report to parents diagnostic? . . .
7. Is your report to parents constructive? Does it direct their attention to the future? . . .
8. Does your report accentuate the positive? . . .
9. Does your report provide ample space for comments? . . .
10. Is your report to parents closely related to the cumulative pupil-personnel record? . . .
11. Is your report easily understood by the different parents in your community? Does it speak their language? . . .
12. Can your report to parents be prepared without putting too great a burden on the teacher? . . .
13. Do pupils share in the writing of their own reports of progress? . . .
14. Is the philosophy underlying your report to parents consistent with the educational philosophy and procedure of the whole school? . . .
15. Are the parents and teachers given help in using the report for guidance purposes? . . .

The second Harvard-Carnegie Study (2) of reading included a survey of practices used in reporting to parents. Results showed that three practices were used most frequently: progress reports or report cards, parent-teacher conferences, and a combination of progress reports and parent-teacher conferences. Other practices are parent-teacher-pupil conferences, letters to parents, home visits, anecdotal records, check lists, rating scales, and various combinations of these methods.

All of the methods mentioned serve a purpose and should be used on occasion. The one that seems most appropriate is the parent-teacher-pupil report-card technique. Teaching and learning is a cooperative affair, and the principal participants in any one learner instance are the school (teacher and administrator) and the home (parents and child). In the interest of sound pedagogy and sound human relations, the pupil should be a participant in each interview report. This keeps all communication lines open and avoids the "secrets" anxieties.

Ask any pupil in a classroom who is the best reader and most likely he can tell you. Or, ask who needs the most help and again he can tell you. Ask any pupil to tell you what he thinks about his reading ability and his needs, and the likelihood is considerable that he can give you a fairly accurate account. Pupils know where they stand; they know what it means to run a good race; they know the meaning of competition; and, above all, they know when they are being dealt with honestly. In short, teachers need not be concerned about giving grades if they do so openly and honestly and let sincerity and knowledge be their guide.

Parent conferences in school seem to be the most common practice. They have many advantages. They bring the parents to school. Pupil work can be displayed as supporting evidence. Comparisons among pupils can be made readily. The school principal is available. A teacher can see more parents on a visitation day than would otherwise be true. All too often, though, only mother can come for a visit, and this is unfortunate. Interview time should be planned so that at least on some occasions father can come too. Pupil progress and plans can be viewed jointly and this in turn may produce more cooperative action.

Parents should not come away from an interview feeling that they were on the spot. When home visits are made by teachers, parents should not be led to feel that they are the ones who are being examined and rated. To avoid such reactions requires tact and know-how on the part of the teacher. Obviously she must be the leader in this regard.

SUMMARY

A number of impressions should be created by this chapter. Once again the significant role of the teacher should be apparent. The kind and quality of evaluation and reporting that may occur in a classroom or school depend primarily upon the teacher. Much of the burden of responsibility and action also lies heavily upon the shoulders of the school principal and the school administrators. The hard-to-measure outcomes of critical and creative reading led to the publication of tests that measured only superficial evidences of quality reading performances. As a result, these tests encouraged a teaching of reading that focused primarily on eliminating symptoms of inefficient reading, rather than on reading as a thinking process. It is a truism that the accuracy of the measuring rod pretty well determines what will be brought forth to be measured. As long as both informal and formal tests focus primarily on symptoms, the teaching they stimulated will also. Norms did become standards, and the misuse of grade-equivalent scores made a major contribution in this regard.

Recent advances are most encouraging. The "band" score idea should do much to break the norm-standard whip. Building tests such as the *SCAT-STEP* combination and the *Diagnostic Reading Tests* through joint action of teachers, reading specialists, and test specialists will result in better tests and, in turn, in better teaching. Reporting to pupils should be the focus of all testing and evaluation of progress. This keeps attention centered on the learner, on the learning-teaching act as a cooperative venture, and on more careful documentation of ratings. Reports to pupils should be the foundation for reports to parents.

What does a good test measure? What it is intended to measure. But this is the rub! What is intended and what is done are, as has been shown herein, often quite different. Test validity can be determined in a number of ways, but certainly team effort will result in greater suitability. If test authors and producers provide a specific description of what each test question is intended to measure, the likelihood is considerable that the test will better fit the desired teaching and will have content validity.

Not all aspects of testing in reading are discussed in this chapter. However, if the references listed are consulted, the reader can find additional information as needed. He can also find certain special items. For example, the Ebel (6) text provides in the appendix an excellent glossary of terms used in educational measurement. The Chauncey and Dobbin (5) text provides an excellent appendix on multiple-choice questions: a close book. And, of course, The *Mental Measurements Yearbook* (4) makes available an excellent listing of tests, along with insightful reviews of many of them.

It is hoped that soon now—perhaps very soon—we may take long strides toward achieving the goal of testing the changes in children who have been taught from the very beginning of their school lives in the reading-thinking approach.

REFERENCES

1. American Association of School Administrators, *Testing, Testing, Testing,* Washington, D.C., 1962.
2. Austin, Mary C., and Coleman Morrison, *The First R: The Harvard Report on Reading in Elementary Schools,* New York, Macmillan, 1963.
3. Bloom, Benjamin S., "Testing Cognitive Ability and Achievement," *Handbook of Research on Teaching,* N. L. Gage, ed., Chicago, Rand McNally, 1963.
4. Buros, Oscar Krisen, ed., *The Sixth Mental Measurements Yearbook,* Highland Park, N.J., Gryphon, 1965.
5. Chauncey, Henry, and John E. Dobbin, *Testing: Its Place in Education Today,* New York, Harper & Row, 1963.
6. Ebel, Robert L., *Measuring Educational Achievement,* Englewood Cliffs, N.J., Prentice-Hall, 1965.
7. Good, Carter V., A. S. Barr, and Douglas E. Scates, "The Nature of Scientific Think-

ing," *The Methodology of Educational Research*, New York, Appleton-Century-Crofts, 1935.

8. Goodlad, John I., and Robert H. Anderson, *The Non-graded Elementary School*, New York, Harcourt, Brace & World, 1959.

9. Otto, Henry J., *et al.*, *Four Methods of Reporting to Parents*, Bureau of Laboratory Schools Publication No. 7, Austin, Tex., University of Texas, 1957.

10. Strang, Ruth, *Reporting to Parents*, Practical Suggestions for Teaching, No. 10, New York, Teachers College, Columbia University, 1947

11. Thomas, R. Murray, *Judging Student Progress*, New York, Longmans, Green, 1954.

INDEX

68 69 70 71   7 6 5 4 3 2 1